Debate as Global Pedagogy

Debate as Global Pedagogy

Rwanda Rising

Ben Voth

LEXINGTON BOOKS
Lanham • Boulder • New York • London

Published by Lexington Books
An imprint of The Rowman & Littlefield Publishing Group, Inc.
4501 Forbes Boulevard, Suite 200, Lanham, Maryland 20706
www.rowman.com

6 Tinworth Street, London SE11 5AL, United Kingdom

Copyright © 2021 by The Rowman & Littlefield Publishing Group, Inc.

All rights reserved. No part of this book may be reproduced in any form or by any electronic or mechanical means, including information storage and retrieval systems, without written permission from the publisher, except by a reviewer who may quote passages in a review.

British Library Cataloguing in Publication Information Available

Library of Congress Cataloging-in-Publication Data

Names: Voth, Ben, 1967– author.
Title: Debate as global pedagogy : Rwanda rising / Ben Voth.
Description: Lanham : Lexington Books, 2021. | Includes bibliographical references and index. | Summary: "In Debate as Global Pedagogy, Voth illustrates how Rwanda's debate instruction and several other international examples of deliberative and argumentation practices demonstrate the power of debate to address the problem and ongoing risk of genocide"— Provided by publisher.
Identifiers: LCCN 2020047833 (print) | LCCN 2020047834 (ebook) | ISBN 9781793629371 (cloth) | ISBN 9781793629395 (pbk) | ISBN 9781793629388 (epub)
Subjects: LCSH: Debates and debating—Study and teaching—Rwanda. | Debates and debating—Social aspects—Rwanda. | Communication—Political aspects—Rwanda. | Genocide—Prevention.
Classification: LCC PN4191.R95 V67 2021 (print) | LCC PN4191.R95 (ebook) | DDC 808.530967571—dc23
LC record available at https://lccn.loc.gov/2020047833
LC ebook record available at https://lccn.loc.gov/2020047834

Contents

Acknowledgments		vii
Introduction: The Communication Roots of Injustice and Genocide and Rwanda as a Model		ix
1	Darkness before the Dawn of the Twenty-First Century: Rwanda 1994	1
2	Discursive Complexity and the Global Renaissance for Justice	19
3	Debate Training in Rwanda among Security Forces	43
4	Deconstructing Anti-Colonialism and Anti-Imperialism as Jacobin Predicates of Violence	57
5	Debate as Pedagogical Empowerment at HBCUs in the United States (Christopher Medina, Sean Allen, Drake Pough, and Ben Voth)	75
6	The Global Ecological Museum and the Climate Debate	97
7	Rwanda Rising: Rwanda as a Global Model for Success (Jean Michel Habineza and Ben Voth)	113
8	Guatemala Rising with the Creative Peace Process (Rebecca Voth and Ben Voth)	131
9	China Rising: Debate Programs across China	151
10	Debate as a Global Empowerment Tool for Ending Injustice and Genocide	169
11	Coolidge Debate Pedagogy: A Historic and Inclusive Model for Today (Matthew Lucci and Ben Voth)	189
12	Conclusions: How Debate Helps the Global Human Community	207
Bibliography		231
Index		247
About the Author		253

Acknowledgments

There are so many people who deserve heartfelt thanks in the creation of this book. Jean Michel Habineza is a grand architect of an incredible debate program in Rwanda. His years of friendship and collegial labors are continually inspiring and his heart can be seen in his direct contributions to this manuscript. His college coaches Chris Baron and Beth Skinner worked closely with me in Rwanda during December 2019. It was an enduring Christmas present to see what collegiate debate in the early 1990s wrought among so many young people in Africa. Chris Medina is another hero of debate who has endured for the cause of debate and speech at Historically Black Colleges and Universities (HBCUs). Rebecca Voth created great content on Guatemala based on her impressive research on the issue. Matthew Lucci is more than a great American debate champion and we have done many great debate projects together.

Incredible students do more to convince me that debate and speech are powerful tools with their incredible choices in life after they graduate. Not all of these great examples can make it into a book like this but I am grateful to all of them. Terri Donofrio, Aaron Noland, Jieun Pyun, Allison Fisher Bodkin, and many more deserve acknowledgment. One student who must remain unnamed was willing to share her powerful story for readers and she continues to inspire me. The many debaters I met in Rwanda in 2019 were inspiring. So many of them were willing to be coaches at a young age and this moved me. Every day there was made more joyful by their efforts and support.

Many institutions supported elements of this project. The United States Holocaust Memorial Museum was the catalyst to my now longstanding interest in stopping genocide. Terri Donofrio and Ellen Blalock created the speaking workshops that sparked much of the imagination that now informs this book. The Calvin Coolidge Presidential Foundation has for many years supported a vision for reintroducing debate to high school students. Amity Shlaes and Matthew Denhart have been incredible leaders for the foundation and the related debate work. More recent friends like Jared Rhoads and Rob Hammer have also been indispensable to this ongoing debate work reaching so many people. The Bush Center here at Southern Methodist University (SMU) has been supportive and creative for many years and continues to encourage service and positive deliberations in the public. The SMU Dispute Resolution program under the leadership of Dr. Betty Gilmore helped me realize that Rwanda was a realistic place for work, and professor Gilmore is a great campus leader on these issues. Lori Shaw who collaborated in 2017 continues to do great work. Wiley College and its debate program have been stalwart about the high importance of debate and the significant history that abides on that campus with regard to the Great Debaters. The SMU debate team and program is flexible and demonstrative of the need for debate locally and worldwide. The U.S. State Department was helpful and supportive by providing a generous grant to make the iDebate program more successful. Peter Vrooman is the U.S. Ambassador to Rwanda and his participation in debate as a young person clearly influenced his generosity and support of the Rwanda debate project. Much thanks to him and his office.

In the conclusion I note how Rwanda is incredibly guided more by women in its politics than any other nation. That is an important development since they were so marginalized prior to the genocide. In my own life, I am buoyed by four exceptional and strong women—my wife Kelli and three incredible daughters Rebecca, Sarah, and Anna. Kelli's edits make her an equal in all of my written work. Rebecca, Sarah, and Anna each uniquely encouraged me in the midst of many complicated problems compounded by the pandemic. Kelli and my daughters are patient enough for me to spend many days out of the country helping others and this speaks to their generous spirits. I am profoundly blessed by the four of them.

Introduction

The Communication Roots of Injustice and Genocide and Rwanda as a Model

When I wrote my first book, *The Rhetoric of Genocide* (2014), it was in response to the inspiring work of now professor Dr. Teresa Donofrio who conceptualized the public speaking workshop for our collaboration with roughly thirty-five Holocaust survivors at the United States Holocaust Memorial Museum (USHMM) in Washington, D.C., during the summers of 2006 and 2007. Their collective ambitions to use personal stories to help bring genocide to an end melded with my own passions for public speaking and debate. The human voice has the power to arrest and overcome genocide's fatal fuel of propaganda. My consultation with profound American institutions such as USHMM, the U.S. State Department, the George W. Bush Presidential Center, and the Calvin Coolidge Presidential Foundation, and so many other groups pointed to a path where the human voice can resist, prevent, and overcome genocide. All of what harms humanity most in the way of injustice can be overcome in the axiom I discovered from Elie Wiesel at USHMM: "What hurts the victim most, is not the cruelty of the oppressor, but the silence of the bystander."[1] All of my classes and scholarship aim to disable that risk of the silent bystander. In twenty-five years of working on projects like this I have seen and heard hundreds of heroes on their way to these human fires of injustice. This is another rhetorical step in that journey that can lead to the end of genocide in this century.

As a communication scholar, I have taught and researched particularly with regard to argumentation and debate studies for more than 25 years. Anthropological studies of human life suggest that one symbolic habit that connects humanity with regard to communication over thousands of communities and thousands of years in various mythic histories is killing one another.[2] E. O. Wilson documents in *The Social Conquest of the Earth* that human societies are marked by a passion for killing our fellow human beings.[3] Additionally, knowledge is power.[4] This truism is bedrock to all academic thinking and justifications. Ironically, it also is the heart of global violence as knowledge forms biopower over human bodies toward rationalized acts of mass violence. The advance of communication technologies has vastly accelerated the propensity for propaganda. Propaganda forms the foundational communication fuel for genocide. Propaganda is a typical yet unfortunate pattern of human communication.[5] The commonplace nature of propaganda can give rise to a pattern of normalcy surrounding this communication distortion. As examined in my first book, *The Rhetoric of Genocide*, discursive complexity exists as both theory and praxis for the abolition of genocide.[6] Discursive complexity is defined as: "The capacity of an individual, group, society, and/or culture to encourage and maintain multiple points of view and free expression." The ethic of discursive complexity dispensed by debate instruction should be globally disseminated in order to prevent the conventional pattern of normativity establishing the negative symbolic valence of an ethnic or political target, propaganda in the form of intensive communication aimed at dehumanization, and culminating in mass violence where an ethnic or political target is annihilated without mercy.

The continent of Africa offers one provocative example of this problem and solution. In 2003, the African nation of Liberia emerged from sociological nightmare orchestrated by genocidaire Charles Taylor. Among his many important and subordinate agents was General "Butt Naked." The general engaged in bizarre but inhumane rituals that lead to more than 250,000 deaths—nearly 10 percent of the domestic population—in the small nation of Liberia populated with three million people. In 2008, General Butt Naked confessed to killing more than twenty thousand of his fellow citizens. His outrageous battlefield alias was drawn from his common habit of marching into civilian annihilations wearing nothing but a pair of boots. According to the general and other observers, these mass slaughters began with the ritualistic killing of a young child, cutting out the heart, and feeding it to his loyal troops. While not in combat, his soldiers would kick around human skulls in soccer matches. The regular international demands for Taylor's removal reached a crescendo in the spring of 2003. President Bush's speech at Senegal in the same year, about global slavery was an important era of time for administrative decision-making about Liberia. The argument made in Senegal was significant and was the first of an American president to be broadcast live to a global audience. In the speech, President Bush argued for the timeless ideal of human freedom and its persistence in impossible inhumane conditions like slavery:

> For 250 years the captives endured an assault on their culture and their dignity. The spirit of Africans in America did not break. Yet the spirit of their captors was corrupted. Small men took on the powers and airs of tyrants and masters. Years of unpunished brutality and bullying and rape produced a dullness and hardness of conscience. Christian men and women became blind to the clearest commands of their faith and added hypocrisy to injustice. A republic founded on equality for all became a prison for millions. And yet in the words of the African proverb, "no fist is big enough to hide the sky." All the generations of

oppression under the laws of man could not crush the hope of freedom and defeat the purposes of God.[7]

President Bush connected the injustice of American slavery to the identity of the African continent. The rhetoric tended to reverse the conventional notions of a "white man's burden" and suggested that Africa held an original repository for the cause of justice. Bush's fire metaphor originally offered on a cold inaugural in January 2005 in America came burning through on a balmy Goree Island at Senegal. In his conclusion to the speech directed primarily at his African delegation he stated:

> We know that these challenges can be overcome, because history moves in the direction of justice. The evils of slavery were accepted and unchanged for centuries. Yet, eventually, the human heart would not abide them. There is a voice of conscience and hope in every man and woman that will not be silenced—what Martin Luther King called a certain kind of fire that no water could put out. That flame could not be extinguished at the Birmingham jail. It could not be stamped out at Robben Island Prison. It was seen in the darkness here at Goree Island, where no chain could bind the soul. This untamed fire of justice continues to burn in the affairs of man, and it lights the way before us.[8]

Bush wove the intimacies of African suffering spelled out in the lives of men like Martin Luther King Jr. in the Birmingham jail and Nelson Mandela in a Robben Island, a South African prison, to create a global image of hope against tyranny and violence. Ultimately, after much deliberation the Bush administration in 2003 made an important decision to allow U.S. troops to support African troops in Monrovia in the removal of Charles Taylor.[9] The transition compared favorably with the results in the neighboring French colonial holding of the Ivory Coast. Elections in Liberia would later install the first female president on the continent of Africa: Ellen Johnson Sirleaf who was educated at Harvard.[10]

In the main exhibit of the George W. Bush Presidential Library on the campus of Southern Methodist University in Dallas, Ellen Johnson Sirleaf's ascendancy to the presidency of Liberia is noted as an important change in Africa during the Bush presidency. However, little explanation of how she came to power is provided. Charles Taylor's persistence in Liberia was well established by human rights proponents who sought his departure. The American presidential effort broke the common but misguided maxim offered by critics of President Bush that he acted unilaterally and without a plan for local success.[11] In the spring of 2003, with massive troop deployments moving against genocidaire Saddam Hussein in Iraq and rising apprehensions at home and abroad, President Bush sent hundreds of American troops into the capital of Liberia to ease the transition of Taylor out of power and to usher in an African Union peace coalition led by Nigeria. The effort was masterful in the secondary role U.S. troops played while providing a powerful diplomatic and military backstop for African troops that did not want to experience the same backlash and disruptions seen in the neighboring French colony of the Ivory Coast. The abrupt American military mission also violated another principle of intellectual reactionaries analyzing U.S./Africa relations: the United States only invades nations that have resources, such as oil, at stake.[12] Liberia was historically connected to the United States as a unique state founded by former American slaves, there was no great financial or mineral treasure trove to be colonially exported to America after the invasion. The fact that American military planners were wary of the shadows cast from the 1992 Somalia mission points to the axioms noted by genocide expert and the former UN ambassador Samantha Power in her important tome on the question.[13] By breaking the taboo of sending American soldiers into Africa, President Bush was bolstering the broader continental argument for combatting genocide.

The incredible success of the American and African Union military liberation of Liberia in 2003 takes place in a deliberative backdrop where African leaders and American leaders considered what the best options were for defeating a wide array of discursive cynics including Charles Taylor, colonial rejectionists, Islamic supremacists, American rejectionists, and so many more who might have rallied deadly attacks on the rescuing military forces and the infant project of true democracy in Liberia. In her 2017 memoir, former National Security advisor Condoleeza Rice explained a complex set of deliberations that led the emergence of the first female president on the continent of Africa in 2005, Ellen Johnson Sirleaf. On June 28, 2003, Rice took a photo of one of Charles Taylor's child soldiers carrying an AK-47 and a teddy bear backpack to the Oval Office to make an argument for change in Liberia. Ultimately, further deliberations with UN secretary general Kofi Annan and African heads of state such as John Kufour of Ghana and Olusegun Obasanjo of Nigeria led to the military removal of Charles Taylor.[14] The *New York Times* described the situation this way on July 4, 2003: "President Bush, enmeshed in an internal *debate* in his administration over whether and how to send American peacekeeping troops to Liberia, strongly implied today that no soldiers would be deployed until the Liberian president, Charles Taylor, steps down [emphasis added]."[15] The *Los Angeles Times* also focused on the debate necessary to achieve the decision: "But, after intense *debate* by President Bush's foreign policy team, the administration on Wednesday signaled its willingness to play a role in Liberia. 'The humanitarian crisis clearly calls for some type of response,' said a senior administration official who briefed reporters [emphasis added]."[16] It is this deliberative framework created by debate that is highlighted and the focal point of this book. As noted initially in *The Rhetoric of Genocide*, the abolition of genocide is possible with a concerted agenda of discursive complexity most recognizable in the pedagogy of debate.[17] Debate is the foundry of deliberation.

Some definitions of debate are in order given its primacy in this analysis. Debate is "the process of inquiry and advocacy; the seeking of a reasoned judgment on a proposition."[18] Debate is a process of inquiry that requires argumentation among its practitioners. This means that competing ideas will be presented by the debaters and reconsiderations will be made in a chronological dialogue between the sides. Debate typically observes at least four characteristics: (1) a resolution or proposition that establishes what is being debated, (2) two assigned sides of advocacy often named as affirmative and negative or proposition and opposition, (3) times limits for speeches by the advocate that typically range in length from three to ten minutes, and (4) a decision-making tool usually recognized as the ballot. The variety in types of propositions, lengths of speeches, and numbers of debaters arguing on each side gives rise to a wide variety of debate formats. Nonetheless, this definition and these characteristics are a consistent basis for recognizing what debate is and even how it can be tailored for many different situations around the world. Because debate is the intellectual foundry of deliberation, it is also the engine of discursive complexity and the ultimate enemy of propaganda. Debating will cause both the debaters and a listening audience to recognize rather immediately that there is more than one side to a controversy. This speaking and listening habit of observing competing sides of argument diminishes the acceptability of propaganda and raises the commitment and presence of discursive complexity within societies.

At the heart of this academic analysis of debate is Jean Michel Habineza. Habineza is the director of iDebate Rwanda—a compelling nonprofit enterprise that teaches debate through workshops, competitions, and global travel events. In 2014, when I met Jean Michel I asked him how he learned to debate—eager to know the pedagogical sources of his inspiration and passion. He told me how he travelled from Rwanda to Maryland in order to attend Towson University where he met his collegiate debate coaches Beth Skinner and Chris Baron. He spoke reverently of them, and he probably could not fully perceive why I was smiling so warmly to his wonderful story of their dedicated efforts to teach collegiate debate. I explained that almost thirty years prior in 1990, Chris and Beth were two of my first undergraduate debaters when I was only a doctoral graduate student debate coach at the University of Kansas. Beth and Chris were highly motivated undergraduate debaters who were intensely idealistic about the activity—pursuing far more than the acclaim of winning trophies or accolades. I was not surprised to find such a profound practitioner of debate borne of their later passions to be debate coaches themselves. I would like to believe my smile in that moment was as inspiring as a Rwandan smile that has become so trademark and infectious in my mind as I become more immersed year to year in their beautiful culture. Jean Michel and I were sure that debate empowers the margins of any society like nothing else could. Our shared Christian convictions made us fierce in a desire to make debate work for anyone and everyone around the world. This book is a pact for demonstrating how debate pedagogy is changing the world and can remake the globe into a place without genocide. This book is a story of how debate can abolish genocide in the twenty-first century. We can know this because the empirical path is already clear. Genocide is on the decline as a practice. Genocidaires are on the run, stepping down, and being replaced by life affirming alternatives. This academic analysis solidifies the procedures of deliberation leading to debate as pedagogy and the liberatory results that can be expected based upon empirical examinations.

Later in this book, readers will discover a remarkable case study toward this goal of abolishing genocide: the Dreamers Academy of 2019. In December of 2019, in the twenty-fifth anniversary year of the Rwandan genocide, a team of more than forty staff and coaches, met more than four hundred young students and more than fifty teachers from Uganda, Burundi, and Rwanda for three weeks of debate instruction partly funded by the U.S. State Department. Four American debate coaches joined this endeavor and laid further foundations for the rising nation of Rwanda. One Ugandan art and design teacher could not stop describing how stimulating the entire environment was, and though he had no background in debate before he came to the event, he was eager to go back to Uganda and teach students debate. He felt sure that debate would ignite in his students a fierce appreciation and practice of critical thinking that would ultimately make them better artists and better citizens. He showed me a handwritten research note confirming his conviction—a quotation from American presidential candidate Hubert Humphrey: "Freedom is hammered out on the anvil of discussion, dissent, and debate."[19] Over the course of several weeks we all collaborated to make the world less violent and less prone to its worst vice of genocide. We did it in the sociological shadows of one of the worst genocides of the twentieth century and abounding about us were hundreds of young souls celebrating their impending debates with rivals on topics as diverse as universal basic income, corporal punishment, and primary education.

I found as I taught and coached hundreds of eager students that as I shared my usual optimism and idealism about the human condition, I was met not with the usual American academic skepticism and doubt but a boundless enthusiasm that rivaled and surpassed my own. Each day I felt as though I were climbing a ladder of hope and getting a clearer and clearer view of this bright green land of a thousand hills. The world needs debate. That truth was clearest in Rwanda where the aftermath of genocide left a successive generation hungry for idealistic alternatives. There are real and powerful constraints against meeting this need. For that reason, this book combines the theoretical templates laid out in 2014 in *The Rhetoric of Genocide*, with practical implementations of discursive complexity. How do individuals implement the capacity to consider multiple points of view? How do groups and communities teach debate and argumentation? How do societies educate toward this critically thinking culture? This book establishes those answers. The following chapters outline empirical examples of how debate instruction and praxis lead to the elements of profound positive social change necessary to arrest and end genocide. These answers and examples exist across continents—Central America, Africa, Asia, and North America.

DEATH AS A TEXT: THE GLOBAL REALITY

This optimistic introduction cannot and should not look past the harsh realities of the past and the ongoing cruelties of the present. There are many great scholars who lay out the dreadful case of humanity killing her fellow innocent human beings in all too significant slaughters.[20] In my classes I have tried to insulate my students from the horror by primarily considering the death tolls of the twentieth century: the African Hereroes, the Armenians, the Jews, the Ukrainians, the Chinese, the Russians, the Cambodians, the Tutsis, and many, many more. One of the most comprehensive academic treatments in terms of time and culture is anthropologist E. O. Wilson in his 2011 work *The Social Conquest of the Earth*.[21] Wilson demonstrates through empirical anthropological study that humanity has an intrinsically common bond: the shared desire to kill the innocent. The interconnections of thousands of years of data with tens of thousands of human cultures share an intrinsic flaw: The Kill.[22] Humanity desires to kill one another, and confronting that ugly reality makes any individual mind recoil. Any class on genocide, whether it limits itself to one episode or a selective survey, will find students overwhelmed by the steady human diet for unjust violence against innocent peers. In my initial efforts to understand the problem with the American civil rights movement and moving to work at the United States Holocaust Memorial Museum in 2006, I noticed an ominous reflex in my mind. How can we muzzle and restrain the forces of revenge? How can we confine our own sense of indignation and self-righteousness that we would never allow our noble selves to do this same thing? This is the delicate art of pedagogy focused upon the most ominous ramifications of oppression: genocide. Candidly, as much as I admire Wilson's incredible panoptic review of human crimes, I cringed at his reactionary solution: abolition of religion from the mind of humanity.[23] I sensed the intuition and logic of it. Yet, I recognized immediately that some of the deadliest human political reformations of the twentieth century—iterations of communism—held the very same predicate of a solution as Wilson. I sometimes ask my students: How can we take our solutions and prevent them from becoming a creed whereby anyone who disagrees must die? One of the most popular courses I teach is a class called Ethnoviolence. Students encounter the deadly habits of humanity and walk around in local histories of violence before attempting to answer about what can be done to stop all of this violence. In multiple semesters, I have had students originating from a geographic home where they knew these risks were high and ongoing but they were personally afraid to challenge them in a published book created by the class.

Debate represents an important and necessary answer to the dilemma of closed societies. We must develop a pedagogical discipline of listening that is not closed. We must recognize the profound instability of knowledge lest we become intoxicated with the "knowledge is power" maxim that makes us ready to rid the world of its fools. Debate is empowering and humbling in a concurrent manner that offers a good educational step forward to remedying the risks of genocide. Some of life's most important lessons can be learned losing a debate such as "I was not listening," "I was too sure of myself," "I was not respectful enough of my opponent." The costs are not so high that recovery and growth are impossible. In fact, the genuine stakes of debate will motivate the student more than the challenges of rote memorization or recitation. This academic analysis provides a mixture of steps toward higher discursive complexity in a world of richer, more robust argumentation. Chapters on anti-colonialism, the Ecological Museum, Guatemala, and China provide corrective analysis of how restraints on argumentation and deliberation are limiting human potential. Chapters on debate training of security forces in Rwanda, debate training at HBCUs, Rwanda's Dreamer Academy, impactful projects with students and the Coolidge debate program provide examples of how debate instruction increasing the voices of people worked in empirical settings around the world. Chapter 10 includes several small examples around the world, including the work with the Bush Center. The conclusion chapter provides a summary and charge for further action to successfully implement debate instruction as a global corrective to genocide. All of the material is interconnected with a theory of discursive complexity maintaining that communication openness is best for the human condition and can be achieved through the teaching of debate and deliberation.

BOOK OVERVIEW

In this book, I provide, in consultation with a number of academic thinkers, a state of the art globally with regard to argumentation and debate. This is an important summary to have as we access the important human resource of discursive complexity to confront a range of human problems from pandemics to genocide. Following from this introduction are chapters providing a comprehensive review of prominent global locations and their relations to argumentation and debate study. The chapters following this introduction:

Chapter 1: Darkness before the Dawn of the Twenty-First Century: Rwanda 1994

This chapter by Jean Michel Habineza (director of Rwanda debate) and Dr. Ben Voth describes the basic logistics of the Rwandan genocide in 1994. In one hundred days, more than one million Rwandans were killed in one of the most significant genocides of the twentieth century. The chapter connects communication and argument practices like propaganda with the result of genocide. The chapter explains the communication causes behind the genocide.

Chapter 2: Discursive Complexity and the Global Renaissance for Justice

Discursive complexity is the capacity of a group, individual or society to consider multiple points of view.[24] The First Amendment is the American textualization and foundation of this political ideal. The promotion of this theoretical distinctive is the basis for believing that genocide can be abolished in the twenty-first century. Teaching debate is an ideal pedagogy for instilling social respect for differences of opinion. This chapter documents on a global level the status of discursive complexity and connect the concept to argumentation and debate instruction. The chapter builds upon lesser known notions of "Beloved Community" explained by civil rights leaders like James Farmer Jr. and Martin Luther King Jr. These American civil rights leaders traveled around the globe trying both to learn and ensure that this model for nonviolence would continue worldwide.

Chapter 3: Debate Training in Rwanda among Security Forces

Training in nonviolent conflict resolution is an important method for genocide prevention. In 2017, the SMU Conflict Resolution program went to Kigali to work with security forces in a training program aimed at improving their nonviolent conflict resolution skills. Conflict resolution is an important academic area that utilizes communication strategies to reduce conflict around the world. This chapter details those efforts and results. This effort focused on communication approaches to help officers communicate with local residents and better understand the conflicts leading to crime and social problems through debate related instruction. The training utilized the techniques developed in the American civil rights movement by the Great Debater James Farmer Jr.

Chapter 4: Deconstructing Anti-Colonialism and Anti-Imperialism as Jacobin Predicates of Violence

Discerning what arguments will help or hurt human societies is as complicated as human individuals themselves. Collegiate and high school debate praxis creates a normativity surrounding ideographs of "imperialism," "colonialism," and related descriptions of political power expressed internationally. Ideology can always form the pretext to propaganda and violence. Examining how in the twenty-first-century arguments against colonialism grant rhetorical refuge to serious human rights abuses in places as diverse as Venezuela, Sudan, Zimbabwe, Iran, and Hong Kong, allows the reader to see how caution, discernment, and debate are essential to prevent "liberation" from becoming genocide. Case studies in recent dictator declines witnessed with leaders such as Bashir (Sudan), Mugabe (Zimbabwe), Morales (Bolivia), and Chavez/Maduro (Venezuela) help make sense of an impending discursively complex world where individuals are free to form both individual property rights and socially significant civil rights such as freedom of speech. This chapter explains how the critique of colonialism can be abused to further genocidal conditions—especially in places in Africa.

Chapter 5: Debate as Pedagogical Empowerment at HBCUs in the United States (Christopher Medina, Sean Allen, Drake Pough, and Ben Voth)

Historically Black Colleges and Universities (HBCUs) occupy an important pedagogical legacy in debate instruction. Medina's background as director of debate at Wiley gives him exceptional insights into this contemporary culture especially as it relates to HBCUs. Medina explains how Black competitors overcome problems of racism within the forensics community. At Wiley, he oversaw an important implementation of debate pedagogy known as "debate across the curriculum." Debate across the curriculum allows debate instruction to be used in many different academic subfields, and dramatically increase the number of students positively impacted by this form of instruction. The successful details of this curriculum are included here.

Chapter 6: The Global Ecological Museum and the Climate Debate

One of the most supreme utopian notions of our time is climate change. A distinct notion of urgency suggests that we cannot indulge the luxury of debate regarding global warming because of the extreme impacts worldwide. Disagreement is referred to as "climate denial." The term is designed to connote analogy to Holocaust denial—an important problem in the academic field of genocide study. This chapter offers an argumentation critique of the climate debate and examines the scientific and credible reasons for being skeptical and even hopeful about climate change.

All of these items connect with a larger critical framework of how an intellectual elite wants to maintain the undeveloped world as an ecological museum wherein millions will die from malaria, infectious diseases, the dangers of unclean water, contaminated food, and reduced communication networks that combine to make human life more violent, dangerous, and ugly. These genocidal engines of democide (Rummel) and eliminationism (Goldhagen) are recast rhetorically as pristine cleansings and protections of a better earth.[25] The notion of humanity as a "global infection" rationalizes genocide as a therapeutic avenue of elite policy making that we should resist going forward in the twenty-first century.

Chapter 7: Rwanda Rising: Rwanda as a Global Model for Success (Jean Michel Habineza and Ben Voth)

This chapter details the efforts of iDebate Rwanda to establish debate instruction within the nation since 2014. There is a focus on the post genocide generation and building a national pedagogy valuing debate for young people. The project reaches communities throughout the region including dozens of teachers and hundreds of students from additional nations such as Uganda and Burundi. The description culminates in the recent debate camp Dreamers Academy held in December of 2019. The analysis includes important pedagogical content on how debate works toward healing a nation.

Chapter 8: Guatemala Rising with the Creative Peace Process (Rebecca Voth and Ben Voth)

Guatemala is an important Central American example for conflict resolution and the problem of eliminationism. Guatemala's civil war saw a rise of political eliminationism[26] that led to the killing of thousands. This chapter details current reconciliation efforts within the nation. The chapter also provides historical study of how past conflicts led to the current reconciliation efforts. The chapter establishes how the human condition can be improved with conflict resolution efforts. The country's use of deliberative models in pursuit of transitional justice exemplifies the importance of argumentation and political discourse to build democratic institutions. Trials represent a deliberative function that serve to provide a forum for argumentation and truth-seeking as a practical application of discursive complexity where victim and perpetrator meet public spaces that mute the cycle of violence. This chapter formalizes a case study in how this process is working in Central America.

Chapter 9: China Rising: Debate Programs across China

This chapter grapples with China's complex history of violence, both as a victim in Japanese Shinto supremacy of the early twentieth century along with the violent legacy of Mao Tse Tung in Communist politics of China. The ongoing controversy of Chinese human rights is also surveyed for twenty-first-century events. Included in this analysis is an important and extended consideration of how China's closed society contributed to the current pandemic crisis. Stefan Bauschard's work is offered as an important global initiative in debate for China. He helps place debate coaches throughout the most populated nation in the world. The unique challenges faced in the political limits of China are described in this chapter. The chapter provides an excellent example of how debate can thrive as an educational practice in a relatively closed political order.

Chapter 10: Debate as a Global Empowerment Tool for Ending Injustice and Genocide

This chapter organizes a variety of empirical examples of argument instruction and presents the broad case for why debate pedagogy is needed to end human injustice and especially genocide. Voth's experiences in India; the United States Holocaust Museum; the Bush Human Freedom initiative for North Korea and Burma, Rwanda, India, and Israel form practical examples for a theory about how argumentation can reduce human harms. References to empirical studies on these questions from experts like Hans Rosling and Stephen Pinker form a research basis for believing that debate can make the positive difference.

Chapter 11: Coolidge Debate Pedagogy: A Historic and Inclusive Model for Today (Matthew Lucci and Ben Voth)

This chapter contains the primary ingredients to a recent debate format revision known as Coolidge debate. Calvin Coolidge was transformed by debate instruction in college at Amherst. This instruction allowed him to believe he could be a leader and animated his capacities as president of the United States. The chapter explains the Coolidge Cup and debate tournament. The Coolidge debate format suggests a valuable approach to argument that treats opponents with dignified respect rather than withering contempt and scorn. These latter aspects of contemporary argument practice indicate our unfortunate trend toward cancel culture that must be reversed.

Chapter 12: Conclusions: How Debate Helps the Global Human Community

This chapter provides a theoretical summary of why debate is important and how it empowers individuals. The research clarifies a better future that is possible. Drawing upon the operational analogy of the book—Rwanda—this chapter explains that in the same way that this small nation has risen from desperate throes of violence to continental leader, the global community can engage a growing middle class to create a new communication infrastructure rooted in dialogue. This dialogue features aspects of respect, listening, empiricism, and deliberation. When these features are present, human thriving commences.

For readers, the goal of this analysis is to provide an understanding of discursive complexity as a communication-based theory for addressing and defeating propaganda as a means to cause genocide. Additionally, this analysis offers a variety of case studies in how argumentation and debate instruction encourage this desired discursive complexity. Mixed into this analysis is academic analysis of important argumentation areas such as environmentalism and colonialism. These argumentation areas are important conversations that risk impairing necessary communication openness that commences with discursive complexity. Rigid Jacobin commitments to rejectionist rhetoric can increase the prevalence of propaganda and the risk of genocidal outbreaks around the world. In total, readers can expect to complete a thorough justification of debate as a global pedagogy for furthering the end of genocide as seen through the pivotal history and contemporary academic practices of Rwanda—a nation on the rise because of its unique appreciation of debate.

NOTES

1. Elie Wiesel, foreword, in C. Rittmer and S. Myers (Eds.), *The Courage to Care* (New York: New York University Press, 1986).
2. Kenneth Burke, *A Rhetoric of Motives*, 1st ed. (New York: Prentice-Hall, 1950): 252–59.
3. Edward O. Wilson, *The Social Conquest of Earth*, 1st ed. (New York: Liveright Pub. Corp., 2012).
4. Michel Foucault and A. M. Sheridan Smith, *The Archaeology of Knowledge*, translated from the French by A. M. Sheridan Smith, 1st American ed. (New York: Pantheon Books, 1972).
5. Jacques Ellul, *Propaganda: The Formation of Men's Attitudes*, translated from the French by Konrad Kellen and Jean Lerner, with an introduction by Konrad Kellen (New York: Vintage Books, 1974).
6. Ben Voth, *The Rhetoric of Genocide: Death as a Text* (Lanham, MD: Lexington Books, 2014).
7. George W. Bush, "President Bush Speaks at Goree Island in Senegal," *White House*, July 8, 2003, accessed August 1, 2020, https://georgewbush-whitehouse.archives.gov/news/releases/2003/07/20030708-1.html.
8. Bush, "President Bush Speaks at Goree Island in Senegal."
9. "Goodbye to All That? Liberia (Liberia's Despot Resigns)," *The Economist* (US) 368, no. 8337 (August 16, 2003).
10. "#83 Ellen Johnson Sirleaf," *Forbes*, accessed August 5, 2020, https://www.forbes.com/profile/ellen-johnson-sirleaf/#6f20c5a044fb.

11. Strobe Talbott, "Unilateralism: Anatomy of a Foreign Policy Disaster," *Brookings Institute*, 2007, accessed July 20, 2020, https://www.brookings.edu/opinions/unilateralism-anatomy-of-a-foreign-policy-disaster/.

12. Adam Weinstein, "Blood for Oil Is Official US Policy Now," *The New Republic*, October 28, 2019, accessed August 5, 2020, https://newrepublic.com/article/155507/blood-oil-official-us-policy-now.

13. Samantha Power, *A Problem from Hell: America and the Age of Genocide* (New York: Harper Collins, 2002); Wilson, *The Social Conquest of Earth*.

14. Condoleeza Rice, *Stories from the Long Road to Freedom* (New York: Twelve, 2017): 405–6.

15. Elisabeth Bumiller and Eric Schmitt, "Bush Insists Liberian President Go before Troops Come In," *New York Times*, July 4, 2003: A3.

16. Robin Wright and Esther Schrader, "U.S. Willing to Send Troops to Help Liberia," *Los Angeles Times*, July 3, 2003, accessed July 28, 2020, https://www.latimes.com/archives/la-xpm-2003-jul-03-fg-liberia-story.html.

17. Voth, *The Rhetoric of Genocide*.

18. Austin J. Freeley and David Steinberg, *Argumentation and Debate: Critical Thinking for Reasoned Decision Making*, 12th ed. (Boston: Wadsworth Pub. Co., 2008).

19. Robert Pearl, "American Healthcare 2040," *Fortune*, October 1, 2019, accessed July 20, 2020, https://www.forbes.com/sites/robertpearl/2019/10/01/american-healthcare-2040/#25ae29ff71b0.

20. Power, *A Problem from Hell: America and the Age of Genocide*; Wilson, *The Social Conquest of Earth*; Rudolph J. Rummel, *Power Kills: Democracy as a Method of Nonviolence* (New Brunswick, NJ: Transaction Publishers, 1997); and Daniel Jonah Goldhagen, *Worse than War: Genocide, Eliminationism, and the Ongoing Assault on Humanity*, 1st ed. (New York: PublicAffairs, 2009).

21. Wilson, *The Social Conquest of Earth*.

22. Kenneth Burke, *A Rhetoric of Motives*, 1st ed. (New York: Prentice-Hall, 1950): 252–59.

23. Wilson, *The Social Conquest of Earth*, 293.

24. Voth, *The Rhetoric of Genocide*.

25. Rummel, *Power Kills*; and Goldhagen, *Worse than War*.

26. Goldhagen, *Worse than War*.

ONE
Darkness before the Dawn of the Twenty-First Century

Rwanda 1994

Genocide is arguably the deadliest threat to humanity. In the twentieth century alone, more than 180 million innocent people were killed in genocidal slaughters. Those killings ranged from the Hereros in Africa, to Armenians in Turkey, to Jews in the Holocaust of Europe, to the deadly actions of the Khmer Rouge in Cambodia, and the Rwandan genocide of 1994. These killings are intimately important to the communication thesis examined in this book: the communication form of argumentation and debate can make a world safer from genocide. Comparatively, the death toll of all wars in the twentieth century amounts to one fourth of that of all genocidal deaths in the same period. In those acts of violence, armed uniformed soldiers engaged in direct contests knowing the stakes and having clear moral boundaries on who was or was not an enemy. In genocide, the boundaries and rules of war are antithetical to the gross immoral character of the action. Killing the innocent is very much the symbolic point. The Rwandan genocide represents an important capstone to the larger human infliction of mass genocide that took place across continents and time throughout the twentieth century—to say even less about the centuries before. Roughly twenty-five years later, the Rwandan genocide continues to provide a proximity for learning and anticipating a better world without genocide.

THE BASICS OF THE RWANDAN GENOCIDE

Of course, every genocide is infinitely complex and ultimately inexplicable. Why would neighbor kill neighbor? Why are children killed despite their apparent vulnerability? These and so many other questions are unanswerable. These crimes should leave the world ashamed and fearful that by the right communication circumstances the same dreadful crimes will be repeated in this century. This book is not primarily about the Rwandan genocide. It is, in fact, more about overcoming that genocide and committing to the kinds of antithetical communication behaviors that not only prevent genocide but heal the wounds genocide leaves behind in human societies. To excavate this more important knowledge set, it is useful to begin with a genocidal crime that is a prelude to our present century: the genocide in Rwanda in 1994.

What happened? In the period of one hundred days beginning on April 7, 1994, 1.4 million Rwandans were killed amid a total national population of six million people.[1] Almost 25 percent of the population was killed in a genocidal event that remains one of the most swift genocides of an already blood-bathed century. Beyond this essential statistical nightmare, the details have murky characteristics that are continually subject to challenge. These features are at least largely true: First, a predominant Hutu majority of the nation targeted and dehumanized a Tutsi minority. There are important exceptions to this rule that Hutus dominated Tutsis, but it remains a primary pretext to the action of genocide. Second, the death of the Hutu president Habyarimana in a plane crash the day before the genocide started is deemed a key catalyst to the orders by Hutu warlords to carry out the dreadful annihilation of the Tutsi minority, who were blamed for the assassination of the leader. Third, the world watched the progression of these tensions for months and refused to take necessary steps to prevent, interrupt, or effectively rectify the genocide. The prominent aspects of this global failure were found in the United Nations peacekeeping operation nobly headed by the Canadian commander, Romeo Dallaire. Despite Dallaire's repeated calls for help and further resources, the global community refused to act to prevent or stop the genocide. Various international state actors, such as the United States and France, did act to remove their own local nationals upon the eve of the genocide, leaving the local population behind to endure near certain slaughters. Finally, the genocide was carried out in large measure with tools such as machetes. In one hundred days, the world stood by while Rwandans pleaded and begged for help. Ultimately the mass killings would not end until nearly 25 percent of the nation was murdered in a gross ethnic purge.

By the end of 1994, the average life expectancy of a Rwandan was twenty-six—a testament to how many children were killed in the genocide. The tragedy eviscerated the moral frameworks against genocide built by the international community in the aftermath of World War II, rendering them hollow and meaningless—perhaps still binding in some grossly racist ethic to save Europeans from similar fates. By July 1994, the world could only be embarrassed for its failure to act. All of this can be rendered with greater detail and sophisticated interrogation of motives and means. To some extent, this chapter will continue to do that, but the goal is to validate an emerging ethic among the Rwandans themselves, and formerly shared in the global community, that these things should never happen again.

THE COMMUNICATION PRETEXT TO GENOCIDE: PROPAGANDA

Whenever such horrific crimes against humanity happen, a morally serious culture should stop and ask "why?" A genuinely inquisitive culture should be unafraid to find a simple, direct, and rectifiable answer, despite the scope of the crime. In this case, the answer is propaganda. Propaganda is the antithesis of discursive complexity. Discursive complexity is the capacity among individuals and a society to endure and encourage dissent. Propaganda is the antithesis of a lively argumentation process and debate is the direct methodological threat to propaganda. The *New Oxford American Dictionary* provides specifics on what propaganda is: "information, especially of a biased or misleading nature, used to promote or publicize a particular political cause or point of view."[2] Miscommunication in the form of propaganda is an important, if not foundational, step on the dark path to genocide. Political leadership makes pejorative symbolic misrepresentations of an internal public group, and the repetition of these symbolic misrepresentations forms the foundation of individual action collectively galvanized toward the common act of genocide. It is important to understand this primary cause to recognize how argumentation and debate is the antithesis, and therefore the antidote, to genocide. A public that is committed to and practiced in debate is less receptive to or willing to participate in propaganda.[3] Debate is a unique pedagogical antidote to the problem of genocide:

> Argumentation and communication scholars are better equipped than most experts to understand that humans rarely kill in random ways. They are motivated by words. Their actions are shaped by public arguments that establish the reasons for the Kill. The simple and persistent creation of human scapegoats—while common—is not inevitable. Human beings can reconsider and advocates can suggest alternatives.[4]

Debate requires symbolic reflexivity and the ability to see not only two sides but multiple sides. Debate will not allow its practitioners to see only the simple answer or the easy exclusions. A more in-depth view of the Rwandan genocide is critical in order to understand more directly how propaganda worked in the case of Rwanda to galvanize portions of the public to kill one another.

The propaganda utilized by Hutu leaders was not brief or simplistic. Adolf Hitler made a number of observations on propaganda in his opening treatise to the German public and the larger case for the Holocaust in his book *Mein Kampf*. He observed the failures of propaganda for Germany in World War I and explained how it must be oriented for his own genocidal vision:

> All propaganda must be popular and its intellectual level must be adjusted to the most limited intelligence among those it is addressed to. Consequently, the greater the mass it is intended to reach, the lower its purely intellectual level will have to be. But if, as in propaganda for sticking out a war, the aim is to influence a whole people, we must avoid excessive intellectual demands on our public, and too much caution cannot be extended in this direction.[5]

Here, Hitler highlights the rhetorical demands for a less deliberative communication environment and the lower intellectual life necessary to its success. Jacques Ellul explains the process with greater depth:

> [M]odern man does not think about current problems; he feels them. He reacts, but he does not understand them any more than he takes responsibility for them. He is even less capable of spotting any inconsistency between successive facts; man's capacity to forget is unlimited. This is one of the most important useful points for the propagandist, who can always be sure that a particular propaganda theme, statement, or even event will be forgotten within a few weeks.[6]

The urgent need for, yet absence of critical thinking is apparent in these propaganda formulations. The Rwandan propaganda, like all genocidal pretexts, was sustained and multifaceted. At the essential core was a simple assertion of ethnic supremacy: Hutus are better than Tutsis. The origin of this idea is its own rhetorical quagmire. In the most exhaustive studies, the colonial traditions dating back more than one hundred years, established Belgian colonizers as accentuating perceived differences between local populations in the Rwandan region. This, however, did not establish an inevitable path to genocide. Beginning in the 1950s, the most contemporary rhetorical rifts began to form a pattern for Rwandan society. Hutus, as a majority, had a natural social advantage to define the terms of conversation as handed to them by European colonizers. One of the most famous and essential statements of propaganda in the immediate prelude to the genocide was the statement: "Tutsis are cockroaches."[7] Over radio broadcasts, Rwandans could hear the dehumanizing terminology of comparing the ethnic group of Tutsis to insects. Dehumanization is an important and essential characteristic of genocide propaganda. The symbols begin to position the genocidaires and genocide perpetrators toward the comfortable psychological disposition that they are not killing fellow human beings, but some form of nonhuman entities. Radio, print, and various forms of major media began to consistently portray the Tutsis as social interlopers and a threat to the general well-being.[8]

Scholars and other observers may wonder why people did not try to resist this decades-long spiral of cynicism that would position human beings to kill their neighbors. Such problem is at the heart of this study. Argumentation and debate study and practice can raise up individuals that resist these common human communication patterns characterized by scapegoating. Noted Holocaust survivor and genocide commentator Elie Wiesel famously observed: "What hurts the victim most is not the physical cruelty of the oppressor, but the silence of the bystander."[9] The bystander effect—whereby public individuals are willing to be passive while the spiral of cynicism fueled by propaganda winds greater and greater social tension into a community until the spring snaps forward toward democide, eliminationism, and genocide—is the fundamental social danger. A natural resistance toward hateful action must be built into all human communities. Debate and argumentation practice can mitigate these risks and create a community of upstanders, rather than bystanders. The distinction was originally contemplated in Samantha Power's seminal work introducing this century of genocide: *A Problem from Hell: America in the Age of Genocide*.[10] The *New Oxford American Dictionary* defines an upstander as "a person who speaks or acts in support of an individual or cause, particularly someone who intervenes on behalf of a person being attacked or bullied." Holocaust museums around the world including Yad Vashem in Jerusalem, USHMM in Washington, D.C., and the Dallas Holocaust Museum emphasize educational missions to shift the public from passive observers of genocide to active "upstanders" willing to resist the processes being described here.[11]

In the case of Rwanda, the problem was politically bound as well. There was a minority Tutsi community that wrestled with political control among a dominant Hutu political body. In 1973, a military group installed Major General Juvenal Habyarimana, a moderate Hutu, in power. In the weeks, months, and years leading to the events of April 1994, the moderate Hutu leader compromised with the Tutsi minority seeking to reestablish their place in Rwandan society. The Tutsi minority was primarily represented by a group known as the Rwandan Patriotic Front (RPF). Between 1990 and 1993, government officials directed massacres of the Tutsi, killing hundreds. A cease-fire in these hostilities led to negotiations between the government and RPF in 1992. In August 1993, Habyarimana signed an agreement at Arusha, Tanzania, calling for a transition government that would include the RPF. The Arusha Accords signed between the leadership of the Hutu government and the RPF was a way of mitigating the conflict within Rwanda between the two groups. Hutu hardliners who did not want peace between the two groups were likely responsible for the shooting down of the aircraft that had the Rwandan president and Burundi's president Cyprien Ntaryamira onboard. Though these events remain a matter of historical debate, these are the likely causes to the immediate events of April 1994 and ascendant violence. It is vital to examine this delicate history because all genocides have a basis in a notion of historical grievance. This is why genocides are often cyclical. Ethnic groups often take revenge upon each other decades later based upon a sense of history that they were unfairly treated by the rival ethnicity. For Rwanda, there were prior instances of ethnic violence, such as in the 1970s.

Even earlier, in 1959, Joseph Habyarimana Gitera, a leader of the radical Hutu political party Aprosoma, openly called for the elimination of the Tutsi "vermin." The winding of an internal genocide spring within a society takes time and there were decades of dehumanizing forms of rhetoric directed at the Tutsis. Ever more clever terms for delegitimizing the Tutsis created a social sport whereby practitioners earned a sense of ethnic pride while the targets of the impending genocide became resigned to patterns of silence. The stigmatization and dehumanization of the Tutsi had begun. When the first of the many anti-Tutsi pogroms broke out that year, Gitera was overjoyed.[12] These groups continue to affect regional African politics in places such as Burundi and the Congo. Discursive complexity is vital to enable further discovery of accurate history while minimizing the risk of a future genocide or ethnic violence.

WHY DID FOREIGN GOVERNMENTS FAIL TO HELP?

In examining the global passivity to this outrageous crime, it is also important to understand this as a cause to the genocide. The genocide could have been prevented, or even interrupted, by outside agents. Outside nations and institutions were also bystanders in the manner noted by Wiesel. Initially, it is important to recognize Rwanda in 1994 as primarily a part of Francophone Africa. This means that Rwanda was primarily a nation influenced and directed by French political interests. French was and remains one of the foundational languages of Rwanda. Close relations between France and Rwanda led the French government to provide weapons and arms to Rwanda that were indispensable to the action of genocide. An initial analysis of how outsiders contributed to or failed to act must begin with the government of France. The government of France understood internal Rwandan politics as well or better than any other foreign government, and their decisions to continue supporting the Hutu supremacism without limits is an essential component to how this genocide ultimately unfolded. A communique from the French ambassador to French officials in Paris communicated the following apparent concern in January of 1994:

The French Ambassador to Rwanda Jean Michel Marlaud wrote a telegram to the French Minister of Foreign Affairs explaining the atmosphere in Rwanda. Ambassador Marlaud explained that he received some reliable information with tangible evidence that there's a plan of killing Tutsis in the country. Ambassador Marlaud said that the plan will be preceded by provoking RPA forces stationed in Kigali so that as they try to defend themselves, this will be a pretext to kill Tutsis beginning with those in Kigali. The Ambassador adds that the national army organised the plan and more than 1,700 Interahamwe in Kigali city have been provided with training and weapons to kill Tutsis, and have capacity to kill around 1,000 people in the first hour of the killings.[13]

Despite this direct knowledge of an impending genocide to be committed by the Hutus against the Tutsi minority, France did not immediately act to stop this event from unfolding. France did not seek to mobilize international restraints on the activity. When France finally authorized a military intervention in June 1994 as the genocide was coming to a close, many experts believe that the humanitarian zone they created in the southwest corner of the nation helped Hutu war criminals to escape while protecting some civilians.

The United Nations was founded in 1945 in large measure to counter war crimes and genocide around the world. The popular imagination was that this body could prevent atrocities like the one that would ultimately transpire in Rwanda. The United Nations had more than two thousand military forces in Rwanda that were operating with a mission to minimize and prevent ethnic conflict in the nation. In this regard, the United Nations was an active government agency working to prevent the genocide. The dominant criticism offered in hindsight is that the parameters for military engagement were so confined and narrowed by the leadership of the United Nations that the local military force could not reasonably stop the genocide. The killing of Belgian peacekeepers by Hutu military leaders in the immediate prelude to the genocide was one of the clearest global communication signals that Rwanda was on the brink of genocide, and far more dramatic rules of engagement and military forces would be necessary to prevent this outcome. Romeo Dallaire made constant pleas in the months leading to the genocide for precisely this increase in force and mission operability, but those requests were denied. Ultimately, he and other forces would largely look on as bystanders while more than one million people were killed in the genocide. Today Dallaire travels the world offering a grim but important reminder of the profound costs to inaction in the face of impending genocide. He is the respected existential character who provided an unheeded warning about the impending atrocity.

The United States must also be examined as a potential solution and apparent bystander. President Clinton was careful to prevent his State Department officials from describing events in Rwanda as a "genocide."

This careful avoidance of the G-word at a White House briefing in 1994 still stands as one of the greatest communication paradoxes of this terrible tragedy.[14] The American government knew what genocide was and the inherent obligations that the term entailed but it was careful to avoid referencing the term and the inherent responsibilities that came with it. Why was this the case? The simplest and clearest answer would be provided by genocide commentator Samantha Power. That simple answer was this: Somalia. In her Pulitzer prize winning book, Power explains:

> Although Dallaire gravely underestimated the tensions brewing in Rwanda, he still believed that he would need a force of 5,000 to help the parties implement the terms of the Arusha Accords. But the United States was unenthused about sending any U.N. mission to Rwanda. "Anytime you mentioned peacekeeping in Africa," one U.S. official remembers, "the crucifixes and garlic would come up on every door." Washington was nervous that the Rwanda mission would sour like those in Bosnia, Somalia and Haiti were then doing. Multilateral initiatives for humanitarian purposes seemed like quagmires in the making. But President Habyarimana had traveled to Washington in 1993 to offer assurances that his government was committeed to carrying out the terms of the Arusha Accords. In the end, after strenuous lobbying by France (Rwanda's chief diplomatic and military patron), U.S. officials accepted the proposition that UNAMIR could be the rare "UN winner." Even so, U.S. officials made it clear that Washington would give no consideration to sending U.S. troops to Rwanda and would not pay for 5,000 troops. Dallaire reluctantly trimmed his written request to 2,500. He remembers, "I was told, 'Don't ask for a brigade, because it ain't there.'" On October 5, 1993, two days after the Somalia firefight, the United States reluctantly voted in the Security Council to authorize Dallaire's mission.[15]

Power's research indicates the powerful historical constraints creating an exigence for failed leadership against the Rwandan genocide.

In 1992, President George H. W. Bush enacted a humanitarian mission to confront warlords in Somalia who were promoting food deprivation in the Horn of Africa. The mission would ultimately be handed off to the Clinton administration and the struggle devolved into a relatively famous incident now often referred to as "Blackhawk Down." An American film popularized the events wherein U.S. military Blackhawk helicopters were shot down in Mogadishu—the capital of Somalia—during a mission to capture warlord leaders instigating mass starvation and political instability in the small African nation. Eighteen American soldiers were killed in the incident and one dead soldier was dragged through the streets of Mogadishu like a prize. This imagery conveyed on CNN became a public catalyst for military withdrawal and an informal, but firm, conviction that the U.S. military should not engage in dangerous missions of primarily humanitarian goals. The incident was an important rhetorical basis to Osama bin Laden's famous claim that America was "a paper tiger" that no one would follow in the world because of a preference for "the strong man on the horse." In short, American foreign policy analysts and advisors in 1994 were much in favor of avoiding a repeat of the international humiliation perceived in the U.S. military withdrawal from Somalia. The escalating events in Rwanda were viewed through this paradigm, and the U.S. State Department worked to defuse global expectations that the United States would resolve this problem.

All of these ingredients, and many more beyond the scope of this analysis, led to a situation where Rwanda was left alone to receive whatever outcomes would spring from decades of escalating ethnic bigotry and political anger within the Hutu leadership of the nation. There were moderate Hutus who opposed the violence. These individuals would themselves face the same violent demise as their fellow Rwandan Tutsis. Their sacrifices should not be ignored in the broad cultural sweep of ethnic rivalry that naturally fueled this genocide in 1994.

THE DEADLY EXTENT OF THE RWANDAN GENOCIDE IN 1994

At the United States Holocaust Memorial Museum in Washington, D.C., there are some exhibits where television displays are laid into the floor and surrounded by four-foot walls. These unusual configurations are made to insure that children are not able to see some of the worst atrocities that happened during the Holocaust. Genocides bring with them the worst that humanity has to offer—terrible acts of violence that hopefully make us all recoil in the present. They are nonetheless real and recurring. When we observe them today, we should not view them as a kind of ethical pornography—something we enjoy considering because it provides for us a sense of moral satisfaction. Perhaps we imagine that we are so much better than such actions. We are not. We also do not want to trivialize these events and become numb to those radical symbolic acts of dehumanization that are clearly overwhelming. Somehow, in order to stop these crimes in the future, we must be balanced in our considerations of what really happened. Recognizing these terrible rhetorical calculations confer no privilege upon us now, nor do they justify a callous sense of inevitability that such brutal prevarications cannot ever be stopped. We must resolve ourselves to a steady middle path between these psychological poles. In examining atrocities within the Rwandan genocide, no special claim of guilt is being made beyond the realization that all of us are capable of these crimes. The horrific details of these events are not an ongoing excuse toward cynicism that such things can never be stopped—they can. With these intellectual boundaries established, let us examine the horrific details of this genocide.

Statistically speaking, this genocide was uniquely bad. Happening in one hundred days and killing nearly one-fourth of the entire national population, it stands out as one of the most rapid genocides in twentieth-century history, though its magnitude is not as large as events like the Holocaust that took more than ten million lives. Rwanda had a population of six million people when the genocide began. The nation is approximately the size of the state of Maryland; therefore, its geography is rather confined in comparison to other nations that we might examine. Between 1985 and 1994, the average life expectancy of Rwandans declined from fifty-one to twenty-six. This tells us that though the most violent aspects of the genocide took place in the one hundred days spawned from April 1994, there were systemic problems apparent in the decade before. The systemic blinding hold of authoritarian conviction was strangling the people of the nation, much like Robert Mugabe in Zimbabwe.

Among the first victims of the genocide were moderate Hutu prime minister Agathe Uwilingiyimana and ten Belgian peacekeepers, killed on April 7. A Rwandan commentator provided this description of the ensuing events in April 1994:

> Hordes of members of the Hutu ethnic majority, armed with machetes, spears, nail-studded clubs, and other rudimentary weapons, moved house to house in villages, hunting for Tutsis, the second largest of Rwanda's three ethnic groups. The radio station RTLM, allied with leaders of the government, had been inciting Hutus against the Tutsi minority, repeatedly describing the latter as *inyenzi*, or "cockroaches," and as *inzoka*, or "snakes." The station, unfortunately, had many listeners.
>
> The promoters of genocide used other metaphors to turn people against their neighbors. Hutus, by reputation, are shorter than Tutsis; radio broadcasters also urged Hutus to "cut down the tall trees."[16]

The use of metaphors stands out as a mechanism of dehumanization, and Rwandans resorted to primitive weapons in their quick task of annihilation. Political leader Noël Hitimana, speaking on a private radio station, provided this ominous warning not long before the genocide:

> "On the day when people rise up and don't want you Tutsi anymore, when they hate you as one and from the bottom of their hearts . . . I wonder how you will escape." One month later, "blood was flowing on the streets; Tutsi were hunted down without mercy; they were killed in schools, churches, hospitals, and even prisons."[17]

With meticulous organization, lists of government opponents were handed to militias who went and killed them, along with all of their families. According to a BBC report at the twenty-year-year anniversary:

> Neighbours killed neighbours and some husbands even killed their Tutsi wives, saying they would be killed if they refused. At the time, ID cards had people's ethnic group on them, so militias set up roadblocks

where Tutsis were slaughtered, often with machetes which most Rwandans kept around the house.[18]

A key ingredient to the energetic and frenetic slaughter was a group known as Interahamwe; "Those Who Attack Together." This Hutu government-sponsored youth group was converted into militia activity that would, during the one hundred days, carry out many of the vicious slaughters. The names of people to be killed were read out on radio.

The *New York Times* provides a recent recollection of the terrible events from a perpetrator and victim:

> On a patch of property shaded by yellow flowering trees, Jacqueline Mukamana and Mathias Sendegeya sat side by side shelling peanuts and tossing them into a metal pan. At first glance, the pair could be mistaken for husband and wife, leaning against each other with ease as they shucked the nuts. They were neighbors before the genocide and have known each other most of their lives, after growing up in a nearby village. In 1994, Ms. Mukamana was 17. Her father, six brothers, five sisters, and nine uncles were killed that April. She fled to Burundi. When she returned, her family home was destroyed. Mr. Sendegeya was among the group that killed her father and four other members of her family, a fact that both speak about frankly but without much detail. While Mr. Sendegeya takes responsibility for the murders, he believes that the political leaders of the past orchestrated the killings and that without that influence, his life would have been very different. "That was the fault of the then government that pushed us to kill Tutsis," he said, his eyes gazing steadily ahead as he echoed a sentiment heard throughout the community from both perpetrators and survivors. "We massacred them, killed and ate their cows. I offended them gravely."[19]

In 2020, A 102-year-old survivor relayed her story of how fifteen of her seventeen children were killed in the genocide:

> Save for two of her children who died lost when they were so young, all the others, their father, and her three grandchildren were killed during the 1994 Genocide against the Tutsi. Her eldest son was working for the former National University of Rwanda, something seen as a major accomplishment for a Tutsi at the time. He too was killed. "I will never forget the attack by Nikodemu (an Interahamwe militia) that killed my son," she says, breaking down into tears. One of her daughters was thrown into a pit latrine alive "because she had refused to sleep with an Interahamwe militia." Mutumwinka doesn't like to share the story of how she lost all of her family, because it triggers deep grief and a loud cry. For that reason, she was reluctant to share the story about how she survived the slaughter herself, or anything more about how her husband and children were killed.[20]

Her reticence twenty-five years later is an enduring tribute to how cruel and evil the actions of genocide were for her and her family. We must try to understand the incomprehensible loss of such individuals, not for our own satisfaction, but for the formation of an enduring moral reserve that these things never happen again.

A 2015 research summary based upon more than one hundred thousand documents about the genocide and reviewed by a librarian for African, Global and International Studies at the University of Kansas provided this painfully detailed glossary of atrocities witnessed by children:

> These handwritten testimonies reveal that children witnessed firsthand the following atrocities being committed to fellow children or to other people: Torture and being beaten was common; People being killed using machetes, guns, knives, bows, spears and arrows; Women and girls being raped; People being undressed and left to walk naked along the road; while some of the victims were drowned in river Nyabarongo. It was also common for perpetrators to disembowel pregnant Tutsi women or Hutu women married to Tutsi men that they came across. Some toddlers were killed by being smashed onto walls while others were killed by strangulation with their necks twisted between metal bars. Destruction of property belonging to Tutsi and moderate Hutus was prevalent and some of it was either burnt down or got looted. Perpetrators and members of the killer gangs extorted money from Tutsis and moderate Hutus either through brute force or by promising to spare their lives. It was not uncommon for those who were targeted to pay bribes only to be killed later or even be killed instantly. Those who did not have anything to bribe the perpetrators tended to be killed instantly. Perpetrators also coerced some of the people they arrested to participate in killing fellow Tutsis or moderate Hutus. Other victims were first forced to witness people being killed before they themselves got killed. Among those who were being killed happened to be relatives or family members of the survivors.
>
> It was just by sheer chance that any children survived this genocide. Some hid among dead bodies while others hid in swamps, in pit latrines, in deep pits, or were on the move trying to escape. Some were given refuge by relatives or strangers while others sought refuge in churches or hid in forests.[21]

This excerpt of genocide accounts allows us to peer into the deepest depravity of human cruelty as we confront how genocide attacks children—even unborn children. These are deaths authored and intended by decades of symbolic dehumanization of the targets conditioning perpetrators to view their acts of violence as inevitable and necessary. These exceptional deaths as texts authored by genocidaires spell out for us the intensity of rhetorical venom that rejects even a distant future of Tutsi presence in Rwanda. Not even moral conventions of deference for innocence and vulnerability of children prevented the attackers from carrying out heinous crimes day after day in broad daylight before many public peers. This obvious general moral sanction attached to having more than one hundred thousand killers unleashed to cleanse a society of those deemed "unacceptable" must register for us all at a deep moral and ethical level, if we are to reconcile ourselves to a possible future without such terrible acts.

ENDING THE GENOCIDE

It is tempting, in analyzing an existential human crisis like the Rwandan genocide, to refrain from looking for heroes. One may imagine that such a rhetorical designation will lay the groundwork for revenge and enduring anger. Wiesel's axiology about genocide provides a means for understanding the error of that paradigm. There are those who were not silent. There were those who were not passive. There were those that resisted. Under the leadership of Paul Kagame, the Rwandan Patriotic Front represented the human interests of the victims. RPF was a political and military force that was more than a voice for those being silenced in killings. RPF was a military response to genocidal massacres. Almost immediately, this relatively small force in comparison to the Hutu government forces, and associated Interwahame, fought back and seized the landscape of Rwanda in growing segments to provide relief and safety for victims. Recognizing Kagame and the RPF as heroes is not the predicate to another genocide against Hutus. Recognizing the military response to save the Tutsis and associated Hutu sympathizers is not a call for more or vengeful violence. The recognition of Kagame's heroic military and political forces is an empirical witness of how genocide comes to an end and how peace may endure. By July 1994, RPF was successful in liberating the capital city Kigali from control of the dominant Hutu forces and declare July 4 as their new Independence Day. A 2012 academic summary provides this rather straightforward conclusion: "It is only through the victory of the largely Tutsi rebel group that the slaughter ends. The Hutu genocidaires are pushed out of Rwanda, mostly into the D.R.C., where elements continue a low-grade insurgency against Rwanda's new government (event R6)."[22] Intellectual honesty about this atrocity requires us to acknowledge how the genocide ended. Without this knowledge in hand, we are at risk for perpetuating the spiral of hopelessness that has tended to allow genocides to continue decade upon decade.

JUSTICE FOR THE GENOCIDE

A difficult challenge was seeking justice for this genocide. The devastation of Rwanda provided little in the way of resources to bring the suitable prosecutions. In 1996, the *Christian Science Monitor* provided this effective summation of the practical problems facing the nation:

Hutu militia leaders in 1994 tried to spread responsibility among so many villagers that there may have been as many as 100,000 murderers. Nor could there be any mistake about motive. No society could mount an adequate response to a crime of this magnitude, least of all Rwanda. Only 12 of the country's 800 judges survived the massacres, and although aid programs have trained another 300, there are still not enough judges to prosecute common criminals, let alone genocidaires. The prosecutors' offices are even more impoverished.[23]

More recently, the U.S. State Department provides this summary of the justice process culminating in Rwanda:

> In November 1994, the U.N. Security Council established the International Criminal Tribunal for Rwanda (ICTR), based in Arusha, Tanzania, to prosecute high-level genocide perpetrators. The ICTR, which received U.S. funding, concluded its work in 2012, having convicted 62 individuals. An appeals chamber continues to hear challenges, while a follow-on "mechanism" continues to seek the arrest and trial of three accused fugitives. The Rwandan government and survivor groups have criticized aspects of the ICTR's proceedings, including early releases granted to some convicts. Domestically, Rwanda organized grassroots "gacaca" trials, drawing on traditional justice mechanisms, to identify and try over a million low-level perpetrators. Rwanda continues to seek the arrest and extradition of alleged perpetrators abroad; in recent years, U.S. federal attorneys have prosecuted several Rwandans in the United States for immigration fraud, citing their involvement in the genocide.[24]

The year 2019 constituted an important step in the justice timeline. Ultimately the maximum prison sentence for those convicted of genocide crimes was twenty-five years. The anniversary poses practical questions today about justice. Was twenty-five years of prison enough? How does a perpetrator feel upon release? Are the motives and animus gone or are they accentuated and hardened? What is reconciliation? What is something as profound as forgiveness? Who can require or teach such things and upon what authority? These questions continue to haunt as they must. Chapter 3 details the emergence of *gacaca* courts. These courts were important to the necessary process of reconciling a nation so profoundly wounded. Perpetrators are now emerging from prison sentences and not every mind was changed from its violent dispositions. The problem of trained ethnic hatred remains.

CONCLUSION

The incredible sociological study completed by E. O. Wilson, *The Social Conquest of the Earth*, details the one enduring rhetorical thread that connects humanity across time and culture: the public killing of the innocent.[25] Utilizing vast anthropological literatures touching upon more than seventy thousand social groups worldwide and thousands of years of human history, Wilson concludes that our love of killing is what we have most in common. The book leaves little room for hope and it piles the bodies resulting from genocide so high that we may not be able to see the hopeful thesis imagined in this book. Millions upon millions of innocent human beings have been killed since the beginning of human societies. Innocent people continue to be killed today in places as diverse as Burma, Nigeria, and Syria. Scholars can begin in this dark valley of the human consciousness not to be proud or even differentiated. The intellectual community can begin here to be honest and to confess. This is our humanity. This is what human societies have done and what they continue to do. The Rwandan genocide, only twenty-five years old, is a reminder of failed intellectual sophistication. The intensity and brutality of the 1994 genocide is a grim conclusion to humanity's bloodiest century. In 2021, it is not too early or too late to think about whether this century can be different or perhaps the first to put an end to such brutality. This conclusion gathers the causes, and even preliminary solutions, to the Rwandan genocide as we begin to stake out the argumentation and debate pedagogy that might lead humanity out of this dark valley.

At the heart of the cause of genocide is a well-understood and researched communication problem: propaganda. Genocidaires and their associated political partners deliberately deceive a public in order to lead them into an atrocity against their fellow innocent human beings. Teachers and educators have experience in recognizing these things and we know the characteristics at a distance. In order to best stop genocide in the future academics must firmly grasp this root. Genocides begin with propaganda. This book argues for the most antithetical communication practice with regard to propaganda: debate. When individuals debate, they feel the sense of importance attached to their own voice.

C. S. Lewis provided an excellent entry to this project when he juxtaposes the powers of argument and propaganda in his fictional theological examination of good and evil in *The Screwtape Letters*. In Lewis's fictional plot, he imagines the devil training a junior apprentice and providing advice on the promotion of evil in the world. In the opening of chapter 1, as authored by an imaginary devil trying to bring the world to a collective demise, senior demon Screwtape explains our own present paradox to his junior demon Wormwood:

> My dear Wormwood,
> I note what you say about guiding your patient's reading and taking care that he sees a good deal of his materialist friend. But are you not being a trifle naive? It sounds as if you supposed that argument was the way to keep him out of the Enemy's clutches. That might have been so if he had lived a few centuries earlier. At that time the humans still knew pretty well when a thing was proved and when it was not; and if it was proved they really believed it. They still connected thinking with

doing and were prepared to alter their way of life as the result of a chain of reasoning. But what with the weekly press and other such weapons we have largely altered that. Your man has been accustomed, ever since he was a boy, to have a dozen incompatible philosophies dancing about together inside his head.

He doesn't think of doctrines as primarily "true" or "false," but as "academic" or "practical" "outworn" or "contemporary," conventional or ruthless. Jargon, *not argument* is your best ally in keeping him from the Church. Don't waste time trying to make him think that materialism is true! Make him think it is strong, or stark, or courageous—that is the philosophy of the future. That's the sort of thing he cares about.

The trouble about argument is that it moves the whole struggle on to the Enemy's own ground. He can argue too; whereas in really practical propaganda of the kind I am suggesting He has been shown for centuries to be greatly the inferior of Our Father Below. By the very act of arguing, you awake the patient's reason; and once it is awake, who can foresee the result? . . .
Your affectionate uncle
Screwtape [emphasis added][26]

Lewis's profound suggestion reminds readers of the enduring possibilities found in argumentation. Argumentation has at its intrinsic nature and core a human capacity to dispel the magic of propaganda and derive a truer world free of the most profound injustices. Written in some of the darkest moments of World War II and the formative years of the Holocaust, Lewis reminds us of the profound human capacity found in argumentation. As much as any episode of genocide has ever come to an end, it is educationally fair for us to pursue the goal of ending genocide.

Empirically, this century does have encouragement to offer beyond suggestion or mere metaphysics. This century is witnessing the decline of genocide. Researchers like Steven Pinker document dramatic declines of all forms of human violence including the most granular act of genocide: murder. Theoretically and empirically, we are justified in continuing with our examination of Rwanda rising because 1994 is only the beginning of this central anecdote. What transpired twenty-five years hence is a portal to a potential future without genocide. We will find that around the world the methodology of discursive complexity is winning a world without genocide—where it is able to take hold. This holding stretches well beyond the borders of Rwanda and into the educational habits of billions. The following chapters document episodes in a grander picture of armies of nonviolence animated by argumentation as a practice to lay down the sword of propaganda and take up the deliberation of societies at peace. This deliberative model can be achieved by teaching and encouraging debate. Debate as a public ethic in the education of the young can create robust minds unwilling to be silent in the face of threats created by propaganda. Such an educational emphasis creates a proliferation of discursive complexity. In the next chapter, we will examine the empirically successful models of discursive complexity and the theoretical underpinnings of how this argumentation approach rejects the world guided by propaganda while creating the preconditions of abundant human life.

NOTES

1. Musa Wakhungu Olaka, "Collaborating to Preserve and Disseminate Testimonies of Childsurvivors of the 1994 Genocide in Rwanda," *Cape Town IFLA WLIC* (June 2015): 1–12, accessed August 1, 2020, http://library.ifla.org/1161/7/206-olaka-en.pdf.

2. Angus Stevenson and Christine A. Lindberg, "Propaganda" in the *New American Oxford Dictionary* (Oxford University Press, 2018).

3. Ben Voth and Aaron Noland, "Argumentation and the International Problem of Genocide," *Contemporary Argumentation and Debate* 28 (September 2007): 38–46, http://search.ebscohost.com.proxy.libraries.smu.edu/login.aspx?direct=true&db=cms&AN=40305088&site=ehost-live&scope=site.

4. Voth and Noland, "Argumentation and the International Problem of Genocide," 38–46.

5. Adolf Hitler, *Mein Kampf,* translated by Ralph Manheim (Boston: Houghton Mifflin Company, 1943).

6. Jacques Ellul, *Propaganda: The Formation of Men's Attitudes* (New York: Random House, 1965): 47.

7. "Dehumanisation—How Tutsis Were Reduced to Cockroaches, Snakes to Be Killed," *Africa News Service*, COMTEX News Network, Inc, March 14, 2014.

8. Kennedy Ndahiro, "In Rwanda, We Know All about Dehumanizing Language: Years of Cultivated Hatred Led to Death on a Horrifying Scale," *The Atlantic*, April 13, 2019, https://www.theatlantic.com/ideas/archive/2019/04/rwanda-shows-how-hateful-speech-leads-violence/587041/.

9. Elie Wiesel, foreword, in C. Rittmer and S. Myers (Eds.), *The Courage to Care* (New York: New York University Press, 1986).

10. Samantha Power, *A Problem from Hell: America and the Age of Genocide* (New York: Harper Collins, 2002).

11. Dallas Holocaust Museum, https://www.dhhrm.org/about/; Paul Bartrop, *Resisting the Holocaust: Upstanders, Partisans, and Survivors* (Santa Barbara, CA: ABC CLIO, 2016).

12. Ndahiro, "In Rwanda, We Know All about Dehumanizing Language."

13. Bizimana Jean Damascene, "Some Key Activities that Characterized the Preparation of Genocide against Tutsi between Dates of 13–19 January 1991–1994," *KGM*, January 16, 2020, accessed July 15, 2020, https://www.kgm.rw/some-key-activities-that-characterized-the-preparation-of-genocide-against-tutsi-between-dates-of-13-19-january-1991-1994/.

14. Eric Heinze, "The Rhetoric of Genocide in U.S. Foreign Policy: Rwanda and Darfur Compared," *Political Science Quarterly* 122, no. 3 (2007): 359–83, accessed August 17, 2020, www.jstor.org/stable/20202884.

15. Power, *A Problem from Hell: America and the Age of Genocide*, 340–41.

16. Ndahiro, "In Rwanda, We Know All about Dehumanizing Language."

17. Ndahiro, "In Rwanda, We Know All about Dehumanizing Language."

18. "Rwanda Genocide: 100 Days of Slaughter," BBC, April 4, 2019, accessed August 1, 2020, https://www.bbc.com/news/world-africa-26875506.

19. Megan Specia, "How a Nation Reconciles after Genocide Killed Nearly a Million People," *New York Times*, April 25, 2017, accessed July 20, 2020, https://www.nytimes.com/2017/04/25/world/africa/rwandans-carry-on-side-by-side-two-decades-after-genocide.html?smid=fb-share&referer=http://m.facebook.com.

20. Glory Iribagiza, "102-Year-Old Genocide Survivor Who Lost All Her 17 Children Reminisces about Meeting the King, Old Times," *The New Times*, March 9, 2020, accessed July 15, 2020, https://www.newtimes.co.rw/news/102-year-old-genocide-survivor-who-lost-all-her-17-children-reminisces-about-meeting-king-old.

21. Olaka, "Collaborating to Preserve and Disseminate Testimonies of Child Survivors of the 1994 Genocide in Rwanda."

22. Omar Shahabudin Mcdoom, "War and Genocide in Africa's Great Lakes Region since Independence," *ResearchGate* (January 2012): 1–41, accessed July 14, 2020, https://www.researchgate.net/publication/48911153_War_and_genocide_in_Africa's_Great_Lakes_region_since_independence.

23. Iain Guest, "For Rwandan Genocide Survivors, It's Pragmatism vs. Revenge," *The Christian Science Monitor*, August 30, 1996, accessed July 15, 2020, https://www.csmonitor.com/1996/0830/083096.opin.opin.1.html.

24. "Rwanda: In Brief," Congressional Research Service, updated May 14, 2019, accessed July 10, 2020, https://fas.org/sgp/crs/row/R44402.pdf.

25. Edward O. Wilson, *The Social Conquest of the Earth* (New York: W.W. Norton & Co., 2012).

26. C. S. Lewis, *The Screwtape Letters* (New York: MacMillan Co., 1943): 1–4.

TWO

Discursive Complexity and the Global Renaissance for Justice

Discursive complexity is the theoretical foundation of this book. It is upon this basis that the teaching and instruction in debate can make profound and positive changes in our world. The book *Rhetoric of Genocide* provides this definition of discursive complexity in 2014:

> Discursive complexity can be defined and recognized as the capacity of an individual or group to encourage and allow dissent. Furthermore, discursive complexity is a principle recognizing the value of various expressed viewpoints. The notion of discursive complexity is highly contrasted with a diminished notion of discursive simplicity whereby an individual or group demands or insists upon a limited capacity of expression. Argumentation inherently valorizes discursive complexity by emphasizing the study and teaching of contrasting and competing ideas. Discursive complexity represents a moral point of view since we can prefer individuals and groups that make greater provision for free expression. Such environments encourage critical thinking and diminish the expectation and need for violence. [1]

One of the most practical examples of discursive complexity is the profound statement of its essence in the First Amendment of the U.S. Constitution. In the twenty-first century, the U.S. Constitution remains one of the most recognized and important statements about the propensity of human freedom. The rhetorical essence of the U.S. Constitution is to provide a social contract between people and government which limits the government while ensuring basic peace and tranquility available in central forms of governance. In striking this balance in 1791, constitutional writers grappled with whether the formula spelled out in the document was sufficient in its definition of the roles or whether additional stipulations should be made to prevent the government from growing into an abusive form that they recognized as stemming from the British monarchy of their day. Fearing that any specification of rights may foster an illusion that government creates rights, some writers urged that amendments to the Constitution should not be created.[2] Ultimately, voices in favor of specifications prevailed and the amendments to the U.S. Constitution began with the First Amendment. It is not a coincidence that among the first rights listed as not to be encroached upon by the government were rights emanating from the central idea of freedom of speech. These notions conflate well with this definition of discursive complexity. As a practical example, one may consider the freedom to dissent within various geographic settings. Am I free to dissent in the United States? Am I free to dissent in the Gaza Strip? Am I free to dissent in Tel Aviv? Am I free to dissent in Hong Kong? Am I free to dissent in Moscow? While there is no absolute right to dissent, the greater degree to which a person may dissent in any particular place is a measure of discursive complexity. That is the particular idea of freedom this work is addressed toward. With regard to the international focus of this book, "freedom of speech" is growing in popularity in the global community.[3] This global popularity suggests that it is among the most intrinsic desires among human beings—to be able to speak and to be heard. There are five freedoms indicated in the First Amendment to the United States Constitution: freedom of religion, freedom of speech, freedom of press, freedom of petition, and freedom of assembly. All five of these freedoms constitute a civil rights hand that any reasonable advocate should be aware of in order to change their society for the better. The more than two hundred years of American struggles about their meaning and practice represent an important global question about whether human beings are free, and how the practice of that freedom can bring individuals under threat from their own government. This hand can grasp the public policy options necessary for changing the world for the better. In teaching and educating people to debate, the individual capacity to reshape political environs is dramatically increased. Debaters are likely to become the legislators, the lawyers, advocates, and most simply—the least silent members of a society. Debate does not merely enable them to change the world, but to change the world for the better because we are reducing the probability of silent bystanders.

This later point is important. World changing happens all the time. But does the world change for the better or for the worse? It is a central moral and ethical contention of this analysis that a better world will be had in those instances where changes make people freer. How can such freedom be measured? Analysis of the manifest realities of discursive complexity like those already outlined above are helpful. What are some further and prominent indicators of this greater freedom and greater discursive complexity?

There are a number of NGOs (nongovernmental organizations) dedicated to the national and international studies of these First Amendment freedoms and we can create a rather empirical review of these characteristics.[4] It is the goal of this analysis to create a community of individuals committed in principle and practice to these five freedoms. Though these five freedoms do work in tandem, freedom of speech is the most well recognized of these rights both inside the United States and worldwide.[5] There are three major theories about freedom of speech and its importance. These theories arguably apply to the broader set of rights noted here as well. The three theoretical perspectives are: (1) marketplace of ideas, (2) free speech helps democracy, and (3) free speech increases individual autonomy.[6] All of these theoretical perspectives justify a global promotion of discursive complexity and explain how the five freedoms of the First Amendment tend to enable ideal political outcomes both for the society and the individual. There are certainly more intimate civic values contained within these broad theories including values such as justice.[7]

These theoretical matters are empirically measured. Organizations as noted earlier—like Freedom House—provide explicit localized measures of many nations worldwide.[8] These denotations are made on an annual basis and allow us to recognize both progression and regression with regard to the forums that enable debate and discursive complexity through mechanisms such as newspaper. In their most recent report for 2020, Freedom House notes that fifteen democracies have declined with regard to important internal commitments like those noted here while nine have made progress.[9] While this is discouraging, it both highlights the need for pedagogical tools to improve these conditions and a confidence that we will be able to observe the results. Debate is well understood as a primary educational tool that can accomplish this goal even in international settings.[10]

Even if discursive complexity is defined and understood as means of measuring such freedom, it is challenging to demonstrate that discursive complexity is ethical. In the earliest explanation of this concept, a chronological delineation of the ethical progression is made. One of the most intuitive examples is that of the Korean Peninsula. The common ethnic makeup of this geography suggests a relatively homogenous probability with regard to discursive complexity and the broader panoply of civic rights that might exist there. The differences between the divided sovereignty of North and South Korea is among the starkest in all the world. The people of North Korea have a lower life expectancy—by ten years.[11] The North Koreans are substantially shorter than South Koreans. These are minor health indicators of a larger more serious problem with regard to the right of dissent. North Korea operates dangerous and massive labor concentration camps. An American who tried to take a propaganda poster from North Korea was recently returned to the United States in a comatose state resulting from such a detention. He ultimately died from his injuries suffered at the hands of this brutal government.[12] Many of the borders of the world established in the past century were deadly results brought at tremendous costs of violence. The twentieth century was epistemologically governed by the metaphor of the AK-47. Individuals confined in these closed societies recited propaganda compelled upon them by way of violent weapons like the AK-47. This Russian military weapon is one of the most prolific pieces of military hardware ever made. An individual who owns such a weapon can kill another human being with relative ease, and such threats compel consent to all kinds of inhumane forms of governance including the most extreme demands of democide, eliminationism, and genocide.[13] Millions of people professed to believe an idea—even an ideology—for the sake of not being killed in a brutal slaughter or ritualistic public killing. The problem of rhetorical intensity and its tendency to lead to mass killings is well observed in studies of argumentation and rhetoric.[14] "Certainty leads us to attack evil; being less sure we would but resist it. The difference between attack and resistance is the difference between violence and argument, the thread on which our lives dangle."[15] The dangling thread of argument is one which must be fortified by the pedagogy of debate if we are to erase the threat of genocide in the twenty-first century.

Rule by force is low discursive complexity within any notion of a social contract between a public and government. It is clearly and manifestly unethical, and even evil. At the heart of the contest between the governors and the governed is the problem of dissent. Disagreement with governing authorities can lead to being beaten, jailed, attacked, and perhaps killed. This is the immoral world of propaganda and genocide that captured the governing imagination in the twentieth century and killed nearly two hundred million people. The immoral condition is driven by the need to constrain free and open communication as expressed in the five freedoms already noted.

As a matter of profound moral and ethical contrast, we have the matter of societies of open communication. This society is metaphorically governed by the cell phone. Though the cell phone also shoots, its weaponization is one of media capture and a means of betraying the propagandistic world that seeks to make all communication an undue devotion to the super-intending state. Individuals can show the ideological monstrosities of public killings, lynchings, stonings, and so many ruthless forms of execution and punishment dealt out by unreasonable sovereigns by simply using the camera features of their cell phone. The universal audience,[16] potentially connected in the openness of a technological network, can judge more fairly what is happening within the closed system of propaganda offered by a group like ISIS. From 2012 to 2019, ISIS was able to build an ever-expansive AK-47 eliminationist supremacist worldview largely within the geographic realms of Syria and Iraq. Their sovereignty killed more than fifty thousand innocent people—mostly Muslims—in an effort to communicate their death as text ruthless unethical ideology. ISIS is but one of hundreds of human societies that one might lay upon a grid of discursive complexity and discover its lack of moral concern.

The well-known and a much-cited Frankfurt School thinker Jurgen Habermas laid out an elegant global trajectory of this theory in *Communication and the Evolution of Society*.[17] Communication is a key ingredient by which the world can measure her progress from injustice toward justice. From the intimate concerns of how an individual might come to grasp "communication competence" to the larger quests for elusive abstractions such as "justice," Habermas details a formula for judgment founded upon communication. For this work, communication competence at the individual level is best secure through the teaching and practice of debate. Students will master the elements of a given society as described by Habermas. In so doing, they will be intimately able to form a more just union for governance among their fellow human beings.

Habermas's break from the Frankfurt School was in many respects driven by his frustration with exceedingly materialist explanations for the inadequacies of equality and justice within human societies. Departing from the notion of "capital" and "dialectic materialism," Habermas supposes that there are some bootstraps by which the individual may rise within a society: the ability to communicate. Studies documenting limitations to Habermas's notion of a public sphere inhabited by reasonable beings underscore the need to make debate instruction and argumentation training more broad based.[18] Habermas's notion has fallen under intense attack from critical theorists who highlight how elite members have access to the public sphere. This special access makes justice difficult to obtain for marginalized communities. The solution is not the abolition of the public sphere or reification of irrational identity-based claims, but to distribute the means more broadly to communication competence outlined by Habermas. Habermas's rejection of the materialist thesis of the Frankfurt School was bound up in a conviction that injustice has intrinsic connection to failed access to communication. Material standing does not explain social outcomes as well as communication standing. Individuals with an ability to lay aside silence can improve the social condition and in fact these are the individuals in history who have done so. Professor Ferry provides this review of Habermas's theorizing on the force of good arguments:

> The first step is to define a rational action or a rational opinion with regard to one's ability to give sound reasons in support of it (Habermas, 1984, p. 8–17). The second step is, in turn, to define argumentation as the means by which one can evaluate the rationality of his/her opinion and action (Habermas, 1984, p. 18–22). The third step is to consider that this evaluation can only happen if the argumentative process were conducted in respect of certain rules, such as symmetry between the

arguers (Habermas, 1984, p. 25–26). Those rules are supposed to ensure the compliance with the force of the better argument.[19]

These points are drawn from Habermas's key work *The Theory of Communicative Action*.[20] Argumentation study and critical theorists worry what the "force of good reason" is and lament its possible abuse.[21] There is of course no reasonable alternative to this process. There are ways to improve the process whereby reason giving is built but it remains hazardous to press the well-being of humanity toward something more in line with Plato's Republic of Philosopher Kings. It is important to realize that where Habermas's theory leaves ambiguity, debate as a practice and pedagogy provides answer to fill the vacuum. The important vagaries arise over the "rules" and the "symmetry of arguers." This is precisely what debate does best even as debate allows for a variety of styles and formats. The activity of debate is itself rather fluid and unstable apart from the four criteria already noted. Debate provides the symmetry of arguers and elaborates the rules for argument. Professors Platt and Majdik make the point that Habermas's view of the underlying questions of ethics proceed from Christian origin: "Christianity, and nothing else, is the ultimate foundation of liberty, conscience, human rights, and democracy, the benchmarks of western civilization."[22] Christianity's iterative dialectic relationship with viewpoints through Judaism, Samaritan derivations of Judaism, Gentile acceptance, Roman appropriation of Christian belief in AD 320, and many more iterative phases point to a deliberative process that accords with Habermas's ever expanding and more inclusive public sphere.

In concert with Habermas's thesis, this book establishes an international path for the better world and a manner by which the organic intellectual described by Anthony Gramsci might enact a true and actually effective "pedagogy of the oppressed."[23] Injustice and equality are not functions of material deficits—though material can impact the larger sources—such inadequacies are the function of communication deficits. Martin Luther King Jr. described the communication deficits with his usual rhetorical elegance: "Men often hate each other because they fear each other; they fear each other because they don't know each other; they don't know each other because they cannot communicate."[24] This connects well with our earlier premise provided by Wiesel. The opposite of communication—silence can hurt the victim most. This communication deficit is the necessary aim as an intellectual community in order to raise the human standard with regard to any possible ethical outcome in the twenty-first century.

The theory of discursive complexity may appear to have coherence. Discursive complexity can be defined, textualized, and taught in the pedagogy of debate. How can we as readers be sure this teaching of debate will work? There are so many interconnected problems, and humanity's history of pain is so great, that this all may be insurmountable even for a good idea. We can be confident that this plan will work because it already has. Moreover, the plan is already in place and working. Debate director and researcher Gordon Mitchell highlights how collegiate debate empowers human agency in the ways noted in this analysis in this credo for the American Forensics Association (forensics is the academic umbrella term for speech and debate instruction):

> Our principle is the power of individuals to participate with others in shaping their world through the human capacity of language;
> Our commitment to argument expresses our faith in reason-giving as a key to that power; Our commitment to advocacy expresses our faith in oral expression as a means to empower people in situations of their lives; Our research studies the place of argument and advocacy in these situations of empowerment;
> Our teaching seeks to expand students' appreciation for the place of argument and advocacy in shaping their world, and to prepare students through classrooms, forums, and competition for participation in their world through the power of expression; and
> Our public involvement seeks to empower through argument and advocacy.
> —American Forensic Association Credo [25]

The lofty goals enumerated in the American Forensic Association's credo have long served as beacons that steer pedagogical practice in argumentation and debate. The credo's expression of faith in "reason giving," "oral expression," and critical thinking as formulas for student "empowerment" is reflected in the many textbooks that have been written to guide the academic study of argumentation. "The relevance of skill in argumentation seems self-evident to anyone living in a democratic society," write George W. Ziegelmueller and Jack Kay in *Argumentation: Inquiry and Advocacy*, and they go further to say "The notion of full and free public debate on the vital issues facing society is deeply rooted in the documents and ideas comprising the American conscience." [26] Making a similar point in the introduction to their textbook *Argumentation and Critical Decision Making*, Richard D. Rieke and Malcolm O. Sillars suggest that "the ability to participate effectively in reasoned discourse leading to critical decision making is required in virtually every aspect of life in a democracy." [27] "We need debate not only in the legislature and the courtroom but in every other area of society as well," echoes Austin J. Freeley in *Argumentation and Debate*, "since most of our rights are directly dependent on debate." [28]

We need to do more to accelerate the success of debate praxis like that described by Professor Mitchell and other debate educators like Ziegelmueller, Rieke, and Sillars. The good news is that a research trajectory of more than a decade including discernible rubrics and results are available in the present. This research gathers upon the empirically harsh realities from the twentieth century that documented so many genocidal consequences created by communication failure and propaganda. Key discoveries include: (1) the genocidaire, (2) the relationship of the individual and the State, and (3) the dramatic success of the American civil rights movement as fueled by debate praxis.

THE GENOCIDAIRE

Noted rhetorical theorist Kenneth Burke discussed in his symbolic study of human interactions the intense fascination with killing as a symbolic human act.[29] Professor Aaron Noland, originally examined the initial rhetorical textures of genocide in 2007.[30] Only the French language seems to have a term for the perpetrator of genocide: the Genocidaire. This linguistic limitation is significant, since from a Burkean standpoint, it limits our capacity to understand the agent and the act. The habit of viewing genocides as a *scenic feature* is detrimental to the victims and our capacity to seek justice. Media coverage tends to emphasize the place of genocide rather than the agents and agency. Tragedies in Sudan and Rwanda leave observers more familiar with the place than the crime. This scene/agency ratio creates the public impression that genocide is endemic to certain parts of the world. False generalizations become acceptable "understandings" of genocide such as: "Africa will always be this way." "We cannot change Somalia, Rwanda, and Sudan." "*Those* people over there are always. . . ." The reduction of human actions to geographical motion is a selection and therefore deflects reality.[31]

Individuals have chosen to give orders to kill. Individuals and groups have taken up arms in response to propaganda for the purpose of carrying out genocides. It is possible to communicate with reference to agents and agency and reestablish the agent/scene ratio.[32] This distinction is vital to the operation of international law. Establishing motive and action remains a critical distinction in the prosecution of genocide as a crime. So long as perpetrators can rely upon communication patterns emphasizing the scene, they will know that identification will be limited and the risk of prosecution low.

An early twenty-first-century example can be found in the case of Sudan. The difficult struggle over naming the Sudanese violence ended abruptly in 2003 when U.S. Secretary of State Colin Powell said in public to the U.S. Congress that the violence in Sudan constituted "genocide." In an instant, the scene/act ratio reversed itself and became act/scene. The world saw an argument that the government of Sudan was committing genocide. This public argument stood in contrast to the State Department's careful avoidance of the term during the 1994 Rwandan genocide.[33]

A consistent pattern of communicating about violence as instigated and caused, rather than serially inevitable, will convert motion back into action. The genocides in Africa do not arise out of the soil or elements of the continent. The genocides there and around the world are the consequences of public arguments made to individuals who then carry out the crimes—whether in Cambodia, Kosovo, Rwanda, Iraq, or Turkey. Communication and argumentation scholars can identify proponents of genocide. Individuals can be named and the rhetoric they employ can be critiqued. This should displace the pedestrian "place is violent" pattern, which encourages students of the global public sphere to believe nothing can change. The Joseph Kony campaign of 2012 is a great example of how communication can target an aspirant genocidaire like Kony and destabilize an emergent danger rooted in propaganda. Kony was recruiting child soldiers into his "Lord's Army" and committing incredible atrocities across Uganda and the region.[34] A global campaign to identify and shame ultimately led to a U.S. military collaboration to cripple his genocidal activity and force him into hiding.[35]

In the case of Sudan, in 2019, the genocidaire Omar Bashir abruptly stepped aside.[36] The action of this ICC convicted genocidaire was prompted by broad public protests within the nation. Sudan was hardly the ideal communication public sphere that Habermas or any other critical theorists would dream about. Nonetheless, public arguments removed the dictator from power and now multiple legislative acts are repealing draconian social codes aimed at marginalizing women and members of nondominant religious groups.[37] The naming of the genocide and identification of the genocidaire in the early twenty-first century put in motion the current opening of the public sphere. Sudan is a dramatic case study in how closed societies can abruptly open—especially in those cases where the global community remains committed to openness and a willingness to be candid about the causes and consequences of closed propaganda societies.

THE STATE VERSUS THE INDIVIDUAL

A second remedy from the communication sphere regarding genocide is the building of a broad critique of state's rights. Building on the analogy of civil rights, critics can ask questions about state sovereignty and the privilege of killing domestic civilians accorded to state leaders. The peculiar intensity of this privilege in places such as North Korea and Zimbabwe should draw critical attention. International law presently provides privilege to states over individuals.[38] International interference in state's rights is construed as an act of war and leaves individuals without refuge from brutal violations of their humanity.

The boundaries drawn by colonial powers become the lines of a discursive prison wherein an individual's humanity becomes profoundly contingent upon the wishes of the state.

A difficult issue in this discussion is an understanding of the differences between war and genocide. When military personnel from one sovereign engage in combat with military personnel from another sovereign, this is war. When military personnel or state sponsored militias attack and kill their own domestic populations, this is genocide. There is a difference and that difference is profoundly moral. The civic power position of civilians is inherently limited compared to military personnel. Discursive complexity in civilian/military relations is thus low. The capacity to resist and disagree with militarized states is marginal. Consequently, the moral outrage regarding genocide must exceed the moral outrage surrounding war. At present, it is difficult to discern that global moral sense, even among academic and international experts.

The dramatic reduction of state to state violence suggests that the world does perceive the state as more valuable than the individual. A broad critique of this preference should be supported by communication scholars due to intrinsic limits genocide imposes on public expression for the attacked population.

BELOVED COMMUNITY: DEBATE TEACHING THAT WORKED

One of these more pernicious human problems noted above is racism. Humanity has always formed, and in fact continues to form, pejorative judgments about one another on the basis of race. These judgments bring with them injustice, inequality, violence, and even genocide. There is no easy solution to racism. Nonetheless, there are successful efforts from which to glean a path forward. Various significant and additional perspectives on anti-Black racism emerged in the mid-twentieth century. Great Debater James Farmer Jr. set in motion his advocacy of the Congress of Racial Equality (CORE) in 1942. CORE put John Lewis on the Freedom Rides bus in 1961. Malcolm X was originally an Afro-pessimist advocate in the early 1960s. James Meredith has a uniquely American idealist approach to the problem. Stokely Carmichael led a major Afro-pessimist break away in the late 1960s. These and many more set into motion different forms of advocacy that can be arrayed in a spectrum of idealist and pessimist frameworks. An Afro-idealist project that did succeed in dismantling a key feature of racism known as segregation in the United States is historically apparent.

It is worth pausing on this notion of Afro-idealism. The theories of Afro-pessimism—the evident antithesis of this notion—is well established. This scholarly summary is provided by professors Brar and Sharma:

Gathering their ideas under the banner of Afro-Pessimism, Wilderson and Sexton have sought to dismantle a liberal consensus in Black Studies by taking apart the logics of multiculturalism and solidarity through common lines of racial oppression. Shaped by a particular reading of Frantz Fanon, as well as selective interpretations of Achille Mbembe, Orlando Patterson and Lewis Gordon, Wilderson and Sexton have assembled a virulent account of blackness (47). For them, blackness is exclusively tied to the Middle Passage and the slave trade, and as such it does not travel. The black is the sole unit for the paradigm (as opposed to experience) of blackness, because what it concentrates are historical modes of dispossession and alienation that amount to social death. Such conceptual moves allow Wilderson and Sexton to distinguish between generalised racism (directed by whites and experienced by all non-whites) and the more categorical violence of anti-blackness (which is generated both by whites and all non-black people of colour and directed towards all black people). The engine for the production of anti-blackness is civil society, a hegemonic structure which reproduces and sustains the white/non-black through a libidinal drive for the public spectacle of black social death.[39]

Afro-pessimism supposes at an intimate human level—so intimate as to be a psychological subtext—we are all *hopelessly* racist. We have no real choice but to perhaps "burn it all down." Social destruction is not a mechanism for political change working within an existing order. In this respect destructive calls like these are revolutionary and derivative to movements like the French revolution. The radical notions of the French revolutionaries are referred to as Jacobinism. Jacobin politics as initiated by key practitioners like Saul Alinsky and Stokely Carmichael may be burning itself out. The radical notion offered by Black power advocates like Carmichael may finally yield to the enduring idealism of men like James Meredith. African American race politics burns brightest in America today with regard to what the future of Jacobin politics may be. California academic radical Dr. Frank Wilderson also urges students to "burn it all down."[40] However, what happens when we are surrounded by those hollowed out and de-institutionalized scenes? In other words, we should destroy all notions of social order, knowing that every order brings with it the subconscious, yet powerfully destructive, force of racism. Taneshi Coates is one of the most coherent and profound thinkers in the realm of Afro-pessimism. He concedes the problems associated with this intellectual life and knowledge in 2019:

> I have no teaching advice at all. I was a terrible student. I failed my way through high school. I don't know how I got into Howard University, but I failed my way through that too. I just—I don't know. I have horrible advice, in terms of teaching, I'm serious because one of the things that annoys me is, people act like they know everything. . . . Come on, be clear about what you know and what you don't know. I'm gonna talk about what I don't know. And listen, here's the thing that

happens. You are well-researched and knowledgeable about one thing that you've been thinking about a long time and you've been reading about a long time. That does not make you well-researched and knowledgeable about all things.... I get this title, "public intellectual," and I don't like it, because what it sounds to me is, like, people who B.S. They're smart about one thing, and so they play into this notion that they're smart about everything else.... If you want to ask me about writing, I can [talk about it] up one side, down the other. I got you. I'm with you, because I've struggled with that.[41]

The impossibility of knowing is an important pre-text to more humble beginnings of a world without genocide. In her summary of debate as a mechanism for solving the problems of Afro-pessimism, Amber Kelsie concludes: "In studying debate's (im)possibility, we might theorize at the End of the World as a praxis oriented toward its abolition."[42] A too simple explanation of Kelsie's analysis is that the indeterminate nature of debate allows knowledge to refrain from the hard-edged threats of propaganda that continually threaten innocent and vulnerable human life. Knowledge is power. The intoxication of this power is difficult to resist toward the ends of genocide. Coates's confession contains the seed of our Afro-idealist project to leave knowledge both indeterminate and productive for human life. Cross-examination revealing the limits of our knowledge and the public accountability of saying when you do not know the answer are some of the first steps in any reasonable debating process.

"Beloved Community" is an important alternative to Afro-pessimism, having a grounding both in past and future orientations. Beloved Community is an organizing telos to the civil rights movement.[43] Drawn from the Christian teachings of Jesus urging his followers to "love one another," civil rights advocates argued that we "love" each other when we meet one another's needs. The particular problem of racism was broadly confronted in the civil rights movement. The role of debate in forming successful advocates against the human problem of racism is an important justification for further drawing upon this pedagogy to address the many motives, including racism, toward the problem of genocide and a broader array of human injustices.

Several key American civil rights figures were developed in their advocacy through teaching in argumentation and debate. These leaders include: Martin Luther King Jr., James Farmer Jr., Lula Farmer, James Meredith, Malcolm X, and Medgar Evers. Between the years of 1934 and 1967, there was a discreet era of debate training that impacted these individuals toward changing the world away from racist structural violence and toward just human relations predicated on love for one another. Predating King and forming the key pedagogy for the movement were James and Lula Farmer. James and Lula were a Black and White couple married in the 1940s in an era where such interracial marriage was deemed scandalous, if not illegal, in many parts of the world. Their personal convictions married to their experiences in debate yielded advocacy in the form of the Congress of Racial Equality (CORE) created in 1942. An important historical figure and advocate within CORE, Bernice Fisher described Farmer's role in the inception this way: "All of us [the CORE members] were determined believers in the equality of man. And we were activists. Simultaneous with our first experiments of non-violence in America's racial problems came Jim Farmer of New York, with his thesis on 'Brotherhood Mobilization.' The radical son of a theological teacher, Jim was our natural leader."[44] Farmer's experience with debate was, by his own explanation, the formative basis of his moral and intellectual reasoning. He referenced an incident of segregation clarified with his debate coach Melvin Tolson in describing his post graduate work at Howard University with Professor Howard Thurman. Thurman was a highly influential seminary professor who worked with many key civil rights leaders including Farmer and King.[45] He was especially expert on the integration of nonviolent activism like that described by Thoreau as it applied to Christian ministry. Farmer describe the environment of Thurman's classroom in his biography *Lay Bare the Heart*:

> [Thurman] would wait for a response. My hand usually was up first with a question: "Dr. Thurman, are you saying that if a soldier kills the enemy, he is a murderer, or at least a killer? Or if one accepts an assigned status of inferiority—let us say, sits in the balcony of a Jim Crow theater—he *is* inferior?"
>
> Thurman would say, "Ah," and recognize one of the several hands now held aloft.
>
> We would leave the class with no answer, but many intriguing questions that had not occurred to us before. It was Thurman's belief that answers must come from within, from the bit of God in each of us. Perhaps I partly agree with him. I did not want answers. I wanted only questions. The answers could I find for myself, but not from God; from my own powers to reason. If those came from God, then so be it.[46]

A statue of Thurman was added in 2006 to the National Cathedral in Washington, D.C., to commemorate his formative role toward the creation of the nonviolent methodologies embraced by the movement.[47] His statue has greater prominence and size within the cathedral than the small statue for Martin Luther King Jr. located over an arched door. This is a symbolic testament to the power of good teaching toward shaping a better world. By his graduation from Howard University in 1941, Farmer was able to tell his professor father what he wanted to do with his collegiate education: "Destroy Segregation." Between 1942 and 1967, Farmer's civil rights organization of CORE grew from less than a dozen activists to more than eighty thousand in the era culminating in sweeping federal laws like the Civil Rights Act of 1964 and the Voting Rights Act of 1965. These laws were passed after he sat shoulder to shoulder with King and Johnson in the White House to bring such legislation as a powerful ax against the segregationist habits of the nation. By 1967, de facto segregation as indicated by various local signages was abolished in the United States. Farmer's 1961 Freedom Rides were one rather dramatic effort that effectively abolished segregation in interstate travel after two Supreme Court decisions specifying this result had been substantially ignored. The Freedom Rides directly confronted racial animus in the form of terrorism directed against integrated bus riders in Aniston, Alabama. By the fall of 1961, the Interstate Commerce Commission issued rulings perfectly in compliance with James Farmer Jr.'s insistence in a letter for President Kennedy in April 1961.[48] The intrinsic patterns of debate: listening, speaking, structure, and refutation all contributed to the specific advocacy rules of CORE. Farmer's vision came true through nonviolence aimed at communicating the needs of the Black community to a larger community that was in many specific situations and topics denying equality under the law. His wife, Lula Peterson Farmer was also a debater in high school while growing up in the Chicago area.[49] She was the clerical backbone of CORE and undoubtedly sharpened the mind of her husband and co-collaborator in founding the civil rights organization. Argumentation and debate worked to remove powerful state and local obstacles to racial justice through the work of this interracial couple.

James Meredith, the first Black man to attend the University of Mississippi, pursued a distinct but similarly successful agenda aimed at confronting racism. Meredith specifically rejected the movement methodology of Farmer and King. He nonetheless was formed by debate in his collegiate life and used it to engage the legal sphere with arguments that Blacks should be as free to attend White schools as any other American. Meredith's unique legal argument strategy precipitated the verge of a second Civil War in 1962.[50] Meredith's biographies clarify that he never agreed with the social movement activism of organizations like SNCC (Student Nonviolent Coordinating Committee), SCLC (Southern Christian Leadership Council), CORE (Congress of Racial Equality), and other organizations. Meredith believed that *individuals* had rights under the U.S. Constitution that could compel structural changes to the Jim Crow South. In his 2019 biography he provided this insight based on a paper he wrote at Jackson State University titled "My Philosophy of Life":

> Why are men afraid to speak in a society whose very existence is based on freedom of expression? Why are men afraid to meet when the law says that freedom of assembly is an undeniable right? . . . Three days after the paper was completed, I wrote a letter to the students and faculty at Jackson State College, suggesting the organization of a debating group on campus. And three weeks later the Jackson State Debaters Club had been organized and its temporary officers selected.[51]

In Meredith's chronology of activism, his application to University of Mississippi proceeded immediately after founding the debate program at

Jackson State. For Meredith, the long effort to be enrolled at the University of Mississippi was a protracted game of legal chess wherein he maneuvered the segregationists into an untenable position. Ultimately, courts did find a constitutional right for Meredith to attend the school but the only practical way to accomplish this was for U.S. military forces to compel his entry secured by his constitutional right to be there.

Also in Mississippi was NAACP field secretary Medgar Evers. His assassination in 1963 was an important escalation in the struggle to confront and confine racial violence. While a student at Alcorn State University, Evers helped lead a debate program on campus. This was an important part of his brave character in leading a chapter of the NAACP in one of the most dangerous places of intense segregation in the South—Philadelphia, Mississippi. His killing was a prominent motivation for other activists against the problem of White supremacist terrorism. Debate in college was a formative part of his leadership development and personal courage.[52]

Malcolm X is another relatively famous case of a civil rights activist who was deeply trained in debate. While in prison as a young man, a local college had an outreach program for inmates that taught and encouraged debate. Upon joining an unusual prison debate program where he was held in Norfolk, Virginia, Malcolm described the magical moment this way:

> I will tell you that right there, in the prison, debating, speaking to a crowd, was as exhilarating to me as the discovery of knowledge through reading had been. Standing up there, the faces looking up at me, the things in my head coming out of my mouth, while my brain searched for the next best thing to follow what I was saying, and if I could sway them to my side by handling it right, then I had won the debate—once my feet got wet, I was gone on debating.[53]

The program's reach was extraordinary—allowing Malcolm to debate teams from Harvard, Yale, Boston University, and MIT. Noted debate expert Austin Freeley trained teams from Boston University that debated in the prison debates.[54] It is little wonder that the program transformed Malcolm Little into the feared advocate more commonly known as Malcolm X. Malcolm X and James Farmer Jr. debated several times. In one debate, they squared off at Cornell University where Malcolm X defended segregation and James Farmer Jr. argued against it. They also debated on television on the day that Medgar Evers was assassinated. That debate was revisited with the surviving panel members thirty years later—with only Wyatt T. Walker and James Farmer Jr. still alive.[55]

All of this debate activity connected and empowered these activists. Thomas Freeman, who remained the debate director emeritus at the important Houston HBCU (Historically Black Colleges and Universities) Texas Southern University until his death in 2020, taught both Barbara

Jordan and Martin Luther King Jr. debate and argumentation skills. The *New York Times* offered this summary of his life's work:

> [O]ver time, as he wove together his power as a preacher and his skills as an educator, Dr. Freeman went on to establish, build and coach the award-winning debate team at Texas Southern University, a historically black university in Houston, where he reigned as the chief of forensics—the study and practice of public speaking and debate—for an astonishing six decades.[56]

The *New York Times* explained the argumentation instruction of Martin Luther King Jr. by Freeman:

> One was an 18-year-old named Martin Luther King Jr. Dr. Freeman, who was a guest lecturer at Morehouse College in 1947, did not recall teaching him until Dr. King saw him years later at a restaurant and went up and introduced himself. "You don't remember me," Dr. King told him, "but I remember you."

Barbara Jordan described Freeman's impact on her advocacy skills that were decisive in the Watergate hearings: "I cannot overestimate the impact and influence that Dr. Freeman had on my life. He stretches your mind. He places you on your own, teaches you to stand on your feet, think, and open your mouth and talk."[57] This was why Freeman was an important advisor to Denzel Washington's 2007 film *The Great Debaters* that dramatized another African American debate coach, Melvin Tolson, in his role of shaping young James Farmer Jr., who attended college beginning at age fourteen. In summarizing his own work Freeman said, "I had the conviction then as I have now that God wanted me to carry the word, and that is what I do."[58] Debate coaches like Freeman and Tolson can deploy enough human advocacy power to easily topple social fixtures like racial segregation within a single generation.

It is important to understand that while debate was a common ingredient to the leadership development of all these great advocates, their methodologies for arriving at a more just world varied wildly. Malcolm X famously referred to the "March on Washington" in 1963 as the "Farce on Washington." As already noted, Meredith rejected the civil rights movement explicitly. In his own memoir *A Mission from God*, Meredith recounts picking up MLK from the airport for a campus talk and then being thrown out of a town hall meeting with King when he challenged the notion of nonviolence. Other Black students were so angered by his arguments that they picked him up and threw him out of the hall where King was speaking. The divergence of methods surrounding the problem of racism is a testament to the ultimate fluidity and creative destruction possible with discursive complexity. The infinite resource of human imagination in constructing arguments is the deeper resource for dislodging seemingly permanent structures of injustice. It is, to paraphrase King, the "justice flowing like waters." These collective human endeavors motivated by words composing arguments can in time erode the features of human cruelty. This is not a theory. It is an observation about these great debaters. Discursive complexity did not require monolithic agreement among these various advocates. In fact, the multitude of voices in the civil rights movement created a rhetorical tapestry knit together by the strong tools of debate training.

It is also important in observing this empirical model that we recognize the potentially lost international sources of this approach. The primary components of the civil rights movement with regard to nonviolent civil disobedience were explicitly drawn from Gandhi in India. His interpretation of Satyagraha, or "soul force," formed the foundations of resistance to British colonialism. For James Farmer Jr. and ultimately King and other major leaders, the book *War without Violence*, by Kṛshṇalāla Śrīdharāṇī written in 1939 to distill the Hindu principles used by Gandhi to reject British colonialism for American and Western audiences, was a foundational resource to their movement.

The African contributions to American civil rights actions can also be lost. Of course, African Americans recognized that their ethnic origins were in the continent of Africa and true freedom would necessarily involve the recovery of lost African identities. Freedom Schools, which were a lesser known component of Freedom Summer 1964, aimed to restore a sense of African identity to young Blacks in the South. Civil rights leaders like James Farmer Jr. and Martin Luther King Jr. traveled to Africa during key junctures of the 1950s and 1960s to understand Pan African movements and the nationalist movements against colonialism. All of this informed the efforts and arguments presented in America. Stokely Carmichael, who formulated the notion of "black power," would become so centered on the African experience that he joined African nationalist struggles on the continent.

The debate model found in these advocates, and so many beyond what can be listed here, integrates global politics and a wide range of religious perspectives. This discursive complexity can embrace a diversity of perspectives as a praxis for improving the human condition anywhere in the world. Teaching debate around the world can benefit all participants regardless of geography, race, or background. Learning to increase discursive complexity through debate can lessen the adverse impact of propaganda that leads to violence. In the case of the American civil rights movement it is clear that this was transcontinental knowledge with regard to the processes of civil disobedience.

Known as the "Great Debater," James Farmer Jr. pioneered the more central practical points of the prominently known American civil rights movement. Nonviolent direct action was the full name given to this methodology. Originating in the early 1940s, CORE leaders such as Bernice Fisher, George Houser, and Farmer focused on refining a variety of intellectual presuppositions that would guide much of what became more famous in events like the Montgomery bus boycott and sit-ins across the nation. Arguably, the first major organized sit-in took place on the south side of Chicago at a restaurant known as Jack Spratt in 1942. The successful sit-in is described by Farmer in a lecture given at Mary Washington University in 1983:

> We went in with a group of about twenty-five—this was a small place that seats thirty or thirty-five comfortably at the counter and in the booths—and occupied just about all of the available seats and waited for service. The woman was in charge again [the manager they had encountered on a previous visit]. She ordered the waitress to serve two whites who were seated at the counter, and she served them. Then she told the blacks, "I'm sorry, we can't serve you, you'll have to leave." And they, of course, declined to leave and continued to sit there. By this time the other customers who were in there were aware of what was going on and were watching, and most of these were university people, University of Chicago, who were more or less sympathetic with us. And they stopped eating and the two people at the counter she had served and those whites in the booth she had served were not eating. There was no turnover. People were coming in and standing around for a few minutes and walking out. There were no seats available.[59]

Ultimately, both Blacks and Whites were served. Farmer and his CORE activists called the police before they staged the sit-in and this likely factored into the police's unsympathetic response to the owner when he called. Since Farmer and CORE were not breaking a law, the police encouraged the owner to provide service and even warned that he should stop repeatedly calling them or expect to be arrested himself. Such techniques would become famous and more dramatically successful in the Montgomery bus boycotts of the 1950s and the Greensboro, North Carolina, sit-ins of 1960. Farmer's training in argumentation and debate was at the heart of a patient process that idealistically held that careful argumentation could change minds. This is, in fact, what happened in dozens of establishments across the United States long before Federal laws became intrusive upon the question. It is arguably an important misunderstanding about how justice arrives in a society to suppose that justice only arrives in a deductive form of high-power government legislation requiring the change. In fact, the inductive process of small group actions predicated on the power of argument necessarily make it possible for such edicts to solve problems like these.

The CORE methodology was carefully thought out and continually refined over more than two decades of operations. There were thirteen rules that anyone involved had to agree to in order to participate:

1. A CORE member will investigate the facts carefully before deciding whether or not racial injustice exists in a given situation.

2. A CORE member will seek at all times to understand the attitude of the person responsible for a policy of racial discrimination and the social situation which engendered the attitude. The CORE member will be flexible and creative, showing a willingness to participate in experiments which seem constructive, while being careful not to compromise CORE's principles.
3. A CORE member will make a sincere effort to avoid malice and hatred toward any group or individual.
4. A CORE member will never use malicious slogans or labels to discredit any opponent.
5. A CORE member will be willing to admit mistakes.
6. A member will meet the anger of any individual or group in the spirit of good will and creative reconciliation: he will submit to assault and will not retaliate in kind, either by act or word.
7. A member will never engage in any action in the name of the group except when authorized by the group or one of its action units.
8. When in an action project, a CORE member will obey the orders issued by the authorized leader or spokesman of the project, whether these orders please him or not. If he does not approve such orders, he shall later relay the criticism back to the group or to the committee which was the source of the project plan.
9. No member, after once accepting the discipline of the group for a particular project, shall have the right to withdraw. However, should a participant feel that, under further pressure, he will no longer be able to adhere to the Rules for Action, he shall then withdraw from the project and leave the scene immediately after notifying the project leader.
10. Only a person who is a recognized member of the group or a participant accepted by the group leader shall be permitted to take part in that group action.
11. Each member has the right to dissent from any group decision and, if dissenting, need not participate in the specific action planned.
12. Each member shall understand that all decisions on general policy shall be arrived at only through democratic group discussion.
13. A CORE member shall receive the uncompromising support of his CORE group as he faces any difficulties resulting from his authorized CORE activities.[60]

All of these rules spelled out an argumentation paradigm where those implementing unjust actions are invited by public challenge to change. The profound success of this praxis from 1942 to 1967 in removing rules segregating Blacks and Whites suggest that, in some form, argumentation study can form new leaders for similar successes in this century.

CONCLUSION

Between 1940 and 1970, the conditions for African Americans was dramatically improved by way of discursive complexity implemented in the methodologies of CORE and affiliated civil rights advocacy groups. Groups as diverse as the NAACP and the Nation of Islam were positively impacted by the pedagogy of debate to synthesize the diminution of injustice and the improvement of the human condition. Though figures as diverse as James Meredith, Barbara Jordan, James Farmer Jr., Malcolm X, Lula Farmer, and Medgar Evers took different rhetorical approaches to the same problem of racial injustice, the common thread of debate pedagogy caused them to imagine a world without racism. They were unleashed upon segregated America by idealistic debate coaches such as Melvin Tolson and Thomas Freeman. Of course, our world of the twenty-first century continues to suffer from the problems of racism. That cannot diminish the progress made. The explicit affirmations of segregation indicated by laws, rules, and signifiers telling Blacks to drink, sit, and otherwise occupy public life in separate settings from Whites, were dismantled by efforts like those specifically embraced and enacted by CORE and various civil rights activists. For purposes of this book, the power of debate is the primary pretext that will allow the emergence of dozens of approaches to improve the human condition and reduce the incidence of injustice. Between 1940 and 1970, it is not only the Jim Crow legal infrastructure that was abolished. The murder rate of Black men fell substantially. The unemployment of African Americans fell. The poverty rate for African Americans fell substantially. Habermas's elusive communication competence is found in the teaching of debaters so they are able to apprehend and resist propaganda denying the humanity of Black Americans. The low discursive complexity of a world without debaters breeds violence, injustice, and ultimately genocide. These are broader ramifications to specific solutions sought in the imaginative minds of debaters. We must build, more broadly, a pedagogy of debate that disseminates discursive complexity. In this new pedagogy, the individual tendency to shrink and be silent in the face of cruelty and crimes diminishes, and the bravery and courage common to efforts to stop the worst of human harms rises. This chapter provides the theoretical template for future chapters as different episodes of human problems are visited with an intellectual eye for how discursive complexity might ameliorate and even resolve the underlying problems. We will see specific examples in the twenty-first century of this theory at work around the world.

NOTES

1. Ben Voth, *The Rhetoric of Genocide: Death as a Text* (Lanham, MD: Lexington Press, 2014).
2. Kirby Goidel, Craig Freeman, and Smentkowski, *Misreading the Bill of Rights Top Ten Myths Concerning Your Rights and Liberties* (Oxford: Praeger, 2015).
3. Richard Wike and Shannon Schumacher, "Democratic Rights Popular Globally, but Commitment to Them Not Always Strong," *Pew Research* (February 27, 2020), accessed August 11, 2020, https://www.pewresearch.org/global/2020/02/27/democratic-rights-popular-globally-but-commitment-to-them-not-always-strong/.
4. Examples of these NGOs include: Freedom House, Freedom of the Press Foundation, Alliance Defending Freedom, Amnesty International, Human Rights House, and many more.
5. Goidel, Freeman, and Smentkowski, *Misreading the Bill of Rights Top Ten Myths Concerning Your Rights and Liberties*.
6. Shannon M. Oltmann, "Intellectual Freedom and Freedom of Speech: Three Theoretical Perspectives," *The Library Quarterly* 86, no. 2 (April 2016): 153–71.
7. Steven Shiffrin, "Dissent, Democratic Participation, and First Amendment Methodology," *Virginia Law Review* 97, no. 3 (2011): 559–65, accessed August 10, 2020, www.jstor.org/stable/41261522.
8. Goidel, Freeman, and Smentkowski, *Misreading the Bill of Rights Top Ten Myths Concerning Your Rights and Liberties*.
9. Zselyke Csaky, "Dropping the Democratic Façade," Freedom House, accessed August 10, 2020, https://freedomhouse.org/report/nations-transit/2020/dropping-democratic-facade.
10. Kevin Johnson, "Speech and Debate as Civic Education," *Argumentation and Advocacy* 55, no. 1–2 (2019): 82+. *Gale Academic OneFile*, accessed August 10, 2020, https://link-gale-com.proxy.libraries.smu.edu/apps/doc/A615915869/AONE?u=txshracd2548&sid=AONE&xid=15fb55e4.
11. H. J. Kim, et al., "Health Development Experience in North and South Korea," *Asia-Pacific Journal of Public Health*, vol. 13 Suppl (2001): S51–7.
12. "Otto Warmbier, American Recently Released by North Korea, Dies at 22," Morning Edition, National Public Radio, Inc. (NPR), June 20, 2017.
13. Samantha Power, *A Problem from Hell: America and the Age of Genocide* (New York: Harper Collins, 2002).
14. Gregory Desilet, *Cult of the Kill: Traditional Metaphysics of Rhetoric, Truth, and Violence in a Postmodern World* (New York: Xlibris Corporation, 2002).
15. Alien Wheelis, cited in B. Brummett (1976), "Some Implications of 'Process' or 'Intersubjectivity': Postmodern Rhetoric," *Philosophy and Rhetoric* 9 (1976): 39–40.
16. Chaim Perelman and L. Olbrechts-Tyteca, *The New Rhetoric: A Treatise on Argumentation* (Notre Dame: [Ind.] University of Notre Dame Press, 1969).
17. Jurgen Habermas, *Communication and the Evolution of Society* (Boston: Beacon Press, 1979).
18. Soo-Hye Han and Colene J. Lind, "Putting Powerfulness in Its Place: A Study on Discursive Style in Public Discussion and Its Impact," *Argumentation and Advocacy* 53, no. 3–4 (2017): 216+. *Gale Academic OneFile*, accessed August 10, 2020, https://link.gale.com/apps/doc/A543611048/AONE?u=txshracd2548&sid=AONE&xid=2af50b41.
19. Victor Ferry, "What is Habermas's 'Better Argument' Good For?" *Argumentation and Advocacy* 49, no. 2 (2012): 144+. *Gale Academic OneFile*, accessed August 10, 2020, https://link.gale.com/apps/doc/A332892402/AONE?u=txshracd2548&sid=AONE&xid=2ed30c90.
20. Jurgen Habermas, *The Theory of Communicative Action* (Cambridge, England: Polity Press, 1984).
21. Erik Doxtader, "The Entwinement of Argument and Rhetoric: A Dialectical Reading of Habermas' Theory of Communicative Action," *Argumentation and Advocacy*

28, no. 2 (1991): 51+. *Gale Academic OneFile*, accessed August 10, 2020, https://link.gale.com/apps/doc/A12983009/AONE?u=txshracd2548&sid=AONE&xid=9d012d1f.

22. Carrie Anne Platt and Zoltan P. Majdik, "The Place of Religion in Habermas's Transformed Public Sphere," *Argumentation and Advocacy* 49, no. 2 (2012): 138+. *Gale Academic OneFile*, accessed August 10, 2020, https://link.gale.com/apps/doc/A332892400/AONE?u=txshracd2548&sid=AONE&xid=29f70fdb. The quote from Habermas they note here comes from C. Case, "Germans Reconsider Religion: Pope Benedict XVI's Challenge to Secularism Meets with Receptivity during His German Visit," *The Christian Science Monitor*, September 15, 2006, accessed August 10, 2020, http://www.csmonitor.com/2006/0915/p01s01-woeu.html.

23. Paulo Freire, *Pedagogy of the Oppressed* (New York: Continuum, 2000).

24. Martin Luther King Jr., An Address by the Reverend Dr. Martin Luther King Jr., Cornell College, Mount Vernon, Iowa, October 15, 1962, accessed on August 10, 2020, https://news.cornellcollege.edu/dr-martin-luther-kings-visit-to-cornell-college/.

25. Gordon Mitchell, "Pedagogical Possibilities for Argumentative Agency in Academic Debate," *Argumentation and Advocacy* 35, no. 2 (1998): 41+. *Gale Academic OneFile*, accessed August 10, 2020, https://link.gale.com/apps/doc/A53650192/AONE?u=txshracd2548&sid=AONE&xid=34d0a1a7.

26. George W. Ziegelmueller and Jack Kay, *Argumentation: Inquiry and Advocacy* (Allyn & Bacon, 1997): 6.

27. Richard D. Rieke and Malcolm O. Sillars, *Argumentation and Critical Decision Making* (New York: Pearson, 1997): xvii.

28. Gordon Mitchell, "Pedagogical Possibilities for Argumentative Agency in Academic Debate," *Argumentation and Advocacy* 35, no. 2 (1998): 41+. *Gale Academic OneFile*, accessed August 10, 2020, https://link.gale.com/apps/doc/A53650192/AONE?u=txshracd2548&sid=AONE&xid=34d0a1a7.

29. Kenneth Burke, *A Grammar of Motives* (Berkeley: University of California Press, 1969).

30. Ben Voth and Aaron Noland, "Argumentation and the International Problem of Genocide," *Contemporary Argumentation and Debate* 28 (2009): 38–46.

31. Burke, *A Grammar of Motives*.

32. Burke, *A Grammar of Motives*.

33. Power, *A Problem from Hell: America and the Age of Genocide*; Simon Tisdall, "Sudan Fears US Military Action over Darfur Clinton Warns of 'Need to Sound Alarm' over Crisis: Obama Urged to Keep Pledge to End Genocide," *Guardian*, January 16, 2009.

34. David A. Hoekema, "Risking Peace: How Religious Leaders Helped End Uganda's Civil War," *Commonwealth* (January 25, 2019): 10+. *Gale Academic OneFile*, accessed August 10, 2020, https://link.gale.com/apps/doc/A573715695/AONE?u=txshracd2548&sid=AONE&xid=333f8703.

35. Sonya Nigam, "The Internet Campaign Urging Capture of Ugandan Rebel Leader Joseph Kony Is a Good Thing," *Internet Activism* (Detroit: Greenhaven Press, 2013).

36. "Omar Al-Bashir Steps Down, Transitional Government Announced: *Al-Arabiya TV*," *TCA Regional News* (Chicago: Tribune Content Agency LLC, April 11, 2019).

37. "Sudan Repeals Omar Al-Bashir-Era Law Regulating Women's Behaviour and Dissolves Former Ruling Party," *The Telegraph Online*, Telegraph Group Ltd, November 29, 2019.

38. Sascha-Dominik Dov Bachmann and Naa A. Sowatey-Adjei, "The African Union-ICC Controversy before the ICJ: A Way Forward to Strengthen International Criminal Justice?" *Washington International Law Journal* 29, no. 2 (2020): 247+. *Gale Academic OneFile*, accessed August 10, 2020, https://link.gale.com/apps/doc/A629150909/AONE?u=txshracd2548&sid=AONE&xid=50e95ee2.

39. Dhanveer Singh Brar and Ashwani Sharma, "What Is This 'Black' in Black Studies? From Black British Cultural Studies to Black Critical Thought in UK Arts and

Higher Education," *New Formations*, no. 99 (2019): 88+. *Gale Academic OneFile*, accessed August 10, 2020, https://link.gale.com/apps/doc/A626207381/AONE?u=txshracd2548&sid=AONE&xid=9d678ae9.

40. Frank Wilderson, *Red, White and Black: Cinema and the Structure of U.S. Antagonisms* (Durham, NC: Duke University Press, 2010); Amber Kelsie, "Blackened Debate at the End of the World," *Philosophy and Rhetoric* 52, no. 1 (2019): 63–70; Colin Jenkins, "Burning Down the American Plantation: An Interview with the Revolutionary Abolitionist Movement," *Truth Out*, September 16, 2017.

41. Hanna Hart, "How to Say 'I Don't Know' with Grace and Authority: A Leadership Lesson from Ta-Nehisi Coates," *Forbes*, October 31, 2019.

42. Kelsie, "Blackened Debate at the End of the World," 63–70.

43. "The Beloved Community," The King Center, accessed March 1, 2016, http://www.thekingcenter.org/king-philosophy#sub4 .

44. Bernice Fisher, "Confessions of an Ex-Liberal," James Leonard Jr., and Lula Peterson Farmer papers, Dolph Briscoe Center for American History, The University of Texas at Austin, Box 2R648.

45. Michelle N.-K. Collison, "Ressurecting the Thurman Legacy for the Next Millennium," *Black Issues in Higher Education* (November 11, 1999): 24. *Gale Academic OneFile*, accessed August 11, 2020, https://link.gale.com/apps/doc/A58036234/AONE?u=txshracd2548&sid=AONE&xid=2dba1bc3.

46. James Farmer Jr., *Lay Bare the Heart* (Fort Worth: TCU Press, 1985): 136.

47. "Howard Thurman," National Cathedral website, accessed August 11, 2020, https://cathedral.org/what-to-see/interior/howard-thurman/.

48. Catherine Barnes, *Journey from Jim Crow: The Desegregation of Southern Transit* (New York: Columbia University Press, 1983): 178.

49. *Lula Peterson High School Yearbook*, James Leonard, Jr., and Lula Peterson Farmer papers, Dolph Briscoe Center for American History, The University of Texas at Austin, Austin, Box3U250.

50. James Meredith with William Doyle, *A Mission from God: A Memoir and Challenge for America* (New York: Atria Books, 2012); and James Meredith, *Three Years in Mississippi* (Jackson: University of Mississippi Press, 2019).

51. Meredith, *Three Years in Mississippi*, 43.

52. Mississippi Writers website, "Medgar Evers," University of Mississippi English Department (2015), accessed August 11, 2020, http://mwp.olemiss.edu//dir/evers_medgar/.

53. Malcolm X and Alex Haley, *The Autobiography of Malcolm X* (New York: Grove Press, 1965): 184.

54. James Branham, "I Was Gone on Debating: Malcolm X Prison Debates and Public Confrontations," *Argumentation and Advocacy* 31 (1995): 117–37.

55. "The Open Mind: Race Relations in Crisis," PBS, June 1963 and 1993 [video], accessed August 5, 2020, https://www.pbs.org/video/the-open-mind-race-relations-in-crisis/.

56. Katharine Seelye, "Thomas Freeman Debate Coach with Broad Influence Dies at 100," *New York Times* (June 16, 2020), accessed July 15, 2020, https://www.nytimes.com/2020/06/16/us/thomas-freeman-debate-coach-with-broad-influence-dies-at-100.html.

57. Seelye, "Thomas Freeman Debate Coach with Broad Influence Dies at 100."

58. James H. Ford, *The Peddler's Son* (BLURB incorporated, 2016).

59. "James Farmer Jr. Lectures," Mary Washington University, accessed August 11, 2020, https://jamesfarmerlectures.umwblogs.org/lectures-audio/.

60. James Farmer Jr., 1945, "Plan for a Two Month or Three Month Full Time Campaign Against Jim Crow," James Leonard, Jr., and Lula Peterson Farmer papers, Dolph Briscoe Center for American History, The University of Texas at Austin, Austin, Box 2R566.

THREE

Debate Training in Rwanda among Security Forces

It is one thing to imagine and theorize about a world without genocide. It is another thing to observe great moments in history where past individuals succeed in the struggle for justice. It is still another more difficult thing to go about this work in a direct and contemporaneous manner. This chapter grapples with such an effort and concentrates upon the important academic field of conflict resolution. Conflict resolution is a popular area of study around the world and focuses at the heart of problems central to the matter of genocide. Hatred, disagreement, anger, resentment, and general confusion about social expectations are all topics within the important study area of conflict resolution. Most of these techniques have important and substantial connection to communication study and even argumentation study.

In 2017, I accompanied the director of SMU Conflict Resolution program on a trip to Rwanda in order to take students from this program of study to key sites pertaining to the genocide and also conduct a multi-day training seminar for Rwandan security forces stationed in Kigali. The instruction involved a combination of my pedagogical work in debate with two colleagues and their pedagogical training in conflict resolution practices. The student-centered touring of the genocide sites allowed for a distillation of the impact of genocide as well as first-hand accounts of post genocide reconciliation processes that aided in the rebuilding of the country. The first portion of this chapter contains narratives of what we saw and experienced followed by a compilation of key components taught in the training that were directly derived from the ideas presented in the previous chapter. By presenting it in this way, a practical direct observation of how debate instruction can be carried out is accomplished. This trip embodied some of my first major steps toward implementing theories surrounding discursive complexity and utilizing debate instruction as a direct means to those ends. This trip was an incredible opportunity to put theory into direct and actual practice.

Dr. Betty Gilmore, director of the SMU Conflict Resolution program, describes the beginning of our trip:

> Our first day, we visited a church in Nyamata, the site of a massacre and where 50,000 people were buried. Although we thought we were prepared for what we were about to see, we were wrong. We saw clothes and belongings of the victims. Most striking to me was a tiny lone shoe from a toddler nestled among the piles. In another part of the church, stains marked the spots where infants were murdered. Our guide's pain in telling the story was palpable.[1]

The first genocide site was devastating—thousands of lives lost in an ethnic supremacist fantasy. The essential premises common to civil society—a church, a schoolhouse—were now housing thousands of human remains. At one point in the tour, the guide calmly indicated a faded red stain on the wall of a schoolroom within the church grounds. The guide explained that the stain was the blood of a small child whose skull was smashed against the wall. At that moment, one of our female Muslim graduate students ran from the room. It was impossibly horrifying. The annihilation of innocence was amplified by displays of table tops filled in neat orderly rows of human skulls. That alone was shocking beyond common reason, but the eye was soon drawn to a more deeply disturbing reality: so many of the skulls were too small to be adults. This mass killing was focused upon children. This disturbing memorial recalled something for us about being human that we can barely allow our minds to consider: a willingness to kill the innocent. The incredible natural beauty of Rwanda was illuminated by bright sunlight, gorgeous greenery, and set upon a luscious dark soil. The broken-down brick buildings and dark Christian crosses marked the landscape for the peculiar human festivities of killing the innocent that interrupted the placid landscape in 1994. The morality tale laid so starkly before us at Nyamata was enough to consider the lesson learned and return home, but we pressed on in Rwanda.

We proceeded in the afternoon to visit a village that was home to one of many dedicated political efforts toward reconciliation:

> We heard the testimonies of people from both sides of the conflict. Survivors told of how they learned to forgive. And those who participated in the murders, most who have served time in prison for their crimes, spoke of making amends. Humility was a common theme in their stories. One woman sat silently in her tears while we were having these conversations. Another survivor talked about how hard it is, on a daily basis, to forgive those who harmed her family members. Trauma and unity bind together. Although we left with heavy hearts, we were

both astounded and inspired by the resiliency, hope and unfathomable strength that we were seeing in the Rwandan people.[2]

The stories were translated for us from the Rwandan language (Kinyarwanda) while we sat on wooden benches in the shade of a modest new home. The conversation reached a climax when one woman explained that the house we were sitting near was built by a man who participated in the genocide. The woman had lost her husband and sons in the genocide. The man had served twenty years in prison for his participation in the crime of genocide, his release was not a release from responsibility. The reconciliation program required that he work to serve constructively the community he had helped destroy. There we sat in the shade of the home he had built for a woman who had lost everything. She stood shoulder to shoulder with him and told us she had *forgiven* him. That was difficult to comprehend. In that moment, every petty grudge I held in my heart against my fellow human beings felt like a too heavy piece of luggage containing worthless weight. The willful demonstration and explanation of grace was yet another shocking contrast in Rwanda. Somehow, grace was defeating judgment in Rwanda, and we were seeing this in their words and actions.

The Rwandan reconciliation courts (Gacaca) are an important feature of the larger trajectory of discursive complexity that can heal human communities devastated by crimes as vicious as genocide. As previously noted, the genocide killed hundreds of judges in the small nation of Rwanda in 1994. In the aftermath, the logistical prospects for justice were as dismal as the raw emotions of the moment. There was not a court system to deliver a form of justice in the aftermath. Rwandans created their own, extensive though ostensibly less formal, court system modeled after the Truth and Reconciliation Commissions of South Africa. More than twelve thousand courts were established across the nation in the aftermath of this mass slaughter.[3] The Gacaca courts were an important accomplishment in the quest for justice:

> Gacaca has reoriented the course of Rwandan justice by emphasizing confession, apology, and forgiveness. The alternative—the continued imprisonment of 125,000 genocide suspects—was both untenable and undesirable.[4]

It is important to realize the deliberative ingredients inherent to this justice. Less formal notions of a plaintiff and defendant meet before an independent third party who judges the case. This form of discursive complexity was an important step away from the natural impulse of revenge and toward reconciliation and collective healing. It is also important to understand empirically that Rwanda has one of the highest incarceration rates of any nation in the world.[5] The abstract intellectual desire for justice that simply finds anyone and everyone innocent, rather than culpable and responsible, is not a reasonable action to take in the aftermath of a genocide. Rwandans settled on a maximum punishment for genocide of twenty-five years. That means that many of these perpetrators will soon or have already been released. Part of their judgment includes the reconciliation work noted in this 2017 example. It is also important to understand that not every heart of a perpetrator is changed by twenty-five years in prison. Sometimes those hearts are hardened and sometimes those released return to ethnically hateful crimes like the ones that led them to prison. Humanity remains human despite our best intentions combined with good actions. Nothing here is a panacea.[6]

The *Washington Post* summary of Chakravaty's book offers the following contemporary summary:

> Chakravarty's findings suggest the need for much more scholarly work on the "tacit bargains" that govern relations between elites and mass publics in the aftermath of atrocity crimes; as she notes, the bargain expressed in and built through the *gacaca* process is not an inter-elite legislative or ruling party bargain, but rather "an informal elite-mass social contract that consolidated the new order by tying the new elites to their social constituents, and demonstrating to them ('clients') the benefits of cooperating with and advancing within the system." Of particular interest is a question Chakravarty raises in the context of comparison with Nazi Germany's postwar accountability and justice processes: the ways that individual citizens having a choice of patrons rather than being forced to rely on a sole patron (as in Rwandan) influences outcomes in modern transitional justice processes.[7]

Nonetheless, there were client alternatives for Hutu perpetrators and, of course, this has proven an ongoing problem for Rwanda as many Hutu perpetrators fled into the Congo or took more silent positions in places such as nearby Burundi. As previously noted in chapter 1, the French established an important sovereignty zone toward the end of the genocide that allowed potential perpetrators to go free. In all of these complexities, further deliberation and discursive complexity can help current and future ethnic conflicts to be better reconciled. The Rwandan accomplishment of twelve thousand deliberative centers, after losing more than eight hundred judges, is an amazing accomplishment and an ongoing communication force contributing to the rise of Rwanda out of hatred and into the light of Beloved Community.[8] A world without genocide as this book envisions will entail the kind of courts utilized by Rwanda in the aftermath. The corrections and idealization of such courts will depend on deliberative questions and suggestions like those prompted by Chakravaty.

CONFLICT RESOLUTION TRAINING OF SECURITY FORCES

After visiting a genocide memorial site and meeting with a reconciliation community, our academic group divided into different collections of service in Rwanda. Gilmore, Shaw, and myself stayed at the ALARM (African Leadership and Reconciliation Ministries) compound to begin the training of Rwandan security forces. Two student groups traveled to different orphanages in the region and provided leadership in daily activities such as arts, singing, and sports. Chris Snyder had incredibly brought guitars to Rwanda in order to allow children an opportunity to learn and play electric guitars. One of our graduate student team members had played in the NFL and he was incredible at helping children learn and enjoy sports activities.

Approximately fifty members of the Rwandan security forces arrived at the ALARM facility for training in conflict resolution. Our teaching team relied mainly upon the considerable expertise and experience of Dr. Betty Gilmore who leads an excellent master's program in conflict resolution on the SMU main campus in Dallas. Dr. Shaw from Abilene Christian University had worked in Kenya and had considerable academic and professional background in conflict resolution. I came to offer methodologies in conflict resolution rooted in the experiences of American civil rights hero and "Great Debater" James Farmer Jr. as well as my background with debate. Our presentations were translated into Rwandan (Kinyarwanda) and the security forces were excellent audience members. Their bright green uniforms and smiling faces constituted the front line of a new Rwanda. They were, in fact, the lowest level of security in the state, below both the army and the police. They do not have firearms, and their primary weapons are dialogue within the communities they serve each day. In many respects, they are the initial human face of discursive complexity in the new Rwanda trying to observe and resolve conflicts at the grassroots level.

Our activities focused upon a mixture of strategy explanation, small group discussions, and security force leader reports. These reports presented their local discernment of how the conflict resolution strategies would work best in Rwanda. The presentations by security force members were often offered in English, and it was apparent that while fluent in the Rwandan language, many members also spoke or were literate in English. For me, it was striking to see the workbook we had prepared printed in the Rwandan language (Kinyarwanda). Seeing our slides and lecture notes in Kinyarwanda was a reminder of the importance and potential of communication. We could understand one another and recognize our common experiences with some effort toward communication. We could learn from each other. It was powerfully apparent that Rwanda was rising upon the words, deeds, and actions of these men and women serving their local communities. Every minute was exhilarating to work toward that common goal. Shaw and Gilmore were brilliant in the manner by which they played off one another in role playing. They demonstrated how people can talk to one another and use words to deescalate tense situations. Security forces smiled and laughed about the communication problems they illustrated so masterfully. Their small group discussions were thoughtful and intelligent—showing a seriousness about getting better at their jobs and an appreciation for our sharing of potential insights.

One of the most pivotal portions of my presentation involved a distillation of James Farmer Jr.'s thirteen rules for nonviolent direct action. I chose to focus on the American civil rights movement as a model in order to mitigate the standard problems of cultural imposition. I wanted our hosts to understand that Americans struggled to overcome violence in their recent history and that our heroes even traveled to Africa in order to gain insight about how to help resolve violence best. This established a more culturally mutual basis for our dialogue. I wrote out on poster paper four of the rules used in the American civil rights group founded by Farmer (CORE) that I thought would be most helpful to them in resolving conflicts:

1. Get the facts first.
2. Do not respond with hurtful words.
3. Understand why they are hurt.
4. Seek creative solutions.

I explained that principles like these allowed the American civil rights movement to overcome ethnic violence directed at African Americans in the United States. Most knew who Martin Luther King Jr. was; however, none had heard of his friend and predecessor in the movement—James Farmer Jr. They appreciated that I considered him a hero and were pleased to hear how Farmer traveled often to Africa to learn more about how discrimination might best be defeated as a human habit.

The rules were tempered to fit the place and time of Rwanda 2017. Rule one in the original CORE guidelines drawn from *War without Violence* stated: "A CORE member will investigate the facts carefully before deciding whether or not racial injustice exists in a given situation." Notice that this first rule fits well with Chakravaty's concern about false accusations in the Gacaca courts. By training the officers to get both sides, and maybe three sides or more of a community conflict, it would increase the chances that they would discover the most accurate account of events in question. Farmer explained on different occasions about how his group of CORE sometimes initially misunderstood incidents as being racist in origin while later discovering they were not. On one occasion, Farmer apologized for an accusation against the police that he later discovered to be untrue. This is an important principle to preventing the politicization of knowledge common to the rival epistemic system proposed by Saul Alinsky. Saul Alinsky was a contemporary of James Farmer Jr. In his book *Rules for Radicals*, Alinsky urged activists to adopt a closed discursive mindset that justified cynical actions of personal destruction in order to destroy opponents.[9]

The original rule two was a synthesis of multiple CORE rules: "A CORE member will seek at all times to understand the attitude of the person responsible for a policy of racial discrimination and the social situation which engendered the attitude. The CORE member will be flexible and creative, showing a willingness to participate in experiments which seem constructive, while being careful not to compromise CORE's principles." The other rule was rule four, stating: "A CORE member will never use malicious slogans or labels to discredit any opponent." These rules characterized the practice of nonviolent direct action more than any of the thirteen rules. Rhetorically, we naturally respond to hurtful words uttered in a time of crisis with more hurtful words. Breaking this cycle at the discursive level is vital. The CORE methodology is again dialectic morally with regard to the Alinsky model of trying to destroy an opponent at a personal and intimate level through combative discourse such as ridicule. Training and practicing realistic scenarios, where events like this will happen, helps key players like security force members defuse, rather than add to, conflict situations found in twenty-first-century Rwandan society.

Argument theorist Wayne Brockriede wrote in an article entitled "Arguers as Lovers" that we must clarify our motives as we indulge in argumentation.[10] Why are we arguing? If we seek to force our viewpoint on someone else, we might do well to metaphorically view our rhetorical relationship as comparable to "rape." Good argument is by contrast mutually edifying and has a shared goal of discovering the truth. There are contemporary efforts to reconcile traditionally competitive models of argumentation study to those based upon mutuality as Professors Mallin and Anderson explain:

> Our notion of constructive argument is significant as a tool of argumentation pedagogy. Argumentation is traditionally taught via a win-lose debate model. There are significant risks to adopting this orientation as the only one in which argumentation is taught. As Palmerton (1992) contends, teaching communicative practice entails "teaching students not just how to think, but the very structures of thought that shape their thinking" (p. 335). If the only structures of thought to which we are exposed when we learn about having disagreements or offering reasons are adversarial and monologic, then we are not equipped for the overwhelming majority of situations in which we engage in those practices. Treating everything a disputant says as an argument to be refuted may be appropriate when liberty or property is at stake, as in courtroom practice. It is, however, much less appropriate when the

disputant is someone with whom you need to have an ongoing relationship, such as a spouse, employer, or colleague.[11]

It is clear that models like this are at work in the conflict resolution training utilized in Rwanda. An overly competitive model would encourage self-defeating competition among practitioners.

The third rule given to the security force members encapsulated advice in rule two of the CORE rules and the larger ethos of the thirteen rules. Farmer's paradigm aimed to achieve understanding. This may differ in many respects from knowledge. As the truism goes, knowledge is power. This formation of explanation can bring with it political risks and vulnerability to future conflict. One of the most distinctive aspects of CORE activism from 1942 to 1967 was the tenacious patience of the participants in confronting racial prejudice. In one instance, James Farmer Jr. was observed to have stood in a restaurant with a small container seeking the condiment of mayonnaise. Because the restaurant would not serve Blacks, Farmer stood for forty-five minutes waiting to be served. Everyone in the restaurant was a witness to the passive act of resistance. When enough time had passed a young man working at the restaurant went back and brought a small serving of mayonnaise to Farmer. The people eating at the restaurant erupted in applause. In another case, Farmer and CORE activists interviewed a restaurant owner about why they would not serve Black people. They explained that they personally supported the idea but feared their patrons did not, so they followed the implicit wishes of the patrons. Farmer and his group asked if he could survey the patrons discretely. The owner agreed and the survey showed that patrons actually wanted to have integrated food service. The owner happily complied with the argument made by CORE. Many cases of reconciliation on the important question of racism were resolved through a goal of mutual understanding rather than a knowledge power goal that would confer upon CORE members the power to label their opponents as "racists." This goal of understanding versus knowledge remains imperative to the path forward in the twenty-first century.

The fourth rule given to security force members was also an extrapolation of the second rule from CORE. In particular, we wanted to encourage security force members to "be flexible and creative, showing a willingness to participate in experiments which seem constructive." Solutions must be tailored to the unique situation found with those human beings in conflict. This openness and creativity can establish further examples for future problems that are similar while building trust with the security force members. This trust is important in building stronger communities. One of the common points of analysis in many American debate rounds centers upon a recurring question that emerges in the middle of many debates: "What is the alternative?" Most advocates and most complainants in social situations can identify readily the problem. The alternative requires competing advocates to suggest how to solve the problem. An additional strategy is asking two angry disputants in a local matter to pause for moments of silence before continuing with an angry loud argument. Knowing that their complaint will still be heard after a time of rest is an alternative solution to continuing the verbal combat in the same high stakes interpersonal fashion. This rule worked well with the role-playing activities that were used in other parts of the training.

RELIGION AND COMMUNITY BUILDING

One of the most awkward divides to navigate as an academic is the secular/religious divide. American academics tend to prefer and emphasize the solution bearing strength of secularism and downplay religion as a source of conflict. CORE was formed as a secular organization, while derived from Christian convictions like the Methodist Social Gospel. CORE stood in contrast to the Southern Christian Leadership Center led by Martin Luther King Jr. It is important to note that while these two groups had different designs, they cooperated with great success. Similarly, American academic projects aimed at global audiences should manage more fairly this divide. The world is not only predominantly religious, it is increasingly religious. With that in mind, I also emphasized spiritual and religious components of the instruction. Farmer's work was significantly based upon the Methodist conception of the "Social Gospel" drawn from Matthew 25, in the New Testament of the Bible. The key parts of that parable provided by Jesus say this:

> [37]Then the righteous will answer Him, "Lord, when did we see You hungry, and feed You, or thirsty, and give You *something* to drink? [38]And when did we see You a stranger, and invite You in, or naked, and clothe You? [39]When did we see You sick, or in prison, and come to You?" [40]The King will answer and say to them, "Truly I say to you, to the extent that you did it to one of these brothers of Mine, *even* the least *of them*, you did it to Me."[12]

The security forces were deeply religious, and their prayers and singing amplified the enduring Christian convictions of their labor as community members. It was delightful to participate in a community profoundly committed to loving one another.

It is important to understand that while Farmer's group was secular, it was possible to cooperate without great difficulty among secular, Jewish, Hindu, Muslim, and Christian leaders. A broad notion of loving one another as exemplified in the terminology of "Beloved Community" allowed, and even encouraged, productive cooperation. I found this again in Rwanda and in other locations, such as India, where I have done similar work in the years since.

When we completed the training, there were many celebrations. Governing dignitaries and commanders came to present certificates to the security force members who completed the class. In honor of my great hero James Farmer Jr., I was given a commemorative Rwandan spear and shield. With these, I was told I could be a valiant champion anywhere. The smiles and laughter were another chorus in the days of community we enjoyed together loving one another. There was strong pleading that we return to Rwanda whenever possible. We were delighted to receive word from government authorities a month later that they found our training had observably improved the conduct of those members who took the training. They were eager to find a way to extend the training to more than two thousand similar members throughout the nation.

RWANDA'S DEBATE COMMUNITY

The night before I was to leave Rwanda, members of the Rwandan debate team, iDebate Rwanda, whom I had hosted in Dallas in 2014 and 2015, invited me to a member's home for a traditional dinner. The home was near the American consulate, and they picked me up from ALARM to take me to a wonderful gathering of more than a dozen Rwandan debate team members. I recognized most of them, but some were new team members. The meal was delicious. The conversation was infectious and enlightening. I listened to them politely discuss and argue Rwandan politics in English. It was amazing and inspiring. I could see the bright future of Rwanda before my eyes. It was hard to not feel the optimism and the overwhelming potential of passionate minds who loved debate because it was an ideal way of resolving difference. As happened so often while I was there, I wanted to weep openly with joy, but I did not want to embarrass and confuse my excellent hosts. I saved those tears for night as I fell asleep and dreamed of what Rwanda, and the world, might become. They were beautiful and wonderful thoughts bound in the words, laughter, and smiles of the Rwandan people.

Building youthful communities of dialogue like the one found in Rwanda through programs like iDebate Rwanda is an imperative for a better global future. Every global society should have a community of hundreds of young people who recognize that in the rhetorical exploration and discussion of difference, these conversations can be conducted not only peacefully but with an enthusiasm for the future and freedom from fear. Debate instruction builds that future and creates the resilient advocates less willing to rely on propaganda and cynicism to have their way in a less ideal public sphere. Studies with State Department employees demonstrates that debate can improve cross cultural contacts and provide improvements to the broader debate community as well.[13] Professor Benton explains the benefits: "With growing student populations in India and China showing interest in educational attainment in the U.S., the number of international students promises to increase even further in the coming years. Considering that both U.S. students and international students will be part of an increasingly linked and interdependent world, activities that foster communication and relationship building such as debate should be as diverse as possible."[14] Benton's important work on this topic is further detailed in *The Challenge of Working for Americans: Perspectives of an International Workforce* written in 2014.[15] As the global community trends toward greater diversity, debate is an ideal communication conduit for improving the ethnic relations that can easily fray in such intensive periods of immigration.

MEMORIALS TO GENOCIDE

On the day of our departure, we still had time to visit the official national memorial to the genocide in Kigali. The museum was an excellent and impressive display. It reminded me of the work I had done at the United States Holocaust Memorial Museum in Washington, D.C., ten years prior. This museum communicated with grave seriousness and precision what had transpired in Rwanda during the genocide in 1994. Memorials like this one are fraught with rhetorical peril. The inclusion and exclusions of memory are themselves political, as well observed by Dr. Terri Donofrio in her study of memorials surrounding the American 9/11 tragedy.[16] While the emotions of Nyamata were present in this museum too, it was matched by a scholarly excellence that stressed that this was more than an emotional event. The genocide was an intellectually orchestrated crime against humanity. There was shrewdness, both on the part of the perpetrators, but also on the part of the international community that deliberately stood by and did nothing while more than one million Rwandans were killed. It was not easy to take in the harsh realities of American inaction. It was not easy to see the clear evidence of European and United Nations leadership failing again and again as the crisis spiraled deeper and deeper into death. Though muted, the nationalism of Kagame's resistance to the genocide was evident and well explained. It echoed some of the concerns of the Rwandan debaters who wondered why there is not more public record of his success and heroism. One is left with the obvious unease of how political triumphalism can become its own treacherous slope toward certitude and political abuse. Rwanda negotiated that intellectual and political terrain in the museum at Kigali. The museum negotiates the politics of genocide very well. I was struck by workers on the perimeter of the museum grounds cleansing the concrete surfaces of mass graves holding the bodies of thousands of Rwandan people. It is likely that the cleanings go on daily. The ritual seemed to be an ideal visual metaphor for the travels of my heart through Rwanda in the past several days.

CONCLUSION

The 2017 project to train Rwandan security forces provides an excellent starting point for case studies in how discursive complexity as an academic pedagogy should continue to perform in a twenty-first century aimed at reducing the practice of genocide to zero. Recent international focus on the treatment of police suspect George Floyd underscores the vital need for communication training among police forces so that misunderstandings do not end in death and violence. Debate as an inherent crucible of crisis communication is an ideal pedagogy for helping security team members avoid dangerous misunderstandings.

Before we left Rwanda in 2017, we also visited the famous "Hotel Rwanda," where many individuals were saved from genocide and many critical events transpired. Our lunch there was wonderful and the scene again betrayed the historical sense that somehow this is where life and death was played out almost twenty-five years ago. As we prepared our belongings to go back to the Kigali airport and begin the journey back to Texas, I set aside the wooden spear given to me by the Rwandan security forces. My colleagues joked that I would never be able to get the spear back to the United States through all the security. I decided I would carry it by hand and try to argue my way back, face to face with the various security measures we would encounter along the journey.

As we approached the first security checkpoint at the airport, a group of young security forces approached me. One young man motioned at my spear. I ominously sensed that the parting of me and the spear was about to take an early adverse turn. I reluctantly handed him the spear. He motioned to his friends and he took a mock aggressive stance with the spear and began to prowl about the perimeter looking for an unseen threat. His Rwandan colleagues began to smile and laugh and ask for the spear so they could improve upon his performance. With laughter, the spear was returned to me—though no English was spoken. It was a consistent example of the positive ironies that continually surrounded me in Kigali while I was there: my provincial fear—their boundless joy. In Amsterdam, I took the added step of wrapping the spear in a thick layer of bubble wrap to hide its possibly menacing symbolism. That did not stop the airport security agent from making a query about the odd object as I was about to leave the long, tedious zone. I weakly told him that it was "a spear" and his eyes got huge. "I will have to check with my supervisor about this." I asked if he was sure as I saw my gate for departure nearby and time fading fast. With the supervisor came the judgment I would have to check the spear and take another turn through security. I was nearly late for my U.S. flight. When I landed in Minneapolis, I stripped the spear bare and walked bravely to the security agent. She asked, "What is that?" I said, "It is an African walking stick," she smiled and waved me through and this appeared to be the final rhetorical design to successfully bring the spear home. The spear continually reminds me, every time I see it, of Rwanda rising, and the endless possibility of humanity defeating death as a text in the agonizing reality of genocide.

The spear and my communication about it, is a powerful illustration of what debate has to offer the global community. Prior to becoming president, Calvin Coolidge observed, "Since the dawn of civilization, the triumphs of the tongue have rivaled, if not surpassed, those of the sword."[17] The security forces that laughed and played along with the spear in my hand at the Kigali airport and the struggle of European and American security screeners to understand this "weapon of war" points to the powerful role of communication and the fears and violence that can arise in our misunderstandings. That was indicative of another lesson I realized once I got the spear home to my office in Dallas. With each encounter between myself with the spear and local security forces in Kigali, Brussels, and Minneapolis, I was compelled to rhetorically adapt my argument about the spear. At Brussels, I tried to wrap my spear in bubble wrap, but this argument was not convincing. Not until I got to Minneapolis did I successfully formulate an argument that kept the spear with me personally and out of the hands of the airline baggage handlers. This trip with educational colleagues to utilize communication tools like argumentation pedagogy to strengthen nonviolence as the means of social resolution underscores the truth of Coolidge's insight. Educators need ideal tools like debate to ensure that this continues to be true in the twenty-first century.

NOTES

1. Betty Gilmore, "Going to Rwanda to Train Security Forces in Dispute Resolution," April 2017, https://www.smu.edu/News/2017/betty-gilmore-rwanda-18april2017Gk.

2. Gilmore, "Going to Rwanda to Train Security Forces in Dispute Resolution."

3. Laura Seay, "Rwanda's Gacaca Courts Are Hailed as a Post-Genocide Success. The Reality Is More Complicated," *Washington Post*, June 2, 2017, accessed August 10, 2020, https://www.washingtonpost.com/news/monkey-cage/wp/2017/06/02/59162/.

4. Max Rettig, "Gacaca: Truth, Justice, and Reconciliation in Postconflict Rwanda?" *African Studies Review*, no. 3 (December 2008): 25–50, accessed April 1, 2020, www.jstor.org/stable/27667378.

5. Sintia Radu, "Countries with the Highest Incarceration Rates," *U.S. News and World Report*, May 13, 2019, accessed August 10, 2020, https://www.usnews.com/news/best-countries/articles/2019-05-13/10-countries-with-the-highest-incarceration-rates.

6. Anuradha Chakravarty, *Investing in Authoritarian Rule: Punishment and Patronage in Rwanda's Gacaca Courts for Genocide Crimes* (New York: Cambridge University Press, 2016).

7. Seay, "Rwanda's Gacaca Courts Are Hailed as a Post-Genocide Success. The Reality Is More Complicated."

8. Robert Denton and Ben Voth, "What Can We do? An American Renaissance Predicated on Communicative Idealism," in *Social Fragmentation and the Decline of American Democracy*, edited by Robert Denton (London: Pagrave Macmillan, 2016): 161–65.

9. Saul Alinsky, *Rules for Radicals: A Practical Primer for Realistic Radicals* (New York: Random House, 1971).

10. Wayne Brockriede, "Arguers as Lovers," *Philosophy and Rhetoric* 5, no. 1 (Winter 1972): 1–11.

11. Irwin Mallin and Karrin Vasby Anderson, "Inviting Constructive Argument," *Argumentation and Advocacy* 36, no. 3 (2000): 120. *Gale Academic OneFile*, accessed August 12, 2020, https://link-gale-com.proxy.libraries.smu.edu/apps/doc/A59044832/AONE?u=txshracd2548&sid=AONE&xid=e85d2d6e.

12. Matthew 25: 37–40. *New American Standard Bible*.

13. Bond Benton, "Debate, Diversity, and Adult Learners: The Experiences of Foreign Nationals in the U.S. State Department," *Argumentation and Advocacy* 49, no. 2 (2012): 100+. *Gale Academic OneFile*, accessed August 12, 2020, https://link.gale.com/apps/doc/A332892396/AONE?u=txshracd2548&sid=AONE&xid=5662644e.

14. Benton, "Debate, Diversity, and Adult Learners: The Experiences of Foreign Nationals in the U.S. State Department," 100+.

15. Bond Benton, *The Challenge of Working for Americans: Perspectives of an International Workforce* (New York: Palgrave Macmillan, 2014).

16. Theresa Ann Donofrio, "Ground Zero and Place-Making Authority: The Conservative Metaphors in 9/11 Families' 'Take Back the Memorial' Rhetoric," *Western Journal of Communication* 74, no. 2 (March 2010): 150–69.

17. Calvin Coolidge, "Black River Academy Commencement," (May 1890), from the Calvin Coolidge Presidential Foundation website, accessed August 12, 2020, https://www.coolidgefoundation.org/resources/oratory-in-history/.

FOUR

Deconstructing Anti-Colonialism and Anti-Imperialism as Jacobin Predicates of Violence

Chapter 3 examined a case study in argumentation pedagogy as practiced in Rwanda. The conflict resolution program sought to empower local security forces to make their own judgments and arguments within their society. All societies, including the one in Kigali are imbued with political histories that guide current thinking and paradigms. Within the continent of Africa, one of the most influential arguments contributing to current thinking is colonialism. Discerning what arguments will help or hurt human societies is as complicated as human individuals themselves. Collegiate and high school debate praxis creates a normativity surrounding ideographs of "imperialism," "colonialism," and related descriptions of political power expressed internationally. Ideology can always form the pretext to propaganda and violence. Examining how, in the twenty-first century, arguments against colonialism and imperialism grant rhetorical refuge to serious human rights abuses in places as diverse as Venezuela, Sudan, Zimbabwe, Iran, and Hong Kong, allows the reader to see how caution, discernment, and debate are essential to prevent "liberation" from becoming genocide. Case studies in recent dictator declines witnessed with leaders such as Bashir (Sudan), Mugabe (Zimbabwe), Morales (Bolivia), and Chavez/Maduro (Venezuela) help make sense of an impending discursively complex world where individuals are free to form both individual property rights and socially significant civil rights, such as freedom of speech.

UNDERSTANDING THE COLONIALISM ARGUMENT

Colonialism is an important global argument. The *New Oxford Dictionary* provides this basic definition of colonialism: "the policy or practice of acquiring full or partial political control over another country, occupying it with settlers, and exploiting it economically." For the continent of Africa, colonialism represents one of the most meaningful signifiers for ongoing politics. An initial but deeper understanding of colonialism is justified. In the nineteenth century, European sovereigns convened a Berlin Conference to establish how they might control and exploit the regions in Africa.[1] This broad mapmaking meeting that divided the African continent for the political intentions of European powers such as Belgium, Germany, France and Britain remains iconic to present considerations of the future of the world, and even the global order. The power exercised in drawing those maps is integral to the moral challenge posed by the critique of colonialism. Colonialism today is a uniquely pejorative term that connotes the abuse of human rights and the reality of slavery and other methods for abusing the human condition that go well beyond the power to draw those maps in Berlin. Put simply, much of late twentieth century and current political thinking centers upon the question of colonialism and how policy makers might undo the potentially subconscious effects of this protracted policy relationship between Africa and the world.

Frantz Fanon's work on global politics titled *The Wretched of the Earth* serves as essential primer on the colonialism critique. Fanon explains the moral cause to be taken up by his readers:

> In order to achieve real action, you must yourself be a living part of Africa and of her thought; you must be an element of that popular energy which is entirely called forth for the freeing, the progress, and the happiness of Africa. There is no place outside that fight for the artist or for the intellectual who is not himself concerned with and completely at one with the people in the great battle of Africa and of suffering humanity.
> —Sékou Touré[2]

In this introductory quotation, Fanon references the important leader of Africa, Sékou Touré. Touré was for decades a powerful pan-African thinker and political leader on the continent. His thinking and arguments were so powerful that he attracted American civil rights leader and former CORE participant Stokely Carmichael to the African continent so he could be a personal governmental aid.[3] In fact, Carmichael changed his English name to Ture in deference to this new leader. This quotation and introduction by Fanon is integral to why an analysis of argumentation and debate—especially in an African context cannot ignore the critique of colonialism like the one detailed here by Fanon. Fanon continues:

> Each generation must out of relative obscurity discover its mission, fulfill it, or betray it. In underdeveloped countries the preceding generations have both resisted the work or erosion carried by colonialism and also helped on the maturing of the struggles of today. We must rid ourselves of the habit, now that we are in the thick of the fight, of minimizing the action of our fathers or of feigning incomprehension when considering their silence and passivity. They fought as well as they could, with the arms that they possessed then; and if the echoes of their struggle have not resounded in the international arena, we must realize that the reason for this silence lies less in their lack of heroism than in the fundamentally different international situation of our time. It needed more than one native to say "We've had enough"; more than one peasant rising crushed, more than one demonstration put down before we could today hold our own, certain in our victory. As for we who have decided to break the back of colonialism, our historic mission is to sanction all revolts, all desperate actions, all those abortive attempts drowned in rivers of blood.
>
> In this chapter, we shall analyze the problem, which is felt to be fundamental, of the legitimacy of the claims of a nation. It must be recognized that the political party which mobilizes the people hardly touches on this problem of legitimacy....
>
> Today, we know that in the first phase of the national struggle, colonialism tries to disarm national demands by putting forward economic doctrines. As soon as the first demands are set out, colonialism pretends to consider them, recognizing with ostentatious humility that the territory is suffering from serious underdevelopment which necessitates a great economic and social effort. And, in fact, it so happens that certain spectacular measures (centers of work for the unemployed which are opened here and there, for example) delay the crystallization of national consciousness for a few years. But, sooner or later, colonialism sees that it is not within its powers to put into practice a project of economic and social reforms which will satisfy the aspirations of the colonized people. Even where food supplies are concerned, colonialism gives proof of its inherent incapability. The colonialist state quickly discovers that if it wishes to disarm the nationalist parties on strictly economic questions then it will have to do in the colonies exactly what it has refused to do in its own country.[4]

Fanon's protracted argument is part of the ascendant independence movements in Africa as multiple indigenous parties throw off the European boundaries and political orders drawn up in the nineteenth century. Fanon further explains:

> "[In] the colonial context," he wrote, "it is evident that what parcels out the world . . . is . . . the fact of belonging to . . . a race. . . . [In] the colonies the economic substructure is also a superstructure. The cause is the consequence; you are rich because you are white, you are white because you are rich. The governing race first and foremost are those

who come from elsewhere, those who are like the original inhabitants 'the others.'"[5]

The deference to socialism derived from the materialist theorizing and reciprocal attack on capitalism makes this analysis an important continuation of Marx's original positions. There is an inherent idealism in the proposal to reject oppression and deceptions. Nonetheless, as with any idea, there is potential to form a schema of certitude such that discursive complexity is publicly suffocated. This problem arises in many instances that proceed from the origin of Fanon's critique. It is not unimportant to note that the long lines of analysis offered here often serve as major arguments in American policy debate in the twenty-first century as debaters deliberate over which side is contributing more to the ongoing social pathology that is colonialism.

The critique of colonialism remains a dominant concern of conventional twenty-first-century academic scholarship. An important intellectual leader in this realm is Mbembe. He makes this analysis of colonialism and Africa that is indicative of the broad critiques:

> But the question of the violence of tyranny was already posed to Africans by their remote and their recent past, a past slow to end. This obsession is found in African awareness in the nineteenth century. The slave trade had ramifications that remain unknown to us; to a large extent, the trade was the event through which Africa was born to modernity. Colonialism also, in both its forms and its substance, posit the issue of contingent human violence. Indeed, the slave trade and colonialism echoed one another with the lingering doubt of the very possibility of self-government, and with the risk, which has never disappeared, of the continent and Africans being again consigned for a long time to a degrading condition. In many ways, the form of domination imposed during both the slave trade and colonialism in Africa should be called phallic. During the colonial era and its aftermath, phallic domination has been all the more strategic in power relationships, not only because it is based on a mobilization of the subjective foundations of masculinity and femininity but also because it has direct, close connections with the general economy of sexuality. In fact, the phallus has been the focus of ways of constructing masculinity and power.[6]

Mbembe's argument certainly recognizes the harm of colonialism and its close political tandem with slavery. His academic analysis is an exercise of a common twentieth century ideological trope: the Freudian critique. In essence, deep psychological needs, which only a privileged few academics can see, create the latent but enduring structures of injustice. Through loyal adherence to the reiteration of the critique, the potential of liberation is held out as a possibility. Freud's psychoanalytic schema remains an important paradigm for conducting intellectual critiques in the twenty-first century.[7] It does, however, create a tautological presence in argument to which the public is largely blocked from assessing the assumptions of the critique by way of the psychoanalytic predicates that guide the critique. Anyone who denies the latent power (colonialism) alleged to be controlling contemporary affairs and events is accused of engaging in denial—a subconscious desire to promote the domineering force. Those denying the alleged oppression are rhetorically reformulated as agents of the oppression. This makes it a powerful deception within argumentation practice. It therefore remains an important irony, although perhaps predictable in the Lacanian and Freudian critiques, that African strong-men have made the consistent rhetorical ploy that they alone can fight the "Colonial masters" and, therefore, all individual rights of dissent must be suspended. Bashir, Amin, Mugabe, Khadaffi, and Taylor all offered themselves as anti-colonial prefects needing unscrupulous obedience to throw off the European masters.[8] Situations as dreadful as genocide have arisen in concert with their anti-colonial propaganda. Millions died so their nations could be free from "colonialism." It is a dreadful circular argument.

MANAGING THE COLONIAL/POST-COLONIAL DIALECTIC

The awkward deliberative point of this chapter is a consideration of how anti-colonialism is subject to its own low discursive complexity abuses as it tries to find the simple answer for the history of colonialism. George Ayittey's work *Africa Unchained: The Blueprint for Africa's Future* (2005) is an important productive starting point for this analysis.[9] Ayittey's argument is that the simple dialect of colonialism versus anti-colonialism produces its own lack of discursive complexity denying the potentially better future for Africa. In this seminal framework for the twenty-first-century Africa, Ayittey challenges convention:

> Incredible as it may sound to many, the colonialists did not really introduce any new institutions into Africa. What they introduced were merely more efficient forms of already existing institutions—both good and bad. It was probably for this reason the colonialism lasted for nearly a century. Had it introduced institutions that were diametrically antithetical to the existing ones, the demise of colonialism would have come sooner. The introduction of different forms of the same institutions did not mean the colonialists "invented" those institutions—an extremely important distinction. There were weapons in indigenous Africa; spears, bows, and arrows. The Europeans introduced guns which were more efficient in their killing, although the "primitive" weapons did occasionally trump in the Ashanti and Zulu wars in the nineteenth century. But it is incorrect to assert that the colonialists "invented" weapons and the institution of war. Similarly, in precolonial Africa, the natives gathered under a tree or at the village market square and debated an issue until they reached a consensus. When the colonialists came, they erected a building and called it "parliament" which

means a "place to talk." It did not mean the colonialists "invented" the institution of public debate and free speech.[10]

The implications of this analysis are at least two-fold: (1) there is an essential intellectual nature to African life that predates the colonial era and (2) that free speech and debate were part of that essential African character and identity. Ayittey consistently defends in his work the value of deliberative means to correct the corruption of African elites in modern Africa. This analysis seeks to empower that process by seeing indigenous debate spread across the continent.

Ayittey continues with this line of analysis:

> The onslaught against the "colonial" institutions, more generally, showed a woeful lack of understanding of the purpose of those institutions. The purpose of "parliament," for example, was to provide a forum to debate national issues. Such a forum existed in indigenous Africa under a tree. To expunge all reminders of the hated episode of colonialism is understandable. But it did not require, for example, a destruction of the "parliament" building. A mere name change to say, "Indaba" would have sufficed (just as several African countries adopted African names after independence: Gold Coast to Ghana, Rhodesia to Zimbabwe), and the "parliament" building, whatever it was called afterward, would have continued to serve its purpose. But in blowing up the colonial parliament without providing an alternative forum, many African leaders denied their people public discourse of national issues and participation in the decision-making process—an African tradition.[11]

Ayittey highlights the problem of a reactionary anti-colonialist rhetoric which makes deliberation appear to be a Western concept and therefore alien and offensive to the African identity. This is not the case, and the need for African renderings of the same parliament places and forums is worth considering and developing. Anti-colonialism can in its dialectic origin be its own formula for lower discursive complexity and the inherent manifestations of propaganda and injustice. In 2020, we are able to see further down the road imagined by Ayittey.

Conventional communication scholarship tends to operate within a terministic screen bounded by coloniality and anti-coloniality. An example can be observed in this recent point of scholarship:

> In line with the decolonial thrust, this study has demonstrated the relevance and analytical power of African conceptual tools as exemplified by Ekeh and Mbembe's writings in terms of theorizing popular communication. "Contrary to radical decolonial discourse, which tends to promote a theoretical cul-de-sac anchored in cultural essentialism, this article has highlighted the overlaps and interstices between Western scholars' concept of the subaltern public sphere (see Fraser, 1992) and African scholars notions of primordial publics and alternative popular publics (Ekeh, 1975; Mbembe, 2001). These analytical toolkits feed

off and into Western conceptual lenses in complex but very enlightening ways. Given the unavoidable reductionist and in-ward looking agenda of the dewesternization discourse, focusing on the overlaps and interstices between the 'Western' and 'African' has the potential to promote what Waisbord (2016) calls 'cosmopolitan scholarship' in communication studies that is open to the globalization of problems and academic production."[12]

Mare's work acknowledges the reductionist tendencies of the Western/African dichotomy offered in postcolonial scholarship. It initiates an understanding based upon a growing consensus toward "decoloniality." In this way, intellectuals offer an interpretive path for removing the symbolic impact of colonialism on the African mind.

ANTI-COLONIALISM AS LOW DISCURSIVE COMPLEXITY

The problem is most vivid in the incredible case of a scholar threatened with death for writing and publishing a pro-colonialism research article. In August 2017, Professor Bruce Gilley of Portland State University published "The Case for Colonialism" in *Third World Quarterly*. The abstract for the article explained:

> For the last 100 years, Western colonialism has had a bad name. It is high time to question this orthodoxy. Western colonialism was, as a general rule, both objectively beneficial and subjectively legitimate in most of the places where it was found, using realistic measures of those concepts. The countries that embraced their colonial inheritance, by and large, did better than those that spurned it. Anti-colonial ideology imposed grave harms on subject peoples and continues to thwart sustained development and a fruitful encounter with modernity in many places. Colonialism can be recovered by weak and fragile states today in three ways: by reclaiming colonial modes of governance; by recolonising some areas; and by creating new Western colonies from scratch.[13]

The article gave rise to an incredible movement within academic circles to physically threaten the author and ultimately he requested that the article be withdrawn. Half of the editorial board for the journal resigned in protest over the article. Taylor and Francis, the publishing company, provided this explanation about the article's withdrawal:

> This Viewpoint essay has been withdrawn at the request of the academic journal editor, and in agreement with the author of the essay. Following a number of complaints, Taylor & Francis conducted a thorough investigation into the peer review process on this article. Whilst this clearly demonstrated the essay had undergone double-blind peer review, in line with the journal's editorial policy, the journal editor has subsequently received serious and credible threats of personal violence. These threats are linked to the publication of this essay.

As the publisher, we must take this seriously. Taylor & Francis has a strong and supportive duty of care to all our academic editorial teams, and this is why we are withdrawing this essay.[14]

The incident is indicative of the lack of discursive complexity that can easily arise in academic circles. This is censorship engaged in response to threats of violence against the author. It is important to understand that acts of violence are regularly predicated on a perceived sense of justice being fulfilled in the act. This kind of low discursive complexity should not be the goal of our educational activity.

INTERNATIONAL EXAMPLES OF ANTI-COLONIALIST RHETORIC AS PATHOLOGICAL

These threats of violence are rhetorically contiguous to the violent threats emanating from genocidal regimes in Africa like that of the former Omar Bashir of Sudan or the former Mohamar Khadaffi of Libya. Violent dictatorial tactics across the continent of Africa are regularly justified in terminologies of anti-colonialism. The clever nature of this dilemma constrained American military interventions to stop a wide array of humanitarian abuses across the continent from Somalia, to Sudan, to Liberia, to Rwanda.[15] In essence, military interventions to stop human rights abuses could easily be stopped by rhetorically inferring that the interruption was merely a resurgence of colonialism. This is the essential component of Ayittey's analysis that explains how reactionary rhetoric gilded with anti-colonial trappings justifies an array of modern abuses in Africa against the people of the continent.

Omar Bashir utilized anti-colonialist rhetoric to his ultimate end in politics in 2019. In 2017, news reports explained: "Sudanese President Omar Al-Bashir has accused the International Criminal Court (ICC) of being a politicised colonisation tool geared to undermine the African continent. In his speech to the first Conference of the Chiefs Justice and Heads of the Supreme Courts in Africa, Al-Bashir said Sunday when the African nations realised that the ICC was an unjust colonial tool, the African Union decided to collectively withdraw from the ICC, *Anadolu* agency reported."[16]

THE RHETORICAL INTERSECTION OF AMERICAN CIVIL RIGHTS AND ANTI-COLONIALISM

The travels of American civil rights activists like Malcolm X and James Farmer Jr. were important rhetorical precursors and knowledge gaining enterprises in the era of African nationalism. Black power proponent Stokely Carmichael famously left the American movement to take a personal struggle against colonialism in Africa. He took a new name. NPR provides this summary of his change in thinking and activism centered around Africa: "Hounded by the FBI at home, tracked by the CIA when he went abroad, Carmichael had had enough. He changed his name to Kwame Ture in homage to two African heroes—his friend Kwame Nkrumah (the first president of independent Ghana), and Sékou Touré, the president of Guinea, the country that had welcomed the former civil rights worker as an honored citizen."[17]

Ture believed that America could not be understood until you are outside of it.[18] In October of 1969, Carmichael returned from Africa to give a speech at Malcolm X Liberation University in New York: "We are all working toward building a strong, united African nation wherever we may be, the concept that we must work toward the unification of Africa—in other words, the concept of Pan-Africanism."[19] By contrast, Carmichael explained in an essay in 1969: "There are political divisions and economic divisions that are imposed upon us from Europe."[20] Ture would live for another three decades, visiting the United States frequently as he traveled the globe preaching the merits of pan-Africanism and scientific socialism. People listened—but not in the same numbers as they had in the early days. Ture, with his modest lifestyle and reminders of communal responsibility seemed ... quaint. "It's interesting," biographer Joseph Peniel notes: "Times changed, but Stokely didn't."[21] Ture was arrested in 1986 by the military government of Guinea and jailed three days for attempting to overthrow the government.[22] Ture's cynicism went so far that when he died in 1998, he believed the U.S. government had infected him with cancer.

Similarly, the status of the Sudanese people was an important starting point for the thinking of Malcolm X:

> In July 1959, Malcolm X took his first trip to Africa. Travelling as an ambassador for the Nation of Islam and with a passport issued in his new name, Malik el-Shabazz, the young minister visited Sudan, Nigeria, and Egypt—and a few months later Ghana, Syria and Saudi Arabia. Malcolm X's sojourn in Sudan seems to have been formative, leaving a powerful impression on the 34-year-old. Until the end of his life he praised the Sudanese for their kindness and solidarity, and recalled the wonders of the city of Omdurman. His travel diaries and letters are sprinkled with references to the Sudanese. In one entry in April 1964, he writes of the "quiet confidence" of the Sudanese—in another, he says, "I never cease to be impressed by the Sudanese." On August 22, 1959, Malcolm X wired a letter to The New York Amsterdam News stating that people in Africa seemed more concerned about the plight of their "brothers in America" than their own conditions; and that Africans saw America's treatment of black people as a "yardstick" by which to measure the sincerity of America's offer of assistance. He often mentioned the Sudanese as evidence of Africa's support for the African American struggle.[23]

The experiences of Malcolm X, James Farmer Jr., Martin Luther King Jr., and so many other American Civil Rights advocates traveling in Africa, points to the importance of Africa in shaping the new American consciousness by way of a mutual understanding between the United States and the emergent postcolonial nationalism of Africa. In the fifty years since those visits, the various nationalist projects of postcolonialism have yielded disparate, and often disappointing, results. One of the most important genocides concluding the twentieth century after the Rwandan genocide was the genocide in the Darfur region of Sudan. The genocidal propaganda of sovereign leader Omar Bashir was often phrased in terms of stopping the colonialism of the West. The stubborn persistence of Bashir, despite prosecution by the International Criminal Court, yielded to his surprise decision to step down from governance in 2019. The removal of Omar Bashir in 2019 stands as an important current marker in the struggle for greater freedom on the continent. Young people making internet-based arguments were an important part of the revolution.[24] Less than a year prior to this event, most experts would not have expected any change in Sudanese politics. A grassroots movement pushed the military dictator aside and the slow march of international law like the ICC tribunal was swept away by local advocacy in Khartoum that changed the draconian Islamic supremacist state to one of increasing openness and growing potential for more discursive complexity.

TWENTY-FIRST-CENTURY AFRICAN DISCURSIVE COMPLEXITY

The abrupt and arguably unexpected success of efforts inside Sudan to remove Omar Bashir, point to an evident and not easily denied trend on the continent to shed the low discursive complexity propaganda of mechanistic anti-colonialism toward the often female- and internet-led interpretation of compelling local needs against authoritarian centralization. The blueprint of Africa appears to be yielding tangible alternatives to neo-colonialism and authoritarian anti-colonialism. The delicate balance of this rhetorical ecosystem should be understood with reference to each unique context. The list of declining or defeated twenty-first-century anti-colonialist propagandists is difficult to ignore: Khaddaffi, Taylor, Morsi, Mugabe, and Bashir. These five nations—Libya, Liberia, Egypt, Zimbabwe, and Sudan—represent 150 million individuals with considerations of an alternative of greater discursive complexity. This is not to say that in the ensuing chaos of nations without leaders that something worse such as ISIS or Boko Haram could fill the void, but the reality that local individuals in Africa are taking responsibility for removing bad leadership lies at the heart of a potentially better world. Already, the revolutions of Arab Spring in 2011 look less robust than the 2019 revolution to remove Bashir. This suggests that internal movements are learning and appropriating the values of discursive complexity. Africa is an exceptionally young continent demographically, and an educated youth has the potential to build solid political alternatives to the unipolar descriptions of their authoritarian forbearers.

The potential collapse of the rhetorical dialectic between colonialism and anti-colonialism improves the ability to interrogate authoritarianism offered in the name of anti-colonialism. A corrupt leader of Equatorial Guinea was recently caught in a financial sting against his plundering of the sovereign treasury to buy extravagant American mansions and exotic cars:

> It was not just politicians. Western bankers, lawyers and middlemen were happy to help Africa's looters first hide their money in shell companies and tax havens and then splurge it on super yachts, private jets, luxury cars and multi-million pound properties across the rich world. But a change in attitudes has slowly been brought about by pressure from campaigners and a realisation by Western governments that there was an inherent contradiction in doling out aid to Africa only to see vast quantities of stolen cash seep back to the West. The United States, Britain and Switzerland—some of the favoured destinations for the stolen cash—have led the way, tightening up laws to make it easier to seize suspect assets and search properties.[25]

Previously, such autocrats could deflect criticism of their luxuries by supposing that such censure was an overreach of the imperialist. The theft of public monies does not prosper the local populations anywhere, and the cooperation between Africa and Western powers yields positive human results.

The 2003 removal of Charles Taylor from Liberia is an instructive positive case for how tyranny and human rights abuse can end and be replaced with a positive alternative. Charles Taylor had for decades abused the people of Liberia with little restraint. As noted in the introduction, a famous general in his ruthless anti-civilian military was "General Butt Naked." The general testified later that he was responsible for the killing of thousands of Liberians in a larger war against civilians that killed about 250,000. In 2003, Liberians appealed to President Bush for military relief. The chances for the nation appeared slim, as the United States was already deeply embroiled in major military operations in Afghanistan and Iraq. The War on Terror already occupied tens of thousands of U.S. soldiers, and there were many other high value theaters of that war around the world. Moreover, Liberia as a continental member, faced the quandary of U.S. failure in Somalia in 1992 and 1993, all contributing to U.S. inaction during the 1994 Rwandan genocide. The invasion of U.S. troops in Liberia would likely be heralded by Taylor and other African sympathizers as "imperialism" and "colonialist." Nonetheless, President George W. Bush authorized a small deployment to Monrovia, the capital of Liberia. More importantly, he secured, by diplomatic means, assurances of support from the African Union—a conglomeration of African states. This provided a predominantly Nigerian military force of about six thousand. This muted the colonial rhetorical features of Taylor's removal from power by military force.

As noted in the introduction, the vacuum of Taylor's departure was filled by something much better. Liberians elected the first female president on the continent of Africa. Ellen Johnson Sirleaf was educated at Harvard, but came with powerful acclaim to rule her homeland. More recently, Liberians made another successful electoral handoff, electing George Weah in 2017.[26] Liberia was the origin of the Ebola outbreak in 2014 that killed roughly ten thousand Liberians. The greater discursive complexity of the nation compared to the dictatorship of Taylor, allowed relief hospitals and medical education to limit the impact of the virus and save Liberians and people around the world from a larger Ebola pandemic. Between 1990 and 2015, life expectancy in Liberia rose from forty-six to sixty-three. This 27 percent improvement in the human condition is paved by the growing discursive complexity of the nation. Liberia made a 10 percent improvement in its literacy rate between 1985 and 2008 going from 32 to 43 percent. Additionally, since the fall of Taylor, Liberian GDP has increased from $750 million to almost $3.2 billion.[27]

COLONIALISM AS ARGUMENT OUTSIDE OF AFRICA

The use of colonialism dialectics is not limited to Africa, despite the apparent pretexts to such arguments. In South America, this discursive struggle is also apparent. The recent ousters of Maduro in Venezuela and Morales in Bolivia point to the impending fragility of centralizing authoritarians offering themselves as anti-colonialist saviors. The lexis of such conversation has important pretexts in American academics like Noam Chomsky, who consistently championed these authoritarians as morally imperative counters to the American discursive model of global politics. Chomsky was comfortable traveling to Venezuela and seeking direct embrace of flamboyant Venezuelan strongman Hugo Chavez. Venezuela is an important case study in the rupture of anti-colonialist ideology.

Venezuela was, prior to its anti-colonialist socialist insurgency, one of the most prosperous nations in the hemisphere. After his election in 1998, Hugo Chavez commenced toward one of the most destructive reigns of sovereignty in the past seventy years of global history.[28] Venezuela set new records for inflation, comparable to disasters in Zimbabwe. Venezuela entered into a hyperinflationary spiral from November 2016, when monthly inflation surpassed 50 percent. Annual inflation for 2017 was estimated at 2,616 percent, the highest in the world, with December inflation recorded at 85 percent.[29] There were 30 percent and 65 percent increases in infant and maternal mortality, respectively, and a sharp rise in incidents of preventable diseases including diphtheria, dengue, pneumonia, HIV, measles, and Zika. Incidences of malaria rose by 76 percent year-over-year to nearly 250,000 cases. Infant mortality claimed 11,500 lives in 2016, while maternal mortality totaled 756 cases. More than 13,000 doctors left the country. The national poverty rate reached 82 percent in 2017. The official homicide rate was 21,752 murders in 2016, or 60 violent deaths per day. Among these, fifteen of those violent deaths per day were committed by police forces of Venezuela.[30] This summary of the Chavez revolution was offered in 2018:

> As had been the case since Hugo Chávez was first elected in 1998, the fractured opposition movement was an explanatory factor in the survival of the Bolivarian Revolution, even as progress toward the Revolution's original goals of social justice, participation, economic development, and communal-level democracy were reversed. The overt militarization of governance was the most salient trend of 2017, and this opened-up potentially irreconcilable schisms within the Chavista movement and between Venezuelan civil society and the country's security forces.[31]

Despite the overwhelming failure of the Bolivarian revolution as led by Chavez and Maduro, the academic reframing of "success" abounds in academic literature. In a 2019 analysis, we find this ringing rebuke of criticism:

> The Bolivarian Revolution has been vilified by the western bourgeoisie because it has tried to break away from this cycle of dependency. Venezuela, like Cuba, Vietnam, Nicaragua, Grenada, Iran, Egypt, Libya and more before it has tried to break away from colonial exploitation. The only thing the Bolivarian Revolution is guilty of is caring more for its own people than the whims of capital and the global elite. Hugo Chavez ignited the spirit and fire of the Venezuelan people to throw off the chains of imperialism.[32]

In the United States, popular 2020 Democratic Party presidential candidate Senator Bernie Sanders was reluctant to criticize the obvious failures of the socialist fantasy pursued by Chavez and Maduro.[33]

In Bolivia, strongman Evo Morales resigned from power in 2019.[34] Despite his socialist and indigenous origins, even the *New York Times* conceded that Morales's authoritarian habits made him increasingly unpopular. Ultimately, he fled the country under pressure to resign. Jeanine Añez Chavez, an opposition leader, declared herself president as the nation moved toward new elections. The complicated circumstance and path forward continue to emphasize the reality of discursive complexity as a human political need. Appeals to ideological tropes such as imperialism and colonialism no longer suffice to rally the public to support in a predictable manner that increasingly resembles propaganda more than deliberation.

SETTLER COLONIALISM

A more recent extension of original African colonialism and pioneered within collegiate debate in the United States is a notion of settler colonialism. The central agency of a settler is offered in the stead of profound sovereign or central authority. Settlers, according to this rhetorical theory, are imbued through argument with a self-righteous design to take the land from the noble indigenous population. A recent introduction to the topic in *Fordham Law Review* provides a sample of the argument:

> The United States sits on invaded Indigenous (1) lands. European settler colonizers invaded Indigenous lands with the intent to permanently settle and form new ethnic and religious sovereign communities on the newly acquired land. (2) These settler colonizers have continued to occupy invaded Indigenous lands by establishing an ongoing complex social structure of invasion called "settler colonialism." (3) This structure of invasion functions through the ongoing processes of Indigenous elimination and subordination of racialized outsiders (4)—as well as through the creation and enforcement of laws that maintain the ongoing invasion. (5) U.S. settler colonialism's invasion may have started in the past, but it is a continuing structure of elimination and subordination that is happening now.[35]

A broader treatment of the issue and extending beyond the United States is offered by Walter Hixon.[36]

Settler colonialism critiques are built upon two faulty assumptions: (1) all land has an original owner and (2) the original owner was cheated of current ownership. In the United States more than five hundred Native American tribes are recognized by the U.S. Federal Government.[37] In the telling of grand academic narrators such as professor Ward Churchill, Native Americans lived in innocence and without property conflicts. Occasionally, the public is offered "maps" of where these original communities lived. Anthropological studies and thousands embedded within the field like those offered by E. O. Wilson document a plainly violent property frenzy enveloping every corner of the globe and every historical culture.[38] The faulty supposition that an Edenic placid scene of human relations was disrupted by "the colonizer," misses the reality that humanity has not witnessed an era of pure cooperation. Slavery, exploitation, theft, and genocide are the human story. These and so many other human exploits of evil do not appear suddenly in one human culture or in a rupture of some specially selected historical moment. Humanity is habitually evil. Deliberation can reveal to us the unfair moments and intensive deliberation in the way of courts and formal consideration, which can slow and ultimately arrest such cruelty. Settler colonialism as a critique sets in motion essential motives for genocide by imagining a pure and original race that is "unsettled" by foreigners and invaders. The vision for restoration can establish pretexts to violence and cleansing the land. These determinations are subjectively ascertained and delineated from a standpoint of privilege that determines who may speak for the group.

Civil rights advocate James Meredith explains his own complicated family tree traceable to native American populations of Mississippi and White supremacists. He laughs at his original history and emphasizes the need to understand our individual location in the present not bound by narratives of the past.[39] In fact, contemporary White supremacists have used their roots in native narrative indigeneity to rationalize their own contemporary discrimination and anti-Blackness.[40] The artificial imposition by critiques utilizing the settler colonialism argument to invoke an "innocent past" is used to decenter the present. In cases such as economic development within the United States, an arbitrary locus of chronology prior to the development is accepted as preeminent and an assumed voice speaks for the past with tautological certitude. All resistance to the voice of the past is deemed further settlement and discrimination. It is not considered appropriate to contemplate the infinite nature of land forfeiture or pre-assimilated claims that predate the current selected voice.

CONCLUSION: ANTI-COLONIALISM WITHOUT PRE-TEXT TO GENOCIDE

The iterations of colonialism critique can give rise to nationalist and ethnic supremacism. Once communication competency is established toward recognizing isolated voices for speaking on behalf of the past, a privileged tautology emerges where a conversation presupposes that the one who is speaking for the past will decide both the present and the future. Our awkward rhetorical grasp of history points to its reality as almost immediately murky. Anti-colonialism projects in politics within Africa, the broader globe, and in the United States can and have been used toward genocidal ends like those embraced by Omar Bashir in Sudan and White supremacists connecting with their Cherokee roots in Mississippi. Narratives must remain subject to challenge in the rhetorical presence of reason and deliberation. Voicelessness is a human intuition and it does not need rationalization as "reason is whiteness" or some other cultural ideograph. The silence of individuals jeopardizes any notion of collective justice. The colonialism critique can be utilized like all arguments as a pretext toward genocide. Humanity should remain vigilant and committed to inquiry challenging such master narratives.

NOTES

1. Thomas E. Smith, *Emancipation without Equality: Pan-African Activism and the Global Color Line* (Amherst: University of Massachusetts Press, 2018).
2. Frantz Fanon, *The Wretched of the Earth* (New York: Grove Press, 1963): 206.
3. Stokely Carmichael and Ekwueme Michael Thelwell, *Ready for Revolution: The Life and Struggles of Stokely Carmichael* (Kwame Ture) (New York: Scribner, 2003).
4. Fanon, *The Wretched of the Earth*, 206–7.
5. Frantz Fanon and Constance Farrington, *The Wretched of the Earth*, preface by Jean-Paul Sartre, translated from the French by Constance Farrington (New York: Grove Press, 1967): 40.
6. Achille Mbembe, *On the Postcolony* (Berkeley: University of California Press, 2001): 13.
7. Rudolf Allers and Sigmund Freud, *The Successful Error: A Critical Study of Freudian Psychoanalysis*, by Rudolf Allers (London: Sheed & Ward, 1940).
8. "The 10 African Strongmen Who Left Power since 2011," *Agency France Press*, April 25, 2019, accessed August 10, 2020, https://www.france24.com/en/20190423-timeline-10-african-strongmen-deposed-gaddafi-bashir-mugabe-bouteflika.
9. George Ayittey, *Africa Unchained: The Blueprint for Africa's Future* (New York: Palgrave Macmillan, 2005).
10. Ayittey, *Africa Unchained: The Blueprint for Africa's Future*, 116.
11. Ayittey, *Africa Unchained: The Blueprint for Africa's Future*, 119.
12. Admire Mare, "Popular Communication in Africa: An Empirical and Theoretical Exposition," *Annals of the International Communication Association* 44, no. 1 (2020): 81–99.
13. Bruce Gilley, "The Case for Colonialism," *Academic Questions* 31 (2017): 167–85.
14. Bruce Gilley, "The Case for Colonialism," *Third World Quarterly* (2017). DOI: 10.1080/01436597.2017.1369037 [Taylor & Francis statement].
15. Ben Voth, "President Bush's Rhetoric and Policy against Genocide" in *The George W. Bush Presidency, Foreign Policy*, Volume 3, ed. Meena Bose and Paul Fritz (New York: Nova Publishers, 2016): 161–74.
16. "Sudan's Bashir Accuses ICC of Facilitating Colonisation in Africa," *Middle East Monitor*, April 3, 2017, accessed August 1, 2020, https://www.middleeastmonitor.com/20170403-sudans-bashir-accuses-icc-of-facilitating-colonisation-in-africa/.
17. Karen Grigsby Bates, "Stokely Carmichael, a Philosopher behind the Black Power Movement," NPR, March 10, 2014, accessed August 1, 2020 https://www.npr.org/sections/codeswitch/2014/03/10/287320160/stokely-carmichael-a-philosopher-behind-the-black-power-movement.
18. Charles Cobb, "From Stokely Carmichael to Kwame Ture," *Callaloo* 34, no. 1 (2011): 89–97.
19. Kwame Ture, "We Are All Africans: A Speech by Stokely Carmichael to Malcolm X Liberation University," *Black Scholar* 1, no. 7 (1970): 65.
20. Stokely Carmichael, "Pan Africanism: Land and Power," *Black Scholar* 27, no. 3/4 (1969): 38.
21. Karen Grigsby Bates, "Stokely Carmichael, a Philosopher behind the Black Power Movement."
22. "Kwame Ture: 1941–1998," *Race and History*, November 15, 1999, retrieved from http://www.raceandhistory.com/historicalviews/111599.htm.
23. Hisham Aidi, "Malcolm X and the Sudanese," *Al Jazeera*, March 19, 2020.
24. Isma'il Kushkush, "Protesters in Sudan and Algeria Have Learned from the Arab Spring," *The Atlantic*, April 13, 2019, accessed August 10, 2020, https://www.theatlantic.com/international/archive/2019/04/protesters-sudan-and-algeria-have-learned-arab-spring/587113/.
25. Adrian Blomfield, "Going, Going, Gone: African Dictators Losing Luxury Lifestyle amid Money Laundering Crackdown," *Telegraph*, October 6, 2019, accessed Au-

gust 10, 2020, https://www.telegraph.co.uk/news/2019/10/06/going-going-gone-african-dictators-losing-luxury-lifestyle-amid/.

26. Clair MacDougall and Helene Cooper, "George Weah Wins Liberia Election," *New York Times*, December 28, 2017, accessed August 10, 2020, https://www.nytimes.com/2017/12/28/world/africa/george-weah-liberia-election.html.

27. "Liberia," *World Bank*, accessed July 21, 2020, https://data.worldbank.org/country/liberia.

28. Julia Buxton, "Venezuela: Deeper into the Abyss/Venezuela: a las puertas del abismo," *Revista de Ciencia Politica 38*, no. 2 (2018): 409+.

29. "Venezuela 2017 Annual Inflation at 2,616 Percent: Opposition Lawmakers," *Reuters*, January 8, 2018, accesed February 10 2018, https://www.reuters.com/article/us-venezuela-economy-inflation/venezuela-2017-annual-inflation-at-2616-per-cent-opposition-lawmakers-idUSKBN1EX23B.

30. Buxton, "Venezuela: Deeper into the Abyss/Venezuela: a las puertas del abismo," 409+.

31. Buxton, "Venezuela: Deeper into the Abyss/Venezuela: a las puertas del abismo," 409+.

32. Sam Parry, "US Imperialism in Venezuela, and the Legacy of Colonialism," *Undod*, January 29, 2019, accessed August 10, 2020, https://undod.cymru/en/2019/01/29/venezuela/.

33. Marc Caputo, "'He Is Not Going to Be the Nominee': Dems Slam Sanders over Maduro Stance: The Just-Announced 2020 Contender Declines to Say Whether the Socialist Venezuelan Dictator Should Go," *Politico*, February 21, 2019.

34. Anatoly Kurmanaev, "Evo Morales and Bolivia: What We Know about the President's Resignation," *New York Times*, November 12, 2019, retrieved from https://www.nytimes.com/2019/11/12/world/americas/evo-morales-resignation-bolivia-facts.html.

35. Monika Batra Kashyap, "Unsettling Immigration Laws: Settler Colonialism and the U.S. Immigration Legal System," *Fordham Urban Law Journal* (June 2019): 548+. *Gale Academic OneFile*, accessed July 28, 2020, https://link-gale-com.proxy.libraries.smu.edu/apps/doc/A592339979/AONE?u=txshracd2548&sid=AONE&xid=fba3ca73.

36. Walter Hixson, *American Settler Colonialism: A History*, 1st edition (New York: Palgrave Macmillan, 2013).

37. "List of Federal and State Recognized Tribes," *National Conference of State Legislatures*, accessed July 28, 2020, https://www.ncsl.org/research/state-tribal-institute/list-of-federal-and-state-recognized-tribes.aspx.

38. Edward O. Wilson, *The Social Conquest of Earth*, 1st ed. (New York: Liveright Pub. Corp., 2012).

39. James Meredith and William Doyle, *A Mission from God: A Memoir and Challenge for America* (New York: Atria, 2012).

40. Jodi Byrd, "Weather with You: Settler Colonialism, Antiblackness, and the Grounded Relationalities of Resistance," *Journal of the Critical Ethnic Studies Association* 5, no. 1–2 (2019): 207+. *Gale Academic OneFile*, accessed July 28, 2020.https://link-gale-com.proxy.libraries.smu.edu/apps/doc/A608784113/AONE?u=txshracd2548&sid=AONE&xid=b677b2e7.

FIVE

Debate as Pedagogical Empowerment at HBCUs in the United States (Christopher Medina, Sean Allen, Drake Pough, and Ben Voth)

One of the most significant recent developments in the field of American debate is the emergence of a new debate national tournament for Historically Black Colleges and Universities (HBCUs) in January of 2018. This tournament completed three successful annual competitions. America is home to dozens of HBCUs that represent an important legacy and future orientation for maximizing the Black voice. Despite their profound creation in the United States in the aftermath of the Civil War against slavery during the 1870s, HBCUs were not welcomed with regard to debate and speech practice in the larger collegiate community. Hundreds of HBCUs were created by Baptists, Methodists, Presbyterians, and Congregationalists between 1870 and 1890.[1] Michael Bartannen and Robert Littlefield documented this exclusion in their excellent work, *Forensics in America: A History*. They note that specific provisions were made in the 1920s to exclude African American competitors in the national Forensics Constitution: "The candidate, who shall not be of the African race, shall be a regular college student . . . a graduate . . . an instructor . . . or a coach" (243). This kind of exclusion damaged the emergence of Black voices. HBCUs did not give up on the effort to develop the Black voice within the United States despite this exclusion. Wake Forest professor and former debate coach Al Louden researched extensively the archives of HBCUs to uncover the type of academic work that continued debate and speech practice.[2] Records indicate that the first debate among Black colleges in the United States took place around 1905. For America, and the world, the heroic struggle for the Black voice within the arena of debate was brought to prominence in a film by Denzel Washington in 2007, *The Great Debaters*. The film focused upon the experiences of the 1934–1938 Wiley College debate team led by coaching legend Melvin Tolson. Tolson led an exceptional debate squad that may have been the first to cross the color line in debate with an event in Oklahoma. They also defeated national champions USC, in Los Angeles, before an audience of more than two thousand observers. The movie depicted this culminating interracial event as being against Harvard University. The movie played a pivotal role in reigniting debate at HBCUs, particularly at Wiley College. In 2012, Wiley implemented, under the leadership of director Chris Medina, a Quality Enhancement Plan in its curriculum known as "Communicate through Debate," which was a Debate across the Curriculum program. The details of that effort are contained later in this chapter. It is important to understand how HBCU debate activity equipped the American civil rights movement in order to better understand how debate is a global pedagogy necessary for improving international conditions for humanity around the world.

INTEGRATING VOICES IN FORENSICS

As noted earlier, there is a long struggle for the competitive Forensics (Speech and Debate) community to accept Black competitors. It is not a simple matter to announce the end to such discrimination. Teaching should include a strategy to help the marginalized feel confident and comfortable in the steps needed to achieve such success. This section is a description of an observed model within the Wiley Speech and Debate team between 2013 and 2018.

Forensics competitors are often admonished by their coaches that competition begins before they step foot on the campus at a tournament. Coaches remind students that judging happens when they are observed at the hotel, between rounds, in the student lounge, or even at a restaurant where teams meet by happenstance. Coaches caution students that they may never know who is listening and anything negative should be reserved as "van talk," discussions which should take place out of earshot of anyone who may negatively perceive the conversation. Judges scrutinize words or actions, inside or outside of a round, to factor in their decision calculus; some judges may do this consciously and others unconsciously. Moreover, competitors graduate and become judges. The interactions that took place among peers can become rationale or justification for rankings when a competitor becomes a judge. As a result, students must take great care to ensure a perception of professionalism and earnestness with all in the forensics community.

A judge is charged with the ranking of student presentations within a particular round of competition; however, individual perceptions and opinions can obscure the decision-making process. Because of the subjective nature of forensics events, social interactions between competitors and judges, student interactions, or even the external observation of interactions, can alter discernment of an individual, and consequently alter the judgment and ranking of any critic. Thus, it is important for students to create a strong interpersonal and social connection with judges, students, and tournament staff; whether in a round of competition, or outside.

Forensics teaches many skills that are indispensable to professional success; the ability to think critically, to communicate effectively, the ability to work in teams, as well as research and leadership skills. Moreover, forensics alumnae understand the skills developed competing at the highest level, and former competitors may be in a position of distinction, corporate authority, or in a position that may be mutually beneficial within a professional network. Thus, building a healthy professional network can be an integral part of career and business development. The central message is that maintaining good relationships is important in the forensics community.

Relationship development in the forensics community can be theoretically explained and described through various interpersonal communication models. However, the communication theories which are used to define the relational development among individuals cannot be adequately or generally applied to students of color. Though no specific or reliable racial demographic information about forensics competitors has been explicitly studied or published, forensics in America has been described as an activity that is largely dominated by the White, upper–middle class students. Among this forensics community, there is a meager presence of students of color, many ethnicities and cultures are underrepresented, or virtually nonexistent.[3]

As a result of the homogeneity of the forensics community, there are unique and observable disparities and struggles in interpersonal relationship building for students of color. Because of increased anxiety and in-group/out-group categorization, social identity theories indicate that visible differences reduce communicative interaction.[4] Thus, for students of color to successfully develop interpersonal relationships and foster acceptance in the White-dominated activity of forensics, they must increase their communication initiations, and diverge from the typical interpersonal communication models. In order to identify the divergence from the traditional interpersonal communication models, the observation of successful students of color serve as a case study in the adaptation and building of relationships in the forensics community.

Chapter 5

THE CASE STUDY OF THE GREAT DEBATERS

Though racial diversity in forensics continues to grow, its genesis can be traced to Tolson and the debaters of Wiley College. In 2014, Wiley College was the first HBCU team to win a national championship tournament, winning the Pi Kappa Delta National Comprehensive Tournament. This is the same tournament that excluded Tolson and his debaters in the 1920s and 1930s. Because this demonstrated their ability to build interpersonal relationships and achieve success in the primarily White activity of forensics, the Great Debaters of Wiley College serve as an ideal case study in the examination of interpersonal communication and relationship building in forensics. As noted in chapter 2, a variety of debaters, including James Farmer Jr. as coached by Tolson, came to construct powerful advocacy against segregation and other persistent problems of racism. Farmer's common rival, Malcolm X, also learned debate and it transformed him while in prison. *The Great Debaters* film well captured debate instruction as it occurred at the HBCU of Wiley College. Wiley rightly serves as an important historical touchstone for our current struggle to utilize debate for liberating goals directed at contemporary problems like those encountered in Rwanda. It is not surprising and it makes this discussion particularly relevant that the earliest efforts to conduct debate training in Rwanda in 2014 utilized key dialogue from the movie, *The Great Debaters*. In one scene, Tolson is speaking to Wiley debaters outdoors on a riverbank. The following dialogue takes place: "Debaters: The Judge is God! Tolson: Why is he God? Debaters: Because he decides who wins or loses not my opponent! Tolson: Who is your opponent? Debaters: He does not exist! Tolson: Why does he not exist? Debaters: Because he is a merely a dissenting opposing voice to the truth I speak."[5]

The movie and the underlying history of the Great Debaters did inspire the Rwandan debate program at its inception. It is important to understand that the movie also inspired the re-creation of Wiley College debate in 2008. The program had been inactive for decades and when the film was made, Denzel Washington donated one million dollars to reform the program. Consequently, the history of the Great Debaters is inceptional, both to the Wiley program in the twenty-first century and the debate camp in Rwanda begun in 2014. Although both communities face ethnic struggles a continent and ocean away, they are connected by this common point of history drawn from the consequences of the translatlantic slave trade that brought Africans involuntarily to the United States in too many cases. The common problem of prejudice and discrimination connects Rwanda and Wiley. For their trips to the United States where they visit dozens of American colleges and universities, the visit to Wiley is especially important.

It is further important to understand that the Debate across the Curriculum plan enacted by Wiley and discussed here is a national and international model for implementing debate. Debate can cross the curriculum. It does not have to be a stand-alone course or extracurricular club. Much like the training of the security forces discussed in chapter 3, debate can be an instructional mode in many academic settings. These interdisciplinary implementations may lead to a separate course or extracurricular program but this model shown here is a useful potential starting point.

INTERRACIAL COMMUNICATION

Discussions regarding race and ethnicity issues remain difficult, in part, due to the significantly different perceptions and realities.[6] The interference in communication between people of color and individuals who are not of color, stems from fundamental perceptions that are shaped by experiences that are not common among the groups attempting to communicate. The lack of common experiences creates a divide between racial groups, which causes distrust among group members. Trust is an important ingredient in meaningful communication between racial groups.[7]

In the American forensics community, there are inherent disparities that exist between racial groups that keeps these groups from complete trust, and therefore meaningful communication interaction. The first issue is the lack of representation. Because students of color are the numerical minority in the forensics community, there is a required adaptation in communication. This adaptation can erode a student's racial identity and self-perception; particularly, if they feel their culture is not respected.

Moreover, different experiences between racial groups in the forensics community, many of which may be socioeconomic, social, or political in nature, may affect students' self-determination. As a result, there is an inherent misunderstanding of the experiences of the socially marginalized, which can affect meaningful communication. As noted by communication scholars, "Communication obstacles and interaction problems are exacerbated by the fact that Whites and Blacks have fundamentally different perspectives on the attitudes implied and the actions demonstrated by Whites during these interactions."[8]

Because of the number of students of color in forensics, and the socially political nature of the activity, most students of color are forced to interact with others. As a result, in order to assist in the effective communication and reduction of message interference, people of color are often required to adopt language, idioms, mannerisms, and expression of those not of color. Thus, rendering students of color in the forensics community a "muted group."[9] The Muted Group Theory was originally a feminist theory and adapted to African Americans by Mark Orbe. However, this muted group theory can also be applied to forensics students of color in their interactions with Whites. As a result, many students of color feel they do not have a voice within the forensics community, making it difficult to create change and inclusivity.

THE GREAT DEBATERS' STEPS FOR EFFECTIVE RELATIONSHIP BUILDING

A common trope among people of color is, "You have to be twice as good, to get half as much." This perspective about society at large is drilled into the consciousness of students of color and is reflected in their values and actions. This principle is not only apparent in the everyday lives of students of color, but is persistent in their journey as forensics competitors.

A survey of students in the forensics community attempted to quantify the number of students of color who felt they had to "prove their racial equality at forensics tournaments." Of the respondents who self-identified as an ethnicity other than White, 75 percent answered they feel this way sometimes, fairly often, or very often.[10] Specifically, for the Great Debaters, the mindset of proving racial equality in the forensics community was often mentioned and in the forefront of the mind of competitors.

Whether the belief in racial disparity in forensics is founded in reality, or simply in the perspectives of these forensics competitors of color, the Great Debaters often espoused their belief that their presentations must be more practiced, more effective, and their behavior must be more professional, than their White counterparts. This certainty of racial disparity is not a social indictment or even an accusation of White students or judges in the forensics community, but a matter of perspective and experiences of members of the forensics community, based on their racial backgrounds. Though the easiest way to integrate into the dominant culture of the forensics community is assimilation, there are three primary goals of students of color in their relationship development and interpersonal communication: (1) relationship building, (2) promotion of inclusion and racial equality, and (3) avoiding the erosion of racial identity. The observation of regular relationship building and interpersonal interactions between the Great Debaters and White students in the forensics community has yielded a unique model. These interactions have typically followed a five-step process of communication in the achievement of racial equality, without the degradation or loss of cultural identity. It should be noted that this process is the observed behavior of interactions between Great Debaters and White students rather than a prescribed behavior methodology.

THE PROCESS OF SELF DISCLOSURE AND RELATIONSHIP BUILDING

In 1973, psychologists Irwin Altman and Dalmas Taylor advanced the Social Penetration Theory, which explains how individuals self-disclose information to one another.[11] Altman and Taylor described the process of self-disclosure as peeling back the layers of an onion, with a depth and breadth of information being disclosed through interactions, with more intimate information being disclosed in the deeper layers of the onion. Though there is a process of self-disclosure when students of color communicate, in a forensics setting, with judges, coaches, or competitors of color, the process outlined by Altman and Taylor does not adequately describe such interactions.

Altman and Taylor describe a five-step process of self-disclosure in the Social Penetration Theory. The various stages are known as the Orientation Stage, Exploratory Affective Stage, Affective Stage, Stable Stage, and De-penetration Stage. Though Altman and Taylor describe the depth and breadth of information that is disclosed, little attention is paid to how that information is communicated, and how the student of color's work interplays with the effectiveness of communication.

Socialization

Altman and Taylor describe the first step as the Orientation Stage, where individuals engage in small talk and exchange non-intimate information about themselves. Though the initial stages that Altman and Taylor describe the depth of information that is exchanged, little attention is paid to the manner in which that information is communicated. Specifically, when one communicator is a person of color and the other is White.

The process of socialization is similar to the Orientation Stage and occurs during initial interactions between the communicators. This initial phase is described as socialization because this is the point when social interaction begins and these interactions are executed in a way that adheres to social norms, as the term socialization indicates.

Students of color have often been faced with the possibility that during many initial interactions, outside of the forensics community, cultural immersion can be unsettling to Whites and might be met with rejection or distancing. Because first impressions are lasting impressions, many students of color will resort to almost exclusively "code-switching" during this period of initial interactions, increasing the likelihood of acceptance and continued interaction.

Code-switching is the idiomatic term for the Communication Accommodation Theory (CAT), developed by Howard Giles, professor of communication at the University of California, Santa Barbara. Code-switching is characterized through the change in communication approach, to minimize social differences. Giles theorized that when speakers seek to gain acceptance and approval in social situations, they are likely to assimilate to the speech and manner of the other speaker. Communicative alterations may be verbal or nonverbal and may include changes to language choice, accent, dialect, mannerisms, and gestures.[12]

Though maintaining code-switching during all interactions may be effective in achieving the goal of relationship building, it does not meaningfully promote inclusion, racial equality, or avoid the erosion of racial identity for students of color. Additionally, the reliance on code-switching for all interactions is not personally fulfilling, and in some cases offensive, to students of color, who feel they are always responsible to change who they are to accommodate others. Students of color often feel their cultural identity is being ignored, they are not recognized as a complex individual, especially when being required to code-switch for extended periods of time.

Thus, once students of color feel confident that some familiarity exists between the two parties, then the relationship can move to the acclimation phase.

Acclimation

Altman and Taylor describe the second stage of their process as the Exploratory Affective Stage in which information about political affiliations and concerns are exchanged. Though the acclimation phase is similar in the depth of information exchanged, the difference is the way the information is communicated. The acclimation period is characterized by students of color moving from code-switching to "code-meshing."

Editors Vershawn Ashanti Young and Aja Y. Martinez compiled essays from a range of scholars, sociolinguists, and English teachers, which argue that all writers and speakers benefit when we elucidate academic language and encourage students to explore the diversity of the English language, in both unofficial and official spaces. Unlike code-switching, which alters the speech and manner of one speaker to adopt that of another, code-meshing is characterized by the simultaneous use of two language variations within a single context. These scholars argue code-meshing, rather than code-switching leads to cogent, often dynamic communication by native English speakers who speak with "accents," and those whose "home language" or neighborhood dialects are deemed nonstandard.[13]

It is during the acclimation process that people of color begin to introduce elements of their culture through the code-meshing process, acclimating White communicators to cultural differences. Code-meshing allows students of color to begin to acclimate those to whom they are communicating without overwhelming the receiver. Though the acclimation process allows students of color to express culture through language and consistently code-meshing would allow students to achieve the goal of relationship building; however, the goals of inclusion and racial equality are not achieved, while there is also erosion of cultural identity.

Typically, a student of color will recognize when the receiver is ready to move to the next phase of the process when both communicators engage in code-meshing communication. The individual from the majority culture will often mimic the elements of minority culture introduced by the student of color. It is at this point that the student of color will become "human."

Humanization

The third stage of Altman and Taylor's self-disclosure methodology is the Affective Stage, which is characterized by disclosure of more personal matters. It is at this point that Altman and Taylor recognize the use of personal ways of speaking and use of idioms and unconventional language are acceptable. However, Altman and Taylor fail to recognize that people of color are seen as "Human" at this stage.

Often during early interactions, a student of color may be recognized by their school affiliation, their gender, sexuality, skin tone, complexion, or a combination of these group identities, as well as others. During the humanization phase, a student of color is beginning to be seen as "Human"; that is to say, as an individual, as opposed to part of a group identity or part of an organization. Much like the insurance commercial, the agent on the phone is known as "Jake, from State Farm," students may be known as "Drake, from Wiley," or "The tall guy, from TSU." However, during the humanization process, a student of color starts to be called by their name, which becomes their identity, rather than any aspect or identity or intersectionality of identities.

It should be noted that—although a student of color during the humanization process may become an individual within the eyes of White judges, competitors, or coaches—students of color will, predominantly, continue to communicate through code-meshing. Students of color will almost never communicate with "others" entirely in their own code. Students of color will almost entirely communicate with those who are not of color through the use of code-meshing, regardless of the level of comfort. It is during the humanization process that students of color have built a stable relationship, as a forensics competitor, however, complete inclusion in the world of forensics has not been achieved. Once the student of color is seen as an individual, it is then that the forensics work of the student may truly be appreciated.

Appreciation

The previous three stages have been building the relationship to a point where the work and material of a student of color can be evaluated from a perspective of reduced bias. The appreciation stage is when the forensics work of the student of color is no longer clouded by their group identities, and the biases those identities may produce. Once an individual is seen as "Human" their work may be evaluated from an individual perspective.

Because many students of color engage in material that is important or personal to that individual, it is at this point that materials may be seen as the work of the individual and not as a product of the group identity. At this stage the performance may be referred to as "Austin's Dramatic Interpretation" instead of "That Dramatic Interpretation from Wiley" or "That Black Dramatic Interpretation." However, once the student of color is seen as an individual and the material produced by the student is seen as the product of the individual, both can be evaluated from a perspective of reduced bias. During the appreciation process, the talent of the student of color is appreciated. During the acquisition of reputation, stature, and competitive success is when the student and the work reach the admiration phase, and the performance may truly change the perspective of the White audience member.

Admiration

Within most activities or organizations, the individuals who represent the highest achievement, the most prolific, the most revered, are the "icons." This level, in forensics, are typically the national finalists or champions at national tournaments like the American Forensics Association National Individual Event Tournament, National Forensics Association National Championship, Pi Kappa Delta National Championship, Cross Examination Debate Association National Championship, National Debate Tournament Championship, International Public Debate Association National Championship, or the National Parliamentary Tournament of Excellence. All of these championship tournaments are highly regarded, and those who excel at their highest level generally are elevated to the status of icon. The student of color's work may be so appreciated that the student can become an icon within the forensics community. Once a student achieves this iconic status, the student of color has credibility and this allows the student to achieve admiration of the collective forensics community. These icons can then become agents of change. Because of the credibility these students wield, the messages contained within their performances may have the power to cause change in the thoughts and beliefs of audience members. It is at this point that a message about racial inequity or other social critique may be well received and create lasting change. Some students may never achieve the level of icon or admiration, those students may remain at the appreciation phase and may never become a true agent of change.

SUMMARIZING INCLUSION TECHNIQUES FOR STUDENTS OF COLOR IN FORENSICS

Students of color in the American forensics community instinctively communicate in a way that maximize effective relationship building, without racial identity erosion, and may ultimately allow the student to become a change agent. This five-stages of relationship development in forensics is not prescriptive nor is it the only communication method. However, in discussion with Great Debaters of Wiley College, and in observation of the interactions of students of color and "others," this relationship development model of forensics students of color seems largely to follow this course. Much of the code-switching and code-meshing that happens in initial interactions is a result of the muted voices of students of color in the forensics community. If students of color felt greater acceptance within the forensics community, they would not need to alter their communication style, nor feel an endangerment to their culture or cultural identity.

WILEY'S DEBATE ACROSS THE CURRICULUM PEDAGOGY

As noted earlier, with this narrative in mind, Wiley College committed itself to innovating its curriculum by making debate part of all of its classes. As part of its Quality Enhancement Plan (QEP) for the Southern Association of Colleges and Schools Commission on Colleges (SACSCOC) accreditation, the Communicate through Debate program was designed and implemented. The program simultaneously pays homage to Wiley College's debate legacy, while also potentially changing the face of higher education. Wiley College created a foundation of argumentation fundamentals; reinforced and expanded these fundamentals through debate and argument assignments in classes across every classification of every major; created an atmosphere of high-engagement, allowing students to succeed in their academic career; and ultimately, created a campus-wide culture of debate. The plan was conceived by polling all Wiley College stakeholders, including administration, faculty, staff, students, and community. An analysis of student data revealed that Wiley College students tested below national averages in critical thinking, reading, and writing skills.[14]

Wiley College implemented a Debate across the Curriculum (DAC) model, introduced into the College's curriculum beginning with entering first-year students, who are taught the basics of argumentation. Consultants, called Forensics Specialists, collaborated with faculty to create high-engagement debate and discussion assignments, as well as facilitating the assignment and evaluating student performance. Additionally, students participate in an annual capstone event, where they refine and utilize their skills in a practical setting.

Wiley College immersed students in the Communication through Debate model throughout their four years of matriculation. The Communicate through Debate program was first introduced to cohort one, the freshmen class admitted during the 2013–2014 academic year, and continued with the program over the following four years. In order to track the program's effectiveness, extensive benchmarking was used to determine each year cohort's base skill-level and to measure the cohort's progress toward intended learning outcomes. Each subsequent year of the program saw the addition of another freshman class, to ensure every classification, having participated in the program by the academic year 2016–2017.

CONSULTATION AND FACILITATION METHODOLOGY

As the result of faculty feedback and a literature review to establish basic practices of the program, it was determined that "between 63 and 70 percent of new programs fail" (Song, 2009, p. 8).[15] The most common explanation is that organizational inertia effectively blocks the most ambitious changes. Experts argue that because there is no change in culture (Schwartz & Davis, 1981), and there is no change in the structure of organizations,[16] new mandates are perceived by personnel as a burden and create a backlash.[17] Heffron (1968) argued that faculty and staff have a vested interest to continue "business as usual," and new initiatives appear as a burden and as an indictment of the abilities of current personnel.[18] Therefore, Wiley College created a consultation methodology in which debate experts, called "Forensics Specialists," teach the fundamentals of argumentation in the freshman experience classes, as well as act as facilitators of debate or argumentation assignments in classes across the curriculum, utilizing content provided by professors. Forensics Specialists took on the role of collaborators in assignment creation; spearhead facilitation of the assignment; and assess the assignment, in order to minimize the strength of organizational inertia, as well as create momentum for change.

Forensics Specialists meet with professors to design a custom assignment for use within classes assigned by the program director. The Forensics Specialist and the professor collaborate in the creation of the assignment, with Forensics Specialists acting as methodology experts and the professor as the content expert. Assignments are uniquely designed based on the goals of the professor and the professor's desired content. Some sections used traditional debates, some opted for discussions, and others a mock congress style of debate. The assignment is based upon the consultation with the professor, so as not to infringe on the academic freedom of the professor, but also ensures the highest quality of instruction for the assignment.

Once the assignment is designed, the Forensics Specialist acts as a facilitator for the assignment. The Forensics Specialist performs a pre-assignment discussion with the class, explaining research requirements, expectations, assignment particulars, and grading. Following this pre-assignment discussion, Forensics Specialists observe debates and fill out a rubric for grading. The Forensics Specialist then holds an assignment follow-up, in which they discuss the assignment and what students can do to improve and build upon their skills and administer satisfaction surveys. For example, a math class might have a debate about what methods are best for teaching someone the mathematical process of division. A Forensics Specialist would help identify the controversy or competing ways to approach a mathematical problem like division and guide the creation of a debate resolution. The specialist and the math instructor would agree what amount of time might be suitable for debate. Here again the specialist would help design a format that maximizes participation among students. The specialist may help set up a panel of judges to evaluate using a ballot mechanism with agreed upon criteria like clarity and usages of evidence.

INTEGRATION WITHIN THE ACADEMIC CURRICULUM

To ensure Wiley College students master each programmatic learning outcome, a four-level deployment plan was adopted by each academic department. One or more courses from each classification level (freshman through senior), were chosen by each department to incorporate and reinforce each Communicate through Debate–focused student learning outcome. Using Bloom's Taxonomy, Forensics Specialists lead students progressively through the Communicate through Debate curriculum: from learning introductory debate concepts to the critical analysis of arguments presented in a capstone experience.[19]

Integration into Wiley College's pedagogic practice and the academic core was intentionally seamless, so the principles of critical thinking and argument are embedded elements within the liberal arts curriculum, and are deliberately imparted, rather than assuming learner assimilation. In integrating this program into the instruction of the required general education curriculum, every area in the liberal arts faculty included at least one course at each classification level, where these concepts are reinforced, and students are taught to apply them to their major discipline.

The selected freshman and sophomore (1000- and 2000-level) courses present introductory debate concepts of effective research and the identification and evaluation of arguments. Also, Wiley College's Freshman Seminar course, a first-year course required for all matriculating students, began familiarizing students with basic concepts of argumentation, while simultaneously orienting students to rigors of college life and academics. At every level, these introductions to debate, research, and argumentation are presented as skills central to the academic disciplines being explored. At the end of their second year of college, Wiley College students have developed a robust skillset, which they utilize as they acquire mastery in their chosen fields of study.

Junior and senior (3000- and 4000-level) courses reinforce and build upon the foundation laid during the freshman and sophomore years while demonstrating students' mastery of debate skills through the creation and application of well-formulated arguments. As the academic content of their coursework becomes more demanding, students are guided in the application of the foundational argumentation skills and research, in increasingly sophisticated and nuanced ways. At this level, various debate demonstration activities occur within the classroom throughout the semester to help prepare students for public debate exhibitions. In this way, students can display not only their mastery of argumentation but also apply these skills to their field of study.

In order to achieve an effective balance between efficacy and ease of implementation, the following measures are integrated into the Communicate through Debate paradigm:

1. The freshman class only focuses on the first two of the four learning outcomes.
2. The first-year learning outcomes emphasize the lower-order cognitive skills of Bloom's Taxonomy: identification and recognition. In the second year, the learning outcomes elevate to the next level of higher-order thinking: comprehension and application. In the third and fourth years, the level of learning outcomes increases to reflect the higher-order thinking skills of analysis and synthesis, evaluation, and creation or formulation of ideas.
3. Instructors are only required to alter a minimum of two assignments in a course to incorporate argumentation related objectives.
4. In addition to learning the structure of an argument, faculty learn how to integrate various debate, discussion, or information literacy assignments and activities into their curriculum (Wiley College, 2012).

MISSION, GOALS, AND STUDENT LEARNING OUTCOMES

The mission of the Communicate through Debate initiative was to provide students:

1. The skills and experiences that will prepare students to be effective communicators, through the medium of debate and the study of the elements and functions of argumentation.
2. Implement activities that facilitate pedagogy and increase the level of classroom interaction and student engagement within and across disciplines.
3. Training in the skills of debate to be critical thinkers, who have excellent writing and speaking skills, and possess the ability to work in diverse teams and make persuasive professional presentations.

In achieving the mission of improving students' communication and critical thinking skills, the following goals were established:

1. Create a foundation of argumentation fundamentals upon which Wiley students can build communication and critical thinking skills.
2. Reinforce and expand argumentation fundamentals through debate and argument assignments in classes across every classification of every major.
3. Create an atmosphere of high engagement, allowing students to succeed in their academic careers.
4. Create a campus-wide culture of debate.

In order to accomplish the goals of the program, the following students learning outcomes were developed.

Learning Outcome 1:

Students will be able to compile and analyze empirical and expert evidence from diverse media to support a logical claim.[20]

This learning outcome is focused on information literacy. The objective is for students to have the ability not only to research and compile data but also to identify arguments and make judgments about the best sources and data to use. The program teaches students the difference between primary and secondary sources and the best way to use each. Additionally, students will be able to recognize prejudice, deception, and manipulation within the sources they compile.

Learning Outcome 2:

Students will be able to draw conclusions by evaluating an argument to determine the veracity of the evidence and the logic of the idea.[21] This learning outcome focuses on the identification and evaluation of the components of an argument. Students learn a modified version of the Toulmin (1958) model of an argument, which contains a claim (statement of the argument), warrant (empirical evidence that the claim is valid), data (examples that indicate the claim is valid), and impact (what positive or negative impact could result).[22] Each component of the argument can be evaluated to determine the veracity of the entire argument.

Learning Outcome 3:

Students will be able to demonstrate knowledge and application of a well-formulated argument that uses evidence to support a position. This learning outcome requires students to create an argument, with all of its components. In the creation of a case for debate or a position of argumentation, students will be able to incorporate all elements of an argument to create a cogent and coherent thought which justifies their position.

Learning Outcome 4:

Students will be able to recognize opposing viewpoints and utilize researched evidence to champion their position through the exchange of verbal questions and answers. For this learning outcome, students utilize evidence which they have gathered to ask and answer questions. Instructor facilitated question and answer sessions enable students to explore an issue in-depth, extract more information, or attempt to find weaknesses with the opposition's position.

For various fields of study, such as anthropology, sociology, and psychology, there can be differences of opinion about which methodologies work best to study artifacts within that field. Those differences of opinion can be fashioned into in-class debates. As an example, at SMU Dr. Eric Bing teaches anthropology classes that focus on medical care in Africa. He utilizes these debate concepts and approaches to encourage students to research medical solutions for treating mental health across the continent. He has done that for more than five years. In one case, an African national leadership team was following his student debate live in the United States to learn more about potential medical solutions being examined in the debate.

DISCUSSION OF RESULTS

An examination of the results from cohort one's first-year and fourth-year tests establishes that the Debate across the Curriculum creates a significant difference in the test scores from baseline to fourth-year testing.[23]

These results would support the theory that Debate across the Curriculum increases critical thinking scores at a higher rate in higher education students. However, a further examination of the results also implies there are statistically significant critical thinking gains in the national

Table 5.1. Student Group Mean Scores

Student Group	N	M	Variance
Nat. Average Frosh	11,470	1063	20736
Nat. Average Seniors	7,970	1110	19600
Wiley College 1st Year	180	809	21025
Wiley College 4th Year	41	960	19044
AA and Black Frosh	1,564	963	15625
AA and Black Seniors	910	1016	16641

Notes. N = sample size; M = mean

average and the African American and Black national average. Therefore, it can be assumed that there are critical thinking gains as a result of normal matriculation, but those gains are multiplied when a student is part of a Debate across the Curriculum program. Graph one (table 5.1) illustrates that from baseline to exit testing, the mean yield of Wiley College cohort one (first year) is significantly higher than the other two comparison groups. Wiley College cohort one gains were 105 percent greater than the national average and 96 percent higher than the African Americans and Black national average, respectively. Thus, Debate across the Curriculum has a significant effect on critical thinking gains at a rate of almost twice that of the comparison groups. The graph is a visual representation of the critical thinking gains of all three groups displaying the gains through Debate across the Curriculum education more substantial than normal matriculation.

Despite the vast gains in critical thinking scores, further scrutiny determines that Wiley College scores are wholly lower than the comparison groups, particularly the baseline scores. These results may be explained by the fact that Wiley College is an open-enrollment institution, accepting students regardless of college readiness, test scores, or high school grades, this may explain the low baseline and fourth-year scores. Because the raw scores of the baseline and the fourth-year tests of Wiley College cohort one were lower than the national average, future research should be conducted to determine the effect of college readiness on critical thinking skills.

On June 6, 2017, the *Wall Street Journal* published an article entitled, "Exclusive Test Data: Many Colleges Fail to Improve Critical-Thinking Skills." This article provided an analysis of CLA (College Learning Assessment) data across eighty-six public institutions and the findings that most higher education institutions failed to demonstrate significant gains in critical thinking and communication scores on the CLA.[24] The published institutions all tested a sample of seventy-five or more students before their freshman year, as a baseline, and then tested a sample of seventy-five or more seniors. Although the sample sizes exceed the minimum level for statistical analysis; therefore, no specific sample sizes were provided, the only comparison possible is the change percentage and comparison of raw scores.[25]

Table 5.2 presents a comparison of the increase in total score and percentage change from Texas institutions. Though the first-year and fourth-year scores for Wiley College cohort one were the lowest in the state of Texas, the increase in raw scores and the percentage change were the highest in the state. Because there are no sample sizes provided, inferences based upon statistical analysis was impossible; however, further statistical analysis among Texas schools would be beneficial and warranted.[26]

Table 5.3 presents a comparison of the increase in total score and percentage change from the institutions with the highest point increase. Though the first-year and fourth-year students' scores for Wiley College cohort one were the lowest, the increase in raw scores were the fifth highest in the country, and the percentage change was the highest in the country. Because there are no sample sizes provided, inferences based upon statistical analysis was impossible. Though these findings are worthy of note, further statistical analysis would be beneficial and warranted.

This program review indicates that debate training can be a best practice for academic skills improvement, given that preparation for debate requires students to research empirical data to support claims, exercise judgment based upon logic and ethical standards, and work in teams—all of which are attributes attractive to potential employers. Moreover, the heightened student engagement and application of argumentation skills across disciplines, which the Communicate through Debate program emphasizes, prepares students for their next life phase, whether it

Table 5.2. Percentage Change in Texas Institutions

Institution	Freshmen Score	Senior Score	Overall Increase	Percentage Change
Wiley–Cohort 1	809	960	151	18.67%
UT–Pan Am.	1002	1093	91	9.08%
Texas A&M Inter.	965	1052	87	9.02%
Texas State U.	1046	1130	84	8.03%
UT–San Antonio	1064	1128	64	6.02%
UT–Arlington	1083	1134	51	4.71%
UT–Austin	1257	1254	-3	-2.40%
UT–Dallas	1172	1160	-12	-1.02%

Table 5.3. Percentage Change in High Performance Institutions vs. Wiley

Institution	Freshmen Score	Senior Score	Overall Increase	Percentage Change
Plymouth State Un.	1007	1185	178	17.68%
CSU, Sacramento	948	1119	171	18.04%
CSU, Northridge	959	1117	158	16.48%
San Jose State Un.	983	1137	154	15.67%
Wiley College	809	960	151	18.67%

leads to a professional career, graduate education, or community and national service.

The enhancement of argumentation and presentation skills is paramount to students' ability to compete in the world beyond the walls of their respective institutions. As a result, we must not be committed to: persisting in a commitment to this groundbreaking pedagogy, building upon the lessons learned, and to the continued improvement of leadership skills through students' oral communication and critical thinking skills.

CONCLUSION

The results of Debate across the Curriculum at Wiley point to an empirical reality to debate as pedagogy. Within the context of the African American community as experienced at HBCUs we are realizing more than the inspiring biographies of voices like Martin Luther King Jr., Barbara Jordan, James Farmer Jr., James Meredith, and Malcolm X. We have, in view of this successful twenty-first-century experiment at Wiley, the potential for a global impact as all teaching communities consider how to improve critical thinking and other educational outcomes. Education is long considered by deep thinkers on justice as the cornerstone of human progress. At the center of that educational realm is the bright burning flame of debate. Stokely Carmichael became famous in 1966 for advocating for burning it all down. The matter crystalized into a major argument nationally by 1968. Farmer was asked about this Jacobin plan:

> Question: Then we have Mr. Stokely Carmichael, who was quoted as saying that now there won't be any other Negro leader who will tell his brothers not to burn, and he says, "this means it's necessary to fully enter into a revolution." What do you say to Mr. Carmichael?

Farmer: Well, I think Mr. Carmichael is wrong there. I think that there must be voices that say this is not the way, obviously. What we need now is not destruction—we need buildings. The slogan should not be "Burn baby burn" but "learn baby learn" and "build baby build."

We've had enough of destruction. We've had enough of violence...

We should understand that the Black community is not monolithic, nor is the white community monolithic. There are many voices, there are many leaders, there is much debate and dialogue, discussion and disagreement in the Black community; and that's as it should be.[27]

James Farmer Jr. responded to Stokely Carmichael's invocation of "Burn Baby Burn," with the refutation of "Learn Baby Learn."[28] This chapter of how the African American community uses debate as a dramatic empowerment tool within educational settings can serve as a powerful global signal for debate as pedagogy. Learning debate is the constructive pedagogy that builds a post-genocidal world.

NOTES

1. Michael Bartanen and Robert Littlefield, *Forensics in America: A History* (Lanham, MD: Rowman & Littlefield, 2013).
2. Bartanen and Littlefield, *Forensics in America: A History*, 249–50.
3. Andrew Billings, "Increasing Diversity in the 21st Century: Minority Participation in Competitive Individual Events," *Forensic* 85, no. 4 (2000).
4. Frances Milliken and Luis Martins, "Searching for Common Threads: Understanding the Multiple Effects of Diversity in Organisational Groups," *Academy of Management Review* 21, no. 2 (1996): 402–33.
5. Robert Eisele, *The Great Debaters* [screenplay] (Beverly Hills, CA: 2007).
6. Mark Orbe and Tina M. Harris, *Interracial Communication: Theory into Practice* (Los Angeles: Sage Publications, 2013).
7. John Dovidio, Samuel Gaertner, Kerry Kawakami, and Gordon Hodson, "Why Can't We Just Get Along? Interpersonal Biases and Interracial Distrust," *Cultural Diversity and Ethnic Minority Psychology* 8, no. 2 (2002): 88.
8. Dovidio, Gaertner, Kawakami, and Hodson, "Why Can't We Just Get Along? Interpersonal Biases and Interracial Distrust," 88.
9. Orbe and Harris, *Interracial Communication: Theory into Practice*.
10. Christopher Medina, Denise Vaughan, Sean Allen, and Dawn Lowry, "Perceived Racial Discrimination and Its Effects in Collegiate Forensics," manuscript, 2017.
11. Irwin Altman and Dalman Taylor, *Social Penetration: The Development of Interpersonal Relationships* (New York: Holt, Rinehart, and Winston, 1973).
12. Howard Giles, *Communication Accommodation Theory* (Los Angeles: Sage Publications, 2008).
13. Vershawn Ashanti Young and Aja Martinez, *Code-Meshing as World English: Pedagogy, Policy, Performance* (Chicago: National Council of Teachers of English, 2011).
14. "Wiley College's Quality Enhancement Plan" (2012), unpublished manuscript, Wiley College, Marshall.
15. Xiongwei Song, "Why Do Change Management Strategies Fail? Illustrations with Examples," *Journal of Cambridge Studies* 4, no. 1 (2009): 6–15.
16. Howard Schwartz and Stanley Davis, "Matching Corporate Culture and Business Strategy," *Organizational Dynamics* 10, no. 2 (1981).

17. Mark Granovetter, "Economic Action and Social Structure: The Problem of Embeddedness," *American Journal of Sociology* 91, no. 3 (1985): 481–510.

18. Florence Heffron, *Organization Theory and Public Organizations* (Princeton: Princeton University Press, 1968): 154.

19. Benjamin Bloom, Max Englehart, Edward Furst, Walter Hill, and David Krathwohl, *Taxonomy of Educational Objectives, Handbook One* (Nashville, TN: Vanderbilt University, 1956): 201–7, https://cft.vanderbilt.edu/guides-sub-pages/blooms-taxonomy/.

20. "Wiley College's Quality Enhancement Plan."

21. "Wiley College's Quality Enhancement Plan."

22. Stephen Toulmin, *Uses of Argument* (London: Cambridge University Press, 1958).

23. "Wiley College's Quality Enhancement Plan."

24. Douglas Belkin, "Exclusive Test Data: Many Colleges Fail to Improve Critical-Thinking Skills," *Wall Street Journal*, June 5, 2017, https://www.wsj.com/articles/exclusive-test-data-many-colleges-fail-to-improve-critical-thinking-skills-1496686662.

25. "Wiley College's Quality Enhancement Plan."

26. "Wiley College's Quality Enhancement Plan."

27. James Farmer Jr., April 16, 1968, TV Interview, Transcript. James Leonard Jr., and Lula Peterson Farmer papers, Dolph Briscoe Center for American History. The University of Texas at Austin, Austin, Texas, Box 2R635.

28. James Farmer Jr., April 16, 1968, TV Interview, Transcript.

SIX

The Global Ecological Museum and the Climate Debate

One of the most supreme utopian notions of our time is climate change. A distinct notion of urgency suggests that we cannot indulge the luxury of debate regarding global warming because of the extreme impacts worldwide. Disagreement is referred to as "climate denial." The term is designed to connote analogy to Holocaust denial—an important problem in the academic field of genocide study. This chapter offers an argumentation critique of the climate debate and examines the scientific and credible reasons for being skeptical and even hopeful about climate change. Important argument literatures are explored including: (1) how cool temperatures kill many more human beings than warm temperatures, (2) how fossil fuels reduce the destruction of forests, (3) how CO_2 increases plant growth and forest growth, (4) how climate change contributes to record grain harvests to reduce the problems of hunger and starvation, (5) how fossil fuels replace one another to improve economic and environmental conditions, and (6) how renewable energy sources destroy and damage the environment.

All of these items connect with a larger critical framework of how intellectual elites desire to maintain the undeveloped world as an ecological museum wherein millions will die from malaria, infectious diseases, unclean water, contaminated food, and reduced communication networks that combine to make human life more violent, dangerous, and ugly. These genocidal engines of democide (Rummel) and eliminationism (Goldhagen) are recast rhetorically as pristine cleansings and protections of a better earth. The notion of humanity as a "global infection" rationalizes genocide as a therapeutic avenue of elite policy making that we should resist going forward in the twenty-first century.

The recent global pandemic regarding COVID-19 amplifies the clarity by which we may understand the argumentation limits provided by metaphors of disease. James Lovelock, an important academic leader on questions of the environment, explained with ominous rhetoric how humanity might be seen as a disease:

> "Individuals occasionally suffer a disease called polycythaemia, an overpopulation of red blood cells," writes Lovelock, environmentalist, futurologist and creator of the Gaia hypothesis. "By analogy, Gaia's illness could be called polyanthroponemia, where humans overpopulate until they do more harm than good."[1]

One of the most difficult thoughts to confront as an intellectual community united to the task of abolishing genocide, is to properly grapple with the rationalizations that justify the killing of our fellow human beings. Metaphors like these are especially dangerous at a time when public anxiety about diseases are acute and fueled with mystery and suspicion. When one views genocide through the lens of history, it is possible to provide in contemporary terms that those past acts were thoroughly irrational and, thereby, cognitively differentiate this world from the genocidaire who led to those mass killings. The difficulty of this reconsideration away from such a dualistic dialectic of rational and irrational emerges as one thinks about how in the present one might come to participate in the same crimes as the past. In the twenty-first century, there is profound potential for intellectual participation and assent to serial genocides and at least the passive acceptance of millions of our fellow human beings dying. Since at least the intellectual leadership of Thomas Malthus, dystopian orientations in intellectualism have led thinkers to believe that it might be best to allow human beings to die in order to protect the earth. The disjunction between humanity and the earth has been accepted at a relatively metaphysical level.

A dominant intellectual tradition does not treat humanity as part of the earth and therefore the conduct of human beings becomes subject to a critique of how human action implicates the autonomous earth. This initial intellectual move of differentiating the planet from an internal species of animal known as human is its own important hegemony of thought that makes the iterations of dystopian fantasies possible. Lovelock's 2009 book is one of the more important twenty-first-century contributions to our public sphere with diminished discursive complexity because of the impending peril of the inhuman earth.[2] An inhuman earth suggests a rhetorical regard for the planet that imagines that humans are not, and to some degree, should not, be part of the natural earth. From the Malthusian nightmare of overpopulation overwhelming the earth's capacity for food production, to the present ecological crisis prescribed as a climate crisis, there is a shared disdain among these intellectual advocates that the earth likely has "too many people." This chapter challenges these important dystopian assumptions for the purpose of reestablishing a more open public sphere that maximizes and improves upon empirical results that protect a holistic earth—an earth open to all humans and the complete ecology.

A RECENT GENEALOGY OF THE DYSTOPIAN ECOLOGICAL NIGHTMARE

As previously noted, the ecological dystopian intellectual fear can be traced back at least to Thomas Malthus, who published his seminal essay in 1789, "An Essay on the Principle of Population as It Affects the Future Improvement of Society, with Remarks on the Speculations of Mr. Godwin, M. Condorcet, and Other Writers." Therein Malthus joined an emerging scientific community oriented toward human progress and an intellectual management of risks associated with human development. As a component of the mature Enlightenment era, Malthus laid important cornerstones in the paradoxical notion that humanity was killing itself. This enduring argument suggested that so many people would ultimately be born that the earth could not provide sufficient subsistence to prevent catastrophic starvation.[3] This rhetorical framework, like many others that would resemble and follow, suggested that macrochanges needed to be made to the ethics of human behavior. The focus here is not to exhaust the topic historically or establish an absolutely exhaustive genre of this intellectual literature, but rather to observe the contemporary trends of this rhetorical framework, remove the discursive constraints, and ultimately embrace the discursively complex positive options that remain on the table for political considerations of human affairs.

THE SILENT SPRING

One of the most important contemporary manifestations of Malthusian genre is a book written by Rachel Carson: *Silent Spring* (1962).[4] As an American biologist, she theorized that the growing prevalence of pesticides used especially in agriculture would ultimately doom the ecology and create a world of the "silent spring"—a world largely devoid of an active organic season for reemergent ecology after winter. Her descriptions were so vivid and backed by her scientific preeminence as a thinker on ecological matters that the book became a best seller and the arguments contained therein came to shape American and global public policy on the question of pesticide use. Her arguments about pesticides came to bear acutely upon one pesticide: DDT. Carson's argument suggested that pesticides like DDT damaged the ecosystem—especially with regard to birds and their offspring. Concern became so great that DDT would be banned and severely constrained in its usage. DDT, arguably, has saved more human life than any known scientific innovation. Malaria is a disease so endemic to mosquito populations throughout the world that it was thought to be an insurmountable cause of death until the advent of aerial spraying of DDT. In 2015, nearly half a million people died of malaria—primarily in sub-Saharan Africa.[5] Malaria was eradicated from the United States in 1949 after intense usage of DDT.[6] A 1997 CDC study documented that as DDT spraying was reduced worldwide, malaria incidence increased.[7] The study concluded that "hundreds of millions of lives" were in question as a result of deliberate choices not to spray DDT.

The trend from 1975 to 2000 of reducing DDT spraying came at tremendous human cost. More recently, under an innovative American program initiated by President Bush in 2003—PEPFAR (President's Emergency Plan For Aids Relief)—the use of DDT-soaked bed netting and localized DDT house spraying in Africa increased. For the past fifteen years, these measures have reduced the deaths resulting from malaria, and many experts view the PEPFAR policy as one of the most successful global policies in history. Arguably, half a million human lives are saved each year by the reductions, from a million deaths a year at the turn of the century.[8] As noted earlier, the success begs the question of why we have not fully eradicated malaria from the entire continent of Africa. Why not, for example, focus on the one hundred largest cities in Africa and be sure that malaria is not a threat in any of those cities? Are we allowing Africans to die in ways we would not tolerate in other parts of the world? If this is the case, it raises fundamental questions about racism and ethnic discrimination. All of this is haunting an intellectual culture that may be tempted to believe that too much human life may be too much of a good thing. Perhaps Africa would serve humanity better as an untouched garden or even an extravagant botanical museum of an idealized green earth. Such dystopian views, no matter how passively held, must be rejected for the malicious prejudice they represent. Malaria can be eradicated from the continent of Africa in less than two decades if the "precautionary principle" is not allowed to overwhelm humane ethics. The precautionary principle holds that long-term catastrophic risks outweigh taking good short-term policy actions.[9] This errant reasoning lies at the heart of many pathological suppositions in ecological pessimism.

CLIMATE CHANGE

The idea that the earth is approaching her ecological end because of climate change is the ascendant dystopian narrative of the twenty-first century. Most recently, Greta Thunberg embodies the childish ethos asserting: "How dare you?"[10] In essence, the ongoing usage of fossil fuels and general economic development contributing to CO_2 emissions is rhetorically deemed so dangerous that immediate global civic limits must be imposed or all life on the planet will likely be destroyed. At minimum, by the end of this century, aspects of global sea level rise encouraged by polar melts will lead to massive unsustainable destructions of human life across the planet. The assertion is accepted by major research within argumentation study that tautologically assigns disagreement with this argument about climate as inherently unreasonable.[11] The primary evidence offered by researchers urging rejection of climate "skepticism" as unreasonable is an argument articulated by John Cook that "97 percent of scientist agree that the earth is warming" in an article entitled "Quantifying the Consensus on Anthropogenic Global Warming in the Scientific Literature." The abstracts analyzed by Cook do not justify this conclusion, and it is difficult to say what the consensus among scientists on this topic actually is.[12] This argument is a matter of focus in this book because it poses an overriding threat to discursive complexity. Put simply: the debate about climate is over. We do not have time to argue. Collectively, humanity must submit to the solutions as offered by experts or else short-term tendencies toward global warming will warm the earth so rapidly that we will have no reasonable means by which to avoid complete catastrophe at the end of this century. The point of this critique is not to offer an absolute denial of the climate arguments but to clearly suggest that the war against argumentation is definitely a hazard to our collective well-being. The certitude about climate change has the potential to consign millions of people to death in poverty and de-developed economic situations that make life impossible. We must continue to allow arguments and discursive complexity in the conversation about the global climate to maximize all of the best outcomes, both for the earth and the human inhabitants.

THE INCREDIBLE BENEFITS OF ECONOMIC DEVELOPMENT

At no point in human history has poverty been in such a rapid rate of decline. More people are leaving the realms of poverty than ever, and this impacts almost every aspect of a quality of life: life expectancy, access to medicine, freedom of movement, education, cleaner water, and so much more. Between 1982 and 2015, the global rate of extreme poverty has fallen from 42 percent to less than 10 percent.[13] That happened while the world's population was increasing dramatically. The rate of decline is so rapid that extreme poverty will likely be abolished prior to global goals.

All of this translates into important results for human beings. One of the most important statistical indicators to examine is causes of death for children under five years of age. Obviously, these deaths are deeply troubling and represent the greatest loss of human potential. On a wide array of killer causes such as respiratory disease and diarrhea, the death rate has plummeted right alongside reductions in poverty. Total deaths for children under five were 8.5 million a year in 1990. Total deaths under five were 3.6 million a year in 2016.[14] This translates into saving five million children every year among those under five. These are tangible "goods" that are swept up into better and more abundant life because of broader improvements in the human condition.

If the policy solutions to climate change require reductions in economic growth or perhaps bans on economic development, these successes may be slowed or even reversed. The intimate association between economic development and climate change is perhaps best seen in the problem of deforestation. Not always noticed is the important role deforestation can play in climate change considerations. Of course, trees have the capacity to absorb and store carbon. When trees burn, there are few things that can emit CO2 more aggressively. This is why that in some instances, deforestation can be a leading emitter of greenhouse gases. An example from the relatively advanced case of British Columbia is informative:

> Dr. Kurz says that in 2017 about 1.2 million hectares of forest burned in British Columbia, and 1.3 million hectares and counting this year. Compared to the average annual area burned in the province between 1990 and 2015, each of the last two years burned 15 times more than the average area. Forest fires like these release carbon dioxide and other greenhouse gasses, such as methane into the atmosphere. The initial—albeit unofficial—estimate is that the direct fire emissions in 2017 were about 150 (plus/minus 30) million tons of carbon dioxide. This is two to three times the emissions from fossil fuel burning from all other sectors in B.C.
>
> But the impacts on the atmosphere are even greater because the many trees killed by fires will decompose over the next decades, releasing more carbon dioxide into the atmosphere. Also, trees killed by fires will not be removing carbon dioxide from the atmosphere as living trees would. Therefore, the combined impact on the greenhouse gas emission balance is larger than just the direct emissions. Fortunately, most forests affected by wildfires will regrow in future decades, and remove carbon dioxide from the atmosphere again.[15]

Kurz's examples focus on developed national settings and forests set ablaze often by accidents such as a lightning strike. But human causes can also lead to deforestation and the deliberate burning of forests. In Indonesia, forests are intentionally burned by humans.[16] Farmers take advantage of summer conditions to clear vegetation for palm oil, pulp, and paper plantations using the slash-and-burn method. They often spin out of control and spread into protected forested areas. These are the choices compelled by relative agrarian poverty. This is the cheapest and most immediate mechanism for clearing land. These fires can easily elevate Indonesia to among the highest national emitters of greenhouse gases.[17] Helping relatively impoverished parts of the world leave relatively primitive and impoverished farming strategies can improve all global conditions.

FOSSIL FUELS REDUCE CO2 EMISSIONS

This rather counter intuitive fact can be observed by noting the dominant fuel used by humans prior to fossil fuels: wood. It is rather likely that without the development of fossil fuels in the early twentieth century, many parts of the world would be denuded of trees. Trees were a basic human mechanism for creating fire to use in generating warmth and effective cooking of unsafe food. The increase of forest cover in the United States is significantly tied to the reality that the need to cut down trees is greatly reduced by the usage of fossil fuels for these tasks rather than wood.[18] In fact, tree coverage has increased dramatically in the twenty-first century around the world.

The discursive complexity of human ingenuity is more clever with regard to how fossil fuels reduce CO2 emissions. The fracking revolution in the United States that allows more fossil fuels to be extracted in previously unsuspecting locations has dramatically increased the supply of overall fossil fuels, including natural gas.[19] This is fundamentally changing the markets of fossil fuels that originally relied upon coal as the primary industrial method for electrical generation. The change of inefficient coal in favor of more efficient natural gas as an energy source is the largest reason that the United States has for fifteen years been reducing its CO2 emissions. It is also a primary reason that 2019 was the first year in world history that CO2 emissions went flat instead of rising. That trend will likely be accelerated by the economic slowdown of 2020. In fact, the world is already experiencing the largest reduction in CO2 emissions:

> "A pandemic is the worst possible way to reduce emissions. There's nothing to celebrate here," says Samaras, of Carnegie Mellon University. "We have to recognize that, and to recognize that technological, behavioral, and structural change is the best and only way to reduce emissions."
>
> During this unprecedented, deadly global event, millions of people who could stay at home did just that. Cars sat in driveways. Air travel ground to a halt. Manufacturing plants slowed or stopped. Public buildings shut their doors. Even construction slowed down. Nearly every sector of the energy-using economy reacted to the shock in one way or another.
>
> The result was one of the biggest single drops in modern history in the amount of carbon dioxide humans emit.
>
> Over the first few months of 2020, global daily CO_2 emissions averaged about 17 percent lower than in 2019. At the moments of the most restrictive and extensive lockdowns, emissions in some countries hov-

ered nearly 30 percent below last year's averages, says Glen Peters, one of the authors of the *Nature Climate Change* analysis and a climate scientist at Norway's Center for International Climate Research.[20]

This analysis underscores the potentially inhumane ramifications of an obsession to reduce CO2 emissions. A relentless intellectually viral pandemic of growth limits could slow the reduction of poverty and stifle economic growth to the benefit of those already rich but profound harm to those still impoverished.

The world is at the cusp of switching to more efficient fossil fuels and thereby generate more, yet cheaper, energy and releasing less pollution in all forms. This is not technology or innovation that experts were predicting twenty years ago. This radical innovation and change in global energy consumption is a by-product of believing in discursive complexity. The great thinker Julian Simon explains that the reason we cannot trust our predictions of dystopian disaster like those often thought to unfold from ecological origins, is that we continually underestimate the ultimate commodity: human ingenuity.[21] Simon explains the intimate relationship between human progress and discursive complexity this way: "human imagination can flourish only if the economic and political system gives individuals the freedom to exercise their talents and take advantage of opportunities. So another crucial element in the economics of resource and population is the extent to which the political-legal-economic system provides personal freedom from government coercion."[22] Additional research tends to confirm this thesis.[23] Debate is an essential intellectual lever for prying open the naturally closed jaws of governmental systems too strongly driven by ideology to maximize a human conversation properly predicated on an idealistic imagination.

ENVIRONMENTALISM DESTROYS THE ENVIRONMENT

It is not only that human innovation can continually save the globe as observed by thinkers like Steven Pinker. Our gross excess of certitude can destroy the very things we profess to want to protect. We can develop an intellectual Midas touch that seems to be converting material to our desires, but we soon find ourselves on a dangerous trajectory. Renewable energy is one of the important buzzwords in a rhetorical war against fossil fuels. In this intellectual rendering, there are continually renewable sources of energy such as solar and wind that should phase out fossil fuels and thereby save the planet from ecological demise inherent in the burning of fossil fuels. Accepting this premise requires turning an intellectually blind eye to the ecological harms of these same technologies.

Before looking at wind and solar directly, it is important to realize that almost all of these better forms of energy depend upon the emergence of an alternative electrical interface—primarily in the form of batteries. Electrical cars and even solar homes need batteries to store electricity and forego the portable energy found in comparable sources such as gasoline. Put simply, batteries are toxic.[24] More importantly, batteries are not renewable. After a period of time, batteries lose their ability to store an electrical charge. After that cycle of usage, the batteries are largely useless. Their inert cores contain a wide range of toxic metals that are nearly impossible to dispose of without posing an obvious threat to straightforward human needs, such as clean water sources. The rhetorical featuring of battery technology without a candid assessment of how millions of batteries will be disposed of by the end of the twenty-first century is environmental blindness and plainly dangerous to any candid sense of environmentalism. The mere disposal of batteries likely makes electrical storage a net degradation of the environment, but we must initially consider the sourcing and construction of such batteries. What are they made of? Batteries are made of increasingly exotic metals that possess unique and compelling molecular structures for holding charges longer and drawing such charges more quickly. Advanced metals, such as lithium, are presently popular in various iterations of battery technology. Can the mining of extraction of lithium be done without adversely impacting the ecology of the earth? An honest answer would concede it is unlikely. Is there enough of these metals compared to fossil fuels to power the world for decades to come? It is not really known, but the mining of these metals is a highly destructive environmental process that is ignored as imagination of electrical cars and solar powered homes increases. The rhetorical blindness of pretending that these technologies do not have vast damaging potential is an ethical hazard for all of us.

Wind power brings similar environmental hazards. The giant turbine blades are killing millions of birds and bats throughout the world every year. We know that the North American bird population is in decline and researchers are not entirely sure whether massive wind farms may be to blame. These wind industries are actually exempt from legislation protecting birds from slaughter, and this myopic view of the environment is precisely one of the many ways environmentalism destroys the environment. The giant blades on these churning machines do wear out after a period of time. Unfortunately, they are so intensive in their construction that there is no effective place for disposing of these giant blades. They may never return to a natural state as they are buried in ever-larger graveyards around the world. Why is this necessarily better for the environment? A Harvard study of wind power found that they actually increase global warming.[25] This new study explains, when wind turbines extract energy out of the air, they effectively slow down the wind, which alters "the exchange of heat, moisture, and momentum between the surface and the atmosphere."[26]

Solar power requires careful chemical construction of panels that are largely dominated by the Chinese government as an economical process.

Their incredibly cheap production of solar panels brings with it chemical leaching processes that contribute to the destruction of Chinese water supplies. They are able to build these panels at below market costs because they do not adhere to common environmental standards that follow in production facilities elsewhere. Some of the most enduring and respected proponents of solar power concede that the technology is environmentally destructive.[27] The International Renewable Energy Association (IRENA) explains: "in 2016 [IRENA] estimated there was about 250,000 metric tonnes of solar panel waste in the world at the end of that year. IRENA projected that this amount could reach 78 *million* metric tonnes by 2050. Solar panels often contain lead, cadmium, and other toxic chemicals that cannot be removed without breaking apart the entire panel. 'Approximately 90 percent of most PV modules are made up of glass,' notes San Jose State environmental studies professor Dustin Mulvaney. 'However, this glass often cannot be recycled as float glass due to impurities. Common problematic impurities in glass include plastics, lead, cadmium and antimony.'"[28] Shellenberger's broader analysis of environmentalism is important because it explains how alarmism is making for bad policy and bad outcomes for all of humanity.[29]

WARMING SAVES HUMAN LIFE

What are the benefits of a warming earth? Asking such questions in a low discursive complexity environment is difficult, but useful and compelling answers can be discovered by taking this brave path. A 2015 *Lancet* study examining mortality statistics in more than two hundred global cities found that for every degree of warming on the earth, many thousands of human beings did not die of exposure to the cold. Less severe cold is saving human life around the world. It is important to note that this data set is limited only to the urban areas studied around the world. It is likely that these effects are more profound in rural areas not examined by the study, since rural areas often get colder and have less access to secure sites out of the cold. The study found that warming did not produce a reciprocal number of deaths from overheating. In other words, more people die from cold than heat. In fact, the study found that this is true by a factor of seven.

Warming also complicates and hinders the spread of flu viruses like COVID-19.[30] Viruses kill thousands of people every year and the recent bout of COVID-19 was an especially virulent strain. Flu viruses in the northern hemisphere do their greatest affliction and damage during the coldest months of fall and winter. Summer months constitute an existential threat to most viruses. During the Spanish flu epidemic of 1918, studies found that keeping patients outdoors and exposed to sunlight improved infected patient outcomes.[31] Researchers find that a one-degree

Celsius increase in temperature and one percent increase in humidity lower the reproduction rate of viruses like COVID-19.[32] The University of Maryland mapped severe COVID-19 outbreaks with local weather patterns around the world, from the United States to China. They found that the virus thrives in a certain temperature and humidity channel. "The researchers found that all cities experiencing significant outbreaks of COVID-19 have very similar winter climates with an average temperature of 41 to 52 degrees Fahrenheit, an average humidity level of 47 percent to 79 percent with a narrow east-west distribution along the same 30–50 N latitude," said the University of Maryland.[33] It is vitally important to understand all the varying arguments for improving the human condition and not be limited by doctrinaire statements about how "the climate debate is over." Argumentation is an ever-evolving open system of discussion where human discoveries always have the demonstrated possibility of completely changing the previously known world and, more importantly, the human relationship to that world.

CO2 STIMULATES PLANT GROWTH

Anyone can buy a CO2 emitter for their greenhouse to increase production of their plant life. There are powerful indicators that the rising CO2 levels are making the earth greener. Scientific studies suggest that rising CO2 levels will increase the global food supply.[34] These scientific studies suggest grain yields can grow 25 to 60 percent. More CO2 means we have more forests and larger grain crops. All of the largest grain crops in human history have happened in this century.[35] It appears that the available harvestable land is increasing, and that the overall global production of key grains is also increasing. It is possible that this is a coincidence, but it is likely the result of a world no longer bound in ice and increasingly warmed to temperatures suitable for growing. As we examine grain production, it is important to see again how our ecological myopia distorts a simple human need like food.

At the turn of the century, the United States made the provocative decision to begin adding ethanol to its gasoline inventory. In theory, this provided a supplement to short supplies of gasoline and a possible mechanism for reducing the price of gasoline. It also meant that establishing government subsidies to buy corn to turn into ethanol and add to gasoline increased the cost of government for consumers. This makes Iowa farmers and other corn growers economically content, but it also distorts global grain prices. It encourages the overproduction of grain and a higher price on the global market. Today, with gas prices at historic lows both at the gasoline production level and the intake of petroleum barrels, the ethanol policy of the United States makes no environmental sense. The ethanol fuel is less efficient, more destructive to engines, and may increase global warming by the manner of farming that produces the corn. There is no real need to add corn to our gas tanks today, but this continues to happen as a political bribe to farmers in the United States. This is the painful world of low discursive complexity where we are no longer free to consider our best options among many. The primary harm is higher grain prices that make food less able to reach the neediest mouths.

RENEWING DEBATE ABOUT OUR CLIMATE

It is important to reclaim discursive complexity in the debate over climate change. We should reject the simple rhetorical reflex that tends to initially bolster the idea of ending the debate: we are out of time. Climate alarmists suggest that the earth may have roughly a decade left until we are locked in a downward spiral of anthropological doom. Empiricism tells us that this is untrue. Since Malthus, every prediction of complete human destruction relating to the environment has proven to be untrue. Moreover, human life expectancy is still tending upwards and the global population continues to rise. Human civilization is not collapsing into inevitable total death. At the turn of the nineteenth century, experts imagined that London and New York City would soon be drowning in horse manure as a result of excess travel by way of horse.[36] These often mathematical, and even scientific, deductions of accumulation fail to track that intangible but infinite power of human imagination. Julian Simon constantly attempted to remind economists and other social prognosticators about this continually impending idealism. Researchers do not know, nor can they anticipate, human ingenuity as it will shatter highly constraining conventions. Humanity has time—especially time to make the best choices instead of the most rushed choices.

Opinion leaders say the science is settled. Fortunately, science is an open-ended discursive system and it is not bound by our self-imposed limits. One of the inherent and important characteristics of scientific theory is that all scientific theories are falsifiable. This means that our projections, models, and theories about global temperature can be wrong, and can even be proven to be wrong. There are any examples within the climate debate showing evidence of data tampering in order to achieve ideologically preferred outcomes.[37] Never allow fear of being criticized to stifle scientists of varying perspectives from examining different assumptions with regard to any topic, but especially those that are affecting human well-being and benefits most profoundly. Hans Rosling, the great statistician who visually depicted some of the most positive sociological outcomes occurring in the world today was pressured at one time to change his approach to present and justify consistently pessimistic reports on global outcomes. He refused to do this work because he felt it was inaccurate to the empirical realities he was uncovering.[38]

The rhetoric of science is a well-established area of study within communication study.[39] Communication scholars have examined in multiple studies that despite the façade of scientific objectivity, science is necessarily rhetorical. Scientists are making arguments to influence the public sphere and affect their own credibility and public standing within that sphere. Deriving from important writing of thinkers such as Thomas Kuhn, we know that science must make an argument and even the community of who is and is not a scientist is bounded by lines rhetorically determined.[40] Kuhn explained that we would need to understand argumentation better in order to understand how science progresses properly: "To discover how scientific revolutions are effected, we shall therefore have to examine not only the impact of nature and logic, but also the techniques of persuasive argumentation effective within the quite special groups that constitute the community of scientists."[41] Given the pattern of Neo-malthusian accusations that humanity cannot be allowed to live *against* the earth, we need an empirical view of these arguments that can harmonize the two alleged antagonists. This should not be impossible to do since humanity has upon many consecutive decades proven an ability through her imagination and creativity a capacity to overcome these dystopian fantasies. The rhetoric of fear upon which propaganda primarily feeds within the minds of its audience is a prerequisite to the compromises of discursive complexity that make the earth unlivable. In the 1990s, environmentalists created a fear about the toxic nature of gasoline and insisted at great public expense that MTBE should be made an additive so that the fuel could be oxygenated.[42] The cruel reality of this rushed emergency decision was that the gasoline with the additive was found to be much more dangerous than the original forms. This led to widespread water source contaminations. Critical thinkers must refuse the dichotomy offered rhetorically suggesting that there are humans who "hate the environment" and "want to destroy it." This fearmongering reduces reasoning and the better imagination to improve the global condition. Accepting that all human beings are worthy proponents and an ever-larger deliberative sphere improves the stockpile of solutions on a daily basis. The alarmism surrounding the climate debate is obstructing this necessary conversation and holding billions of human beings hostage in regard to critical questions of economic development, public health, and social equality.

There is a rising risk of continents like Africa facing the brunt of an irrational project justified by the mystique of false science. In this false view, Africa will be maintained as an ecological museum free of extensive urbanization, infrastructure development, higher electrical consumption, and fossil fuel usage. All of these limits will make Africa suitable for visits from their industrialized economic superiors who deem the development of Africa—too great a danger to the precautionary principle undergirding claims about climate change. It is not inappropriate to observe that Charles Darwin's first major book on scientific evolution posited in the title about his notions of "favoured races." Science has regularly been used as a propaganda device for insidious agendas ranging from racism to the Holocaust aimed at Jews. Africa must be able to develop in a way that extends the longevity of life as much as it may be in places such as Japan or Sweden. Artificial limits imposed by overzealous environmental assertions must be seen for the ethical implications they entail.[43]

NOTES

1. James Lovelock, *The Vanishing Face of Gaia: A Final Warning* (Basic Books, April 2009).
2. Lovelock, *The Vanishing Face of Gaia: A Final Warning*.
3. Paul R. Ehrlich, *The Population Bomb* (New York: Ballantine Books, 1968).
4. Rachel Carson and Evelyn Oppenheimer, *Silent Spring* (Boston: Houghton Mifflin, 1962).
5. Clyde Haberman, "Rachel Carson, DDT and the Fight against Malaria," *New York Times*, January 22, 2017, accessed August 10, 2020, https://www.nytimes.com/2017/01/22/us/rachel-carson-ddt-malaria-retro-report.html.
6. "Elimination of Malaria in the United States (1947–1951)," *CDC*, March 3, 1997, accessed August 10, 2020, https://www.cdc.gov/malaria/about/history/elimination_us.html.
7. D. R. Roberts, L. L. Laughlin, P. Hsheih, and L. J. Legters, "DDT, Global Strategies, and a Malaria Control Crisis in South America," *Emerging Infectious Diseases* 3, no. 3 (1997): 295–302, https://dx.doi.org/10.3201/eid0303.970305, accessed August 10, 2020, https://wwwnc.cdc.gov/eid/article/3/3/97-0305_article.
8. Aleksandra Jakubowski, et al., "The US President's Malaria Initiative and Under-5 Child Mortality in Sub-Saharan Africa: A Difference-in-Differences Analysis," *PLoS medicine* 14, no. 6 e1002319 (June 13 2017), doi:10.1371/journal.pmed.1002319.
9. Daniel Farber, "Coping with Uncertainty: Cost-Benefit Analysis, the Precautionary Principle, and Climate Change," *Washington Law Review* 90, no. 4 (December 1, 2015): 1659–82.
10. "'How Dare You?' Greta Thunberg Asks World Leaders at UN Summit," *International Business Times* - US Ed. Newsweek Media Group, September 23, 2019.
11. Nicholas Paliewicz and George F. (Guy) McHendry Jr., "When Good Arguments Do Not Work: Post-Dialectics, Argument Assemblages, and the Networks of Climate Skepticism," *Argumentation and Advocacy* 53, no. 3–4 (2017): 287+. *Gale Academic OneFile*, accessed August 10, 2020, https://link.gale.com/apps/doc/A543611053/AONE?u=txshracd2548&sid=AONE&xid=27fb938a.
12. David Henderson, "1.6 Percent, Not 97 Percent, Agree That Humans Are the Main Cause of Global Warming," Econ Log, March 2014, retrieved August 10, 2020. https://www.econlib.org/archives/2014/03/16_not_97_agree.html.
13. Max Roser and Esteban Ortiz-Ospina, "Global Extreme Poverty," *Our World in Data* (2019), accessed July 13, 2020, https://ourworldindata.org/extreme-poverty.
14. Nicholas Kristof, "This Has Been the Best Year," *New York Times*, December 28, 2019, accessed January 10, 2020, https://www.nytimes.com/2019/12/28/opinion/sunday/2019-best-year-poverty.html.
15. "How Do CO2 Emissions from Forest Fires Compare to Those from Fossil Fuels?" *CBC Radio*, September 14, 2018, accessed August 10, 2020, https://www.cbc.ca/radio/quirks/sept-15-2018-summer-science-camping-under-a-volcano-plastic-in

-beluga-bellies-and-more-1.4821942/how-do-co2-emissions-from-forest-fires-compare-to-those-from-fossil-fuels-1.4821944.

16. "Indonesia Haze: Why Do Forests Keep Burning?" BBC, September 16, 2018, accessed August 5, 2020, https://www.bbc.com/news/world-asia-34265922.

17. Ruby Mellen, (September 18, 2019). "Wildfires in Indonesia Have Ravaged 800,000 Acres. Palm Oil Farmers Are Mostly to Blame," *Washington Post*, accessed July 1, 2020, https://www.washingtonpost.com/world/2019/09/18/wildfires-indonesia-have-ravaged-acres-palm-oil-farmers-are-blame/.

18. Xiongwei Song, M. C. Hansen, S. V. Stehman, et al., "Global Land Change from 1982 to 2016," *Nature* 560 (2018): 639–43, https://doi.org/10.1038/s41586-018-0411-9.

19. Stephen Moore, "How Fracking Has Reduced Greenhouse Gases," *Real Clear Politics*, April 16, 2016, retrieved on June 1, 2020, https://www.realclearpolitics.com/articles/2016/04/16/how_fracking_has_reduced_greenhouse_gases_130303.html.

20. "Plunge in Carbon Emissions from Lockdowns Will Not Slow Climate Change," *National Georgraphic*, May 2020, accessed July 13, 2020, https://www.nationalgeographic.com/science/2020/05/plunge-in-carbon-emissions-lock-downs-will-not-slow-climate-change/.

21. Simon authored many major books examining the centrality of human ingenuity on these broad questions including: Julian L. Simon, 1977, *The Economics of Population Growth* (Princeton: Princeton University Press; 1981); *The Ultimate Resource* (Princeton: Princeton University Press, 1986); *Theory of Population and Economic Growth* (Oxford ; New York: Basil Blackwell, 1989); *The Economic Consequences of Immigration* (Oxford: Basil Blackwell); *Population Matters: People, Resources, Environment, Immigration* (New Brunswick, NJ: Transaction Publishers, 1990).

22. Julian Simon, *The Ultimate Resource 2* (Princeton: Princeton University Press, 1996).

23. D. Ahlburg, "Julian Simon and the Population Growth Debate," *Population and Development Review* 24, no. 2 (1998): 317–27, doi:10.2307/2807977.

24. Laura Millan Lombrana, "Saving the Planet with Electric Cars Means Strangling This Desert," *Bloomberg News*, June 11, 2019, accessed July 13, 2020, https://www.bloomberg.com/news/features/2019-06-11/saving-the-planet-with-electric-cars-means-strangling-this-desert; "Electric Cars Pose Environmental Threat," BBC, October 5, 2012, accessed July 13, 2020, https://www.bbc.com/news/business-19830232; Paul Driessen, "Destroying the Environment to Save It," *Townall*, May 30, 2020, accessed July 13, 2020, https://townhall.com/columnists/pauldriessen/2020/05/30/destroying-the-environment-to-save-it-n2569710.

25. Ethan Huff, "Study Finds That Wind Turbines Create MORE Global Warming than the Fossil Fuels They Eliminate—And the Same Is True for Scooters and Electric Cars," *Ecology News*, August 26, 2019, accessed July 13, 2020, https://www.ecology.news/2019-08-26-wind-turbines-create-more-global-warming.html.

26. Huff, "Study Finds That Wind Turbines Create MORE Global Warming than the Fossil Fuels They Eliminate—And the Same Is True for Scooters and Electric Cars."

27. Michael Shellenberger, "If Solar Panels Are So Clean Why Do They Produce So Much Toxic Waste?" *Forbes*, August 28, 2018, accessed July 13, 2020, https://www.forbes.com/sites/michaelshellenberger/2018/05/23/if-solar-panels-are-so-clean-why-do-they-produce-so-much-toxic-waste/#54d0e713121c.

28. Shellenberger, "If Solar Panels Are So Clean Why Do They Produce So Much Toxic Waste?"

29. Michael Shellenberger, *Apocalypse Never: Why Environmental Alarmism Hurts Us All* (New York: Harper Collins, 2020).

30. Ronald Bailey, "Coronavirus Epidemic May Be Slowed by Warm and Humid Weather," *Reason*, March 16, 2020, accessed August 20, 2020, https://reason.com/2020/03/16/coronavirus-epidemic-may-be-slowed-by-warm-and-humid-weather/.

31. A. Richard Hobday and John W. Cason, "The Open-Air Treatment of PANDEMIC INFLUENZA," *American Journal of Public Health* 99, no. S2 (October 1, 2009): S236–S242.

32. S. Lakshmi Priyadarsini and M. Suresh, "Factors Influencing the Epidemiological Characteristics of Pandemic COVID 19: A TISM Approach," *International Journal of Healthcare Management* 13, no. 2 (April 2, 2020): 89–98.

33. "Researchers Predict Potential Spread and Seasonality for COVID-10 Based on Climate Where Virus Appears to Thrive," University of Maryland Medical School, accessed August 10, 2020, https://www.medschool.umaryland.edu/news/2020/Researchers-Predict-Potential-Spread-and-Seasonality-for-COVID-19-Based-on-Climate-Where-Virus-Appears-to-Thrive.html.

34. Craig Idso, "Projecting Impacts Rising CO2 Future Crop Yields in Germany," CATO, 2016, accessed July 13, 2020, https://www.cato.org/blog/projecting-impacts-rising-co2-future-crop-yields-germany.

35. Moses Naim, "The World Is Full of Grain," *The Atlantic*, October 14, 2014, accessed August 10, 2020, https://www.theatlantic.com/international/archive/2014/10/the-world-is-full-of-grain-agriculture-economy/381413/.

36. Steven Davies, "The Great Horse Manure Crisis," *FEE*, September 4, 2004, accessed July 13, 2020, https://fee.org/articles/the-great-horse-manure-crisis-of-1894/.

37. "The Stunning Statistical Fraud behind the Global Warming Scare," *Investor Business Daily Editorial*, March 29, 2018, accessed July 13, 2020, https://www.investors.com/politics/editorials/the-stunning-statistical-fraud-behind-the-global-warming-scare/.

38. Hans Rosling, *Factfulness: Ten Reasons We're Wrong about the World—And Why Things Are Better than You Think*. (New York: Flatiron Books, 2018).

39. Philip C. Wander, "The Rhetoric of Science," *Western Speech Communication* 40, no. 4 (1976): 226–35, DOI: 10.1080/10570317609373907; and A. G. Gross, "The Roles of Rhetoric in the Public Understanding of Science," *Public Understanding of Science* 3, no. 1 (1994): 3–23, https://doi.org/10.1088/0963-6625/3/1/001.

40. Thomas Kuhn, *The Structure of Scientific Revolutions* (London: University of Chicago, 1962).

41. Kuhn, *The Structure of Scientific Revolutions*, 94.

42. "Gasoline and Additives," encyclopedia.com, 2020, accessed July 13, 2020, https://www.encyclopedia.com/environment/encyclopedias-almanacs-transcripts-and-maps/gasoline-and-additives.

43. Charles Darwin, *On the Origin of Species by Means of Natural Selection, or the Preservation of Favored Races in the Struggle for Life* (London: 1859).

SEVEN

Rwanda Rising

*Rwanda as a Global Model for Success
(Jean Michel Habineza and Ben Voth)*

*Most of this chapter is provided from the perspective of iDebate founder, Jean Michel Habineza.

Franz Fanon insightfully observed, "Each generation must, out of relative obscurity, discover its mission, fulfill it, or betray it."[1] Genocide prevention is an important mission for every society. Genocide is a cruel crime against humanity because its impact cannot be measured simply in the number of people that are murdered during the extermination process, but also the way that it impacts the social cohesion and relationship between the groups after all killings have stopped. This is most evident in Rwanda, where Hutus and Tutsis alike had to go back and live on the same hills after the genocide. It is common in Rwanda to hear stories of people living next to people who were hunting them day and night during the 1994 genocide against the Tutsis.

BURDEN OF A POST-GENOCIDE GENERATION

In our continued discussion of the impact of the genocide, one of the most overlooked effects of the genocide is the impact that it has on the Post-Genocide Generation. More than 70 percent of the population in Rwanda is made up of young people under the age of thirty. This means that these are people who were not born during the 1994 genocide against the Tutsis or who were too young to participate in the massacres. This generation might not have had an active role in the genocide, but the genocide shaped their lives and continues to greatly influence their lived experience. Many grew up without grandparents, cousins, or were even orphaned at a young age. Some had to confront the dark past of their family members, and are on a journey of trying to understand and to find new direction in the world. Countless research has been done about the different ways in which the genocide affected this generation through intergenerational trauma.[2]

In our parents' generation, we can talk about victims and perpetrators, but in our generation, we are all victims because we have to bear the consequences of something that we did not create. This creates a dilemma in our generation, how do we ensure that NEVER AGAIN becomes our reality while also ensuring that we are rebuilding the breach that our parents have created? How do we remember while also building a brighter future?

I believe that our mission comes from Isaiah 58:12:

> And your ancient ruins shall be rebuilt;
> you shall raise up the foundations of many generations;
> you shall be called the repairer of the breach,
> the restorer of streets to dwell in.[3]

Our mission at iDebate Rwanda is two-fold: one of creating an environment where NEVER AGAIN is a reality, while also creating a generation of builders and leaders who are committed to their communities and who are working toward its transformation.

UNDERSTANDING OUR CONTEXT AND EXIGENCE

In a post-conflict situation, a prominent question that a generation always asks themselves is *how did we get here?* In chapter 1, we examined prominent aspects of the history leading to the ultimate consequent genocide of 1994. Since that event more than twenty-five years ago, our society has cautiously moved away from this trauma. Staub calls this the "Need for Understanding Reality."[4] The need to comprehend reality is the need to have an understanding of people and the world (what they are like, how they operate) and of our own place in the world; to have views or conceptions that make sense of the world.[5] Scholars such as Walter Fisher have gone further and explained that human beings are *homo-narrans*, meaning that we understand our world through the stories that we tell about ourselves, about others, and about the world. Stories are not only important, but paramount to the human experience.[6] This need for understanding reality, according to Staub, can create a strong potential for people to become caring and helpful, whereas their frustration creates a strong potential for hostility and aggression.[7]

What this shows is that unless we are intentional in allowing for multiple stories and multiple views to be heard in our societies, we are going to succumb to the pressures of propaganda. Propaganda, as noted earlier in the book, is defined as "information, especially of a biased or misleading nature, used to promote or publicize a particular political cause or point of view."[8] Deeper analysis of propaganda and its communication foundations within human psychology and philosophy can be found in the writings of Jacques Ellul.[9] This chapter, will explain how the Rwandan Education System created the underlying conditions that facilitated the spread of propaganda and how we at iDebate are going about changing this system. Many scholars have done work that shows the impact of propaganda on societies but one of the critical elements that scholars tend to leave out in this discussion is the importance of studying the education system as a mechanism of creating and spreading propaganda. Education is a key element of socialization. Formal education can shape understandings, attitudes, values, and the behavior of individuals. Elisabeth King makes the argument that there are three ways in which Education can either lead to conflict or to peace in her book, *From Classroom to Conflict in Rwanda*.[10] She looks at the three concepts that she calls "Access, Content, and Style."[11]

ACCESS TO EDUCATION

McLean, in her research entitled *The Role of Education in Driving Conflict and Building Peace: The Case of Rwanda*, finds that throughout the history of Rwanda, access to education has always been limited to the group that was in power. In the 1950s, the system was set up to favor the Tutsis elites, but this all changed in the aftermath of the 1962 independence as Hutus were in charge. Access to primary education dropped from 63.9 percent in 1964 to about 40.8 percent in the 1970s and secondary enrollment also dropped from 15 percent in 1963 to about 5 percent in the 1970s.[12] Despite the official rhetoric which claimed that the education policies adopted by various governments were inclusive, there seemed to be a trend of bias against the masses by the powerful elite. The lack of equal access to education, McLean argues, created interethnic tension in Rwanda. If education truly is the equalizer and the vehicle through which social mobility could be acquired, then limiting people's access to education frustrates their need for survival and makes them more prone to violence.

EDUCATIONAL CONTENT

If access to education examines WHO is allowed into the school, in education content, Elizabeth King, alongside other scholars, have looked at the impact of WHAT we learn in the classroom. The content of the curriculum shapes our understanding of the *others*. In assessing the impact of curriculum, most authors suggest the need to consider curriculum inclusions, omissions, misrepresentations, and accuracy. The teaching of history is formative to propaganda and the rising dangers of "otherization."[13] A look at the history curriculum tells us that it indoctrinated into the students resentment, hatred, and mistrust of the Tutsi, as encouraged by the political elites of the time, which had the effect of exacerbating the effects of anti-Tutsi extremist propaganda.[14]

The divisive history taught in school made the population more susceptible to extremist propaganda, because for any propaganda to be effective, it must make use of people's prior knowledge and beliefs.[15] Due to how *ubuhake*[16] was taught in school, people were more susceptible to hate propaganda such as the Hutu Ten Commandments, released by the hate newspaper *Kangura*. One of the commandments stated, "All Hutu know that all Tutsis are dishonest . . . their only goal is ethnic superiority. We have learned this from experience."[17] Because this piece of propaganda bore a striking resemblance to the history curriculum, it only reinforced what had already been learned in school. The combination of all these factors is what led Hutu perpetrators to carry out mass violence, and then genocide, against the Tutsi. Therefore, through indoctrination, content played a direct role in solidifying existing classifications between Hutus and Tutsis. Furthermore, it polarized the people while justifying persecution and discrimination against the Tutsi.

EDUCATIONAL STYLE

Pedagogical processes can also play a role in social conflict and peace building. Examining educational processes lets us get at the *hidden curriculum*, meaning the teaching to students of norms, values, and dispositions that goes on simply by their living and coping with the institutional expectations and routines of school's day in and day out for many years.[18] The way in which education was delivered to students and the teacher-student relationships (which can be summarized as teaching style) discouraged critical thinking and open debate.

In Rwanda, from the colonial era to the First and Second Republics, education was mostly done by memorizing content given by the teacher. In this system, the teacher has all the information and the student's role was to accept it without question. As one Hutu man who was a student expressed, "The teacher has to teach what he wants you to learn and what he wants to teach you. So, if you disagree, he will say, 'hey, I'm a teacher, so you have to understand like this; because I'm here to teach you.'"[19] This concept is what Paulo Freire calls the "Banking model of Education."[20] This is a student-teacher relationship that greatly discouraged students to think critically for themselves or disagree with what an authority figure like a teacher said. Another interviewee remarked, "The teacher can just teach. It is very rare that students asked questions." This instills in students a "spirit of submission."[21]

Because the education system discouraged critical thinking by putting all the decision-making power in the teacher's hands, students were not able to reasonably judge for themselves alternatives to the history they were fed by teachers.[22] This in turn heightened the effect of the previously mentioned divisive history curriculum. These classroom practices were transferred into the adult lives of students because propaganda has a higher effect if "schooling instills obedience to authority."[23] This means that the extremist government's divisive anti-Tutsi propaganda was more effective in getting people to participate in the genocide as a result of the poor teaching style. The combination of these factors means that when the order was given for all Hutu to participate in the genocide against the Tutsi in 1994, the perpetrators were ill-equipped to judge for themselves any reasonable alternatives to murder. What this teaches us is that pedagogy aimed at memorialization and learning by rote, the teaching of single narratives and exclusive point of view in closed classrooms that restrict discussion and questions can narrow students' critical thinking and discourage the search for alternatives, thereby reducing their sense of agency in the classroom and in wider society.[24]

OUR EDUCATIONAL ALTERNATIVE: IDEBATE RWANDA

After understanding the causes of the problems that we were faced, it was important for us to establish a pedagogical path by which we can create solutions that are crafted to address each of the different aspects of the problem (access, content, style). Although some of these problems can only be addressed through high-level government policies, we believe that we have a role to play as the emerging Post-Genocide Generation.

Over the last twenty-five years, the government of Rwanda has dealt with the issue of education by expanding access throughout the country. Rwanda is one of the top-performing countries in sub-Saharan Africa in education; having achieved the *Millennium Development Goals* (MDG2) for access to universal primary education, with a net enrolment rate of 97 percent.[25] This was done by the government, putting in place the *12 Years' Basic Education Framework* that allows students to attend school free of charge until their 12th grade.[26] Barriers to access have also been removed. According to the constitution of the Republic of Rwanda, it is now against the law to prevent someone from attending school due to their ethnicity and/or region of birth. By all metrics, the government of Rwanda and the people of Rwanda are on the right path to ensure access to education for everyone regardless of their race. The iDebate Rwanda approach is one that makes a contribution to our society by addressing issues of curriculum (how we study history) and pedagogy.

DEBATE AND MEMORY: ENGAGEMENT AND PROXIMITY

How do we deal with history?[27] Miroslav Volf, in his work *The End of Memory: Remembering Rightly in a Violent World,* states that humans must "remember rightly"[28] and "truthfully"[29] even though the ability to fulfill this obligation is limited by human fallibility[30] and particularity.[31] In other words, all individuals and communities see and remember things from certain perspectives and are always influenced by embodied interests. Everyone sees from here or from there and no one has the ability to step outside of oneself to establish an objective "view from nowhere." As Volf notes, partial perspectives can and should be pursued truthfully as a means of building reconciliation.[32]

Fulfilling Volf's framework for remembering requires us to learn how to disagree and how to acknowledge our own particularity. I believe that debate can provide such a framework. Moreover, debate provides two benefits that are important for Volfian remembering and the prevention of future conflicts: engagement and proximity.[33] In debate, you learn that conflict is inevitable, but that violence is a choice. Embedded into this activity is this idea that a conflict of ideas could lead to a positive outcome that can be revolutionary for societies that are recovering from violent conflicts. In debate, you are forced to engage with a person who is advocating for a position that is contrary to your own beliefs. What great debaters do is listen and find merit in the position of their opponents and learn how to critique their own stances on certain issues.

This critical engagement allows for a few things to happen. The first is that debate allows for dissenting voices to be heard. Staub explains that, "perhaps the most profound effect of a successful totalitarian system is the lack of dissenting voices that offer a perspective different from that cultivated by authorities or engender inner conflict or sympathy with victims."[34] This "lack of dissenting voices" creates echo chambers and the circulation of unquestioned propaganda, thus inviting violence. Communication scholars Voth and Noland describe this as a lack of "discursive complexity" or "the capacity of an individual or group to allow and encourage dissent."[35] The critical engagement offered by debate also allows for participants to perform self-questioning. As stated earlier, each person comes to the table with a "view from somewhere" and their participation in this activity requires that they allow their preconceived assumptions to be questioned. When we allow for our assumptions to be questioned and provide space for dissenting voices, we encounter humility. This is a great trait for people who want not only to learn from the past but also create a brighter future.

Debate also emphasizes proximity. In a post conflict society, polarization is both a cause and an effect. Blinded by fear, hatred, and mistrust, both poles are suspicious of each other. Debate encourages an engagement of ideas and minds, but it also creates spaces for relationships between people from different backgrounds. Our students come from all walks of life, but when they meet with each other, they create relationships that are meaningful, grounded in the sharing of memories, and open to the appreciation of difference. Proximity and engagement also tap into the meaning of King's words quoted earlier—we must know and encounter each other to overcome fear and hate. Encountering each other requires acknowledging that we bring memories of the past into our shared conversations. Thus, memory should be a crucial aspect of debate practice.

DREAMERS ACADEMY: *CHANGING PEDAGOGY*

The Dreamers Academy was started in 2013 as a holiday debate program. Great coaches like Chris Baron came to Rwanda early on to help encourage debate throughout the nation. Our initial plan was to create a holiday program where we can bring students who are part of our debate league together for a period of two weeks for them to be trained in argumentation. In 2015, we noticed that we were attracting students who are not part of the debate leagues. The students who came loved debate as an activity because it allowed them to express themselves, but they were not keen on the competitive side of debate. They did not want to win the World School Debate Championship. They wanted to use the skills and knowledge that debate gives in order for them to do something meaningful with their lives. So, we changed the camp from being a debate camp to the Dreamers Academy.

Changing the name from the debate camp to a Dreamers Academy was the first step in a grander vision of creating a program where we use debate, not as an end in itself, but rather as a means to an end. Our motto was: "We are creating a training ground for World Changers." Our hope was that we could give our students the skills that they need in order to become effective leaders in their schools and their communities at large. This switch was motivated by different factors but one of them was a lecture that we were given in 2015 by Dr. Ben Voth. During our visit to Southern Methodist University, Dr. Voth took us to visit Wiley College, the home of the Great Debaters. All my students had watched the movie *The Great Debaters* and were inspired by the movie. Dr. Voth took us to the Paramount Theater where James Farmer Jr. had gone to watch a movie as a college debater. Dr. Voth then read a passage from Farmer's biography *Lay Bare the Heart,* where Farmer is telling the story to Tolson about going to the movies and having to go through the back door in order to enter the theater. Tolson challenges him: "On Thursday night in your [debate] bull session you tore segregation to bits. Then on Saturday afternoon in the pitiless glare of the sun, you walked downtown in Marshall, Texas, to the Paramount Theater, went around to the side entrance, climbed the back stairs, and sat up in the buzzards' roost. Am I correct?" "Yes." "And you watched the movie. Not only that, you enjoyed it! You had killed segregation two days before. And now, you not only allowed yourself to be segregated, but paid your father's hard-earned money for the privilege. And you enjoyed it!" When later he's asked by his father what he's going to do with his training. He responds, "I'm going to go and destroy segregation." Dr. Voth, after reading this whole passage to myself and the students, asked us the same question "What are you going to do with the training that you received in debate?" He then went on to tell my students that they could change the world by taking the example of the life of James Farmer Jr. At that moment, I had an epiphany. It was never about the trophies; it was never about winning arguments. Rather, it was about creating a world where each child's voice could be heard. So, we made the move from a purely debate camp to a Dreamers Academy, where we train leaders in debate so that they can impact their communities. This change in vision of the camp meant that we had to also change the activities taking place during the camp. The camp has several important aspects.

IMPORTANCE OF VISION

One of the most important parts of the Dreamers Academy is to make sure that we create a common vision for all the people that are at the camp. This is done mostly by explaining to the students a vision that the country has of moving from a low-income country to a middle-income country by 2020,[36] and to move to a high-income country by 2050.[37] Rwanda is trying to accomplish what many developed countries accomplished in four hundred years, and do it in just one generation. Vision is important. The Bible says, "Where there is no vision, the people perish."[38] Throughout the camp, we put in the students' minds the idea that they are part of a country that has a big vision and that the vision of the country is upon their shoulders.

Creating a common vision and debate might sound irreconcilable, but we think that both elements are very important. We believe that it's important to have a common vision in order to counter our history of divisionism. We usually tell students that our destination is the same, but we can debate about "the pathway" to get us to that common destination. This common vision allows us to attract students from all walks of life, all backgrounds, and to make them feel like they are part of something that is larger than themselves. Without a vision, people also are more likely to have bickering—dehumanizing whoever disagrees with them—but we have found that constantly communicating to the students that they are part of something that is much bigger, allows them to passionately disagree on policies and programs without dehumanizing their opponents or whoever disagrees with them. The importance of the post-conflict generation cannot be emphasized enough: this generation can make or break Rwanda. This could be the generation that ends the cycle of violence in our lifetime and we cannot stop communicating that vision to this generation. Vision as a component of our pedagogy is paramount.

DEBATE TRAINING

All the students at the camp must undergo an intensive debate training either at a beginner's level or an advanced level. Through these trainings, students are taught argumentation theory, policy formulation, analysis, and research. This is key in our work of creating informed citizens who will use intellect and research to advocate for change. This creates the lifelong process of carefully considering how to make good decisions and convince others about the good ideas we discover.

DEBATE IN THE WORLD

"Praxis is a reflection and action directed at the structures to be transformed. Through Praxis, oppressed people can acquire a critical awareness of their own condition, and, with teacher-students and students-teachers, struggle for liberation"—Paulo Freire.[39] Debate training should always be coupled with real-world application classes. The debate in the world series is an important component of our program because it helps us to translate our mission of creating world changers into a practical training in different spheres. All the seminars are designed to accommodate student interests in three key areas: arts, business, and politics.

In these seminars, we are committed to turn students from passive recipients of knowledge to active participants in the democratic process. As an example, we have a program that encourages entrepreneurialism among the students by asking them to become parts of groups that research a business idea. They must prepare a convincing "shark tank" presentation for our staff of debate coaches. These projects focus upon feasibility and economic rubrics.

TEACHER TRAINING

Teachers are a foundation to enduring educational practices. Teaching students is a starting point, but teaching teachers is a lasting point. With a considerable body of teachers who know, understand, and value debate, successive generations of debaters can be cultivated within a society. Moreover, as students complete their relatively brief eras of competition, they can see in debate teachers a potential vocation. They themselves can become teachers of debate. This process can begin while they are young as they engage in peer coaching of debate—helping new students acquaint themselves with the characteristics and practice of debate. This is an important part of the iDebate Rwanda Dreamers Academy, where young people work as teaching assistants.

In December 2019, a graphic design teacher from Uganda came to the iDebate Rwanda camp to learn about debate and how to teach it (figure 7.1). At the end he approached Dr. Voth and said, "Sometimes an artist wants to make a project of such a size that he does not have a table big enough to make it. You all [the debate teachers and coaches at iDebate Dreamers Academy] have given us a bigger table upon which to build the future of democracy in Uganda." This insight of how an art teacher was transformed to becoming a teacher of debate epitomizes the process whereby teachers are built for the future of communities, societies, and nations. The teacher explained that over the past week he was encouraged to see so many young people wanting to read, think, argue, and

Figure 7.1. Art Teacher from Uganda trained in debate at iDebate Dreamers Academy. Photo courtesy of author.

prepare their arguments. He knew it would help everything about his school at home.

Melvin Tolson is an important example of how debate teachers can make a difference. Melvin Tolson was the debate coach at Wiley College in Marshall, Texas, during the 1930s. Wiley was one of the nation's most important Historically Black Colleges and Universities. In many respects, it was considered the Black Harvard of the West. Howard University was premiere among HBCUs in the East and Wiley in the West. Tolson is well-known since a 2007 movie, *The Great Debaters*, popularized his work and his persona was played by the great actor Denzel Washington. Though Tolson's primary specialty was poetry, he took his work as debate coach so seriously that he led Wiley College's debate team to the first successful defeat of the national champion school: USC. It is interesting to note that the movie fictionalized the adversary as Harvard.

More than two thousand listened in Los Angeles to a public debate in 1935 where Black students defeated the all-White debate team from USC that had won the national championship in debate. The young alternate for the Wiley team was James Farmer Jr., who went to college at the age of fourteen. He was inspired by the coaching of Tolson to believe that he could destroy racial segregation in the United States. Tolson's personal confrontation with Farmer about the enduring importance of debate as a mechanism for social change formed the backbone of Farmer's conviction that he could abolish Jim Crow racial segregation laws. Between 1942 and 1967, Farmer was able to accomplish this goal by organizing a racial justice advocacy program known as the Congress of Racial Equality that ultimately summoned eighty thousand volunteers to use public argument to bring change in America. Farmer was joined by other Black advocates trained in debate and argumentation including: James Meredith, Medgar Evers, Malcolm X, Barbara Jordan, Martin Luther King Jr., and his own wife Lula Farmer.[40]

The students of debate teaching and coaching are imperative. They represent the inherent future of any society because those students of debate have a unique access to voice—the ability to speak in public. Moreover, these students can break the silence that enables genocidal processes and propaganda. It is useful to hear those young voices in this early era of the twenty-first century. The young voices of the debate programming conducted for seven years in Rwanda can give us a glimpse of a much brighter future for all of global humanity (figure 7.2).

VOICES FROM A POST-GENOCIDE GENERATION

In 2014, Rwanda was commemorating the twentieth anniversary of the genocide against the Tutsis in 1994.[41] As expected, the eyes of the world were on Rwanda. The media held panels about the impact of genocide on

Figure 7.2. Teacher debate training seminar at the Kigali Public Library. Photo courtesy of author.

Rwanda and discussions were held at high levels about whether the world had learned any lessons from the genocide of Rwanda. Amid all those discussions, an important voice was missing. That was the voice of the youth of Rwanda, those affected most by the genocide. As iDebate, we decided to create a project called Voices from a Post-Genocide Generation, which was a two-month tour of the United States with the aim of sharing the story of Rwanda with our American brothers and sisters so that what happened in Rwanda will not happen anywhere else in the world (USA Tour, 2013). This was also because we wanted to bring a human touch to the lessons that students were learning about Rwanda. We believed that bringing to the classroom people who experienced the genocide first-hand or who are living in its aftermath would have a great impact on how American students understand complex issues such as genocide.

We also wanted to share not only the history of Rwanda, but also the rise of Rwanda through the eyes of its youth. We wanted the students to experience the hope that Rwanda represents and for them to be able to see that while Rwandans suffered immensely, they are working hard to rebuild the ruins. We also wanted Rwanda to be a mirror for every person we met; we wanted them to be challenged and inspired to deal with their own issues of prejudice, discrimination, and racism. If Rwandans could live together after a horrific tragedy such as the genocide, then no one in the world has an excuse not to do the same. At iDebate, we have called this "Hope in the valley of dry bones."[42]

All of this points to the crucial role of memory in building the iDebate Rwanda organization and in framing our hopes for the tour. Both understanding history and finding ways to transcend historical crimes through such understanding are critical elements of our project that, we hope, will spill over into debate practices in the United States. Such spillover may assist debaters in the cultivation of knowledge that allows them to speak across lines of difference, respect the important role of individual memory in the construction of arguments, and engage in ethical practices of remembering that both acknowledge the past and make room for building a new future.

For the past five years, the tour has taught my students that the issues of discrimination, polarization, and propaganda are issues that affect not only Rwandans but also Americans. These are human issues. There is an issue in every society on how we treat the "others." We have learned that civil discourse is an imperfect solution, we need to figure out a way to talk to one another without dehumanizing and demonizing each other. Through the various debates that we have had in the sixty universities that we have visited, it's easy to see that, just like my debate coach used to say, "it is through the competition of ideas that better ideas emerge."

As a foreigner looking in, it is easy to see that our American brothers and sisters are making the wrong choices when they live in ideological bubbles and are unable to have cordial and intellectual conversations about the issues that affect the world without resorting to verbal abuse, and sometimes even physical violence. If Rwanda teaches us anything, it teaches us that once the small thread that holds a society together is broken, it will take generations to be able to bring it back together.

CONCLUSION

The iDebate program engages in two primary outreaches to actualize the power of debate as pedagogy: (1) travel to U.S. universities and colleges for campus demonstrations of debate, and (2) debate camps within Rwanda to help hundreds of students and dozens of teachers to learn debate. Our most recent effort in 2019 was further enabled by a generous grant from the U.S. State Department authorized through the U.S. ambassador's office for Rwanda. The U.S. ambassador was himself a former college debater. The large grant allowed up to five American coaches to visit the nation and help convene an expected audience of 125 students and thirty-five teachers. Four coaches ended up being able to make it (figure 7.3). The December experience lasted twenty days and attracted

Figure 7.3. From left: Ben Voth, Chris Baron, Jean Michel Habineza, and Frank Ntambara. Photo courtesy of author.

from Rwanda and surrounding countries about four hundred students and more than forty-five teachers. The top varsity student and top novice student were also qualified to the Coolidge Cup debate tournament held in Vermont in July 2020. They were the first international qualifiers for this American inter-format debate championship among high school debaters. The Rwandan varsity debater finished thirty-forth out of ninety-two competitors at the tournament and missed advancing to the elimination rounds by only two places. The long and far-reaching aspects of iDebate allowed us at the end of the camp to have a picture with four generations of debate: Dr. Ben Voth, Chris Baron, Jean Michel Habineza, and Frank Ntambara. This sequence of individuals taught the next generation how to debate so the chain of learning could reach Rwanda twenty-five years after Dr. Voth coached Chris Baron at the University of Kansas in 1991. The photo was a reminder of the enduring line of pedagogy that debate can represent, and how its pedagogy for the oppressed can liberate around the world and across time. Hundreds of students from Rwanda and neighboring countries such as Uganda, Burundi, and South Sudan are positively impacted by a pedagogy that breaks the cycle of violence and insulates the minds against the dangers of propaganda. In the United States, the dozens of debate exchanges at American Universities also impact hundreds of college students about the dangers of political polarization and the ideal role debate plays in defusing social conflict while encouraging social progress. The iDebate Rwanda represents an escalating pedagogy of idealism laid out by Martin Luther King Jr. that breaks the syllogism of hatred and discrimination, and enables the ascendancy of communication competency and a more noble public sphere.

NOTES

1. Frantz Fanon, *The Wretched of the Earth* (New York: Grove Press, 1963): 40.
2. Check out the work of *Aegis Trust Genocide Research hub*, accessed August 10, 2020, http://www.genocideresearchhub.org.rw/document/?fwp_search_library=Post percent20GEnocide percent20Trauma.
3. Isaiah 58:12, *The Bible*, New International Version (London: Hodder and Stoughton, 1996).
4. Ervin Staub, "Basic Human Needs, Altruism, and Aggression," in A. G. Miller, *The Social Psychology of Good and Evil* (New York: Guilford, 2004).
5. Staub, "Basic Human Needs, Altruism, and Aggression."
6. Walter Fisher, "Homo Narrans—The Narrative Paradigm: In the Beginning," *Journal of Communication* 35, no. 4 (Fall 1985): 74.
7. Staub, "Basic Human Needs, Altruism, and Aggression."
8. *New American Oxford Dictionary*.
9. Jacques Ellul, *Propaganda: The Formation of Men's Attitudes* (New York: Vintage Books, 1974).
10. Elisabeth King, *From Classrooms to Conflict in Rwanda* (Cambridge: Cambridge University Press, 2013).
11. King, *From Classrooms to Conflict in Rwanda*.
12. Lyndsay McLean Hilker, "The Role of Education in Driving Conflict and Building Peace: The Case of Rwanda," *Prospects* 41, no. 2 (2011): 267–82.
13. King, *From Classrooms to Conflict in Rwanda*.
14. David Yanagizawa-Drott, "Propaganda vs. Education: A Case Study of Hate Radio in Rwanda," *Oxford Handbook of Propaganda Studies* (2013).

15. Yanagizawa-Drott, "Propaganda vs. Education: A Case Study of Hate Radio in Rwanda."

16. Luc De Heusch, "Rwanda: Responsibilities for a Genocide," *Anthropology Today* 11, no. 4 (1995): 3–7.

17. King, *From Classrooms to Conflict in Rwanda*, 100.

18. Elisabeth King, "The Role of Education in Violent Conflict and Peacebuilding in Rwanda," PhD Thesis (University of Toronto, 2008): 105–6.

19. King, *From Classrooms to Conflict in Rwanda*, 3.

20. You can learn more about this concept by reading Paulo Freire, *Pedagogy of the oppressed*, 30th Anniversary Edition (New York: Continuum, 2000).

21. King, *From Classrooms to Conflict in Rwanda*, 100.

22. Ellul, *Propaganda: The Formation of Men's Attitudes*, 74.

23. John Lott, "Public Schooling, Indoctrination, and Totalitarianism," *Journal of Political Economy* 107 (1999).

24. Roland Case and Ian Wright, "Taking Seriously the Teaching of Critical Thinking," *Critical Discussions* (1997).

25. "Education," UNICEF, retrieved online at https://www.unicef.org/rwanda/education.html).

26. "Education," UNICEF.

27. This is an excerpt from a paper presented at the National Communication Association annual meeting entitled "The iDebate Rwanda Tour of the U.S.: Cross-Cultural Perspectives on Debate, Memory, and Social Justice" by Jean Michel Habineza, Dr. John Rief, and Rachel Wilson at the National Communication Association Conference, November 7, 2018, Salt Lake City, Utah.

28. Miroslav Volf, *The End of Memory: Remembering Rightly in a Violent World* (Grand Rapids, MI: William B. Eerdmans Publishing Company, 2006): 10–16.

29. Volf, *The End of Memory: Remembering Rightly in a Violent World*, 44–65.

30. Volf, *The End of Memory: Remembering Rightly in a Violent World*, 57, 62, 178

31. Volf, *The End of Memory: Remembering Rightly in a Violent World*, 43–44.

32. Volf, *The End of Memory: Remembering Rightly in a Violent World*, 205–6.

33. Others have noted the crucial role of proximity in cementing human cooperation and understanding. For example, Alan Schroeder (2016) articulates "proximity" as a way to "encourage—at least in theory—a more civilized level of discourse" (para. 12, lines 4–5) in the context of the recent U.S. presidential debates. Alan Schroeder, "Do We Really Need Debate Moderators," *Politico*, September 23, 2016. In addition, in the arena of public memory studies, Edward S. Casey argues in "Public Memory in Place and Time," *Framing Public Memory* (Tuscaloosa: University of Alabama Press, 2004), accessed August 10, 2020, http://escasey.com/Article/Public_Memory_in_Place_and_Time. "Proximity is not for the sake of intimacy—something often sought in social memory—but for the sake of a public presence that can be accomplished only when people congregate for a common purpose. This presence is really a co-presence of each to the other, all within eyeshot and (usually) earshot. This is a specifically interhuman presence, a form of community however brief it may be" (p. 33). In both cases, proximity describes the all-important notion of human contact and interconnectedness needed to promote productive discussion in the public square.

34. Ervin Staub, *The Roots of Evil: The Origins of Genocide and Other Group Violence* (Cambridge: Cambridge University Press, 1989): 125.

35. Ben Voth and Aaron Noland, "Argumentation and the International Problem of Genocide," *Contemporary Argumentation and Debate* 28 (2009): 38–46.

36. Commonly known as Vision 2020.

37. Commonly known as Vision 2050.

38. Proverbs 29:18, *The Bible* (New Americans Standard Version).

39. Paulo Freire, *Pedagogy of the Oppressed*, 30th Anniversary Edition (New York: Continuum, 2000).

40. James Meredith, *Three Years in Mississippi* (Jackson: University of Mississippi Press, 2019): 43; Mississippi Writers Website, "Medgar Evers," University of Mississip-

pi English Department (2015), accessed August 11, 2020, http://mwp.olemiss.edu//dir/evers_medgar/; James Branham, "I Was Gone on Debating: Malcolm X Prison Debates and Public Confrontations," *Argumentation and Advocacy* 31 (1995): 117–37; Katharine Seelye, "Thomas Freeman Debate Coach with Broad Influence Dies at 100," *New York Times* June 16, 2020, accessed July 15, 2020, https://www.nytimes.com/2020/06/16/us/thomas-freeman-debate-coach-with-broad-influence-dies-at-100.html; Ben Voth, *James Farmer Jr.: The Great Debater* (Lanham, MD: Lexingon, 2017).

41. This is an excerpt from a paper presented at the National Communication Association annual meeting in Salt Lake City in 2017 entitled "The iDebate Rwanda Tour of the U.S.: Cross-Cultural Perspectives on Debate, Memory,and Social Justice" by Jean Michel Habineza, Dr. John Rief, and Rachel Wilson.

42. Ezekiel 37:1–14, *The Bible* (The New Jerusalem Bible).

EIGHT

Guatemala Rising with the Creative Peace Process (Rebecca Voth and Ben Voth)

Like those instances noted in Rwanda, every Latin American nation has suffered human rights abuses at the hands of an authoritarian government, and each has developed a different strategy to combat the challenges to democracy that arise in the wake of such abuse. Some governments have offered blanket amnesty to perpetrators and treat the past with oblivion as they seek a forward-looking strategy based on democratic principles and liberal ideology. In some cases, oblivion is easier for a newly transitioning government that faces a mountain of political reform, democratic institution building, and social trust formation.[1] Empirically, however, the strategy of forgetfulness does not work when it comes to building and strengthening a democratic state.[2] The tension and distrust that arise in the face of dramatic human rights abuse demand a strong response. Left unchecked, the damage caused by state-sponsored killing of innocents leaves lasting marks on the electorate that severely impacts the effectiveness and strength of a young democracy.

Citizens of a state that has recently emerged from intrastate conflict experience a deeply divided society, and are likely to have difficulty trusting both their fellow citizens and the government. Transition to democracy requires a state to have a strong sense of unified support from its citizens. When a government lacks legitimacy or approval, citizens fail to participate in the democratic process. Worse, they may actively undermine the regime, and even replace a liberal democracy with an illiberal regime. Empirical evidence shows that regime stability depends heavily upon civil trust and approval, especially following the conclusion of domestic conflict.[3] Given the government's role in political repression during an authoritarian period, citizens will tend to distrust a new government that holds the same position that formerly threatened their lives and basic human rights. Strong institutions that promote civil debate are key to reforming this lost trust and rebuilding a healthy democracy.

Paradoxically, transitioning nations that have recently emerged from the horrors of civil war and human rights abuse have inherently weak institutions; however, only strong institutions can legitimately hold perpetrators accountable. An authoritarian regime leaves democratic institutions devastated: the executive branch has too much power that it wields to oppress opposition; the legislature is left weakened or disbanded altogether with no ability to check the executive's power; and the judicial branch is thoroughly abused by an authoritarian regime that uses the law as a weapon to control citizens, leaving this branch completely incapable of making decisions independent of a dictatorial executive. Building and strengthening these branches is and ought to be the first priority of a new post-authoritarian regime. Institution-building takes time, however, and it is nearly impossible for a young democracy to simultaneously build and strengthen these institutions and effectively bring perpetrators to justice. Although a swift and strong response to the previous regime is necessary, it can often be bungled by nascent democratic institutions that are still contaminated by the very corruption they seek to prosecute and condemn.

Taking a strong stance against the abuses of the old regime sets the tone for a new government based on principles of equality and fairness, one that values the rights of all citizens. Properly implemented transitional justice measures can strengthen the legitimacy of the government if it is able to successfully rebuild trust between citizens and the government; essential in the formation of a strong democracy. A botched attempt at rectifying past abuse, however, can lead to further human rights violations or a loss of legitimacy in the eyes of the people and the international community. It is a precarious activity, and each nation that has successfully made this transition has used slightly different deliberative techniques to approach and address their unique situation. The most successful new democracies have invested in reconciling the realities of the past with their hope for a democratic future by balancing justice with mercy.

This chapter begins with an examination of human rights prosecutions in Latin America and their strengths and weaknesses with regard to strengthening democracy. Next it will explore an alternative transitional justice method known as the creative peace process, which operates on the community level and draws heavily on the ideas of reconciliation and forgiveness in the context of Christian hermeneutics. Finally, using Guatemala as a case study, it will examine how both of these approaches have worked in practice. Emerging from a lengthy and brutal civil war, the nation of Guatemala has struggled to transition to a strong democracy, and has, in the process, attempted to implement a variety of transitional measures. This comparative study will reveal that while human rights prosecutions and the creative peace process each fall short of ideal transitional justice measures, each provides a necessary complementary element of the transitional process: justice and mercy.

BENEFITS OF HUMAN RIGHTS TRIALS

Trials, in their essence, operate on the dualities of right and wrong, justice and injustice, guilty and not guilty, leaving little room for compromise or negotiation. This all-or-nothing nature makes trials a high-risk transitional justice measure. A trial court's inability to find guilty a known war criminal or genocidaire will undermine international perception of that state's rule of law as well as government legitimacy at a domestic level. A well-executed trial can restore confidence in the government for those who have suffered at its hands and felt alienated from the rule of law by demonstrating that the justice system is committed to remaining uninfluenced by political pressure.

Prosecuting complicit government officers, especially heads of state, suggests that no individual is safe from prosecution in the wake of serious violations of human rights in a state, and has implications across international borders. While some have argued that the protection of the head of state and other top officials prevents an endless cycle of retribution, transitional justice scholar Kathryn Sikkink argues that heads of state must be prosecuted, largely to prevent human rights abuse in other nations.[4] Human rights advocates celebrating the advent of individual accountability for human rights violations internationally have echoed this sentiment. Following the conviction of Peruvian leader Alberto Fujimori, a Human Rights Watch scholar noted, "the Peruvian court has shown the world that even former heads of state cannot expect to get away with serious crimes."[5] If one head of state can get away with violating the rights of his citizens, there is nothing to stop others from doing the same. As Hitler stated in justifying his invasion of Poland in World War II, "who still talks nowadays of the extermination of the Armenians?"[6] Prosecuting heads of state provide an example for the world, establishing a record of wrongdoing that will stand as a testament to future would-be abusive leaders. If today's leaders do not defend victims and punitively punish those who commit human rights abuses, there will be no precedent to deter others from taking the same path.

Not only can trials establish a trend of democracy and deter human rights domestically, human rights trials can have positive effects on nations beyond the borders of the country conducting the prosecution. Sikkink calls this phenomenon "deterrence across borders," as the risk of prosecution increases the cost of committing abuses.[7] She argues that these highly publicized human rights trials have resulted in a "cascade of justice" that deters potential perpetrators of human rights violations around the world.[8]

Conversely, when human rights violations in a region go unnoticed, or all actors receive amnesty, heads of state may believe they can get away with committing crimes against their own people with little personal cost. Sikkink's research indicates that citizens in neighboring countries know about nearby foreign prosecutions and easily make connections to their own government's history of abuse.[9]

CRITIQUE OF HUMAN RIGHTS PROSECUTIONS

Human rights prosecutions do not comprehensively address every issue that a transitioning democracy faces, and some aspects of prosecutions may make the transition more challenging. First, it is difficult to determine which perpetrators will be tried and which are allowed to escape consequences.

State-sponsored trials are extremely costly (both in terms of time and money) to a judicial system, and it is, thus, impossible for a state to prosecute every individual who had anything to do with the human rights abuses of a past regime. States run the risk of entering an endless cycle of retribution and overrunning the prison system if they attempt to prosecute every foot soldier that participated in state-sponsored violence. For the sake of stability and the preservation of resources, states must make decisions about whom to prosecute. Handpicking defendants can result in allowing many who are not prosecuted to go without answering for their crimes. It also suggests to the public that there are some above prosecution or perhaps that those who were not tried or not found guilty are innocent in the eyes of the state.

State-sponsored trials also leave significant power in the hands of a judicial system that may not be prepared to determine guilt and mete out sentences to former government agents. In many Latin American states, the judicial branch is the last to fully recover from authoritarian control. Placing a Supreme Court that may or may not be prepared to make impartial decisions at the helm of the state's transitional justice movement could be disastrous for a recovering state if the court proves incapable. Most authoritarian regimes cease to maintain a separation of power between the executive and judicial branches, and it can be difficult for the courts to recover enough to try a case impartially. The Venezuelan Supreme Court, for example, "has ceased to function as an independent branch of government" and simply hands down verdicts that reflect the executive power's political will.[10] If Venezuela or a similarly positioned authoritarian nation attempted to conduct human rights trials in the immediate wake of a democratic transition, the new court would likely be overwhelmed by the task, and risk botching the trial.

While domestic prosecutions can be dangerous in light of biased or inexperienced courts, foreign and international prosecutions risk undermining the new government's authority or exacerbating tensions between the transitioning government and the international community. Foreign prosecutions sometimes take place when a nation is unwilling to extradite a criminal back to their home country for domestic prosecution. Such is the case with Bolivia's former head of state Gonzalo Sánchez de Lozada, who fled to the United States in 2011 and is unlikely ever to be extradited. Instead, victims in the United States are suing him in Federal civil court for reparations on a much smaller scale than the international public eye that would be present for a human rights trial. In this case, Bolivia has no power to try him and could be viewed as impotent in the international community for being unable to properly try and punish a known human rights criminal.[11]

International prosecutions, although less common for Latin American cases, can also undermine the transitioning state's authority and imply that the domestic government is incapable of conducting a proper trial. For example, some have accused the International Criminal Court of bias against Africa, as the large majority of their trials and convictions have been against African leaders. While those convicted are likely guilty of human rights violations, the court's focus on Africa rather than other western nations has built up some resentment between African nations and this international body.[12] Rwanda and Sudan are certainly two prominent examples of this problem more recently.

Perhaps the most significant deficiency in a transitioning democracy's reliance on human rights prosecutions is the failure to address the human aspect of forgiveness and reconciliation. While trials are an effective means to assess guilt and assign blame, they do not necessarily aid in the healing of society. While such factors cannot be summarized in a spreadsheet or graph, creating a strong and stable society built on mutual trust is a pivotal part of any nation's transition to democracy. It is challenging to measure the effect that domestic prosecutions have on social atmosphere, but the protests and demonstrations that inevitably surround courthouses that hold human rights trials suggest that trials can contribute to an environment of division through the establishment and encouragement of a dualistic polarity among members of society. While such division may not manifest itself in intrastate violence, the social divides are stark and cannot be ignored by a newly transitioning democracy. This concern has led many transitional justice researchers to shy away from the idea of domestic prosecutions, as they have viewed them as too dangerous to an already unstable nation. On a philosophical level, prosecutions can never recognize the complexity of human rights abuses and tends to reduce complicated human behavior to the seemingly simplistic categories of guilty and not guilty. For example, there was evidence

Efrain Rios Montt perpetrated violence against the Ixil Indians in Guatemala while later in life supporting aid to the same geographic region.[13]

In light of this critique and in order to better illuminate the effects human rights prosecutions can and do have on transitioning Latin American nations, this analysis now compares the practice of trials as a transitional mechanism with the creative peace process paying special attention to its ability as a nongovernmental solution to strengthen social and government trust.

STRENGTHS OF THE CREATIVE PEACE PROCESS

In his book *The Moral Imagination: the Art and Soul of Building Peace*, John Paul Lederach outlines his theory of the creative peace process.[14] He bases his approach to peace building on decades of work in the field negotiating international peace treaties and collaborations with global leaders to broker peace between various warring or otherwise conflicting groups within a nation. His approach to transition in a post-conflict nation focuses heavily on the need for community healing and forgiveness and prioritizes the rebuilding of social trust among citizens.

Lederach's approach depends on the presence of a willing leader to imagine a world in which the opposing parties live in harmony rather than at odds with one another. One of the key ways in which Lederach observes this ability for parties to imagine a more peaceful future is when leaders of both sides consider the future they envision for their children. Mediation and peace scholars recognize that the beginning of a mediation process requires a tremendous amount of faith on both sides as both parties must trust that the other will not break the terms and take advantage of their weakened position. As peace scholars John Darby and Roger Mac Ginty express, "the pre-negotiation phase of a peace process requires faith. It is nothing less than a high-risk gamble to ascertain the seriousness of other conflict participants."[15]

Acknowledging that need for immense faith, Lederach's approach to peace is theologically based, and draws upon principles of Christian morality. He breaks down the concept of the "moral imagination" into its two terms, explaining their origin and importance. Lederach acknowledges that the term "moral" may make some uncomfortable, as it is associated with religious dogma. Used in this context, however, Lederach insists that morality encourages us to aspire to something higher, "to transcend . . . what exists while still living in it."[16] Lederach's explanation for each person's capacity for imagination originates from the Christian account of creation, or the power to speak life into existence from nothing. Imagination, Lederach describes, "is the art of creating what does not exist."[17] Moral imagination, thus, breaks out of the expected and into the realm of new possibilities where peace is possible. This moral imagination is not simply a naïve ideal, but is "rooted in the day-to-day challenges of violence," yet is "capable of giving birth to that which does not yet exist," and generating "constructive responses and initiatives" in the face of such challenges.[18] The moral imagination paradigm finds an excellent home in debate instruction where participants learn to speak ideas into existence and aspire to arrive at a transcendent truth.

Lederach describes humanity as connected by a web to every other person in the community. This illustration indicates that there is not a single person within a community that is not vital to its survival. This shifts the perspective from that of an individual seeking his own good without consideration for the effects of his actions on other members of the community, to one that recognizes a connected and beloved community.

The web perspective makes human rights violations an irrational choice, as an action that harms a member of society would ultimately harm the leader ordering such abuse. "Violence is the behavior of someone incapable of imagining other solutions to the given problem."[19] The moral imagination, or the injection of discursive complexity into a community, allows a person to embrace multiple viewpoints and reimagine possible solutions to internal strife within a community. The principle goal of the creative peace process is to create a space in which members of a community reeling from a recent conflict can reconsider their position within that web and rebuild the connections necessary to support a thriving community.

Viewed this way, the creative peace process is less about telling a group of people or community the solution to their problem, and more focused on providing them with the discursive tools to express the complexity of their problems and encounter homegrown solutions. This approach has the potential to lead to lasting forgiveness and the strengthening of community trust at a level that is not possible with human rights prosecutions. Placing victims and perpetrators of human rights abuse together in the same room to discuss their differences can result in powerful change. The physical proximity between the two parties adds a human element that neither side can ignore. It is easy, especially once conflict has endured for generations, to simplify the issues to an "us versus them" paradigm that tends to dehumanize the opposing side. Taking on and building the strongest case for the opposing side through a debate exercise can break down such generalizations. The problem of dehumanization was well observed in the argumentation leading to the genocide in Rwanda.[20] Dehumanization rhetoric and argument is an inter-continental problem and we should be unafraid that an argumentation approach can avoid cultural imposition.

Multigenerational conflicts can become an assumed part of culture. Once a long-standing conflict has become entrenched in social identity, the easiest path forward is to perpetuate the status quo of violence. Part of the long-term danger that stems from conflict emerges from the reduction of complex history into "dualistic polarities that attempt to both describe and contain social reality in artificial ways."[21] Anytime a relationship between groups of people is simplified to right versus wrong, politics has been generalized and complexity ignored. It is within this typically ignored intricacy that a pathway toward peace can be found.

Peace building can begin when someone in the midst of a rhetorically oversimplified conflict recognizes the inevitable complexity present in relationships between warring groups. A peacemaker must embrace such intricacies, seek to transcend the norm of violence, and find multifaceted solutions to complex problems. This is where creativity comes in, and allows for the creation of wholeness from brokenness, and peace from hatred and violence. A willingness to risk life and relationships in order to pursue a path other than violence can be all that it takes to assure opposing sides that one is serious about considering a peaceful resolution to shared problems.

COMPARISON TO TRIALS

The creative peace process offers a community-centered approach to transitional justice and has the potential to operate a successful peacebuilding program outside of the confines of a government branch. One of the most important distinctions between human rights prosecutions and the creative peace approach is that Lederach's method does not rely on newly implemented democratic government mechanisms functioning properly under immense scrutiny and strain to guarantee success. Instead, the creative peace process takes place at the individual community level where progress is determined by the willingness of community members to embrace complexity. A grassroots approach *can* incorporate government involvement; however, it does not depend upon democratic institutions. In theory, all that is needed for the creative peace process to begin are a few participants from both sides willing to sit down and engage in meaningful dialogue and make compromises that allow them to live together in a peaceful community. This process can cut out the need for government mediation and instead place community members face-to-face with one another engaging in productive dialogue.

A community focus allows this transitional justice measure to affect social trust in a much more direct way than human rights prosecutions. Creating space in which members of a community can interact face to face allows for a significantly more personal experience than what participants would experience in trials. Where trials carry the risk of international exposure of weak democratic institutions, the creative peace process carries with it the personal reputations and livelihood of each participating member. If my neighbor fails to keep the peace agreement, my children are at risk. The risks involved ensures that nothing other than interpersonal trust can be bred in this process. The creative peace process can also directly affect a greater number of people than trials. While governments are limited by time and resources to a fairly small number of people that can be prosecuted for their crimes, a creative peace process can take place in any size community and encompass all citizens willing to participate.

Lederach's model also encourages participants to recognize the complexity behind conflict and makes them less likely to view problems through the lens of absolutes that domestic prosecutions unavoidably foster. A trial necessarily creates a combative environment in which one side wins at the expense of the other. Legal practice does not leave much room for mercy or forgiveness, and may exacerbate tensions between opponents, forcing them to seek reconciliation outside the courtroom. Within the confines of a courtroom, victims and perpetrators cannot speak directly; instead following a particular set of rules and procedures, and share only the part of their story that supports their desired outcome. Human rights prosecutions leave little room for complex dialogue, as the simplest explanation of the perpetration of a crime is usually the only explanation that makes it into evidence.

The creative peace process, conversely, challenges community members to see beyond easy labels of good and bad, winner and loser, and strike at the root of complex problems. Creating a space in which parties are not constrained by rules of procedure and instead have the freedom to imagine creative solutions is key to the formation of this new, hope-filled future. When widows can sit across the table from soldiers that took the lives of their husbands and children, there is greater potential for restoration and forgiveness than would have been possible through a human rights trial. Creative community peace solutions allow for otherwise impossible dialogue that acknowledges real fear and hurt on both sides.

The creative peace process may have the potential to foster peace that lasts longer than that achieved by a guilty verdict. If community members desire a lasting peace, they must make living together in harmony a reality, as the government will not provide a safety net on which citizens can fall back. When citizens do not trust the government, a community-based solution is likely to be better for all parties. Lederach argues that, "politics, economics, and global structures have become so inauthentic that few of us truly believe in them. We live in a paradox; the things most omnipresent that govern our lives are the very things from which we feel distant."[22]

In the midst of a high-profile human rights prosecution, justice can feel inaccessible to average citizens in a rural village. Providing a process by which citizens of any class can participate in the healing of their own community gives community members a sense of purpose as they aid their nation in the healing process—each of which are essential aspects of the creation of a strong democracy, which depends on proactive citizens.

CRITIQUE OF THE CREATIVE PEACE PROCESS

While Lederach's process has the potential for social healing and political forgiveness at a fundamental level in a transitioning nation, the very nature of this low-risk approach makes it incapable of producing some of the results made possible by human rights trials. The creative peace process could encounter difficulties in nations that lack willing participants or the requisite knowledge for implementation, and instead foster dependency on an outside party. The lack of material consequences surrenders any chance of international deterrence and may not have any repression deterrence effects beyond the immediate community.

In some cases, a third party may be required to initiate the beginnings of the peace process. When this occurs, the presence of an outside mediator could foster a dependency on international assistance. If the two parties expect that the outside mediator will always be present to maintain peace, they have little incentive to create necessary structures that will allow them to broker a durable peace. Encouraging paternalism is dangerous in any situation and especially so when the good exchanged is peace.

One of the main advantages of human rights prosecutions is their public nature as spectacles that can initiate a deterrence effect both domestically and internationally. Material punishment coupled with public exposure of the truth creates an environment hostile to further human rights abuse. The grassroots nature and structure of the creative peace process, by contrast, ensures that effects remain isolated. Using only a creative peace process surrenders the opportunity to use the abuse that has occurred in one nation to set a precedent that human rights violations are not acceptable and will have consequences.

Compared to the research on trials, this creative peace approach lacks the strong empirical evidence to support the creative peace process's effect on democratic institutions. The very nature of a community-centered approach makes it unlikely to influence the development of democracy on a national level. Values like forgiveness and community trust are nearly impossible to quantify, and do not lend themselves to mathematical analysis. While empirical indicators can measure social trust, there are currently no academic, empirical studies that confirm the direct results of a creative peace process in a community as compared to a community that has not undergone a creative peace process.

While this approach is particularly helpful for societies that have undergone a civil war, it may or may not be applicable to state-sponsored violence. If there is a divide between government officials and civilians rather than groups of citizens, the creative peace process may need to take place at the governmental level rather than the community level, which may not see the same results on such a large scale. Shifting the scale of the creative peace process and changing the types of participants involved could render peace negotiation based on forgiveness and individual relationships ineffective.

HUMAN RIGHTS PROSECUTIONS IN GUATEMALA

This section will focus on a case study of the two aforementioned approaches to transitional justice. A side-by-side analysis of a human rights prosecution and a creative peace process in a post-conflict nation will provide insight into the advantages of each approach in practice and point to avenues for further investigation. I will begin with a brief overview of the civil conflict and subsequent human rights abuses that took place in Guatemala before describing the most prominent human rights trial that has taken place in recent years and analyzing its potential effects.

While Guatemala has experienced prosecutions at various levels, the case I will examine in this chapter is its landmark trial of a former head of state.[23] The Ríos Montt trial is the most internationally recognizable transitional justice measure that has come from Guatemala in recent years, and demonstrates the potential a widely publicized human rights trial can have on the strength of democracy within a state and across international borders.

BRIEF HISTORY OF THE GUATEMALAN CIVIL WAR

In 1960 a civil war broke out in Guatemala that would last for thirty-six years, take the lives of over two hundred thousand Guatemalans, and see the disappearance of over fifty thousand citizens, 83 percent of which were indigenous Mayans.[24] During the seventeen-month military rule of General Efraín Ríos Montt, egregious human rights violations took place in the country, especially in the Ixil triangle, where Ríos Montt attempted to destroy the indigenous population. A UN report, indicating the culpability of the national government, showed that between 70 and 90 percent of Ixil communities were wiped out due to the state-sponsored genocidal campaign that took place during the war years.[25] Children were forcibly adopted and assimilated, families were torn apart, women were sexually violated, and many members of Ixil communities were brutally executed in their own homes and communities.

Many killings were politically motivated attempts to rid the nation of communists, keep the indigenous population from joining guerrilla groups, or reclaim historically disputed land. The conflict left the countryside destroyed by scorched earth combat methods, and civil institutions were similarly decimated by authoritarian and military rule throughout the war years. Democratic mechanisms were undermined for years, as Guatemala saw its congress dissolved and reconvened several times during the war. A UN-commissioned report concluded that the state, rather than the guerilla groups it blamed, was responsible for 93 percent of the human rights abuses that took place in the nation during the civil war.[26] In total, reports indicated that the government killed 18.3 percent of the nation's indigenous population, which testimony suggested was comparable to the approximately 20 to 25 percent murder rate present in other acknowledged genocide cases such as in Rwanda and Srebrenica. Military officials reported that their orders were clear: they were to kill any indigenous person they encountered.[27] The Ríos Montt case is a key example of the struggle for justice within a conflicted justice system in Guatemala.

RÍOS MONTT GENOCIDE TRIAL

In January 2012, Ríos Montt was subpoenaed and subsequently charged with genocide and crimes against humanity by the domestic courts along with his chief of military intelligence, José Mauricio Rodríguez Sánchez. After a year of delays by Ríos Montt's defense team, the historic trial began in March 2013. It took two hours to read all of the charges listed on an indictment that went on for over one hundred pages, and the court heard the testimony of one hundred survivors.[28]

Aside from constant procedural attempts of the defense to bring proceedings to an end, the court faced many obstacles and was temporarily suspended three times before the May 10 final verdict. After much delay and two months of testimony, closing arguments were heard on May 8 and 9.

Despite the attempts of the defense to skirt the issue at hand, on May 10, 2013, Ríos Montt became the first head of state convicted of human rights abuses in a domestic court. Thirty years after the end of his rule, Ríos Montt was sentenced to fifty years in prison for genocide and thirty years for crimes against humanity.[29] This verdict was historic not only for Guatemala, but also for the region as a whole, as the Guatemalan court proved that it was possible to overcome the resistance present in a post-conflict society and successfully convict a known war criminal within the domestic court system.

Rejoicing at the historic verdict did not last long, however, as the judgment was annulled only ten days later by the Guatemalan Constitutional Court (the highest judicial body in the nation) on what many view as questionable legal grounds. Despite the annulment, dissenting opinions in the Court's holding injected a spirit of debate and deliberation previously lacking in Guatemalan politics.[30]

In the ensuing retrial, Ríos Montt was declared incompetent, faced no prison time, and did not have to attend the trial proceedings. This was primarily due to his advanced age. By the time of these most contemporary cases, Rios Montt was in his nineties. In short, the verdict in this new trial could only result in a symbolic statement reaffirming the victims and their families that the state recognized the injustice they suffered. Ríos Montt's death on April 1, 2018, put an abrupt end to the proceedings. Following his death, activists in Guatemala, alongside the United Nations, urged the trial court to proceed for the sake of the protection of human rights.[31] Despite these pleas, since his death, the trial has not continued.

The case of General Efraín Ríos Montt illustrates the complex paradox of progress and problems that emerge from human rights prosecutions in Latin America and perhaps globally.

CONTEMPORARY IMPLICATIONS

Challenges, both domestic and international, are endemic to human rights trials, given their high-risk nature. As in Guatemala, inconsistent verdicts and the lengthy process of building a strong enough case to convict a well-known war criminal is not uncommon in the region. Human rights groups seeking justice in Latin America have faced death threats, torture, kidnappings, and bureaucratic resistance at every step. It seems as though the problem lies in the pattern of behavior present among perpetrators of human rights abuses. Individuals that have committed human rights violations have already weighed the options and determined that their actions are or ought to be exempt from the law. Every decision made following the initial decision to violate the fundamental human rights of their citizens is colored by that logic. It is uncomfortable and unfamiliar to be subject to the power of a competing branch of government, and abusive leaders tend to respond to the pressure in the only way they know how: attempting to continue to evade the rule of law. These actors need a new paradigm that fosters deliberation instead of destruction; rational debate instead of killing.

CREATIVE PEACE IN GUATEMALA

While the collection of evidence and preparation for the trial of Ríos Montt and his associates took many years to finally culminate in a trial, several programs have been ongoing since the beginning of the peace process in 1996. Such programs are mostly extra-governmental, but some have seen government sponsorship or support of their community reconciliation work. Programs not involved in complex legal processes or cumbersome governmental oversight have the potential to have a stronger impact at the local level than large human rights prosecutions that take place at the macro level. In Guatemala particularly, the balance of community reconciliation and mediation programs with the national human rights trials has highlighted the key differences between the two approaches to peace after conflict and transitional justice.

Most initiators of these programs have come from within the Catholic Church and Mennonite nonprofits. Beyond religious organizations, however, international bodies such as the United Nations and Organization of American States (OAS) have also taken part in peace building programs in Guatemala and the surrounding region. The religious communities have initiated support groups, community strengthening projects, and truth-telling forums that foster dialogue between community members from both sides of the civil war. International organizations tend to focus on research and truth telling leading to policy recommendations. These remedies often manifest themselves as truth commissions, research studies, or policy memos with recommendations for local government officials. These programs are often small in scale, but have the potential to significantly impact the lives of participants, especially in regard to their relationships with others in the community.

As Julie Hart of Mennonite Central Committee states, "the process of sustainable peace is about rebuilding broken relationships."[32] To that end, Catholic dioceses in Guatemala have formed concerted efforts since the early 2000s to foster reconciliation, truth telling, and forgiveness in communities. There are three main models that the Guatemalan church and other International nongovernmental organizations have used in an attempt to bring healing and reconciliation to scarred communities in Guatemala. First is the Catholic Church's trauma healing project. Launching its own investigation into the human rights violations and violence that took place during the civil war, the church compiled a report (*The Recuperation of Historical Memory Report*) and built a program responsive to the needs identified within that report.[33] The resulting program established small groups led by trained professionals that would lead rehabilitation and self-help sessions for victims of torture and other wartime violence.[34] The groups meet regularly within the dioceses most heavily impacted by the war and provide a variety of services including exhumation and proper reburial of relatives and loved ones, reflection, and group and individual counseling. The program has also begun training community leaders as mental health promoters that can care for many suffering from post-traumatic stress disorder. In many rural communities, where violence was most intensely concentrated during the war, there is no access to professional mental health treatment due to a more general lack of health professionals. These groups have proved a versatile model that can function in a variety of settings to provide an outlet for victims to share their pain in a supportive forum. Despite the lack of formal therapy, the church has found that the simple act of sharing one's story with a sympathetic group and learning that others feel similar pain can be a cathartic and healing experience.[35]

This particular approach is also self-sustaining and efficient. The church provides the initial training of group leaders before sending them into their respective communities for group leadership and may pay any startup fees associated with initiating the meeting of the group. Once groups have begun and formed strong relationships, they require little to no more funding or support from the church that provided the initial training. Relying on the relationships they have built, these groups have all the tools they need to be effective agents of change in their communities. If groups form strong relationships between members and meet regularly to discuss important issues, they will attract the attention of other community members, which could have a multiplying effect locally. In evaluations of the project, researchers discovered that the only weakness of this program is that it has not reached a very large proportion of the victims affected by wartime trauma. So far, the program involves approximately ten thousand participants, which is barely a fraction of those affected by the war.[36] Though there are limitations to this type of peace process, small trauma groups provide a low-cost solution that can yield significant, albeit slow, results.

The second model run by the Mennonite Central Committee seeks to provide education, post-war healing, and a network for peacemakers. The REDPAZ educational organization provides training in topics such as discrimination and genocide, creating communities of peace, and social transformation. Students from diverse communities learn together and form relationships outside of the classroom that can enrich their understanding of peace and the meaning of loving their neighbor. This program aims to equip young leaders with the tools they need to return to their respective communities and foster positive change. Similar to the small groups, this approach focuses on an initial investment of time and resource in hopes that students will multiply the effects of that investment many times over by expanding the reach of the organization through education. At this time, the program has only had approximately 150 students.[37]

Finally, the OAS created a subcommittee following the conclusion of the Guatemalan civil war to regulate and track the application of the peace accords and ensure that peace was maintained. Lacking police powers or the command of a standing army, these international bodies worked in the area in which they could influence Guatemala's peaceful development most: inter-status dialogue. The OAS and UN jointly started several series of dialogue sessions between members of the government and members of communities on topic such as rural development, rights and identity of indigenous people, economic development, and modernizing the armed forces.[38]

One of the groundbreaking aspects of the writing of the peace accords following the conclusion of the civil war was the intentional involvement of "representatives from diverse sectors of the Guatemalan public in defining the substantive agenda of the peace talks."[39] In keeping with the emphasis on diversity of opinion, the UN and OAS followed this same model in creating their dialogues, inviting police officers, university professors, farmers, army officers, and participants from other diverse backgrounds. The meetings took place in three-hour blocks once per week and each included over one hundred participants. Groups were assigned discussion questions, discussed as a large group, broke into smaller groups, and eventually settling on a consensus statement that would then be shared publicly.[40] Placing people from different walks of life in the same room centered on the same discussion helped to rebuild trust between all members of society. Unavoidable in these groups were individuals that had fought on both sides of the war. Not only were members of previously opposing sides interacting with one another, they were working together on tangible solutions to build a peaceful future in their shared nation.

GUATEMALAN TRUTH COMMISSION

It is worth noting that much of the work being done with human rights prosecutions and in the creative mediation and peace process in Guatemala depends upon the information discovered through a nationally sponsored truth commission: the Commission for Historical Clarification. The commission formed in 1994 with the signing of the peace accords and operated for three years collecting testimony and information from thousands of victims and witnesses. This commission was extremely effective in its ability to collect and analyze large amounts of information. The commission was not permitted to name any potential perpetrators they investigated, however, given the pressure from society and the government on those involved with the human rights prosecutions to not accuse certain influential members of society, this mandate made it easier for the commission to tell the truth about what happened. The commission consisted of UN-selected experts with no ties to Guatemala, resulting in a panel that was unbiased, but lacked the language and cultural familiarity to earn the trust of Guatemalans. Some victims doubted a committee of outsiders that spent six months investigating a fourteen-year conflict and lacked the power to name perpetrators could make any difference.[41] This suspicion and lack of trust may have hindered the commission's evidence collection, but their data paved the way for transitional justice.

Behind the veil of anonymity, the commission revealed the key information that has been used in the human rights prosecutions and the aforementioned community-based reconciliation projects such as the fact that the government perpetrated 93 percent of the violence and that 83 percent of victims were Mayan.[42] After compiling the report, the commissioners presented it to the national government on February 25, 1999, providing recommendations and summarized findings to government officials and members of the Guatemalan congress. Calling for judicial reform as well as reparation and efforts dedicated to remembrance at the national level, the commission's report was historic among truth commissions internationally due to the sheer amount of information collected and findings presented.

Twenty-one years after the presentation of findings from the commission, the government has yet to respond to its recommendations. While the slow government response to the findings in the report is disappointing, the publication of a synthesis of so much testimony is significant and paves the way for future advances in the reconciliation process in Guatemala. Without this landmark report, the human rights prosecutions would not have had enough evidence to begin a trial, and the community creative peace process programs would have lacked the public support and general information necessary to garner public participation. Guatemala's journey toward peace has benefitted dramatically from this commission, and it is likely that other nations in the region would do well to begin their peace process with an effective and thorough truth commission similar to Guatemala's.

Following closely on the heels of this report, the Catholic Church issued its own report, *The Recovery of Historical Memory*, which collected the personal testimonies of victims, resulting in the documentation of over fifty-five thousand human rights violations.[43] This report gave voice to victims and provided 1,500 pages of raw material for education and reconciliation. Coming after the Commission for Historical Clarification, this report reinforced their findings and published abridged versions that were more accessible to the common citizen and useful for starting conversations in a community setting.

Both of these attempts to report the truth and consolidate a coherent narrative of the events that took place during the course of Guatemala's civil war are key pieces of the peace and reconciliation process there. In any post-conflict society, public accessibility of a version of events provides the basis from which transitional justice efforts will flow.

CONCLUSION

The peace that Christ preached, according to Christians, is the peace of shalom. That is, the peace of Christ is understood not only as the absence of war, but the product of justice and harmony in the relationships between men, God, and creation. It is a peace that conquers traps, slavery, and death. It is not the peace you would find in the cemetery — the peace of inaction, silence, and death, as Guatemalan Christians have expressed; but it is the peace that is the fruit of justice that is reached in the recognition of the brokenness of humanity.[44]

Human rights prosecutions offer a national, justice-centered approach that can lead to lower rates of domestic repression, stronger judicial institutions, and increased respect for human rights internationally. Despite these benefits, human rights prosecutions fail to address the human need for forgiveness and reconciliation at the community level and can cause deeper divisions that cannot be healed within the confines of a courtroom. The creative peace approach, conversely, offers a community-centered, faith-based approach to transitional justice, allowing community members to build relationships based on renewed trust. This approach does not require involvement of the state, which makes it a low-cost and replicable program, however, the community style of this transitional measure makes it inherently unlikely to influence national policy or areas outside the immediate community.

The insufficiency of either approach alone to eradicate the specter of human rights abuse in Latin American nations suggests that collaboration between these two deliberative approaches is necessary. The strengths of each suggest that a combination is possible, and, perhaps, preferable. This analysis proposes that successful and fair human rights trials of key high-ranking individuals, alongside many opportunities for community members to engage in creative peace settings, would make for the ideal recovery for a transitioning nation in Latin America. Much like the Gacaca courts in Rwanda, such trials are important to social legitimacy. Guatemala's example demonstrates the beginnings of a successful transition. Latin America, in its third wave of democracy, has the potential to strengthen its democratic institutions and enjoy greater freedom and economic success when it operates as a successful liberal democracy that relies on democratic deliberation and debate rather than state coercion. This development will not occur without increased respect for human rights that can only result from reconciliation with history.

The groundwork that has been done to collect truth and testimony, coupled with successful efforts at peace building that have already taken place, indicate that progress in Guatemala's transitional process is both possible and necessary. Creative peace models have the potential to aid in the development of strong and enduring democratic institutions in Latin America by fostering citizen engagement in deliberative truth-seeking.

NOTES

1. Nicaragua, Spain, and Honduras have both relied largely on amnesties to progress post-conflict with few or no efforts to prosecute perpetrators. See: Astrid Bothmann, "Transitional Justice in Nicaragua 1990–2012: Drawing a Line under the Past" (2015); and Kathryn Sikkink and Carrie Booth Walling, "The Impact of Human Rights Trials in Latin America," *Journal of Peace Research* 44, no. 4 (2007): 427–45.
2. Juan E. Mendez, "Accountability for Past Abuses," *Human Rights Quarterly* 19, no. 2 (1997): 255–82, https://doi.org/10.1353/hrq.1997.0018.
3. William Mishler and Richard Rose, "What Are the Origins of Political Trust? Testing Institutional and Cultural Theories in Post-Communist Societies," *Comparative Political Studies* 34, no. 1 (February 1, 2001): 30–62, https://doi.org/10.1177/0010414001034001002.
4. Kathryn Sikkink, *The Justice Cascade: How Human Rights Prosecutions Are Changing World Politics*, 1st ed. (New York: W. W. Norton & Co., 2011).
5. "Peru's Fujimori Gets 25 Years Prison for Massacres," *Reuters*, April 7, 2009, https://www.reuters.com/article/us-peru-fujimori/perus-fujimori-convicted-of-human-rights-crimes-idUSTRE5363RH20090407.
6. Adolf Hitler, 1939. English version of the German document handed to Louis P. Lochner in Berlin. It first appeared in Lochner's *What about Germany?* (New York: Dodd, Mead & Co., 1942): 1–4. The Nuremberg Tribunal later identified the document as L-3 or Exhibit USA-28. For the German original cf. *Akten zur Deutschen Auswärtigen Politik 1918–1945*, Serie D. Band VII (Baden-Baden, 1956): 171–72. http://www.armenian-genocide.org/hitler.html.
7. Hunjoon Kim and Kathryn Sikkink, "Explaining the Deterrence Effect of Human Rights Prosecutions for Transitional Countries," *International Studies Quarterly* 54, no. 4 (December 1, 2010): 939–63.
8. Kim and Sikkink, "Explaining the Deterrence Effect of Human Rights Prosecutions for Transitional Countries," 939–63.
9. Sikkink, *The Justice Cascade*, 175.
10. Human Rights Watch, "Venezuela," Human Rights Watch, January 12, 2017, https://www.hrw.org/world-report/2017/country-chapters/venezuela.
11. "The Legal Case against Gonzalo Sánchez de Lozada Moves into High Gear: The Democracy Center," accessed January 15, 2018, https://democracyctr.org/the-legal-case-against-gonzalo-sanchez-de-lozada-moves-into-high-gear/.
12. "ICC's Toughest Trial: Africa vs. 'Infamous Caucasian Court,'" *Reuters*, October 28, 2016, https://www.reuters.com/article/us-africa-icc/iccs-toughest-trial-africa-vs-infamous-caucasian-court-idUSKCN12S1U3.
13. Chi-Dooh Li. *Buy This Land*. 2012.
14. John Paul Lederach, *The Moral Imagination: The Art and Soul of Building Peace* (New York: Oxford University Press, 2005).
15. J. Darby, Roger Mac Ginty, and Roger Mac Ginty, *Contemporary Peacemaking: Conflict, Peace Processes and Post-War Reconstruction* (London: Palgrave Macmillan Limited, 2008), http://ebookcentral.proquest.com/lib/bayloru/detail.action?docID=4326751, 2.
16. John Paul Lederach, *The Moral Imagination: The Art and Soul of Building Peace* (Oxford ; New York: Oxford University Press, 2005), 28.
17. Lederach, *The Moral Imagination*, 28.
18. Lederach, *The Moral Imagination*, 29.
19. Vicençe Fisas, *La Paz Es Posible* (Barcelona, Spain: Intermon Oxfam, 2002), 58.
20. Kennedy Ndahiro, "In Rwanda, We Know All about Dehumanizing Language: Years of Cultivated Hatred Led to Death on a Horrifying Scale," *The Atlantic*, April 13, 2019.
21. Fisas, *La Paz Es Posible*, 35.
22. Lederach, *The Moral Imagination*, 28.

23. Human Rights Watch, "World Report 2017: Rights Trends in Guatemala," Human Rights Watch, January 12, 2017, https://www.hrw.org/world-report/2017/country-chapters/guatemala.

24. "The Guatemala Genocide Case," *CJA* (blog), accessed March 12, 2018, http://cja.org/what-we-do/litigation/the-guatemala-genocide-case/.

25. Peter Canby, "The Maya Genocide Trial," *The New Yorker*, May 3, 2013, https://www.newyorker.com/news/daily-comment/the-maya-genocide-trial.

26. Canby, "The Maya Genocide Trial."

27. Original quote in Spanish from former soldier Hugo Ramiro Leonardo "Indio visto, indio muerto"; Canby, "The Maya Genocide Trial."

28. International Justice Monitor, "The Guatemala Genocide Case."

29. "After the Verdict: What Ríos Montt's Conviction Means for Guatemala," *WOLA*, accessed March 11, 2018, https://www.wola.org/analysis/after-the-verdict-what-rios-Ríos Montts-conviction-means-for-guatemala/.

30. Corte de Constitucionalidad Guatemala [Guatemalan Constitutional Court] No. 1904–2013, May 20, 2013 at 002067 (Guat.), http://www.right2info.org/resources/publications/votos-razonados-may-21-2013.

31. "United Nations, Activists Urge Guatemala to Continue Trial of Deceased Dictator Efraín Ríos Montt," *Telesur*, April 6, 2018, https://videosenglish.telesurtv.net/video/665736/the-1954-us-coup-in-guatemala/.

32. Julie Hart, "Grassroots Peacebuilding in Post Civil War Guatemala: Three Models of Hope," *Mennonite Life* 60, no. 1, March 2005 (March 18, 2014), https://ml.bethelks.edu/issue/vol-60-no-1/article/grassroots-peacebuilding-in-post-civil-war-guatema/.

33. Jeffrey Haynes, *Routledge Handbook of Religion and Politics* (New York: Routledge, 2008).

34. Haynes, *Routledge Handbook of Religion and Politics*.

35. Haynes, *Routledge Handbook of Religion and Politics*.

36. Hart, "Grassroots Peacebuilding in Post Civil War Guatemala: Three Models of Hope."

37. Hart, "Grassroots Peacebuilding in Post Civil War Guatemala: Three Models of Hope."

38. Hart, "Grassroots Peacebuilding in Post Civil War Guatemala: Three Models of Hope."

39. Enrique Alvarez and Tania Palencia Prado, "Guatemala's Peace Process: Context, Analysis and Evaluation," *Conciliation Resources*, February 7, 2012, http://www.c-r.org/accord/public-participation/guatemala-s-peace-process-context-analysis-and-evaluation.

40. Hart, "Grassroots Peacebuilding in Post Civil War Guatemala: Three Models of Hope."

41. "Roberto Cabrera, Guatemala—The Brudnick Center on Violence and Conflict," accessed April 6, 2018, http://www.northeastern.edu/brudnickcenter/past_conferences/third_world_views-2/transcriptions-of-presentations/roberto-cabrera-guatemala/.

42. "Truth Commission: Guatemala," United States Institute of Peace, accessed March 27, 2018, https://www.usip.org/publications/1997/02/truth-commission-guatemala.

43. "Roberto Cabrera, Guatemala—The Brudnick Center on Violence and Conflict."

44. María Teresa Ruiz, *Los Cristianos Y Los Derechos Humanos En Guatemala*, Colección Análisis, trans. Rebecca Voth (San José, Costa Rica: DEI, 1994).

NINE
China Rising

Debate Programs across China

As the most populated nation in the world, the status of discursive complexity in China is of primary importance. More than one billion people live in the sovereignty of Chinese politics. Recent events regarding the viral epidemic originating in China heighten the concerns over transparency in public policy and the role of critical inquiry in promoting human well-being. This chapter will overview four areas relating to the question of discursive complexity in China: (1) the twentieth century history of China with regard to large scale human violence, (2) the emergence of Chinese Communism in the mid-twentieth century and its violent relationship to the Chinese public, (3) the recent controversy regarding the global pandemic originating from Wuhan, China, and (4) successful efforts to teach debate in China.

The history of China stretches thousands of years, over a vast Asian geography, and involves layers of complexity far beyond the reasonable scope of this analysis. The past one hundred years do provide a reasonable starting point for understanding how discursive complexity—particularly through the pedagogy of debate—can reduce the problems of human violence, eliminationism, and democide in Asia, China, and of course throughout the world, as already noted in these chapters. The twentieth century is sometimes referred to as the age of genocide. It is useful to pause and consider some additional intellectual tools for considering and analyzing the problem of human violence. The terminologies of democide and eliminationism are important.

Genocide is a term that was developed by Raphael Lemkin in the aftermath of the Holocaust in Europe. The term is intended to focus on state-initiated efforts to exterminate an ethnic group.[1] The definition is enshrined in international law and is utilized in a variety of settings such as the International Criminal Court. Of course, there are broader terminologies of violence that consider similar acts of large-scale violence that may not be focused upon ethnicity. In *The Rhetoric of Genocide*, the three terms—genocide, eliminationism, and democide—are described as overlaying circles of description with genocide being the most focused of terms and democide being the broadest.[2] All three share a common intent of killing many people who are enemies of a statist supremacy. This scholarly trajectory, began in 2006 with collaboration at the United States Holocaust Memorial Museum, continues with a goal of utilizing debate as a pedagogy for establishing individual resistance to the inherent fuel of such super-states: propaganda. Propaganda as well, explained by philosophers like Jacques Ellul, are intrinsic human habits that regularly overflow into despotic statist acts jeopardizing human well-being.[3]

Eliminationism is a term coined by Daniel Goldhagen.[4] Perhaps because of the growing international stigma against genocide after World War II, governments became more sensitive to the special focus on extermination of ethnic groups. The goal of eliminating political opponents is the purpose of eliminationism. It is equally deadly and profoundly unjust. Ethnic and political motives may comingle, and in this respect, the boundaries of these two worlds can be blurry. This terminology is necessarily useful in understanding Asian politics, and especially the conditions and preconditions of contemporary China.

The additional terminology that operates at the broadest level for describing state violence against human beings is democide.[5] Rummel's term simply suggests death by state. Any individual dying because of the designs of the state is counted in his well-kept accounting of state sponsored deaths. Rummel's website and scholarship provides one of the most revised scholarly considerations of mass killings around the world over the past few centuries. His calculations garner the opinion of various experts, and therefore provide theoretical ranges of what experts believe is the total loss of life under different political regimes around the world. Rummel's broader consideration gives rise to awkward but still deadly considerations like starvation. Most experts would agree that the starvations taking place during Holmodor in the Ukraine from 1932 to 1933 were the results of state-sponsored attacks on the people of that region by the Soviet Union.[6] These acts are not as easy to identify as soldiers ordered to fire on civilians or gas chambers that can be observed at Treblinka or other major sites of the Holocaust. This broader systemic neglect and enforced deprivations are parts of genocidal motives, but the broader terms allow better descriptions of the relatively obtuse ways that states go about killing the innocent. It is with all three terms in mind—genocide, eliminationism, and democide—that we approach an approximation of the human condition and the striving for discursive complexity in Asia, and particularly in China.

Early twentieth-century Asia was dominated by a straightforward supremacist power: Japan. The unique religion of Shintoism created on the island of Japan a powerful internal ethic about the perceived eternal domination of the Japanese ethnic community. Japan was incredibly violent in its efforts to expel from its shores any efforts to spread Christianity. For hundreds of years, the Japanese preference for Shintoism and disdain for all teleological rivals was violently expressed. By the early twentieth century, Japan's nationalist strength and growing industrial power made it a domineering and deadly force for the entire continent of Asia. Much of twenty-first-century politics in Asia remains dominated by the memory of Japanese violence in Asia stretching fully from the northern to southern reaches of the continent. Chinese and Korean memories of twentieth-century geopolitics focus upon the brutal violence carried out in vicious symbolic actions.[7]

Recent scholarship does focus on the failure to account for Japanese atrocities across Asia:

> One such statement is provided by Roger Baldwin, leader of the American Civil Liberties Union in 1947, when he explains in a letter why Japan's use of mass violence within its colonial empire and the countries occupied by the Imperial Japanese Army were hard to consider as genocide: I do not think you will get very far with the subject of genocide in relation to the Japanese occupation of Korea. That followed the regular old pattern of imperialism except for the single feature that Korea was annexed as an integral part of Japan . . . I doubt whether you will find anything properly relating to genocide in Korean experience. There was no attempt at exterminating a people on racial grounds.
> The obvious fading out of Japanese war crimes from the discussion of genocides after 1945 again highlights the Eurocentric perspective of the definition as it was later accepted by the UN Convention. Many other Asian cases of mass violence would consequently not be considered as genocides, be it due to a lack of interest in the single events or the narrow definition.[8]

Jacob's effort to introduce the broader notions of Japanese atrocities in Asia finds this explanation in his introduction to the book on the topic in 2019:

> While Deborah Mayersen and Annie Pohlman discussed the legacies and possible preventions of genocide and mass atrocities in Asia (in their book of the same name), they failed to include Japan, one of the main perpetrator states in the region, omitting the impact of Japan's colonial empire and the legacies of the war crimes trials in the British Empire in other regions of the continent, that stimulated "fundamental conflicts over the national character" of the postcolonial nation states, and the protagonists in the evolving struggles "were engaged in a struggle to reshape the fundamentals of national character," and therefore began to destroy enemies who represented a different national

idea for the future. In Indonesia, China, and Cambodia, millions of lives were destroyed while the perpetrators, as Robert Cribb put it, "saw themselves as shaping the character of their nation by removing a category of people who could never be a legitimate part of it." This category was defined by membership of the communist party in Indonesia and by imputed class membership in China and Cambodia, but the rationale for purging was similar in all three cases. The nation as it was envisaged by those in charge could not survive the presence of masses of people with different national conceptions.[9]

R. J. Rummel estimates that Japan killed almost six million people across the continent of Asia between 1937 and 1945. Scholars continue to struggle with the naming and cataloging of this violence. Rummel explained the tactical nature of democide:

> the less democratic a regime, the more unchecked and unbalanced power at the center, the more it should commit democide. Democide becomes a device of rule, as in eliminating possible opponents, or a means for achieving one's ideological goal, as in the purification of one's country of an alien race or the reconstruction of society.[10]

Here we find the pretext to Goldhagen's more recent exploration of this violence in the term of "eliminationism." The excruciating detail of Rummel's work with regard to Japanese supremacist violence is apparent in his 1997 work:

> A problem is how to handle the forty-three massacres for which there is a question mark (line 221). For the six massacres in this list for which there are estimates, the average is 1,348 killed. In China, where many more reports of the number massacred were available, the average killed for all the low estimates was 800. Moreover, the average killed in massacres in Indonesia (lines 253–284) for which figures are given is a low of 820 (line 286). Taking the three averages into account (1,348; 800; and 820), I assume an average of 800 for the 43 question marks (line 220). This average times the number of question marks gives a low of 42,000 killed; a high of 85,000 if doubled. These figures are surely conservative, since they do not take into account the many massacres that undoubtedly occurred, but were not reported in the sources. Consider that in the Philippines alone, where after the war American military teams made a special effort to investigate all Japanese massacres, about 90,000 civilians were reported killed (lines 339 and 340).[11]

Rummel provides this summary of the Japanese killings in China:

> we should not ignore the Japanese democide in China. Japanese indiscriminate killing of Chinese became widely known and almost universally condemned as criminal in the late 1930s. World opinion became especially horrified over what became known as "The Rape of Nanking." Nanking was the Nationalist capital and the home of many foreign missionaries, diplomats, and newsmen. As a result, when the Japanese army conquered Nanking and subjected the population to

monstrous indiscriminate killing, looting, and rape, the news was immediately communicated to the international community. Likely some 200,000 Chinese civilians and unarmed soldiers were killed in and around Nanking. And this was not an isolated case. From one village, town, or city to another, the Japanese often killed their inhabitants, executed suspected former Nationalist soldiers, beat to death or buried alive those disobeying their orders or showing insufficient respect, and mistreating many more others. Much of this killing was done in cold blood, and thoughtlessly, as one would swat a fly. An example of this that most sticks in my mind is of one Japanese officer's use of Chinese prisoners for "kill practice" by his inexperienced soldiers. Moreover, the Japanese terror-bombed Chinese cities and towns killing civilians at random (that this was done by the Anglo-American Allies during World War II hardly excuses it—official American protests to Japan at the time condemned such barbarism). And they widely employed germ warfare. Over some major cities, for example, the Japanese released flies infected with deadly plague germs, causing epidemics. Overall and quite aside from those killed in battle, the Japanese probably murdered 3,949,000 Chinese during the war; even possibly as many as 6,325,000. Some readers who were prisoners of the Japanese during the war or remember the Tokyo War Crimes Tribunal revelations after the war will hardly be surprised by these numbers. What is shocking is that the Nationalist likely murdered some 2,000,000 more during the war, and that this toll, or something like it, is virtually unknown. Apparently, the Nationalists got away with murder; responsible Japanese were tried as war criminals.[12]

These atrocities remain an important part of the enduring political psyche of what would supplant Japanese imperialism after World War II: the Communist Party of China. The violence of Japanese nationalism in China points to the critical role debate might play in mitigating the reactionary cycle of violence that ensues in contested realms of ideological supremacy. Chinese nationalists today feel entitled to a violence that matches the disruptive forces imposed upon it by Japanese Shintoism.

THE EMERGENCE OF CHINESE COMMUNISM IN THE MID-TWENTIETH CENTURY AND ITS VIOLENT RELATIONSHIP TO THE CHINESE PUBLIC

The emergence of a new nationalist Chinese identity predicated upon communism as envisioned by Mao Tse Tung is among the most consequential political developments of the twentieth century. By the mid-twentieth century the violent civil war against Chiang Kai-sheck was devolving into the escape of Kai-sheck's forces to the island of Taiwan and the supremacy of the People's Republic of China by 1949 in what was known as mainland China. Taiwan was so essential to the earliest international notions of China in that era that it was granted entry into the

United Nations as the representative of China. The emergence of Mao's dominance in the mainland was powerfully violent and involved democidal violence on an extraordinary scale. Experts estimate that more than forty million civilians were killed in techniques common to communist revolutions in Europe such as mass starvation. More recent estimates by contemporary Chinese scholars enjoying access to more exact archives kept by the party show vastly larger numbers. R. J. Rummel has estimated seventy-seven million deaths. Journalist Ian Johnson, who has lived many years in China, places the estimates closer to fifty million.[13]

Tombstone is an important book by a Chinese journalist Yang Jisheng that documents at least thirty-six million Chinese being killed in the Great Leap Forward. The *Atlantic* provides this description of the book's documentation:

> As a reporter for Xinhua, China's largest state-run news service, Yang was able to access records never intended for public consumption, resulting in a book whose depth of information is coupled with harrowing firsthand accounts of the disaster. Five years after its publication in Hong Kong, the book, entitled *Tombstone*, is now thought to be the most authoritative text about the Great Leap Forward ever published. *Tombstone* has become a best-seller worldwide and, despite being banned in mainland China, has been translated into several languages. For his work in exposing the deadly famine, Yang was recently awarded The Manhattan Institute's Hayek Prize for Literature.
>
> *Tombstone* is more than just a story of how, during a three-year period free from war or natural disaster, at least 36 million people died unnatural deaths. It's also the story of how the political and social environment helmed by Chairman Mao upended the livelihood of China's rural population, punished individuals who didn't echo the party line, and turned a blind eye to the millions who cried out for help.[14]

Yang Jisheng's study is important by the manner in which it documents the unique authoritarian persona of Mao and how it suffocated discursive complexity creating the rhetorical undertow of propaganda taking tens of millions to their deaths under his reign. The problem of propaganda was intimate for Yang:

> As a young high school graduate in early 1960s China, Yang Jisheng, like all young people in China, lacked the means to challenge the Communist Party's interpretation of history. But after he took a job as a reporter for Xinhua, he realized how far his "news" stories were from the truth. Looking back, Yang is displeased with his writing. "I should have burned those articles. I am ashamed of them.[15]

Yang's discoveries led to a new sense of a Chinese ethic: *shi shi qiu shi* (a Chinese aphorism meaning "the fact based search for truth"). This is precisely the goal of debate in securing more accurate understandings of both history and the consequential future that flows from that history.

Yang remains optimistic that perhaps in the next thirty years, democracy will come to the PRC and bring an end to the utopian fantasy of Marxism that dominates the current political mind of the leadership. In 2016, the Chinese government barred Yang Jisheng from going to Harvard to give a speech—an ominous indication of the government's preoccupation with censorship of meaningful criticism.

The most dangerous era of Communist party development is thought to begin in 1959. Agrarian reforms were so intensive that they involved extensive local killings of farmers and anyone disobedient to the imaginations of the "Great Leap Forward" that would transform China into a modern society. Mao had a special disdain for intellectuals, boasting, "What's so unusual about Emperor Shih Huang of the China Dynasty? He had buried alive 460 scholars only, but we have buried alive 46,000 scholars."[16] Mao was referring to a major "accomplishment" of the Great Cultural Revolution, which from 1966 through 1976 transformed China into a great House of Fear. Killing intellectuals and academics by the tens of thousands was a point of pride for Mao. These much smaller acts of democidal violence speak to the heart of discursive complexity under attack. The thinking of Mao became the only thinking of China. Disparate opinions were disloyal and dangerous. The contemporary reification of Mao today continues the violent sense of disparaging dissenting opinions. This creates the anti-critical thinking culture.

THE RECENT CONTROVERSY REGARDING THE GLOBAL PANDEMIC ORIGINATING FROM WUHAN, CHINA

One of the most important global controversies of 2020 was the COVID-19 virus originating in China. The origin of the virus in Wuhan underscores the necessary value of discursive complexity as the communist government of China grappled with how to understand the threat of the virus without jeopardizing a perceived sense of unassailable public policy success. Somewhere in the fall of 2019, the virus is believed to have originated in the vicinity of a wet market. Some evidence has suggested that it may have originated at a biological weapons lab nearby. The fact that, relative to a virus like Ebola in 2014 and more recent outbreaks, we have great difficulty discerning the exact origins of the virus in China, and this is testament to the powerful controls on information exerted by the Chinese government. This hindered public abilities to protect themselves from the virus. For the global community, the pandemic spread without a clear knowledge on how the disease was transmitted or who might be most susceptible. Even the Chinese data on infection numbers and deaths seemed so implausible that experts tended to dismiss them as some measure of propaganda.

The pandemic ushered in a global era of distrust toward the government of China. A number of key instances suggest that the closed nature of the Chinese government played an important role in causing the virus to spread with maximum deadly effect.[17] Important indicators of the government's role in the global crisis include:

1. According to U.S. intelligence assessments, including one published by the Department of Homeland Security and reviewed by *NBC News*, the Chinese government initially covered up the severity of the outbreak. Government officials threatened doctors who warned their colleagues about the virus, weren't candid about human-to-human transmission and still haven't provided virus samples to researchers.[18]
2. A January 24 study published in the medical journal *The Lancet* found that three of the first four cases—including the first known case—didn't provide a documented link to the Wuhan wet market.[19]
3. The bats that carry the family of coronaviruses linked to the new strain are not found within one hundred miles of Wuhan—but they were studied in both labs. Photos and videos have emerged of researchers at both labs collecting samples from bats without wearing protective gear, which experts say poses a risk of human infection. A U.S. State Department expert who visited the WIV (Wuhan Institute of Virology) in 2018 wrote in a cable reported by the *Washington Post*: "During interactions with scientists at the WIV laboratory, [U.S. diplomats] noted the new lab has a serious shortage of appropriately trained technicians and investigators needed to safely operate this high-containment laboratory."[20]
4. According to Senate Intelligence Committee member Tom Cotton, R-Ark., the Chinese military posted its top epidemiologist to the WIV in January. The Shanghai laboratory, where researchers published the world's first genome sequence of the coronavirus, was shut down January 12, according to the *South China Morning Post*.[21]

All of these details point to a habit of secrecy that limited the public's ability to understand the pandemic and plan accordingly. The centralized authority of the Communist party limits the discursive complexity necessary to contain and properly manage such pandemics. The initial control and investigation of the viral outbreak was hampered by the World Health Organization (WHO). WHO is offered to the entire global community as the exemplar of public openness with regard to questions of human health. During this crisis, one of the most important doctors within WHO refused to acknowledge the existence of human beings in the state of Taiwan. Canadian physician Dr. Bruce Aylward, an aide to WHO director-general Dr. Tedros Adhanom refused, in a live interview, to discuss Taiwan's effort to combat the virus.[22] According to WHO, twenty-four million people living in Taiwan do not exist. Taiwan is where the original government of China fled before they were annihilated by Mao Tse Tung. The heroic efforts of this proper government of the Chinese people is not applauded today for its incredible fight against the virus, which is among the most successful in the world, in the shadows of a Communist political party that seeks its annihilation.

The intellectual corruption of the WHO does not end with the arguments of Dr. Aylward. When one examines the charts and data of this organization allegedly protecting all of humanity, it is apparent that the WHO denies the existence of another nation: Israel.[23] More than eight million people who live in Israel are denied their existence by research and public data published by WHO. This is the only Jewish state in the entire world. This prejudice has a name: antisemitism. Because these national inhabitants are Jewish, their existence is denied by a medical community known as WHO. WHO does denote human communities that are non-Jewish in the Occupied Territories. Here again, the heroism and success of Israel are hidden and denied. Director Dr. Tedros Adhanom Ghebreyesus has as an advocacy theme: "Together for a healthier world."[24] Israel and Taiwan and the more than thirty million human beings living in those nations are not part of his global vision or the vision of those working with WHO. On January 14, 2020, WHO tweeted: "Preliminary investigations conducted by the Chinese authorities have found no clear evidence of human-to-human transmission of the novel coronavirus."[25] More than a week later on January 23, 2020, the *New York Times* reported this from Dr. Tedros Adhanom Ghebreyesus: "At this time, there is no evidence of human-to-human transmission outside of China."[26] That was a gross misrepresentation of the facts which lead to a tragedy, killing thousands of Chinese people, and convinced the world that no practical safeguards like those being pursued in Taiwan could be furthered in the global community. Taiwan demonstrates how discursive complexity uniquely equipped it to defeat the pandemic unlike its closed Communist counterpart.[27] The constant battle with its Communist rival across the strait positions Taiwan as continually seeking a defense from viruses and other provocation initiated by the mainland.

One of the more important causes to the present crisis was a false fear of prejudice against Chinese people. Realizing that the virus originated in Wuhan, China, a broad intellectual culture sought to exploit this reality toward a fallacious appeal of prejudice regarding any language acknowledging this point of origin. Anyone who speaks of the virus originating from the state of China is "racist," "xenophobic," and guilty of dangerous "prejudice" that should render them excluded from the public sphere. In Texas, the city of San Antonio adopted regulation establishing that such statements are "hate speech."[28] In Italy, virtue signaling emerged and created calls to "hug a Chinese person."[29] Similar virtue signals were sent in San Francisco and New York City as political figures sought to capitalize on public shows of opposing prejudice with regard to the Chinese community. The greatest source of empirical prejudice and harms against the people of China is in fact the Communist Party of China. Moreover, we have in this moment an opportunity of clarity to see the greatest political champion of the people of China: Taiwan.

Taiwan's political leadership, predicated upon openness, saved lives during the pandemic of 2020: "Taiwan's population is more than 23 million people—and they have 451 cases with only seven deaths," said Tsung-Mei Cheng, a health policy research analyst at Princeton University in July 2020. "That shows how successful they have been at both prevention and control."[30] Health experts noted that the exclusion of Taiwan from WHO protocols hurt the global response to the pandemic:

> William Hsiao, emeritus professor of economics in the Department of Health Policy and Management at the Harvard T. H. Chan School of Public Health, praised Taiwan for its effective early action, noting that health officials had developed a careful advance warning system for diseases around the world. If Taiwan had been a member of the WHO, he said, it might have been able to share its precautions with the organization and help other countries more easily.[31]

All of this points to the manner in which deliberation and discursive complexity improve human outcomes. Long ago, American preacher Henry Ward Beecher observed: "Free speech is to a great people what winds are to oceans and malarial regions, which waft away the elements of disease and bring new elements of health; and where free speech is stopped, miasma is bred, and death comes fast."[32]

A key Chinese doctor acknowledges that the deadly coronavirus originated from an environment of secrecy and clandestine hostility based in a military research lab:

> Yan then claimed that she and her team have produced a scientific report that shows the origin of COVID-19 is the "PLA-owned Zhoushan bat coronavirus." She plans to release the report in the near future, and accuses the WHO of "covering up numerous lies for the CCP." She pointed out that at the end of February, the WHO sent experts, including the controversial Bruce Aylward, who later published a report that praised the Chinese government's handling of the outbreak. However, she claims the WHO "dared not admit Shi Zhengli's RaTG13 virus." The virologist said Wuhan Institute of Virology (WIV) scientist Shi Zhengli, also known as "Bat Woman," deliberately posted a paper on Feb. 3 to draw attention to a coronavirus strain identified as RaTG13, which is a strain she and her team discovered in bats in Yunnan in 2013 and that is 96 percent identical to SARS-CoV-2. Yan claims this was an orchestrated attempt to throw investigators off the Zhoushan bat virus strains, while Shi herself claims the fact that RaTG13 is 4 percent different from SARS-CoV-2 exonerates her lab from being the source of the outbreak.[33]

These allegations point to an absence of transparency and deliberation. Much of the closed nature of the medical science was rooted in an unwillingness to collaborate and support Taiwanese health officials and policy aimed at curbing risks associated with such viruses.

In order to further improve life in China, efforts to educate and foster appreciation for difference of opinion and critical thinking are vital. Debate represents the essential method for disseminating and entrenching this critically thinking viewpoint. This will encourage indicators like life expectancy to rise on the mainland of China and begin to match those of Taiwan which is roughly five years higher in its life expectancy. Debate facilitates the emergence of the Chinese ethic of *shi shi qiu shi*—"the fact based search for truth." Fortunately, there are successful ongoing efforts to teach debate in China.

SUCCESSFUL EFFORTS TO TEACH DEBATE IN THE PEOPLES REPUBLIC OF CHINA

In academic school year 2017–2018, more than 350,000 students from the PRC attended American Universities.[34] Families of these students contribute more than $13 billion to the U.S. economy. For many international students, including those from the PRC, the allure of American universities is profound. An American collegiate education is deemed a gateway to future success wherever that path is grounded. For students from the PRC, there is an inherent intellectual paradox to living life as an American college student: loyalty to the Communist government of China alongside the broad ethos of free expression and critical thinking common to American university life. I have had multiple conversations with PRC students and their own intimate fears about jeopardizing the wellbeing of their family members with critical studies of human rights questions in the PRC. An important prelude to the matriculation from the PRC to the United States is English mastery that will allow students to establish linguistic fluency that maximizes acceptance to selective admission to American universities and improves on campus performance dramatically. Debate is a valuable pedagogy that improves PRC student performance in these areas and indulges the paradox of free expression within the space of Chinese sovereignty.

One of the most important international innovators on this question is debate instructor and coach Stefan Bauschard. His work derived from American debate practices at the high school and collegiate level has created a unique training ground for debate in the PRC, broader reaches of Asia, such as South Korea, and around the world. Bauschard's work in China stands out as an important success in the global trend toward discursive complexity. Bauschard explains in his own research the problem debate seeks to address within conventional Chinese education:

"Chinese students can swarm a problem . . . But when it comes to original thought and invention, we stumble. We are trying hard to make that up. We are trying to make technical education the grounding from which we solve problems."[35] In 2011, Bauschard travelled to China to make the case for debate in China as a powerful educational reform. The collaboration worked with Dipont Education Management (DEM) and Harvard Debate Summer Workshop (HDSW):

> In only seven days in China, I made presentations about the value of debate and the HDSW to DEM (Shanghai), the Wuxi No. 1 School (Wuxi), the Nanjing Foreign Language School (Nanjing), the Hangzhou Foreign Language School (Hangzhou), the Shenzhen Foreign Language School (Shenzhen), and the Shanghai World Foreign Languages School.[36]

In a survey of participants of Bauschard's debate schools in China, he found this self-report result in surveys he created:

> All of the students checked that they joined the program to "learn how to debate and argue." Twenty-two also checked that they chose to participate in the course to "enhance college admissions prospects" and seventeen checked that those chose debate to "enhance college admissions prospects to a US university."[37]

Bauschard's efforts continue to grow rapidly in the PRC:

> Cooperative efforts mean that more than 1,000 students have joined debate in one year. The expectation is that 10,000 students PER YEAR will participate in the DEM organized program within three years.[38]

PRC debate can instill the value of discursive complexity in a political environment dominated by the Communist party. Such educational approaches lay the groundwork for future openness and freedom despite current dispositions and efforts against this intellectual habit.

The Economist in 2019 ironically noted that in Wuhan, China, debate is emerging as powerfully attractive to young people and Chinese families attempting to accelerate student preparation for intensive national exams.[39] On the leading American high school speech and debate website (NSDA) there are often job openings seeking to hire American debate coaches to work in China.[40] These job description note a Chinese educational company looking for such pedagogy:

> ENREACH is a division of Dipont Education, a leading education management group in China and pioneer in development and customization of international language programs for students. Founded in 1990, Dipont is a growing company with a global team of over 1,000 employees and currently operates in 27 learning centers across 18 Chinese cities.[41]

The Dipont effort points to how debate is viewed as a broad national educational accelerator.

In Robert Trapp's debate book, *Building Global Relations through Debate*, created in 2015, major American and Chinese debate coaches describe the reasons for learning to debate toward the conclusion of the introduction:

> In all cases of dispute, individuals who argue well are more likely to succeed in achieving their goals and persuading others to adopt their perspectives. Lawyers, mayors, school board officials, parents, farmers, physicians, employees, employers, artists, children, presidents—all individuals need to be able to think critically, use principles of argument, listen carefully, respond ethically and appropriately, and speak effectively because all individuals use arguments in decision making. In other words, all individuals in a society benefit themselves, their communities, and their societies by knowing how to debate well. The reasons for studying debate and the value of developing debating skills, then, derive from the social need—at the individual level, the community level, and the societal level—to effectively manage individual and group disputes within a society.[42]

Trapp's impressive primer on debate, centered around the World Schools format, is a powerful practical example of debate finding an educational home in China. The conclusion to the introduction to the textbook provides a key challenge of what debating might mean positively for Chinese society. There is a careful deflection away from American notions of individuality and an accentuation of how society will benefit with more practitioners of key trades like lawyers.

Bauschard has also created an online *Global Academic Commons*, an academic tutoring and support service that has already provided more than one thousand hours of instruction for speech, debate, and many other course areas. *Global Academic Commons* provided support for more than 220 students from Canada, China, Korea, Taiwan, and the United States since 2017.[43] This is important educational innovation in the face of new constraints from the COVID-19 virus. The growth of debate in China today indicates a powerful future where more young people will, by the millions, seek to participate in a manner of education that reduces the likelihood of injustice and increase individual freedom.

CONCLUSION

China represents the largest population nation in the world with more than one billion citizens. The future rise of China depends upon an appreciation and practice of discursive complexity best apprehended through the practice of debate. China suffered in the first half of the twentieth century from brutal repression of the Shinto supremacism emanating from the island nation of Japan. Additionally, civil wars have traditionally torn the kingdom of China in violent deadly throes. The second half of the twentieth century was characterized by the most brutal repression of the Chinese people by way of the Maoist supremacism. Tens of millions of people died in a propaganda cult that imagined that a form of nationalism dedicated to a singular national leader could transport the nation forward in its "Great Leap." What died alongside the millions of civilians was an ethos of critical thinking that is vital to all human societies and plays a role in reconciling painful pasts and encouraging maximum social improvement. A Chinese author warned of the present social slowness surrounding the hazards of Chinese Communism:

> The ambivalence and slowness with which persons of Chinese ancestry treat the communist problem can find explanations in a millennia-old Confucian ethos: to actively scold one's government seems unfilial and ungrateful. Coupled with spectacular socioeconomic growth brought about by decades of manufacturing, the Party resembles a savior of the people. Chinese persons, whether mainlander or foreign-born, feel a distinct Chinese success that is hard to rail against.[44]

The dangers of the People's Republic of China, as presently practiced in its Communist politics, was laid bare in the recent pandemic. Closed communication prevented the global public from understanding the threat posed to the general public. Propaganda displaced deliberation, and poor arguments were made about how infectious the disease was and how it originated. Former National Security Advisor Condoleeza Rice recently warned about China's ominous conduct:

> "The Chinese did what authoritarians do," she said. "They silenced those who were trying to sound the alarm, they wanted time to create the narrative that would be blessed by the Communist Party of China, which means it probably had to go to Beijing before you could say anything. It is just the nature of the system. It is a real problem. The Chinese and trying to create a counter-narrative . . . to shift the narrative from their initial responsibility for not fessing up to what was happening, to 'We got on top of it and this is how we helped the world.' That's how they're going to shift the narrative. Don't let it happen." She concluded: "If you keep the focus on how this started, and China's role in that, they will be embarrassed by that. If you let them shift the narrative to all they've done sending out PPE, you're probably not going to make progress."[45]

Scholars may never know accurately how many Chinese people died in the origins of the virus because of the false pride of the Chinese Communist government.

The awkward reality in the twenty-first century in a nation of one billion people where roughly seventy million people are Communist party members, is how does debate thrive and transform this closed society? The deadly results of the COVID-19 pandemic point to the dangers of closed societies with closed communication predicates. Debate does exist in China, however, it is not yet transformative to the highest levels of government and policy.

Debate is an emerging practice for Chinese society. This practice of argumentation instruction can do more than ensure admission to prestigious American universities. The ideals of debate, suggesting that every individual is worthy of being heard with regard to their opinions and insights on matters that affect them, are the best components of this pedagogy. The further trajectory of China as a superpower in the twenty-first century is tied to individual and collective openness. In the former Soviet society, Mikhail Gorbachev referred to this change in Soviet communist closed nature as Glasnost. The new openness of China can bring better opportunities for all of the individuals of China.

NOTES

1. Sergey Sayapin, "Raphael Lemkin: A Tribute," *European Journal of International Law* 20, no. 4 (November 2009): 1157–62.
2. Ben Voth, *The Rhetoric of Genocide: Death as a Text* (Lanham, MD: Lexington Press, 2014).
3. Jacques Ellul, *Propaganda: The Formations of Men's Attitudes*, (New York: Random House, 1965).
4. Daniel Goldhagen, *Worse than War: Genocide, Eliminationism, and the Ongoing Assault on Humanity* (New York: PublicAffairs, 2009).
5. Rudolph Rummel, *Power Kills* (New York: Routledge, 2017).
6. Askold Krushelnycky, "Stalin's Government Created the Ukrainian Famine-Genocide," *Contemporary Issues Companion: Genocide* (New York: Greenhaven, January 1, 2008); Anne Applebaum, *Red Famine: Stalin's War on Ukraine*, first U.S. edition (New York: Doubleday, 2017); Norman M. Naimark, *Stalin's Genocides* (Princeton: Princeton University Press, 2010); "Ukrainians Honour Victims of Stalin-Era Famine," BBC monitoring former Soviet Union (London: BBC Worldwide Limited, November 24, 2018).
7. N. Ganesan and Sung Chull Kim, *State Violence in East Asia* (Lexington: University Press of Kentucky, 2013).
8. Frank Jacob, *Genocide and Mass Violence in Asia* (Berlin: DeGruyter, 2019).
9. Jacob, *Genocide and Mass Violence in Asia*, 8–9.
10. Rudolph Rummel, "Democracy, Power, Genocide, and Mass Murder," *The Journal of Conflict Resolution* 39, no. 1 (1995): 5.
11. Rummel, *Power Kills*.
12. Rummel, *Power Kills*.
13. Ian Johnson, "Who Killed More: Hitler, Stalin, or Mao?" *New York Times Book Review*, February 5, 2018, https://www.nybooks.com/daily/2018/02/05/who-killed-more-hitler-stalin-or-mao/.
14. William Wang, "Meet Yang Jisheng: China's Chronicler of Past Horrors," *The Atlantic*, September 20, 2013, https://www.theatlantic.com/china/archive/2013/09/meet-yang-jisheng-chinas-chronicler-of-past-horrors/279858/.
15. Wang, "Meet Yang Jisheng: China's Chronicler of Past Horrors."
16. Lee Edwards, "The Legacy of Mao Zedong Is Mass Murder," *Heritage Foundation*, February 2, 2010, https://www.heritage.org/asia/commentary/the-legacy-mao-zedong-mass-murder.

17. Ken Dilanian, Courtney Kube, and Carol Lee, "Did the Coronavirus Really Escape from a Chinese Lab? Here's What We Know," *NBC News*, May 4, 2020, https://www.nbcnews.com/politics/national-security/did-coronavirus-really-escape-chinese-lab-here-s-what-we-n1199531.

18. Abigail Williams and Dan De Luce, "DHS Report: China Hid Coronavirus' Severity in Order to Hoard Medical Supplies," *NBC News*, May 4, 2020, https://www.nbcnews.com/politics/national-security/dhs-report-china-hid-coronavirus-severity-order-hoard-medical-supplies-n1199221.

19. Chaolin Huang, et al., "Features of Patients Infected with 2019 Novel Coronavirus in Wuhan, China," *Lancet* 395, no. 10223 (2020): 497–506, https://www.thelancet.com/journals/lancet/article/PIIS0140-6736(20)30183-5/fulltext.

20. Josh Rogin, "State Department Cables Warned of Safety Issues at Wuhan Lab Studying Bat Coronaviruses," *Washington Post*, April 14, 2020, https://www.washingtonpost.com/opinions/2020/04/14/state-department-cables-warned-safety-issues-wuhan-lab-studying-bat-coronaviruses/.

21. Zhuang Pinghui, "Chinese Laboratory that First Shared Coronavirus Genome with World Ordered to Close for 'Rectification', Hindering Its Covid-19 Research," *South China Morning Post*, February 28, 2020, https://www.scmp.com/news/china/society/article/3052966/chinese-laboratory-first-shared-coronavirus-genome-world-ordered.

22. "Why Taiwan Has Become a Problem for WHO," BBC, March 20, 2020, https://www.bbc.com/news/world-asia-52088167.

23. The World Health Organization makes no report on the state of Israel when discussing COVID cases. "Coronavirus Disease 2019 (COVID-19) Situation Report–82," *World Health Organization*, August 15, 2020, https://www.who.int/docs/default-source/coronaviruse/situation-reports/20200411-sitrep-82-covid-19.pdf?sfvrsn=74a5d15_2.

24. Dr. Tedros Adhanom Ghebreyesus, "Director-General Dr Tedros Takes the Helm of WHO: Address to WHO Staff-Director-General of the World Health Organization," *World Health Organization*, Geneva, Switzerland, July 3, 2017, https://www.who.int/dg/speeches/2017/taking-helm-who/en/.

25. Twitter, *World Health Organization*, January 14, 2020, https://twitter.com/who/status/1217043229427761152?lang=en.

26. Denise Grady, "Coronavirus Is Spreading, but W.H.O. Says It's Not a Global Emergency," *New York Times*, January 23, 2020, https://www.nytimes.com/2020/01/23/health/china-virus-who-emergency.html.

27. Evan A. Feigenbaum and Jeremy Smith, "How Taiwan Can Turn Coronavirus Victory into Economic Success: Taiwan Beat the Virus with Efficient Government and Advanced Technology—The Same Ingredients That Power the Economy," *Foreign Policy*, June 1, 2020, https://foreignpolicy.com/author/evan-a-feigenbaum/.

28. Kiara Keane, "Ted Cruz Says San Antonio's Decision to Label the Term 'Chinese Virus' as Hate Speech Is 'Nuts,'" *Business Insider*, New York: Insider Inc, May 9, 2020, US edition.

29. "Italy Launched 'Hug a Chinese' Campaign to Fight Coronavirus-Induced Racism," *The Indian Express*, March 30, 2020.

30. Christina Farr and Michelle Gao, "How Taiwan Beat the Coronavirus," *CNBC*, July 15, 2020, https://www.cnbc.com/2020/07/15/how-taiwan-beat-the-coronavirus.html.

31. Farr and Gao, "How Taiwan Beat the Coronavirus."

32. Henry Ward Beecher as quoted in *Forty Thousand Quotations: Prose and Poetical*, comp. by Charles Noel Douglas (New York: Halcyon House, 1917; Bartleby.com, 2012), www.bartleby.com/348.

33. Keoni Everington, "Chinese Virologist Claims Coronavirus Derived from 'Zhoushan Bat Virus' Whistle Blower Blames WHO for Cover-Up and Implicates White House Health Advisor Dr Anthony Fauci," *Taiwan News*, August 6, 2020, https://www.taiwannews.com.tw/en/news/3981833.

34. "Trade War: How Reliant Are US Colleges on Chinese Students?" *BBC News*, June 12, 2019, https://www.bbc.com/news/world-asia-48542913.

35. Michael Silverstein and Abheek Singhi, "Can US Universities Stay on Top?" *Wall Street Journal*, September 29, 2012, http://online.wsj.com/article/SB10000872396390444358804578018531927856170.html.

36. Stefan Bauschard, "Empowering Achievement: Using Debate to Build Achievement in Western Academic Settings," *4th International Conference on Argumentation, Rhetoric, Debate, and the Pedagogy of Empowerment*, Doha, Qatar, January 12, 2013, 1–27, https://debateus.org/wp-content/uploads/2013/01/cap.pdf.

37. Bauschard, "Empowering Achievement: Using Debate to Build Achievement in Western Academic Settings," 1–27.

38. Bauschard, "Empowering Achievement: Using Debate to Build Achievement in Western Academic Settings," 1–27.

39. "Debating Contests Teach Chinese Students an Argument Has Two Sides," *The Economist*, June 15, 2019, accessed August 10, 2020, https://www.economist.com/china/2019/06/15/debating-contests-teach-chinese-students-an-argument-has-two-sides.

40. National Speech and Debate Website, "Debate and Public Speaking Teacher in China," July 29, 2020, accessed August 10, 2020, https://www.speechanddebate.org/job/enreach-education-china-27-debate-and-public-speaking-teacher-in-china/.

41. National Speech and Debate Website, "Debate and Public Speaking Teacher in China."

42. Robert Trapp, Eric Barnes, Chen Xiangjing, Melissa Franke, Teresa Green, He Jing, Una Kimokeo-Goes, Jackson Miller, Kathleen Spring, and Yang Ge, *Building Global Relations through Debate* (China Education Network, 2015), accessed August 10, 2020, https://debate.uvm.edu/dcpdf/Trappetal_BuildingGlobalRelationsThroughDebate.pdf.

43. "About Us," Global Academic Commons, https://globalacademic.org.

44. Jen Victor, "Will China Ever Be Reined In from Within," *American Thinker*, June 25, 2020, https://www.americanthinker.com/articles/2020/06/will_china_ever_be_reined_in_from_within.html.

45. Condoleeza Rice, "China Wants to Shift the Narrative on COVID 19, Don't Let Them," *Real Clear Politics*, April 15, 2020, https://www.realclearpolitics.com/video/2020/04/16/condoleezza_rice_china_wants_to_shift_the_narrative_on_covid-19_dont_let_them.html.

TEN

Debate as a Global Empowerment Tool for Ending Injustice and Genocide

The twentieth century confounded us with the most detailed documentations of the horrors of human society. The genocides of African Hereroes, Armenian Christians, Jews in the Holocaust, intellectuals in Cambodia, Muslims in Bosnia, and more than any book can contain add up to tens of millions dead and four times as many as those killed in war. Conventional studies of genocide tend to evoke a mysterious awe as to how humans can be so diabolical—perhaps instilling some resignation and revulsion to its ongoing practice. Those numbers and interpretation are sharply contrasted with the accurate and important empirical observations documented in the work of Professor Steven Pinker. Pinker's work on human violence tells a remarkable narrative, heavy with empirical data that humanity is, in fact, overcoming its violent ways. The incredible progress made in these political venues, and our own potential skepticism to this good news, creates a rhetorical vulnerability. Transitions from authoritarianism to representative democracy and the utilization of formal independent judicial tribunals are important steps forward and away from genocide and eliminationism. We may fail to fully capitalize on these positive and ancillary movements in the twenty-first century. These trends include reduced violence, reduced war, reduced hunger, reduced illiteracy and many other social indicators. Pinker explained the problem in a 2011 *Wall Street Journal* editorial:

> Whatever its causes, the implications of the historical decline of violence are profound. So much depends on whether we see our era as a nightmare of crime, terrorism, genocide and war or as a period that, in

the light of the historical and statistical facts, is blessed by unprecedented levels of peaceful coexistence.

Bearers of good news are often advised to keep their mouths shut, lest they lull people into complacency. But this prescription may be backward. The discovery that fewer people are victims of violence can thwart cynicism among compassion-fatigued news readers who might otherwise think that the dangerous parts of the world are irredeemable hell holes. And a better understanding of what drove the numbers down can steer us toward doing things that make people better off rather than congratulating ourselves on how moral we are.[1]

Two prominent idealist empiricists stand out as examples of this approach: Stephen Pinker and Hans Rosling. Their approach operates uniquely from a standpoint of idealism and empiricism. Both professors demonstrate that idealism is both practical and verifiable.

Pinker is a cognitive psychologist who sees tremendous positive potential in humanity from his secular vantage point. Pinker's research makes the compelling case that the worst aspects of human existence—war, murder, crime, genocide, and disease—are all on demonstrable declines for the global human family. Understanding this reality is not a prerequisite to dismissing threats or the disingenuous rhetoric that often drives the most undesirable of human behaviors—violence. In fact, Pinker's empirical approach can help us understand local interruptions to this global trend. His empiricism can also help us better understand how to accentuate and even accelerate these positive trends for humanity. His most recent book, *Enlightenment Now: The Case for Reason, Science, Humanism, and Progress*, illuminates how the intellectual habits of the Enlightenment contribute to positive human outcomes. The book follows his scholarly tradition of defending optimism. The *New York Times Book Review* provided this summary:

> Much of the book is taken up with evidence-based philosophizing, with charts showing a worldwide increase in life expectancy, a decline in life-shattering diseases, ever better education and access to information, greater recognition of female equality and L.G.B.T. rights, and so on—even down to data showing that Americans today are 37 times less likely to be killed by lightning than in 1900, thanks to better weather forecasting, electrical engineering and safety awareness.[2]

This highlights how argumentation scholars can utilize empiricism to document a better world. The wider dissemination of information through freedom of speech allows all of humanity to make better and safer choices that minimize harms. Pinker's work is a good model for current scholarly practice.

A great researcher who unfortunately passed away in 2017, Hans Rosling, is another excellent model of idealistic empiricism. He was a Swedish physician, academic, and statistician who was largely unsurpassed in his capacity to make data illuminating and visually compelling. His TED talks demonstrated rather forcefully and empirically that the human condition is improving along the same lines described by Pinker.[3] We should continue the type of work pioneered by Rosling to make the case for how the world gets better. His specific ability to localize global data and help us see how distinct regions were doing better or worse in terms of economic poverty or life expectancy have profound political implications for our pursuit of the ethical condition known as discursive complexity.

Rosling's work continues with the help of his family and a new company called Gapminder. Rosling provided some insight in how the natural human intuition is inclined toward pessimism as a way of surviving in a complicated world, as this review of his work indicates:

> Swedish top students know statistically significantly less about the world than a chimpanzee who would have scored higher by chance. The problem "was not ignorance, it was preconceived ideas," which are worse. Bad ideas are driven by many -isms, but also by what Rosling calls in the book an "overdramatic" worldview. Humans are nervous by nature. Our tendency to misinterpret facts is instinctive—an evolutionary adaptation to help us make quick decisions to avoid danger . . . Magnified by global, collective anxieties, weaponized by canny mass media, the tendency to pessimism becomes reality, but it's one that is not supported by the data. This kind of argument has become kind of a cottage industry; each presentation must be evaluated on its own merits. Presumably enlightened optimism can be just as oversimplified a view as the darkest pessimism. But Rosling insisted he wasn't an optimist. He was just being "factful."[4]

Rosling's defense of his work highlights the necessary role of debate in creating the better world. Facts must emerge from a contested public space. Rosling notes that a psychological disposition toward pessimism obstructs our mental view of facts. These facts help us elucidate a better world beyond initial fears. Debate allows this fretful exploration to take place beyond psychological walls of negative doubt.

TOWARD DISCURSIVE COMPLEXITY: THE AMERICAN MODEL

The American precept of free speech is one of the most validated theories of public advocacy ever offered in human history. The ability to challenge political utterances for over two hundred years elevated a small band of monarchial resistance to the third most populous nation on the earth with the largest economy and all-volunteer military ever acquired in human history. Moreover, the adversaries of the United States who have generally committed themselves to an innate political rejection of this notion have induced some of the most profound human ethical atrocities in history. These atrocities of the twentieth century include in order of magnitude: Communism, Shinto supremacism, and Nazi fascism.

Communism killed no fewer than one hundred million people across the world in the twentieth century.[5] Shinto supremacism as politically engineered in Japan killed ten to fourteen million people[6] and German Nazi supremacism killed more than ten million people.[7] All three of these political projects made a specific and profound point of rejecting American notions of free speech and relying upon systemic propaganda to suppress political truths and consequent ethical misconduct within their political ranks. Many more ethical case studies in genocide can and should be explored to further validate the political communication theory of discursive complexity.[8]

ENCOUNTERING OUR RHETORICAL PROBLEM AND EXIGENCE: POSTMODERNISM AND SOCIAL FRACTURE

Most scholars and students will readily recognize the First Amendment and its high value essence of free speech. Moreover, they tend to agree that it is a social good and worthy of admiration and respect. However, many scholars remain skeptical of its ongoing reformative power in light of tremendous political disjunctions that prevail not only in spite of the First Amendment but perhaps because of it. More broadly, the American political system seems presently so shrill and divisive that more free speech seems a likely barrier to improvement rather than a therapeutic aid. Dr. Robert Denton commented and diagnosed this condition in our 2017 book, *Social Fragmentation and the Decline of American Democracy*.[9] The path forward in our twenty-first century is to gain a better intellectual mapping of where we are with regard to political intransigence and frustration. Put simply, we are nowhere near both historical and even relatively contemporaneous levels of political frustration. Of course, the inception of the United States under the ideal rubric of the Constitution was, nonetheless, bound by political cynicism and raw violence. Duels that pitted gunslinging politicians to the task of mortal combat in order to settle political disputes were not uncommon. That is not yet apparent today. More contemporaneously, the year of 1968 stands out as an extraordinary era of profound anger and cynicism. The assassinations of Robert Kennedy and Martin Luther King Jr. took place amid major riots in dozens of American cities to make that presidential election year a relative nightmare compared to our present frustration. These observations ought not cause us to accept as benign our present frustrated state. In fact, we ought to peer with some intellectual penetration as to how these miasmic moments were surpassed within the American model.

The path forward is clear. Theoretical and methodological approaches to politics are dominated by an ethic of cynicism. Pessimism is now doctrinaire as a matter of political communication study. A recent study of political affiliation among communication professors at the top forty universities in the United States found that there were 108 faculty members of one political party and not a single faculty member registered to the opposing political party.[10] It is not imperative to recognize which political party was preferred in this 2018 study. If the other party enjoyed the same status, we would recognize the intellectual condition the same: propaganda. The raw cynicism and pessimism that was necessary among those practicing communication study to make this present arrangement of ideology is profoundly disconcerting. Communication study was one of only two disciplines found to not have a single opposing member of the two major political parties in the United States. Not a single discipline, among more than a dozen reviewed was found to have a preponderance of members from the opposing party. The average disparity among all academic disciplines was roughly twenty to one. This brings with it profoundly good news and profoundly bad news. The good news is that almost *any* fundamental reconsideration of communication theory as presently understood is likely to improve our condition of discursive complexity. The bad news is that the entrenchment of negative ideological forces to not only ensure but increase such bad conditions is considerable, if not overwhelming, to any individual student or faculty member. Systemic ostracism and tactics, such as doxing, generally await individuals resisting this present order.

Some intellectual mapping of how we came to be in such an absurd academic position in political communication theory is important to any effort toward removing ourselves from this ethically toxic environment. The year 1968 actually does stand out as a rather profound moment in U.S. political history, as already noted. Approximately fifty years ago, the advent of activist notions of pessimism began to displace the political project of American idealism. King, who was assassinated on a Memphis balcony on April 4, was the leader of a "Beloved Community." His idealistic integrated view of race relations was already being displaced by an Afro-pessimist view of race relations known as Black power.[11] Additional pessimist views of geopolitical relations began to romanticize socialism and communism and demonize the American military as an incorrigible opponent of the Good. Within our economy, enviro-pessimist notions of pesticide poison and overpopulation began to displace the ideas of economic growth, prosperity, and human thriving. The essential practical political strategy reader for these interconnected notions of pessimism is Saul Alinsky's *Rules for Radicals*. At its theoretical heart, Alinsky's tome on tactics for radicals supposes that all aspects of American idealism can be overcome by simply overdemanding of any idealist an adherence to their principle that becomes self-defeating. According to Alinsky's model all idealists should be intensively prompted in a cynical public manner designed to "expose" the idealist as a fraud and unworthy of public respect. This rather simple theory is elaborated into a methodology of twelve rules well explained by Alinsky.[12] The book remains at the heart of most pessimist projects dedicated to decimating the American political experiment in human freedom. The empirical success of the book and its adherents is difficult to deny.

Nonetheless, it is also difficult to deny that America and the world have rebounded from perilous conditions like these, with far fewer resources than are presently enjoyed in twenty-first-century society. Initially, idealist should familiarize themselves with Alinsky's precepts, not with a goal of adhering to them but with an informed desire to overcome them. Secondly, idealists must adopt a strong code of response. Put simply, idealists must become singularly cynical about cynicism. Idealists must understand the American ideals well and in a complementary manner and prepare to be cynical of cynics in a way that reciprocally overdemands their system of praxis. In so doing, neo-idealists can achieve the same implosion of the pessimist model that was achieved since 1968 against the American idealist model.

In actualizing a serial idealism that overcomes the theoretical pessimism orchestrated by Alinsky, it is an emerging reality that the worst crimes of humanity can be overcome. The pattern of urban violence, riots, prejudice, discrimination, civil war, and even genocide can be prevented, interrupted, and recovered from by way of deliberations. The "arguer as lover" is the one who sees argument as an opportunity to listen and understand more—not less.[13] In the next section of analysis, the hermeneutic of understanding aims at the intimate experience of Holocaust survivors and how their voices can comingle with a world struggling to stop genocides in the twenty-first century.

UNITED STATES HOLOCAUST MEMORIAL MUSEUM PROJECT: DISCURSIVE COMPLEXITY AGAINST ANTI-SEMITISM

This section of analysis presents a model on how the disciplinary practice of argumentation study takes human form to resist contemporary anti-Semitism and reverse the cruel maxim: those ignorant of history are doomed to repeat it. Contemporary intellectuals such as Paulo Freire[14] emphasize the role that education should play in practical resistance to modern practices that undermine the human community. Michel Foucault has noted the praxis of the "specific intellectual" dedicated to exposing the relations of power in the immediate situation and circumstances they find themselves.[15] Argumentation and communication study should be engaged to inform humanity of cruel hoaxes in argument which break down the bonds of human community. In this case, workshop procedures implemented rhetorical and argumentation instruction for Holocaust survivors to make it possible for them to effectively give voice to their personal narratives and confront skeptical audiences that occasionally resist their advocacy. Argumentation and forensics pedagogy can be used to empower the human voice toward a critical practice of communication that is both liberating and educational.

In 2006 and 2007, I worked as a public speaking consultant at the United States Holocaust Memorial Museum, working with Holocaust survivors toward improving their public voice. This project started shortly after the president of Iran, Mahmoud Ahmadinejad, began emphasizing, publicly and politically, his firm belief that the Holocaust did not happen.[16] Moreover, the former president of Iran, Ahmadinejad, expressed a desire to erase Israel from the map, and international experts remain increasingly concerned that a nuclear power program would provide the weapons for accomplishing this second Holocaust.[17]

Those weeks spent with Holocaust survivors anchoring that institution forever changed my perspective on the power of communication and what its highest purposes can be. Those seminal moments equipping survivors to better have their voice in telling their own stories about such a profound tragedy provided the moral clarity, inspiration, and intellectual framework for this book. In many respects, the events leading to and following that service at the museum are an important analogy for understanding this book.

Prior to my work at the USHMM, I had not had occasion to visit the museum. It was a young passionate student, Terri Donofrio, who first asked me for advice regarding an internship position in the Survivors Bureau of USHMM. She was graduating in the fall, and unsure about what to do next. I thought it was worth a try. It was not long before I heard she was hired to work within the Survivors Bureau.

Terri quickly became convinced that the survivors needed to have public speaking workshops that mirrored ongoing work with their writing of Holocaust memories. Terri was an exceptional student of rhetoric and excelled in both speech and debate competitions while in college. Communication courses convinced her that being able to express oneself in public was critical. She consulted with me about how to design a public speaking program for the survivors. We corresponded regularly about the project and I presumed that, based upon my recommendations, she would find a local instructor of communication and public speaking in the D.C. area and implement the program. When she contacted me to say that her grant had been approved and the project would proceed, I was happy for her. I was not prepared for her conclusion to the call. She wanted me to fly out and do the training of the Holocaust survivors.

That was a life changing moment for me. Though I loved rhetoric and believed that every person should have their voice, I was in awe of the prospects of working with survivors and trying to shape their voices toward greater use and confidence. How could one evaluate their oral testimonies? Yet, that was inherent in this project designed by Terri. In the following weeks, we collaborated intensely with the director of survivor affairs, Ellen Blalock, to design a four-part program built around lectures and performance practices.

When I arrived on-site in late May of 2006, I remember attending a social event on a Sunday evening honoring the volunteer work of the survivors at the museum. I had no responsibilities for the evening, apart from socializing with the survivors that I would begin working with on Monday morning. I remember a small and slight female survivor grabbing me by the arm that evening:

"Dr. Voth, Dr. Voth, I am so glad you are here."

"I am delighted to be here as well," I responded—surprised at her urgency.

"I have such a hard time telling my story," she continued.

"I can hardly imagine. I know it must be difficult," I offered—beginning to realize the depth of the task I was about to embark upon.

"Every time I try to tell my story, I break down crying. I cannot stop thinking of the children I wanted to have. . . . but I was sterilized by Dr. Mengele."

With those words, my confidence plunged as I pondered in my mind the history of Josef Mengele and the infamous medical experimentation for which he was so well known. I was staggered:

"You know. I would like to hear your story. I imagine many people would like to hear your story. But I want you to know, that these workshops are not mandatory. They are not required. Given the trauma, I am curious to know why you might even want to try to do this?"

She straightened her spine, leveling her eyes toward mine and saying with stern conviction:

"There are people out there saying that the Holocaust didn't happen. And before I die, I want them to know. The Holocaust happened! And it happened to ME!"

Emotions soared within me to see an individual fighting back against cruel cultural graffiti written against her soul. It was heroic and inspiring.

"Well. I guess those are the feelings you will need to hold onto as we go through these workshops."

Her remarks steeled my resolve. If she could rise up against her haunting trauma so cruelly inscribed, then I would manage my own apprehensions about academic pretense prevailing against the sincere memories of survivors.

For most people, the hearing of a Holocaust survivor is a treasured memory of a lifetime. In the work with USHMM, three dozen survivors told their stories week after week, and my soul was seared in the furnaces of human emotions on this question of genocide. After two summers of work at the museum with the survivors, my fundamental perspective about the museum changed. I originally thought of the museum as an epideictic commemoration of one of humanity's most savage acts—a sobering memorial to a terrible tragedy. I now view it as an ongoing heroic story of human voices rising out of the ashes of genocide. It was in the summer of 2007 that I finally noticed a subtle but compelling feature of the museum's flow and architecture. In the midst of an edifice designed to look like Auschwitz sits a small desk staffed by survivors. The survivors are queried by visitors and some will even pull up their sleeves to show the numbers inscribed by Nazis on their bodies. Thinking about the survivor willingness to relive and abide within this memorial of tragedy in an effort to prevent similar tragedies from happening again, led me to the conclusion that the museum has a much more positive message than I originally understood. The survivors are heroes within the defeated scene of the Holocaust. I hope this book will capture that sense of optimism. Many of the specific exercises and discussions enacted with those survivors motivated chapters in this work.

One of the more salient aspects of this memory is the manner by which it was achieved. This was a project envisioned and created by a student. Her original optimism, like so many examples before it and since almost made me giggle as a professor. Is this possible? Students continually challenge me to throw off the blinders of cynicism that cause knowledge to hide the status quo behind a wall as if we know the world cannot change for the better. Terri's vision, like that of so many other young people, did change the world on the important question of genocide.

When the speaker's workshop began, barely ten survivors were willing and comfortable with going outside the museum to tell their story to the public. By the end of 2007, more than twenty-five survivors were prepared to do so. Terri more than doubled the number of survivors that could work so broadly with the public at a time when survivor voices are growing ever scarcer.[18] Each survivor at the D.C. museum that speaks in public reaches an average of ten thousand listeners a year in talks that take place around the nation. Many tens of thousands of people were reached by these stories because of a vision held by a student. Military bases, police trainees, state department employees, churches, synagogues, schools, and a variety of community groups are all reached by oral testimonies given by survivors. The project was a reminder to me about why teaching is so important and inspiring.

Terri's work became a model and inspiration for further work in this area. One of my master's students in Ohio (Allison Fisher Bodkin) went to a doctoral program in Illinois and started a public speaking program for rape survivors. The program had a similar concept and premise. Being able to speak in public about a past trauma was empowering. It was an important step in recovering an identity deformed by a cruel intentional act of hate. Ultimately, the program became self-sustaining.

Another former student, Aaron Noland became a communication instructor at James Madison University and reached out in an academic program to the "lost boys" of Sudan. His heart for preventing genocide was evident and embodied for his students in a way that goes beyond the statistics and the politics.[19] Seeing students act out this serial idealism motivates scholarship like this every day and gradually led to the writing of this book.

As highlighted by these examples, this book is unique in emphasizing the role of debate and argumentation in the subject of genocide. There are several dimensions to this: (1) genocide is a symbolic act that involves defining groups out of existence, (2) genocide is perpetrated through the abuse of symbols by argumentation propagandists known as genocidaires, (3) argumentation is stifled in the prelude to genocide, and (4) argumentation and advocacy is a profound preventative, remedy, and remediation for genocide. The centrality of free speech and the deeper philosophical commitment to the human processes of rhetoric animate the content of this book and make it distinct. Unfortunately, despite the current fascination and appreciation of Holocaust survivors, anti-Semitism that lies at the heart of the Holocaust remains a potent argument in the twenty-first century.

CONTEMPORARY ANTI-SEMITISM

A variety of instances point to the ominous threat of contemporary anti-Semitic argumentation: Louis Farrakhan's invocation of Jews as termites,[20] a past Egyptian president's public "amen" to "Jews as enemies,"[21] capital punishment for selling land to Jews in Palestinian controlled areas of Israel,[22] carving stars of David into the backs of Jewish sympathizers in St. Louis,[23] and a 2007 blockbuster Turkish movie series (Valley of the Wolves) with American icons Billy Zane and Gary Busey promoting the age old notion of blood libel.[24] In 2020, NFL star player DeSean Jackson provided an alleged quotation from Adolf Hitler to support his contention that Jews were controlling the world in dangerous ways.[25] Argumentation scholarship has the potential to identify and prepare audiences to resist the insidious dimensions of this rhetoric. Classic studies like those of "Hitler's Battle" provided by Kenneth Burke[26] provide something of a model on how rhetorical and argumentation studies can undermine pathological viewpoints. This ancient trope organized genocides in the past and is being reenergized to the same type of genocidal activity today.

Jews, like many other groups, have served as convenient scapegoats for the global elite. The famous example of the German Nazis was a strategic amplification of latent attitudes toward Jews that existed for hundreds of years.[27] The dominant educational approach within the United States treats anti-Semitism as a largely historic problem, which rose and fell with the Third Reich. Nonetheless, Jews continue to serve as a rhetorical scapegoat globally, as indicated by the widespread sale of common anti-Semitic propaganda such as *The Protocols of the Elders of Zion*.[28] This book, created in Russia during the early twentieth century, has been widely reproduced throughout the Middle East and the world. The book details a conspiracy by Jewish leaders to control the world and, despite its fictional content, it is widely held as a factual representation of Jewish motives.

Common stereotypes, such as blood libel—which suggests that Jews enjoy drinking the blood of innocents—continue to be utilized throughout the world. In 2007, a Turkish filmmaker employed American actors Billy Zane and Gary Busey to describe how a Jewish doctor (Busey's character) was shipping organs of Iraqis to Jews around the world in Israel, New York, and London. The film's plot was built around global antagonism toward the U.S. war in Iraq. In the story line of the movie, organs were harvested from innocent Iraqis in the notorious Abu Ghraib prison. The film was a huge financial success in Europe, where British and German media conceded its clear anti-Semitic content.[29] Noted civil rights activist Andrew Young scandalized the American public sphere with arguments that Americans should appreciate Walmart putting Jewish, Korean, and Arab merchants out of business. He would later describe his own remarks as "demagogic" and an unfortunate lapse.[30] Ward Churchill's notorious post 9/11 accusations against World Trade Center victims was anchored in a repudiation of Nazi officer Adolf Eichmann's active role in the Holocaust.[31] His comments posed not simply a problem for lost American lives but the potential lessons of deadly anti-Semitism from the past. Unfortunately, anti-Semitism is being deeply amplified in Middle East cultures. Direct English translation services of Middle East media, such as the Middle East Media Research Institute (MEMRI.org), provide the international community with an opportunity to observe the anti-Semitic rants of religious and political leaders in the region.[32]

Chapter 10

GEORGE W. BUSH CENTER: DECISION POINTS AGAINST GENOCIDE

In April of 2013, five living American presidents were in attendance in Dallas as the George W. Bush Center opened on the campus of Southern Methodist University. Since Herbert Hoover, the U.S. Federal government has ensured that each American president has a Federal library dedicated to their papers and history. In the case of President George W. Bush who served from 2001 to 2009, the library also houses the Bush Institute, dedicated to the ongoing work of President Bush. Both the main library exhibit designed to explain historical legacy and the ongoing center for activity are dedicated to a central concept that forms the title of Bush's first major biography on his presidency: Decision Points. Bush's view of the American presidency is predicated on a conviction that presidents must make important decisions for the nation. In the main library exhibit, a Decision Points Theater is dedicated to this notion and guests have an opportunity to complete a five-minute multimedia study of several crises that President Bush faced and instantaneous considerations of data from advisors about how to best resolve the matter in a short amount of time. In his opening remarks, President Clinton noted that this was his favorite feature of the new library.[33] This central concept is indicative of the notion of discursive complexity and the vital role of deliberation. Presidents have many important advisors and they often give conflicting views on profound but complicated matters. The ongoing work of his center since 2013 is dedicated to a similar mindset that deliberation is a prerequisite to good decision-making.

In 2012, I collaborated with the Bush Center to create one of the first initiatives of the new center: The Bush Debates. President Bush and his wife Laura believed that debate was an important characteristic of American civics. These debates, sponsored by the 4% Economic Growth unit of the center, invited local high school debaters to debate about an economic topic. Some of the top debaters got to meet with President Bush, and as a reward for designing the project, I got to have dinner with President Bush and about six of the top speakers from the debate tournament. This event is commemorated in the conclusion of the main library exhibit as visitors leave and give consideration to President Bush's current work.

There are several units that work within the Bush Center besides the economic unit. These initiatives include: Human Freedom, Military Service, Education Reform, Global Health, and Women.[34] All of these initiatives seek to maintain a deliberative stance that enables public conversation and progress on these important topics. In projects focusing on Human Freedom, I conducted multiple public speaking workshops for democracy advocates in places such as North Korea and Burma. Some of the Burmese activists were arrested in early elections of Burma when democracy came to that nation and Aun Sung Kyi was released from prison to become president. North Koreans are protected in their immigration to the United States by legislation originally urged by the Bush administration. Some of these workshops were conducted with translators so students could understand the instruction in their native languages. One of my communication studies students, Jieun Pyun, heads the Human Freedom initiative and the group continues to work toward open societies in North Korea and Burma. Jieun is herself from South Korea. Her collegiate study in communication helped her maintain these programs that stir human capital for discursive complexity within these nations.

During his presidency, George W. Bush was an important advocate against genocide. President Bush's foreign policy throughout the two administrations wove together arguments for global freedom that counteracted genocide and established important human rights progress across the Middle East and Africa. Iraq, Sudan, and Liberia—provides rhetorical and argumentation examples of Bush's statements and policies to clarify a historical record of human rights policy making against genocide. Democracy and freedom appear to not be limited to the European and American spheres of power. They are clearly present and emerging across the Middle East and North Africa. The polarizing effects of President Bush's definitive policies and statements created an initial cloud of objections among global opinion leaders. These three examples noted in this chapter suffice to break the mysterious notion that genocide is inevitable and intractable. If Iraq, Sudan, and Liberia had continued with the death rates they were experiencing during their genocide eras without outside interference, approximately four million additional people would have died in those nations. The consolidation and removal of genocidaires with aggressive diplomacy, and smart military invasions ended eras of "death as a text" written in sovereign locales controlled by the genocidaires of Bashir, Hussein, and Taylor.[35]

Understanding American presidential rhetoric, as it pertains to the question of genocide, is vitally important. After a twentieth century, witnessing more than 150 million victims of genocidal slaughters—roughly four times the lives lost in war—the twenty-first century remains an ongoing opportunity for genocide prevention. The axiom of noted Holocaust survivor Elie Wiesel is applicable here: "What hurts the victim most is not the cruelty of the oppressor but the silence of the bystander."[36] The urgent problem of bystander is well addressed to what many view as the world's most powerful bully pulpit: the American presidency. President Bush filled the potential rhetorical vacuum of silence on genocide with important statements and actions regarding genocidal matters touching Liberia, Sudan, and Iraq. He utilized a mixture of diplomacy and military actions to augment political rhetoric dedicated to the premise of human freedom for individuals in a variety of genocide driven political circumstances. Understanding how President Bush addressed questions of genocide provides models for ongoing action and a basis for refining advocacy against genocide so that the problem might be further reduced in this century.

BUSINESS COMMUNICATION INSTRUCTION FOR EMERGING INDIAN LEADERS

As a part of an international church outreach program in Bangalore, India, to help emerging business leaders learn effective communication strategies to better form businesses in the rapidly growing Indian economy in 2017, I travelled with colleague John Kimmel to conduct on-site education programs. Kimmel was practically skilled as a major salesperson in the United States. He gives many professional talks on how to convince customers more effectively around the world. For my role, I sought to close the rhetorical loop on how argument training originating with James Farmer Jr. in the nonviolent direct-action campaigns of the American civil rights movement were derived from efforts constructed by Mahatma Gandhi. Gandhi's work intersected with the Bangalore community that we primarily worked within while in India. Gandhi's Hindu notion of Satyagraha, or "soul force," was an essential doctrine of nonviolent advocacy both in the Gandhian effort against British colonialism and ultimately the nonviolent techniques utilized by civil rights leaders like Farmer and King. In King's famous "I Have a Dream" speech, he made this allusion to the argument process:

> But there is something that I must say to my people, who stand on the warm threshold which leads into the palace of justice: In the process of gaining our rightful place, we must not be guilty of wrongful deeds. Let us not seek to satisfy our thirst for freedom by drinking from the cup of bitterness and hatred. We must forever conduct our struggle on the high plane of dignity and discipline. We must not allow our creative protest to degenerate into physical violence. Again and again, we must rise to the majestic heights of meeting physical force with soul force. The marvelous new militancy which has engulfed the Negro community must not lead us to a distrust of all white people, for many of our white brothers, as evidenced by their presence here today, have come to realize that their destiny is tied up with our destiny. And they have come to realize that their freedom is inextricably bound to our freedom.[37]

King believed that violence was not essential to meaningful political change. Of course, this movement is now a global model for political activism. In India, I taught hundreds of business leaders how key American ideas for change originated with Gandhi and uniquely Hindu notions. Though these ideas were easily contextualized to Christian contexts like those taught essentially by Jesus, they indicated the global nature of argument and its capacity to bring not only change, but positive developments for human societies. Our communication instruction took place in Bangalore and Coimbatore, and affected more than two hundred leaders. While in Coimbature, I was able to talk with a large population of teachers and graduate students focused on their educational work. One of the interesting questions I received from two graduate students was how I felt the problem Hindu social castes could be best approached. The distinctive social caste system of Hinduism remains a serious challenge to egalitarian goals and I commended Christian views of ironic leadership with regard to a need to be servant leaders and lifting up those who are marginalized. This was also part of my public remarks referencing Jesus's teachings recorded in Matthew 25 and sometimes referred to as the "Methodist Social Gospel."All of this provided a powerful intersection to my work on American civil rights movement activity drawn from activities in this nation of India.

DISCURSIVE COMPLEXITY IN ISRAEL

One of the more interesting programs reaching college students with an international experience is the Passages program, which is based in Chicago. The group allows any Christian college student to make a trip to Israel for a little over one week and experience both the historical and contemporary state of Israel at a cost of approximately $600. Such programs offered through universities utilize faculty guides, and I was able to serve as a faculty guide on trips in 2019 and 2018 with groups of approximately twenty-five college students. In those settings, I was able to contextualize argumentation in that powerful geopolitical and historical setting. We were able to view and study in the precise geographical setting for the famous arguments of Jesus at the Sermon on the Mount.[38] It was possible to engage intensive historical hermeneutic study about those arguments and how they apply in modern contexts. These conversations took place with contemporary controversies, including the Golan Heights—from which the ravages of the Syrian civil war could be observed—and the Gaza Strip—where Palestinian and Israeli identities collide.

Among the most significant events of the two trips was an evening spent with a former student. Her story is fundamentally important in correcting a common myth about why debate should be taught. Students can easily come to the misguided short-term notion that debating has as its terminus: winning. The discipline of losing, and losing in the cause perceived as right is a transcending purpose of debate pedagogy. A student whom we shall call Tikvah, to protect her identity, became a Messianic Jew while she was a college student in the United States. This means that she believes that Y'shua is the Messiah spoken of in Jewish tradition. After college, she became a national youth leader for this community. Nonetheless, she yearned to return and work for her homeland: Israel. Jews are promised a legal right of return and near automatic acceptance in the Israeli immigration system. According to the *Law of Return,* enacted in 1950 as an integral part of Israel's ethos, "Every Jew has the right to come to this country as an *oleh*" [immigrant].[39] As she was entering that legal process she was told by her attorney that she would need to renounce her Messianic faith because immigration authorities in Israel hold that belief in this particular Messiah makes a Jewish person, no longer Jewish. Tikvah made the difficult decision to refuse this renunciation though she confirmed in all verbal and written submissions that she was ethnically a Jew according to Israeli law and tradition. Her refusal to deny her beliefs led her through many difficult deliberative processes and confrontations with immigration authorities. Those circumstances were often fearful, challenging, and isolating. Ultimately, she made the difficult decision to become the third case in history to go to the Israeli Supreme Court on this question. There was considerable basis to believe that the Court might side with her. Messianic Jews do serve in the IDF, the Israeli Defense Force, and commend political activity within the civic sphere of the nation. Ironically, Tikvah would have been guilty of being Jewish from the standpoint of Nazi Germany and yet she was refused her Jewish identity by the Israeli immigration system in 2018. In 1970, Israeli immigration law was amended to clarify that descendants of Jews were also eligible for citizenship. Specifically, the definition was widened in order to ensure that a Jewish person who could be persecuted under the German Nuremberg Laws would be entitled to citizenship in Israel. Consequently, the intent of the law was not to base a person's right to citizenship on his or her Jewish practices or beliefs but simply on his or her Jewish ethnicity.

After hearing a murder case with full deliberations, Tikvah was allowed to bring her case to the judges and the Court. The judges were clearly outraged at Tikvah's attorney and would hardly let the argument proceed. Ultimately, they strongly urged her counsel to withdraw the case so that she would not be inevitably deported by their adverse decision. In a moment of recusal, the attorney asked Tikvah what she wanted to do and she responded that she wanted to press the case and at least speak to the judges. Despite repeated pleas from the attorney, the judges refused to allow her to speak and all she could do was simply stand in the courtroom as an indication of her willful desire to be accepted by her Jewish state of Israel. The Court rejected her claim of Jewish heritage saying that her profession of this Messiah made her no longer of this ethnic and religious category. Ultimately, Tikvah came to this conclusion she wrote in her successful application to law school in the United States:

> In the end, I lost my case and was refused both citizenship and, ultimately, residency. The justices determined that my beliefs were incompatible with the right to identify as a Jew. Though I understood from the very beginning that this result could occur, I could never have imagined the sheer devastation of hearing the justices' conclusion and eventually being deported from a country I loved. After two years of living in Israel, I was given two weeks to leave.
>
> Now that I have returned to the United States, I have taken some time to reflect on my experiences. First, I have developed a deeper, more profound understanding of the sacredness of the rights to freedom of thought, conscience, and religion, and I am committed to fiercely defending these rights. Secondly, the only way that I can accept what happened in Israel is to utilize my experience as a conduit for helping others.
>
> Though I cannot fully understand the pain that refugees and displaced persons endure, I do know what it feels like to live for a prolonged period of time without status or basic rights and to be treated in certain ways like a criminal. I desire to channel this compassion and empathy into pursuing immigration law, where I can gain the ability to advocate for those who are suffering, walk alongside them, and fight for successful outcomes.[40]

Tikvah's experiences underscore a vital essential ingredient to the why of debate: resilience. The losses that debaters face not only in the amicable practices of tournaments but the more demanding recourses of everyday life are the building blocks of a world without genocide. We cannot move forward on political fronts until we have within ourselves the taught empathy acquired in losses. Losses while retaining hope form the character of great advocates and the truly enduring triumphs of historical justice. For my daughter and I to meet with her on a beautiful summer Thursday night in Jerusalem after this loss was the highlight of our first trip to Israel. She remains an enduring model of why the teaching of advocacy, argumentation and debate are so important.

CONCLUSION

All of these examples point to the ready potential of argumentation study and practice to open societies and improve the human condition. The emphasis on American precepts is not a formula for imperialism. America represents a unique international vessel of international concerns. The primary driver of American innovation and diversity of thought for the past one hundred years is immigration. Tens of millions of people from all around the world immigrated to the United States, and the reflective power of these lives lived now reach around the world to touch the original families of these American descendants. As noted in the case of James Farmer Jr., the arguments of the American civil rights movement originated in India. Nonetheless, the ongoing adversity of human rights abuses in the global twenty-first century suggest an urgency to proliferating communication pedagogy that emphasizes argument study and practice. Those practices will necessarily be sensitive to local communities. When I am in foreign nations trying to establish debate topics, I begin the lesson by asking my audience what they think is a good debate topic, rather than imposing my own. While this may not be a permanently sufficient arrangement as the dialogue in our collective education continues, it is a good starting point.

The American context underscores another key international idea. Americans have an exceptional opportunity to engage the world within their own borders because of a large indigenous immigrant population—especially on college campuses. More than almost anywhere else in the world, immigration is a huge part of daily American life and that reality continues in the harsh political lights of immigration policy politics. Conversations in the United States about argumentation have a tremendous potential to travel around the world in unexpected ways. As previously noted, Jean Michel Habineza first learned about debate at the American university in Maryland—Towson University. Habineza also studies in California at Pepperdine University. Millions of students on every campus have a regular opportunity to influence the emergence of argumentation in nations around the world.

Ultimately, these discursive complexity building projects, whether originating in the USHMM, the Bush Center, church missions, or the Passages program, create a global pressure for openness and the end of genocide. The pretext of genocide—propaganda—is destroyed as a genocidal fuel by the deliberative nature of debate. What is the other side of that controversial claim? Where is the best evidence to answer this complicated social question? Pedagogical agendas like those represented in these questions thwart the emergence of authoritarianism and give rise to events like the popular uprising against Omar Bashir in Sudan in 2019. The prospects of abolishing genocide as a social practice are within our human grasp if education can promote debate appropriately as these many examples demonstrate.

NOTES

1. Steven Pinker, "Why Violence Is Vanishing," *Wall Street Journal*, accessed on September 24, 2011, http://www.wsj.com/articles/SB10001424052702304537904577151462937794706420057585321203589408180.

2. Sarah Bakewell, "Steven Pinker Continues to See the Glass Half Full," *New York Times*, March 2, 2018, accessed July 10, 2019, https://www.nytimes.com/2018/03/02/books/review/steven-pinker-enlightenment-now.html.

3. Hans Rosling, "200 Countries in 200 Years," BBC/YouTube, https://www.youtube.com/watch?v=jbkSRLYSojo.

4. "16 Ways the World Is Getting Remarkably Better: Visuals by Statistician Hans Rosling," *Open Culture*, May 26, 2020, http://www.openculture.com/2020/05/16-ways-the-world-is-getting-remarkably-better.html.

5. Stéphane Courtois and Mark Kramer, *The Black Book of Communism: Crimes, Terror, Repression,* . . . [et al.]; translated by Jonathan Murphy and Mark Kramer, consulting editor Mark Kramer (Cambridge, MA: Harvard University Press, 1999).

6. Rudolph Rummel, *Death by Government* (London: Transaction Publishers, 2004); and Rana Mitter, "The World's Wartime Debt to China," *New York Times*, October 17, 2013, https://www.nytimes.com/2013/10/18/opinion/the-worlds-wartime-debt-to-china.html.

7. Laura Levitt, *American Jewish Loss after the Holocaust* (New York: New York University Press, 2007).

8. Ben Voth, *The Rhetoric of Genocide: Death as a Text* (Lanham, MD: Lexington Press, 2014).

9. Robert Denton and Ben Voth, *Social Fragmentation and the Decline of American Democracy* (London: Palgrave Macmillan, 2017).

10. Mitchell Langbert, "Homogenous: The Political Affiliations of Elite Liberal Arts College Faculty," *Academic Questions*, Summer 2018, accessed July 30, 2019, https://www.nas.org/academic-questions/31/2/homogenous_the_political_affiliations_of_elite_liberal_arts_college_faculty.

11. Stokely Carmichael, "Black Power," *Voices of Democracy*, October 29, 1966, accessed September 22, 2019, https://voicesofdemocracy.umd.edu/carmichael-black-power-speech-text/.

12. Saul D. Alinsky, *Rules for Radicals: A Practical Primer for Realistic Radicals* (New York: Random House, 1971).

13. Wayne Brockriede, "Arguers as Lovers," *Philosophy and Rhetoric* 5, no. 1 (January 1, 1972): 1–11.

14. Paulo Freire, *Pedagogy of the Oppressed* (New York: Continuum Publishing Company, 1970).

15. Michel Foucault, "Politics and Reason," in *Politics, Philosophy, Culture: Interviews and Other Writings: 1977–1984* (New York: Routledge, 1988).

16. Daniel Schorr, "Iran's Holocaust-Denial Conference: A Community of Hate; The Iranian Effort to Mount a Holocaust Denial Campaign Is Linked with the Israeli-Palestinian Crisis: ALL Edition," *The Christian Science Monitor* (1983). Boston: The Christian Science Publishing Society (d/b/a "The Christian Science Monitor"), trusteeship under the laws of the Commonwealth of Massachusetts, December 22, 2006.

17. Elihu Richter and Alex Barnea, "Tehran's Genocidal Incitement against Israel," *Middle East Quarterly* 16, no. 3 (June 22, 2009).

18. "Voth Helps Holocaust Survivors Tell Their Stories," *Miami Report*, July 13, 2006, https://miamioh.edu/news/article/view/9919.

19. James Heffernan, "For JMU Students, Refugee Plight Hits Home," *James Madison University News*, November 1, 2012, https://www.jmu.edu/news/2012/11/lost-boys-no-land.shtml.

20. Jeremy Sharon, "Farrakhan Compares Jews to Termites, Says They Are 'Stupid,'" *The Jerusalem Post* (Jerusalem: The Jerusalem Post Ltd, October 18, 2018).

21. David D. Kirkpatrick, "U.S. Criticizes Egypt's Leader for Anti-Semitic Remarks: Foreign Desk," *New York Times* (New York: New York Times Company, January 16, 2013, Late Edition [East Coast] edition).

22. "What's So Sinister about Jews' Buying Land from Arabs?: Final Edition," *Washington Post* (Washington, D.C.: WP Company LLC d/b/a The Washington Post, January 23, 1988).

23. "Attackers Carve Jewish Star into Back of Iraqi Poet in S. Louis," *Israel Faxx*, Electronic World Communications, Inc, 2011.

24. Cem Özdemir, "Controversy over Turkish Movie: Beyond the Valley of the Wolves," *Speigel Online*, February 22, 2006, accessed August 1, 2007, http://www.spiegel.de/international/0,1518,401565,00.html.

25. Kyle Neubeck, "DeSean Jackson Shares Anti-Semitic Quotes Attributed to Hitler on Instagram," *Philly Voice,* July 7, 2020, https://www.phillyvoice.com/eagles-desean-jackson-anti-semitic-instagram-farrakhan-hitler-quotes/.

26. Kenneth Burke, *The Philosophy of Literary Form: Studies in Symbolic Action* (New York: Vintage, 1941): 191–220.

27. Nat Hentoff, "The World's Oldest Hatred Hasn't Gone Away," *Aspen Daily News,* August 20, 2006; and Hilary Krieger, "Jewish World Marks Rise in Antisemitism," *Jerusalem Post,* August 1, 2006.

28. Aaron Hanscom, "Confronting a Worldwide Jew-Hatred," *History News Network,* April 24, 2007.

29. Özdemir, "Controversy over Turkish Movie: Beyond the Valley of the Wolves."

30. Clarence Page, "Learning from Andrew Young's Blunder," *Chicago Tribune,* August 21, 2006.

31. "Professor Fired after 9-11, Nazi Comparison," *NBC News,* July 24, 2007, accessed August 10, 2020, http://www.nbcnews.com/id/19940243/ns/us_news-education/t/professor-fired-after--nazi-comparison/#.UkJL8RY9roM 2013.

32. Middle East Media Research Institute, 2020, Memri.org.

33. "Watch President Clinton Speak at the Dedication of the George W. Bush Presidential Library," PBS/YouTube, April 25, 2013, accessed August 10, 2020, https://www.youtube.com/watch?v=F8zS23nAy5k.

34. George W. Bush Presidential Center, accessed August 17, 2020, https://www.bushcenter.org/explore-our-work/index.html.

35. Voth, *The Rhetoric of Genocide: Death as a Text,* 127.

36. Elie Wiesel, foreword, in *The Courage to Care,* Eds. Carol Rittmer and Sondra Myers (New York: New York University Press, 1986).

37. Martin Luther King Jr., "I Have a Dream Speech," *March on Washington,* August 28, 1963, accessed August 10, 2020, https://www.americanrhetoric.com/speeches/mlkihaveadream.htm.

38. Matthew 5–7, *New American Standard Bible* (Anaheim, CA: Lockman Foundation, 1997).

39. "The Law of Return 5710 (1950)," Article 1, July 5, 1950, https://knesset.gov.il/laws/special/eng/return.htm.

40. Personal statement of Tikvah, August 1, 2020 [name redacted].

ELEVEN

Coolidge Debate Pedagogy

A Historic and Inclusive Model for Today
(Matthew Lucci and Ben Voth)

This chapter contains the primary ingredients to a recent debate format revision known as Coolidge debate (2013–present). Calvin Coolidge was transformed by debate instruction in college at Amherst. This instruction allowed him to believe he could be a leader and animated his capacities as president of the United States. The chapter explains the Coolidge Debate Curriculum used to teach students how to speak and argue as derived from the same rhetorical resources used to teach Calvin Coolidge. The chapter explains the Coolidge format of debate for high school students and its broader implications for debate practice globally. Several key areas are discussed: (1) the significance of debate to the leadership emergence of Calvin Coolidge, (2) the rhetorical training of Calvin Coolidge at Amherst College, (3) the Harding and Coolidge administration arguments against racism, (4) Coolidge's profoundly positive rhetoric on the problem of racism, (5) Coolidge's Birthplace: the historical site of Plymouth Notch, Vermont, and (6) the Coolidge Debate format.

THE SIGNIFICANCE OF DEBATE TO THE LEADERSHIP EMERGENCE OF CALVIN COOLIDGE

American president Calvin Coolidge (1923–1929) is an individual whose leadership potential was positively developed by educational experiences in debate. As a young man of good character, Coolidge was nonetheless not profoundly popular at his college at Amherst.[1] Initially, fraternities that made up an important component of social life for such colleges completely rejected Coolidge's application for membership—rendering him a non-Greek citizen of college life at Amherst.[2] Despite that social setback on his path toward leadership, Coolidge was positively affected by the intellectual opportunity to debate in college. Coolidge arrived at Amherst despite severe setbacks educationally and one student at Amherst described him in thoroughly unimpressive terms: "very eccentric fellow, not particularly brilliant, neither popular nor unpopular, no leader in anything, an honest fellow, a good speaker, could write a good speech and deliver it well, but we boys never looked on him as a leader."[3] Coolidge took three terms of debate while a college student at Amherst, and he wrote home to his father about how profound the experience was for him. Ultimately, as a senior, Coolidge would be accepted by a fraternity.

In 1894, Coolidge debated fellow student Charles Benett on the question: "Do the United States owe more to England or to Holland?" Such debating formed the basis of much of his writing and public speaking activity while in college. He would write while in college, "There is nothing in the world gives me so much pleasure as to feel I have made a good speech and nothing gives me more pain than to feel I have a made a poor one."[4] These educational experiences were transformative to escalating the humble Vermont beginnings of Calvin Coolidge to one of the world's most important historical leaders as a president of the United States. Coolidge's formation through debate is an important model, and his current standing intersects with an important contemporary obstacle in American education: anti-Republican bias. Consequent to a growing ideological disparity among American academics, the intellectual review of Republican political leadership is viewed with increasing reactionary zeal.[5] The Harding/Coolidge administration of 1921 to 1929 is an important era that is presently without fair consideration among academic experts.[6] Understanding his arguments and advocacy can help rectify this problem and insure that our study of debate is not tainted by ideological bias.

THE RHETORICAL TRAINING OF CALVIN COOLIDGE AT AMHERST COLLEGE

A 1962 dissertation at the University of Indiana by Arthur Fleser provides us with an in-depth answer to the particular rhetorical instruction that went into making Calvin Coolidge a formidable political leader for the twentieth century.[7] At the heart of the instruction was an influential professor not unlike Melvin Tolson was for James Farmer Jr. For Coolidge, the key faculty ingredient was Professor Charles Edward Garman. Coolidge wrote six pages in his autobiography about how Professor Garman was a divinely inspiring teacher and one can glean that much of the governing principles of President Coolidge were founded in the classes of Garman.[8] Coolidge learned the principles of careful analysis in argumentation and the proper method of presenting a subject and argument.[9] Garman quoted from the Bible, science, sociology, economics, and other related areas to train Coolidge.[10]

From Coolidge's personal notes taken in college at Amherst this specific methodology of study in rhetorical texts is provided:

Analysis of Orations

1. Give brief sketch of the oration.
2. Give brief sketch of the circumstances which led to the delivery of the oration.
3. Give brief sketch of the attendant circumstances, if noteworthy — audience, place, state of the public mind, favorable or unfavorable conditions.
4. Give the especial end which the orator has in view.
5. Give the orator's general method of attaining this end — how he meets prejudice, or other obstacles.
6. Give AN ABSTRACT — of the oration — the introduction, argument, appeal.
7. Give characteristics of the presentation of the argument or appeal — (a) whether put in a logical or popular form; (b) whether concise or diffuse; (c) whether abstract or concrete; (d) whether sentences are declarative or interrogative, long or short; loose, close or compact, well or ill-adapted for delivery.[11]

This rubric is typical of those found in rhetorical study texts today.[12] This methodology clarifies how Coolidge came to be an effective leader even with carefully chosen and measured words.

THE HARDING AND COOLIDGE'S ADMINISTRATION ARGUMENTS AGAINST RACISM

Coolidge was exceptionally egalitarian in his view of racial equality. The foundations of the arguments were equally rooted in the presidential lead of the ticket in 1920: Warren Harding. Harding as president elected in the aftermath of women's suffrage spoke profoundly on the question of race in 1921 in Birmingham, Alabama:

> "When I suggest the possibility of economic equality between the races, I mean it precisely the same way and to the same extent that I would mean it if I spoke of equality of economic opportunity as between members of the same race," Harding said. "Whether you like it or not, unless our democracy is a lie you must stand for that equality."
>
> Looking at the Black section of the segregated auditorium where he was speaking, he continued, "I want to be looking in their [the Black

audience] direction when I say these things because I am speaking to North and South alike, white and blacks alike. I am never going to say anything that I can't say in every direction and to all people exactly alike."[13]

A variety of Black leaders affirmed the speech as important and positive. Dr. Robert R. Moton of the Tuskegee Institute called the speech the "most important utterance on the question by a President since Lincoln."[14] W. E. B. Du Bois praised the speech as did Marcus Garvey. Harding's position as the first president elected by both White men and women draws attention to one of the important racial controversies and underscores the significance of Harding's racial arguments. One of the key arguments made by opposing Democrat partisans was that Harding was not White, the *New York Times* explained the controversy within his election of 1920: "Will Americans vote for a black president? If the notorious historian William Estabrook Chancellor was right, we already did. In the early 1920s, Chancellor helped assemble a controversial biographical portrait accusing President Warren Harding of covering up his family's 'colored' past. According to the family tree Chancellor created, Harding was actually the great-grandson of a Black woman. Under the one-drop rule of American race relations, Chancellor claimed, the country had inadvertently elected its 'first Negro president.'"[15] Harding publicly challenged the previous norms of the Wilson administration which explicitly introduced racial segregation to the Federal workforce. Harding and Coolidge worked together to support anti-lynching legislation at the Federal level within Congress, but Democrats were always successful in defeating the measure. All of this took place before the untimely death of Harding in the summer of 1923 and the ascendancy of Coolidge to the Presidency. Coolidge left little doubt about his own convictions with regard to race.

COOLIDGE'S PROFOUNDLY POSITIVE RHETORIC ON THE PROBLEM OF RACISM

As of January 2020, most recent public surveys showed that American assessments of race relations were improving in the past few years.[16] This is prior to the sensational events surrounding the death of George Floyd in the custody of Minneapolis police after the use of a knee chokehold. It is nonetheless important to understand where misunderstandings on the important question of race often arise. There is an unfortunate ideological stereotype that Republican presidents are racists and want racism to increase as a matter of political strategy. Such stereotypes factored into the incredible claim by Kanye West in 2005 that President Bush wanted Black people to die in the disaster of Hurricane Katrina that struck New Orleans.[17] More recently, there are common claims by major media commentators, such as Don Lemon, that President Trump is a racist. Regardless of our partisan affiliations, an accurate sense of race relations with regard to the American presidency is highly important to the larger goal of improving race relations, not only in the United States, but worldwide. A profound case study that can help dissipate the Republican president stereotype on race is President Calvin Coolidge. A textual analysis of his speeches demonstrates that President Calvin Coolidge was an exceptional proponent of racial equality in the United States, standing in sharp contrast to his presidential predecessor and ideological rival Woodrow Wilson.

As a Democratic party president, Wilson embodied high ideals of progressivism. In this view, an enlightened view of human progress could begin to supplant the traditions and norms of a constitutional republic. The checks on governance were not as necessary in the case of a highly enlightened intellectual view emerging in the early twentieth century. Wilson thoroughly endorsed racism as a necessary political practice within American governance and one which would lead to "progress" for our society. The Federal workforce was explicitly segregated on the basis of race by Wilson because he believed Whites would better advance the human condition as part of his larger social belief in progressivism. As president of Princeton, Wilson told a Black applicant to the school it is "altogether inadvisable for a colored man to enter Princeton." Wilson's academic textbook *A History of the American People,* described Reconstruction-era efforts to free the South from "the incubus of that ignorant and often hostile" Black vote.[18] The effort to sanitize and isolate Wilson's cynical racist assumptions about America are rooted in equally cynical contemporary efforts to play politics with American presidential rhetoric and valorize through subversive means the inherently racist notions of progressivism that continue to our present day. As a Democrat, Wilson was opposed to the views of his Republican rivals that attracted the American Black vote since the emancipation unleashed by President Abraham Lincoln. In fact, Wilson had praised the film *The Birth of a Nation*, which glorified the Ku Klux Klan. By contrast, Coolidge cast the deciding vote to ban the film in Boston.[19]

Coolidge believed and personally practiced a conviction of equality toward African Americans. This academic hiding of Coolidge and exalting of men like Wilson and FDR are part of a painful ideological suppression designed to create an arc of history in the direction of the blue privilege practiced broadly in academia.[20] Coolidge is ranked #28 among forty-five American presidents in the most recent ranking by scholars while Wilson is ranked #11.[21] Coolidge's Christian humanist upbringing at Amherst College laid the foundation for an exceptional American idealist to begin reversing the "progressivism" of Wilson and defend the dignity of African Americans in the United States. Coolidge's political rhetoric on race in America is remarkable and stands as an ethical beacon of discursive complexity within our intellectual webs of deceit attached to contemporary studies of political rhetoric. Several key incidents of Coolidge's political communication demonstrate the American ethical model.

Initially, at the dedication of a government hospital for colored veterans of the World War, in Tuskegee, Alabama, for Lincoln's Birthday, February 12, 1923, indicated even as vice president the high priority of viewing African Americans not only as equal but exemplary with regard to public services and the highest sacrifices that a fellow American could make in times of war. The dedication of the hospital at Tuskegee was motivated primarily by the aftermath of such sacrifice in World War I. Coolidge provided this analysis of African American combat actions:

> They had the commendation of the secretary of war General Pershing, and former President Roosevelt, Brigadier-General Sherburne, of Massachusetts, who trained and commanded some of the negro artillery, gave me this statement: "Tuskegee, during the war, furnished to the colored artillery regiments some of the finest troops in France. In technical excellence they were unsurpassed. They developed wireless and telephone communication effectively and showed marked ability in the technical lines of artillery. President Moton himself saw the work of the colored artillery and the destruction wrought by it."[22]

Coolidge's remarks contain no hint of paternalistic notions of passionate inferiority to be found in his African American coequals. These African-Americans excel at technical matters at the far forefront of the nation's abilities and even today read as if a near science-fiction-like capacity to conduct the art of war. Moreover, Coolidge derived his own remarks from study and research about their conduct. Coolidge concludes his remarks at this dedication with an impressive integration of Lincoln's emancipatory goals toward the kind of American exceptionalism that distillates a truer notion of "human rights." In our contemporary parlance, Coolidge's remarks ring with a strange twenty-first-century appreciation of justice and the intimate demands of civic dedication to a community of friendship:

> It takes time and patience and perseverance to put into practice our theory of human rights. Lincoln knew that. If there was one virtue that he seemed to possess more than any other, it was that of forbearance. It is well for us, who must live together as Americans, whatever our race or creed may be, constantly to remember his words: "We are not enemies, but friends. We must not be enemies." Those who stir up animosities, those who create any kind of hatred and enmity are not ministering to the public welfare. We have come out of the war with a desire and determination to live at peace with all the world. Out of a common suffering and a common sacrifice there came a new meaning to our common citizenship. Our greatest need is to live in harmony, in friendship, and in good-will not seeking an advantage over each other but all trying to serve each other. In that spirit let us dedicate this hospital and

dedicate ourselves to the service of our country. To do what wisely, patiently, tolerantly, is to show by the discharge of our duties our indisputable title to fellow citizenship with Abraham Lincoln.[23]

These remarks were not isolated or peculiar. They did not constitute some undue obligation handed off to him by President Harding. Even upon his ascendancy to the presidency in that summer, Coolidge would redouble his efforts to speak to and enact a clear public persona that Blacks and Whites were coequal in his vision of America. His remarks did not focus on the enemies of this vision, but rather excavated from the character exploits of African Americans the evidence needed for all Americans to recognize the foolishness of racial bigotry.

As a new president, Coolidge made a deliberate point of speaking at Howard University in 1924 for their commencement ceremonies not long after being elevated from the vice presidency in August of 1923. Howard was, and is, arguably the preeminent HBCU in the United States. His remarks there stand as a stark clarion call against the outrageous racism of Wilson:

> The nation has need of all that can be contributed to it through the best efforts of all its citizens. The colored people have repeatedly proved their devotion to the high ideals of our country. They gave their services to the war with the same patriotism and readiness that other citizens did. The propaganda of prejudice and hatred which sought to keep the colored men from supporting the national cause completely failed. The Black man showed himself the same kind of citizen, moved by the same kind of patriotism as the White man. They were tempted, but not one betrayed his country. They came home with many decorations, and their conduct repeatedly won high commendation from both American and European commanders.[24]

Coolidge's remarks echoed rhetoric offered before the U.S. Congress in 1924:

> Numbered among our population are some 12,000,000 Colored people. Under our Constitution their rights are just as sacred as those of any other citizen. It is both a public and a private duty to protect those rights.[25]

Coolidge would go on in every single State of the Union speech, from 1923 to 1928, to comment for at least one paragraph about racial equality. Coolidge's remarks stand in sharp contrast to those like democratic South Carolina Governor Strom Thurmond who more than twenty years later in 1947 described Wilson's practice of segregation this way:

> I want to tell you, ladies and gentlemen, that there's not enough troops in the army to force the southern people to break down segregation and admit the nigger race into our theatres into our swimming pools into our homes and into our churches.[26]

Coolidge's stance on race was not strategic, cynical, or manipulative. It was consistent with an idealistic notion of American rights and clearly juxtaposed against the increasingly entrenched racist premises of progressivism. Coolidge's ethical stance on race was clear in public remarks he chose to take against members of his own political party. In 1924, political leaders in New York City demanded that a Black man not be allowed to run for public office on the basis of his race. President Coolidge wrote the following letter published in a Brooklyn paper:

> My dear sir,
> Your letter is received, accompanied by a newspaper clipping which discussed the possibility that a colored man may be the Republican nominee from one of the New York districts. Referring to this newspaper statement, you say:
> "It is of some concern whether a Negro is allowed to run for Congress anywhere, at any time, in any party, in this, a White man's country. Repeated ignoring of the growing race problem does not excuse us for allowing encroachments . . ."
>
> Leaving out of consideration the manifest impropriety of the president intruding himself in a local contest for nomination, I was amazed to receive such a letter. During the war 500,000 colored men and boys were called up under the draft, not one of whom sought to evade it. They took their places wherever assigned in defense of the nation of which they are just as truly citizens as are any others. The suggestion of denying any measure of their full political rights to such a great group of our population as the colored people is one which, however it might be received in some other quarters, could not possibly be permitted by one who feels a responsibility for living up to the traditions and maintaining the principles of the Republican Party.
>
> Our Constitution guarantees equal rights to all our citizens, without discrimination on account of race or color. I have taken my oath to support that Constitution. It is the source of your rights and my rights. I purpose to regard it, and administer it, as the source of the rights of all the people, whatever their belief or race. A colored man is precisely as much entitled to submit his candidacy in a party primary, as is any other citizen. The decision must be made by the constituents to whom he offers himself, and by nobody else. You have suggested that in some fashion I should bring influence to bear to prevent the possibility of a colored man being nominated for Congress. In reply, I quote my great predecessor, Theodore Roosevelt: ". . . I cannot consent to take the position that the door of hope—the door of opportunity—is to be shut upon any man, no matter how worthy, purely upon the grounds of race or color."
> Yours very truly, etc.
> Calvin Coolidge[27]

Coolidge's American idealism with regard to race stands in 1924 light-years ahead of many more contemporary utterances on race since that time. The fact that this political communication took place in opposition to the local politics of his own party highlights that Coolidge was communicating from a point of political idealism rather than pragmatism or cynicism. These are at least eight rather prominent examples of the historically ethical and profound political arguments of President Calvin Coolidge who stood in sharp contrast to his "progressive" predecessor President Woodrow Wilson. These instances include four State of the Union messages (1924–1927) that all made mention of negro equality, the speech at Howard commencement, the vice-presidential speech in 1923 at Tuskegee, the New York newspaper letter, and the 1925 Omaha speech. This political advocacy now almost one hundred years old indicts contemporary studies of Coolidge that have ignorantly supposed that Coolidge was "among America's most racist Presidents."[28] Such appellations reveal a blue privilege bias within our intellectual culture that is cynically committed to perpetuating partisan stereotypes that hurt rather than help race relations.[29] It is therefore not surprising that one of the most common nicknames for Coolidge is "Silent Cal"—suggesting that we should not be surprised to find nothing in the historical record for major speeches by Coolidge. Coolidge's public stances were not without moral effect. Noted Coolidge scholar Amity Shlaes documents a significant decline in lynchings during the presidential era of Coolidge. According to *Historical Statistics of the United States: From Colonial Times to the Present* (1975) there were fifty-one racial lynchings reported in the United States in 1922 after reaching a peak of seventy-seven in 1919. By the time Coolidge left office in 1929, reported lynchings declined to just seven annually.[30] Lynchings were nearly 90 percent lower in the United States at the end of Coolidge's presidency than they were at the height of the Wilson presidency.

The implications of Coolidge's strong rhetoric and actions against racism are profound.[31] Initially, the stereotype that Republican presidents aspire to be racist is defied by the profound risk-taking Coolidge engaged in by confronting local prejudices around the nation. Moreover, Coolidge was challenging a normative feature of Democratic party politics that appealed to the supposed virtue of segregation. When partisans use racism as a rhetorical charge to broadly smear an entire party, it damages the largest quest to reduce the human problem of racism. Acknowledging important argument and political actions that reduce racism are as much, and perhaps a more important part toward a solution than consistently pointing to a problem. Coolidge himself summarized this uniquely American political methodology that has consistently moved our nation forward:

> While everyone knows that evil exists, there is yet sufficient good in the people to supply material for most of the comment that needs to be made. The only way I know to drive out evil from the country is by the constructive method of filling it with good. The country is better off

tranquilly considering its blessing and merits, and earnestly striving to secure more of them, than it would be in nursing hostile bitterness about its deficiencies and faults.[32]

COOLIDGE'S BIRTHPLACE: THE HISTORICAL SITE OF PLYMOUTH NOTCH, VERMONT

One of the unusual challenges faced by the Coolidge Presidential Foundation is bringing students to a relatively remote location of Plymouth Notch, Vermont. The site is relatively imperative since it is both the birthplace of Calvin Coolidge and the physical site of the presidential foundation for Calvin Coolidge. The Coolidge site is the last of American presidents provided on the basis of private donations and support. This is in keeping with the famously fiscally conservative arguments of the thirtieth president, Calvin Coolidge. Nonetheless, it is useful to observe that beginning with Herbert Hoover—Coolidge's successor to the presidency—the Federal government funds a repository and physical site for each American president. All presidents since Hoover have Federal government funds dedicated to the building and maintenance of a presidential library.

The Coolidge homestead site, located at the foundation in Plymouth Notch, is the largest intact historical homestead of any American president. An essentially intact small town as it existed in the early twentieth century is maintained at the site. Here, visitors can see the home where on August 3, 1923, Calvin Coolidge's father swore in the new president at 2:00 a.m. He was unique in being sworn in with such an unusual location and the mechanism of his father—a notary public swearing him in. The homestead site contains many interesting elements, including a barn, a cheese factory, a home, a restaurant, a church, gardens, and the more contemporary Coolidge Foundation building. The community church that Coolidge attended has an American flag marking the pew that Coolidge sat in throughout his life. The church served as an important deliberative center of the town, including city governance where a young Coolidge would have witnessed the first civic deliberations of his life along with his father. All of this is situated in the broader geographic context of the rolling Green Mountains of Vermont that provide a spectacular rural setting, dominated by trees and meadows. Visitors are immediately impressed by the humble beginnings of a powerful national leader.

An inescapably important component is the cemetery. The U.S. Federal government lays a wreath on the grave of every American president on their birthday. Coolidge is the only American president born on the fourth of July; therefore, festivities at Plymouth Notch focus upon this annual event. Coolidge's gravestone is provocative for its plain and understated nature. Compared to many other stones in the cemetery it is smaller, plainer, and less elaborate. His stone is nearly identical to that of his wife Grace, who is buried next to him. The burial markers are rhetorically indicative of the kind of humble and simple man that Coolidge was. Varying audiences gather every fourth of July to march about three hundred yards from the Plymouth Notch town to the cemetery site where Coolidge is buried. Around noon, this procession takes place and commemorative remarks are made after a military presentation of the wreath. Taps is played by a lone bugler in the cemetery to commence the event. Fourth of July events for the entire day often include a morning naturalization ceremony for approximately twenty-five inductees and an afternoon of high school debates culminating in an outdoor championship round under a tent with a panel of approximately nine judges. The physical scene of Plymouth Notch, Vermont, is an important part of the overall character of the Coolidge debate series and provides a lasting impression about American political origins.

THE COOLIDGE DEBATE FORMAT

It is with this profound biography in mind that Amity Shlaes and Matthew Denhart committed to leading the Coolidge Presidential Foundation in establishing, with my leadership, a unique debate format in 2013 (figure 11.1). As the only president born on the fourth of July—American Independence Day—the foundation established a national debate tournament for high school students. The content of these debates was founded upon an emphasis on economic topics. Students debated on topics ranging from immigration, to trade, to the impact of COVID-19 stay at home orders. This interest also came alongside an important reform effort directed toward national debate practice: citizen judges.

Conventionally, speech and debate communities over time develop specialized communities of judges—typically composed of coaches and teachers. Those conventions naturally over time develop at least two insidious potentials that are seen in most debate formats: (1) insular debate lingo and (2) rapid delivery rates of arguments. These two factors, along with other social norming, processes create a community of competitive debate that is increasingly impenetrable to the general public. This tends to increase the atrophy of public support for debate as they see it as less inherently meaningful to their own experiences. The Coolidge Cup focuses on defeating that tendency by utilizing citizen judges.

The idea of citizen judges relates well to the larger Coolidge biography and the broader American theme of government by the people and for the people. This point is emphasized in the annual judge training that takes place at Plymouth Notch, Vermont. Coolidge's humble beginnings underscores the important American notion that anyone can be president. The tournament emphasizes the idea that debate is an empowering pedagogy that can make that dream come true for any young person. Similarly, anyone can and should be able to judge debates.

Judge training for the Coolidge Cup seeks to interrupt an important cycle of crisis that inhabits conventional competitive debate forms. Whether parliamentary, policy, Lincoln/Douglas, or Cross Examination Debate Association (CEDA), various formats of debate tend to go through a cycle of reform to technical narrowing. The competitive drive at the heart of debate leads all participants to maximize an effort of rhetorical efficiency. This efficiency quickly leads to shorthand explanations of complex arguments. Single letters like the letter *k* can represent a critique or CP can represent a counterplan. A2 can mean "answers to: ____." Students, coaches, and judges gradually learn that if students speak more quickly opponents are more likely to be overwhelmed by the advocacy in round. College policy debate can easily lead students toward words per minute (wpm) discussions of over four hundred wpm. Standard conversations typically range from 125 to 180 wpm. There is also a spiral of cynicism wherein it is easier to tear down ideas rather than to build them up. Students learn that denouncing ideas rather than affirming them is the most efficient rhetorical path. It is entirely possible in contemporary policy debate for the students to say little to nothing about a topic regarding space or health care and rather dwell on whether their opponents can be successfully cornered as "racists" or perhaps "transphobic." All of this points away from the intellectual idea of discovering better ideas. This driving efficiency and associated characteristics makes the debate activity more technical and less accessible to newcomers. Judge training at Coolidge is centered on the importance of public judges who lack this pattern of initiation. The Coolidge judges imagine an ideal rhetorical space similar to the experiences of Calvin Coolidge and the broader American idealism that imagines intellectual discovery as improving the social condition. The one-hour judge training provided to adults largely inexperienced in college or high school debate focuses on essential rhetorical notions such as delivery, style, and substance. Tabula rasa—the notion of a mental blank slate—is urged as a method for avoiding personal bias while judging. These judges are unable and unwilling to adapt themselves to the shorthand conventions common in other major national formats of debate.

Nonetheless, the Coolidge format is unique for its appeal across debate formats. Any student is welcome to enter, but all are informed that the judges are regular American citizens seeking to hear a persuasive case made by high school students on a topic of current controversy.[33] It is one of the few inter-format championships in the United States. The centrality of the judges makes the format less amenable to the cynical declines of debate reform that tend to discourage novice participation and the larger spread of debate as a social and educational practice. This form of debate is designed to have intrinsic public appeal.

Since 2013, the investment and return on debate as an activity in the remote reaches of Plymouth Notch, Vermont, are profound. More than twenty-five thousand students have debated Coolidge Foundation de-

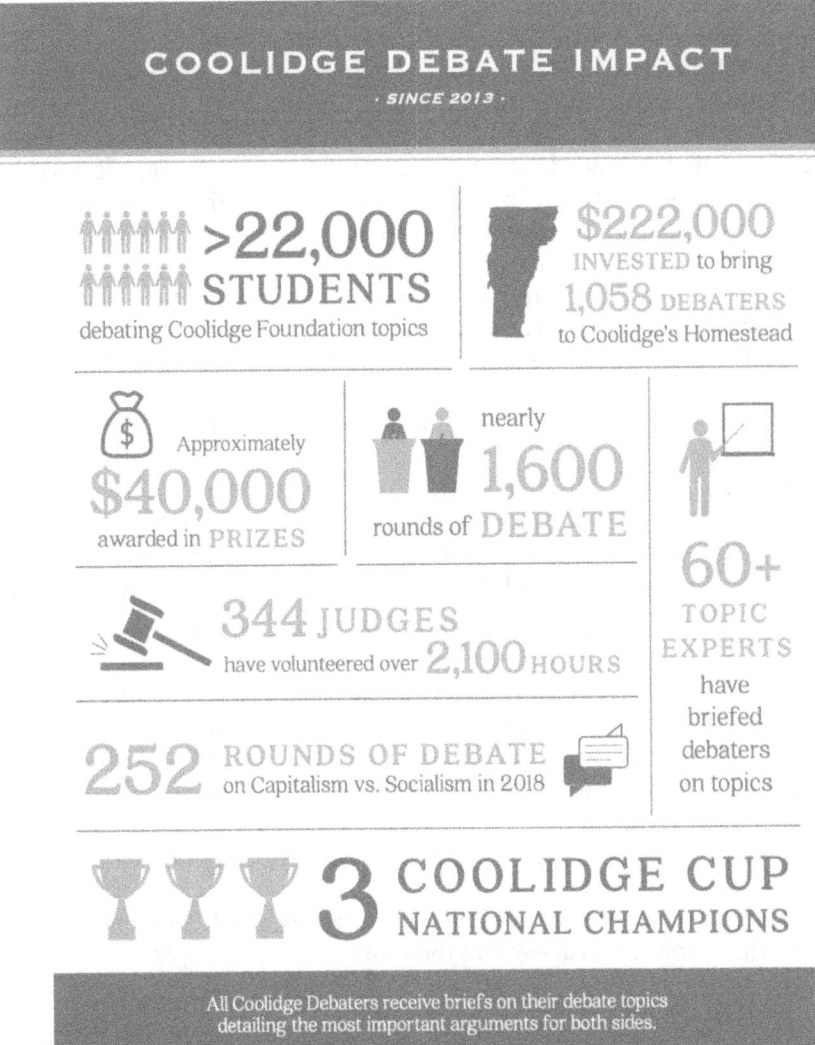

Figure 11.1. Coolidge Debate Impact since 2013.

bate topics. More than $250,000 has been invested to bring students to this competition. More than $60,000 in prize money has been awarded to top high school students from around the nation. There have been more than two thousand rounds of Coolidge debate. More than sixty different topic efforts briefed students including individuals such as Roberto Salinas—a Mexican economist—and Maggie Seidel—the special assistant to Governor Noem of South Dakota. The foundation produced fifteen different topic briefs that were typically fifteen to twenty-five pages of high-quality research about the topics. Roughly one hundred arguments were produced on each side of the affirmative and negative of these resolutions. More than 250 academic articles are references in these briefs. In 2018, for example, the Coolidge Cup conducted more than 250 rounds on the topic of socialism versus capitalism in its summer championship tournament. More than four hundred judges have donated more than 2,500 hours of time to judge high school students debating. Partnering with iDebate Rwanda's Dreamers Academy, for the first time, two students from Rwanda qualified to attend to the Coolidge Cup in 2020—making it an international championship. Rwanda's varsity competitor finished as #34 among more than ninety competitors in the 2020 tournament.

In 2016, the debate activities of the Coolidge Foundation were formalized into the official offer of a Coolidge Cup funded by Bob Luddy. This was the culmination of debate activities that began in 2013 in collaboration with the Bush Institute in Dallas. The resolutions since 2016 were:

2016 *Resolved*: Immigrants contribute to the industry, wealth, and civic culture of the United States.
2017 *Resolved*: The U.S. Federal and state governments should shift the weight of their K–12 education funding in favor of vouchers.
2018 *Resolved*: For the United States, socialism would be a better economic system than capitalism for promoting the well-being of the average person.
2019 *Resolved*: The U.S. Federal government should adopt a policy of unilateral free trade.
2020 *Resolved*: The benefits of the shutdown of the U.S. economy due to the coronavirus are worth the costs.

All of these resolutions sought to emphasize a theme of economics education among young people. Studies on young people show an unusually rapid attrition toward valuing effective economic systems like capitalism and a growing affinity toward deadly and dreadfully unequal economic systems like socialism.[34] Students are able to qualify to the final championship round through regional qualifiers conducted across the United States and online. In 2020, ninety-three students qualified to the Coolidge Cup, including two students from Rwanda in a December tournament qualifier sponsored by the U.S. State Department.

CONCLUSION

The Coolidge debate pedagogy is an important empirical model for the larger global story of how debate can make the world a better place. The Coolidge debate program derives its strength from several key sources: (1) the emphatic and compelling biography of Calvin Coolidge, who was transformed by debate from humble educational beginnings into an individual with a capacity to lead; (2) the rhetorical legacy of President Calvin Coolidge argumentatively dedicated to economic well-being and racial justice; (3) the deliberate design of the Coolidge debate curriculum to encourage wider public participation in the debate process; (4) economic incentives, such as cash prizes, to encourage student motivation; (5) the inter-format nature of this debate tournament, allowing students from a variety of debate formats to join this activity; (6) the root of regional qualifiers to bring the highest quality of debating; (7) the historical site of the Coolidge Presidential Foundation in Plymouth Notch, Vermont as an enduring reminder of how history and legacies further an idealistic future; and (8) high quality programming that brings real-world experts to high school students so they can understand arguments in a proper and realistic context. All of these elements join together in making the Coolidge Cup and associated debate programming a unique and compelling model for debate instruction. Without this unique commitment to the ideals of debate, students would tend to be offered weaker and weaker debate instruction as the natural intellectual processes of cynicism come to dominate competitive practices. Rhetorical shortcuts come to dominate in a way that fewer and fewer schools want to participate and the disjunction between tournament practice and public reception grows wider and wider. Debate can unfortunately become a mechanism where the selfish of a community are attracted in order to magnify their own ambitions and diminish the opportunities of their fellow citizens. It is morally imperative that global debate instruction aim at an inclusive model that makes novices and public observers willing and interested in participation. Debate should naturally encourage discursive complexity—desiring to hear from more voices and not fewer. The style of debate should not be so distinctive or idiosyncratic as to repel the general public or seem out of reach to a new debater. Without this formula of inclusion the life of debate will naturally decline. If debate devolves into a Platonic order where the elite sharpen their minds for rendering a state of servitude among the masses, then the interests of justice and human well-being cannot be well maintained. The narrow band of remaining practitioners will become jaded ideologues denouncing the general inability to appreciate their unusual abilities. The unique approach of the Coolidge Foundation is an exceptional pedagogical model that should be kept in mind as debate pedagogy spreads in more global settings.

NOTES

1. Albert Sargent (August 16, 1923), Boston Traveler, Scrapbook, Forbes Library.
2. Amity Shlaes, *Coolidge*, 1st ed. (New York: Harper, 2013).
3. Sargent, Boston Traveler.
4. Shlaes, *Coolidge*, 54–56.
5. Mitchell Langbert, "Homogenous: The Political Affiliations of Elite Liberal Arts College Faculty," *Academic Questions* 31, no. 2 (Summer 2018).
6. "Ranking America's Worst Presidents," *U.S. News and World Report*, November 6, 2019, accessed August 10, 2020, https://www.usnews.com/news/special-reports/the-worst-presidents/articles/ranking-americas-worst-presidents.
7. Arthur Fleser, *The Rhetoric of Calvin Coolidge* (Dissertation, Indiana University, 1962).
8. Calvin Coolidge (1929), *Autobiography of Calvin Coolidge*, 61–67.
9. Coolidge, *Autobiography of Calvin Coolidge*, 64–65.
10. Garman's letters, lectures and addresses, also pamphlets. Forbes Library. As noted in Fleser, *The Rhetoric of Calvin Coolidge*.
11. Fleser, *The Rhetoric of Calvin Coolidge*.
12. Karlyn Kohrs Campbell and S. Huxman, *The Rhetorical Act*, 3rd ed. (Belmont, CA: Thomson Wadsworth, 2003).
13. Dylan Matthews, "Secret Love Child Aside, Warren Harding Was a Solid President," *Vox*, August 13, 2015.
14. John W. Dean, *Warren G. Harding: The American Presidents Series; The 29th President, 1921–1923* (New York: Times Books, 2004): 126.
15. Beverly Gage, "Our First Black President?" *New York Times*, April 6, 2008.
16. Lydia Saad, "Americans' Take on the U.S. Is Improved, but Still Mixed," *Gallup*, January 27, 2020, accessed August 10, 2020, https://news.gallup.com/poll/284033/americans-improved-mixed.aspx.
17. George W. Bush, *Decision Points* (New York: Broadway, 2010).
18. J. Schuessler, "Woodrow Wilson's Legacy Gets Complicated," *New York Times*, November 29, 2015, accessed August 10, 2020, https://www.nytimes.com/2015/11/30/arts/woodrow-wilsons-legacy-gets-complicated.html.
19. C. Johnson, *Why Coolidge Matters: Leadership Lessons from America's Most Underrated President* (New York: Encounter Books, 2013).
20. Ben Voth, "Academia and Republican Presidents," *American Thinker*, August 21, 2019, accessed August 10, 2020, https://www.americanthinker.com/articles/2019/08/academia_and_republican_presidents.html. Also see R. Denton and B. Voth, "The Epistemological Poisoning of America," *Social Fragmentation and the Decline of American Democracy* (Cham, Switzerland: Palgrave).
21. "Ranking America's Worst Presidents," *US News and World Report*.
22. Calvin Coolidge, "At the Dedication of a Government Hospital for Colored Veterans of the World War, Tuskegee, Alabama, Lincoln's Birthday," February 12, 1923, in *The Price of Freedom: Speeches and Addresses* (Fredonia Books): 276.
23. Coolidge, "At the Dedication of a Government Hospital for Colored Veterans of the World War, Tuskegee, Alabama, Lincoln's Birthday," 279.
24. Calvin Coolidge, *Foundations of the Republic* (Los Angeles: University Press of the Pacific, 2004): 34.
25. Calvin Coolidge, President Calvin Coolidge, First Annual Message to Congress on the State of the Union, December 6, 1923.
26. Taneshi Coates, "Bigotry and the English Language," *The Atlantic*, March 12, 2013, accessed August 10, 2020, https://www.theatlantic.com/national/archive/2013/12/bigotry-and-the-english-language/281935/.
27. David Pietrusza, "Calvin Coolidge and Civil Rights—The Rest of the Story," *The Coolidge Quarterly* 1, no. 3 (November 2016): 10.

28. Ibram X. Kendi, "The 11 Most Racist U.S. Presidents," *Huffington Post*, May 28, 2017, accessed July 10, 2019, https://www.huffpost.com/entry/would-a-president-trump-m_b_10135836.

29. Voth, "Academia and Republican Presidents." Also see Denton and Voth, "The Epistemological Poisoning of America."

30. *Historical Statistics of the United States: From Colonial Times to the Present*, 1975, as reported in K. Schmoke, "The Little Known History of Coolidge and Civil Rights," *Coolidge Quarterly* 1, no. 3 (November 2016): 1–5, accessed May 15, 2020, https://coolidgefoundation.org/wp-content/uploads/2017/01/TheCoolidgeQuarterly_October2016.pdf.

31. J. Blair, "A Time for Parting: The Negro During the Coolidge Years," *Journal of American Studies* 3, no. 2 (1969): 177–99, retrieved fromhttp://www.jstor.org.proxy.libraries.smu.edu/stable/27552892; and A. S. Felzenberg, "Calvin Coolidge and Race: His Record in Dealing with the Racial Tensions of the 1920s," presented at "Calvin Coolidge: Examining the Evidence" conference (Boston: 1998).

32. Coolidge, *Autobiography of Calvin Coolidge*, 186.

33. "The Coolidge Cup," *Calvin Coolidge Presidential Foundation*, 2020, accessed August 10, 2020, https://www.coolidgefoundation.org/debate/coolidge-cup/.

34. Peter Moore, "One Third of Millenials View Socialism Favorably," *Yougov poll*, 2019, accessed August 10, 2020, https://today.yougov.com/topics/politics/articles-reports/2015/05/11/one-third-millennials-like-socialism.

TWELVE

Conclusions

How Debate Helps the Global Human Community

Good debaters are trained to begin reading any source of evidence backwards. This means that a book like this will likely be examined by debaters for its conclusion before its supporting prelude chapters. Debate can bring genocide to an end in the twenty-first century for a number of important reasons: (1) discursive complexity is a key argumentation and debate theoretical construct that diametrically opposes the practice and effectiveness of propaganda; (2) silence among advocates is less likely among those individuals who are taught and coached with debate; (3) various models and examples of debate instruction examined here, including the American civil rights movement, which point to an empirical basis for believing that structural injustices can be diminished and even erased with the skills brought by debate instruction; and (4) many important ongoing models of successful twenty-first century debate instruction are rising in the world, including Historically Black Colleges and Universities (HBCUs), Guatemalan justice methods, Coolidge economic debate, Rwandan high school students learn debate, international conflict resolution curriculums, individual advocacy in front of a national Supreme Court, and Chinese debate leagues. All of these elements justify a conclusion that teaching debate is among the most useful forms of academic instruction any society can endeavor to do for a next generation to improve all social outcomes.

This final chapter provides a theoretical summary of why debate is important and how it empowers individuals. The research clarifies a better future that is possible. This chapter draws upon the operational analogy of the book—Rwanda—and explains that in the same way that this small nation has risen from desperate throes of violence to become a continental leader, the global community can engage a growing middle class to create a new pedagogical communication infrastructure rooted in dialogue and debate. This dialogue features aspects of respect, listening, empirical study, and concentrated deliberations. When these features are present, human thriving commences. This book provides eleven elemental points of analysis aimed at furthering a world dominated by intensive debate instruction in order to achieve better decisions for all of humanity. Those eleven elemental chapters of analysis are: (1) "Darkness before the Dawn of the Twenty-First Century: Rwanda 1994," (2) "Discursive Complexity and the Global Renaissance for Justice," (3) "Debate Training in Rwanda among Security Forces," (4) Deconstructing Anti-Colonialism and Anti-Imperialism as Jacobin Predicates of Violence," (5) "Debate as Pedagogical Empowerment at HBCUs in the United States," (6) "The Global Ecological Museum and the Climate Debate," (7) "Rwanda Rising: Rwanda as a Global Model for Success," (8) "Guatemala Rising with the Creative Peace Process," (9) "China Rising: Debate Programs across China," (10) "Debate as a Global Empowerment Tool for Ending Injustice and Genocide," and (11) "Coolidge Debate Pedagogy: A Historic and Inclusive Model for Today." All of these eleven components illustrate a broad operational theory regarding discursive complexity and an accompanying pedagogical practice whereby genocide can be eliminated in the twenty-first century. This chapter concludes with a prospectus for how this work will proceed based upon this scholarship. Here are some key conclusions from the previous chapters.

DARKNESS BEFORE THE DAWN OF THE TWENTY-FIRST CENTURY: RWANDA 1994

The genocide in Rwanda during the one hundred days beginning in early April of 1994 must stand in the public memory of genocides as one of the worst crimes of the century. Approximately 1.4 million Rwandans were murdered in that short time span, and the direct weapons were often primitive tools and machetes. This human cruelty took place in the midst of a total population of six million Rwandans. Almost one-fourth of the population of the nation was slaughtered in that short span. As a percentage, the loss is twice as large as the population percentage killed for the eleven million of the Holocaust when examined among the approximately eighty million people living in the Nazi controlled realms of Europe. The importance of fully grappling with the horror of the Rwandan genocide, without placing it in some sort of absolute hierarchy is necessary in order to understand how humanity can believe that the abolition of genocide is possible. If a society can overcome something as profoundly hateful and destructive as the one hundred days in Rwanda in the spring of 1994, then all societies can imagine themselves taking up a social task for the amelioration, active prevention, and ultimate end of genocide in the twenty-first century. The humble example of a small African nation as big as Maryland can be a profound example moving forward in the decades to come.

The unique ingredients of propaganda that supplanted reason, discourse, and argument can be seen more clearly than perhaps any genocide of the twentieth century whether we look at the Armenian genocide, the genocide of the Herores, the Holocaust, Holmodor, Yugoslavia, Pol Pot in Cambodia, or any other major eliminationist atrocities. This may be because the Rwandan genocide is one of the last major genocides of the twentieth century. A full understanding of how bad the Rwandan genocide was and the many failures that lined its path are important in galvanizing a prevention plan for going forward. The full evil that was the Rwandan genocide can reassure us that we are not facing something unique that humanity has not faced before. At the heart of this dangerous human problem is a direct and intentional cause: propaganda. Jacques Ellul's insightful analysis of this human problem in *Propaganda: The Formation of Men's Attitudes* lays out a compelling philosophical and linguistic case for how humanity so casually yet consistently misleads itself.[1] Ellul's early insights in 1965 represent a culmination of intellectual concern about mass communication and how it might abuse and even mislead the public. This excellent scholarship nonetheless fails to highlight the true antithesis of propaganda: debate. Debate is not a dialectic result, but a commitment to the dialectic process. Truth is emerging in a trajectory of open human minds conditioned to recognize that all of our fellow human beings are worthy of being understood regardless of whether we ultimately agree. The patient methodology of debate, composed of arguments in a limited time, encourage a heart and mind habit that defeats the natural pathological human psychological patterns described by Ellul. The fact that propaganda is such a profound and central cause of genocide suggests that debate can be the communication safety net that corrects and prevents genocide. The testing of ideas in the laboratories of debate can stifle the formation of genocide and eliminationism. Our indulgence to such pugnacious stated notions as "Tutsis are cockroaches," can be repelled by a deliberative society trained and steeped in debate.

DISCURSIVE COMPLEXITY AND THE GLOBAL RENAISSANCE FOR JUSTICE

Discursive complexity can be defined and recognized as the capacity of an individual or group to encourage and allow dissent. This is the central theoretical premise of this book. Furthermore, discursive complexity is a principle recognizing the value of various expressed viewpoints. The notion of discursive complexity is highly contrasted with a diminished notion of discursive simplicity whereby an individual or group demands or insists upon a limited capacity of expression. Argumentation inherently valorizes discursive complexity by emphasizing the study and teaching of contrasting and competing ideas. Discursive complexity represents a moral point of view since we can prefer individuals and groups that make greater provision for free expression. Such environments encourage critical thinking and diminish the expectation and need for violence.[2]

Understanding how debate furthers discursive complexity involves understanding the broader social and educational practice of debate sought here. Debate is not a singular event. Debate is not even a tournament of several debates. Debate instruction must be more than an occasional habit. Much like the example provided with Wiley College in Marshall, Texas, debate should be threaded throughout all academic instruction to encourage the testing of ideas. The overriding reason for this is an ethical concern: justice. The problem of justice arises from the inequities that are situated in the realm of communication rather than in the material of economics as originally alleged by Marx.

Noted Holocaust survivor Elie Wiesel provides the axiological basis for this conviction when he observed of genocide victims and survivors: "What hurts the victim most is not the physical cruelty of the oppressor but the silence of the bystander."[3] The reason the Holocaust was a viable action of evil was the collective silence of a surrounding German and the broader European society. It is probable that less than 25 percent of the German public was actively a member of the Nazi party. That was, nonetheless, sufficient for a catastrophic cascade of violence and injustice known as the Holocaust to transpire between 1938 and 1944. That cascade was created from a singular source of advocacy in Adolf Hitler to a torrent of social demands by a concomitant silence that did not speak up at appropriate political intervals to interrupt this social building process toward genocide.

The recent surprising social and authoritarian collapse of Omar Bashir's regime in Sudan in 2019 is indicative of the imagination supposed in this book. Bashir is a convicted genocidaire as deliberated by the International Criminal Court. His atrocious crimes in Sudan were contained but not fully prevented. Nonetheless, his rule came to an unexpected end in Sudan when many social voices were lifted against his rule. This surprising action is further evidence of the world that can be pursued despite any apparent authoritarian constraints. The world can be free and humanity can be liberated from the hanging sword of Damocles expressed in the crime of genocide. In Cicero's original telling of a story about the sword of Damocles, political sovereignty made governance an impossible burden because of the continuous and fragile status of peace versus the imminent threat of annihilation metaphorically represented by the sword.[4] The possibility of removing genocide as a probable threat, much like the sword hanging by a thread over the prospective king's head, is a removal within our grasp in the twenty-first century. To modify Cicero's parable, we can strengthen the horse's hair holding that sword over social well-being and make the narrow strand a strong cord of many strands continually being woven by minds galvanized by debate education.

The particular problem of racism in America was broadly confronted in the civil rights movement through processes of argumentation and advocacy. The role of debate in forming successful advocates against the human problem of racism is an important justification for further drawing upon this pedagogy to address the many motives, including racism, toward the problem of genocide and a broader array of human injustices. Several key American civil rights figures were developed in their advocacy through teaching and coaching in argumentation and debate. These leaders include: Martin Luther King Jr., James Farmer Jr., Lula Farmer, James Meredith, Malcolm X, and Medgar Evers. Between the years of 1934 and 1967, great debate coaches and teachers like Melvin Tolson, Howard Thurman, and Thomas Freeman asserted, through teaching, an era of argumentation and debate training for young Blacks in America that impacted individuals toward changing the world away from Jim Crow racist structural violence and toward just human relations predicated on love for one another. The advocates produced by this process were not monolithic. They were individual advocates pulling against one another in a tension that fit a broader vision of a shared goal: ending racism. The creative tensions of their disagreements about methodologies formed the social fabric that every global society needs to resist propaganda, injustice, and even genocide.

Discursive complexity is a mutually reinforcing value within the culture of debate teaching. Our goal is to teach debate because of the inherent value of discursive complexity. The conversations stirred by debate bring about further appreciation in the different ideas of people. This praxis is unnatural and opposed to authoritarianism and propaganda. This is the path of justice that debate and argumentation sets human communities upon for the future.

DEBATE TRAINING IN RWANDA AMONG SECURITY FORCES

The academic debate training of Rwandan security forces in the spring of 2017 is an important initial validation of the larger goal of ending genocide in the twenty-first century by teaching debate. The training took place in the broader academic context of conflict resolution curricula. In 2017, Rwanda is more than two decades beyond the genocide of 1994 and like all societies the risk of a cycle of retaliation and revenge remains real. Using nonviolent teaching techniques derived from the American civil rights movement can be a model for security force training around the world. Security forces in every level need to know how to communicate with their local communities. This communication is fraught with tension and potential conflict that requires the deeper consideration of argument training and how to recognize and defuse a conflict found in words.

This case study is acutely heightened in light of the recent global controversy surrounding Minneapolis police treatment of African American George Floyd. Can security forces deescalate a crisis before it turns deadly? This case study examines how debate methods train the security force member to handle communication strain common in their daily work. Debate's formation around conflict makes it a model pedagogy for helping security force members avoid over reactions among the general public that can turn toward deadly violence when there is misunderstanding. Through communication role play scenarios the Rwandans learned how to deescalate conversations and create a communication environment for effectively resolving disputes in the communities they serve.

The argument training was specifically derived from the thirteen-step method created by the great debater James Farmer Jr.'s organization—the Congress of Racial Equality. Four of those steps were offered as a means to overcome conflicts among individuals. Those rules were originally conceived in the uprisings of Indians against the British Empire. All of this points to the enduring reality that argument and communication study can mitigate problems of injustice and prevent cycles of violence. Security forces members with this type of high-level instruction can serve as a powerful social buffer to future genocides.

DECONSTRUCTING ANTI-COLONIALISM AND ANTI-IMPERIALISM AS JACOBIN PREDICATES OF VIOLENCE

African communities initiated their own significant and indigenous arguments toward achieving justice. Among the most significant were various nationalist movements in the 1950s and 1960s that tore down the political infrastructure of colonialism that dominated the continent of Africa since the nineteenth century. Anti-colonialist arguments today are a reminder that argumentation alone will not solve human injustice. It is not clear that anti-colonialism is a sure path against genocide. It is, in fact, rather clear that genocidaires around the world have adapted anti-colonial rhetorics to foster environments conducive to genocide. Idi Amin of Uganda and Omar Bashir of Sudan are at least two prominent examples of this. Many more could be offered. Rejecting debate as a "western construct" is its own racist and ethnic slur. Ayittey's arguments in *Africa Unchained* are important here.[5] There is a tradition of deliberation rooted in Africa prior to colonialism as documented by Ayittey. Moreover, colonialism did not have a full continental reach. Rwanda's encouragement of debate is not the by-product of White saviors or colonial imposition. Debate is an original African practice and its renewed emphasis is the path returning to justice common to the African experience. This deliberative model will question the anti-colonial ethic that, like all ideas, can produce its own genocides and own systems of propaganda aimed at radical human subordination.

Our awkward rhetorical grasp of history points to its reality as almost immediately murky and malleable to all forms of ideological abuse. Anticolonialism advocacy projects in politics within Africa, the broader globe, and in the United States can and have been used toward genocidal ends like those embraced by Omar Bashir in Sudan and White supremacists connecting with their Cherokee roots in Mississippi. Narratives must remain subject to challenge in the rhetorical presence of a general public sphere of reason and deliberation. Voicelessness is a human intuition and it does not need rationalization as "reason is whiteness" or some other cultural ideograph. The silence of individuals cowering before ideological threats and "cancel culture" jeopardizes any notion of true collective justice. The colonialism critique can be utilized like all arguments as a pretext toward genocide. This analysis derives African answers to this important critique.

Africa, as home to one billion people, is an important source of hope and educational action. Arguments about colonialism are important to the ongoing and emerging realities of this continent. In the heart of the continent is Rwanda, and its experiences can serve as a valuable model throughout the continent.

DEBATE AS PEDAGOGICAL EMPOWERMENT AT HBCUS IN THE UNITED STATES

The African American experience in relation to justice is profound. One of the most moral and significant responses to the evil of enslaving Africans in the United States was the emergence of hundreds of colleges and universities providing free education to former slaves. Born largely of Christian mission efforts by Baptists, Methodists, and Congregationalists, these colleges and universities form the contemporary backbone of what is now known as HBCUs. Beginning in 2018, a generous grant enabled the formation of an HBCU debate nationals. At the heart of this mission is an idea that debate should be available at all HBCUs and students at these universities can reclaim the Black voice best through participation in speech and debate competition. Approximately three hundred thousand students attend HBCUs each year and they represent an important legacy and mechanism for empowering the Black voice.[6] The recent death of HBCU debate coaching legend Thomas Freeman of Texas Southern in Houston underscores the profound impact of debate instruction on Black lives. Denzel Washington's incredible effort to highlight the success of Black debate coach Melvin Tolson in his 1930s endeavor to make Wiley College successful against White universities like USC establishes how paths to equal justice are paved by young minds trained in debate.

Wiley College implemented a unique model for debate instruction known as Debate across the Curriculum. This is an important opportunity for any educator looking to tap into the transformative power of debate within their school community. Believing that all educational areas explore controversies and emerging trends, Debate across the Curriculum encourages educators from all disciplines to identify the controversies in their respective fields and get the students up and debating in class. The 2012 Wiley curriculum demonstrates marked and discernible improvements in student abilities to think critically and to communicate effectively. This research is important for further justifying debate as a global curriculum.

THE GLOBAL ECOLOGICAL MUSEUM AND THE CLIMATE DEBATE

The environment is an important rhetorical signifier. Advocates have continually argued about the natural world as juxtaposed against human existence and the larger civilization. Unfortunately, the allegation of urgency surrounding "climate change" constitutes a threat to debate broadly. Particularly as it relates to human choices as bound by economics, the advocated idea of humanity jeopardizing the ecology by warming the earth through usage of fossil fuels creates an unsavory constraint on public debate. Through iterations of the precautionary principle, debate has been marginalized in favor of fostering closed economic practices that ban fossil fuel extraction and various economic pursuits in deference to the faulty logic that this will reduce CO_2 emissions and thereby "save the planet." Not unlike the anti-colonialism argument, ecologically grounded arguments have both a propensity and demonstrated result of threatening and destroying human life. With regard to Africa, the scourge of deadly malaria is instructive. At the turn of the century, the disease regularly killed almost one million people a year—mostly in Africa. Restraining the efforts to eradicate malaria are rhetorically induced anxieties about pesticides and the environment. Such constraints illustrate how misstatements of science, such as those presented by Rachel Carson in *Silent Spring*, can jeopardize and harm human life. Advocates for a better environment proposition Africa as type of ecological museum that will not be sullied by economic development or industrialized processes like fossil fuel consumption. The garden of Africa can be visited and enjoyed as a type of entertainment as elite global members fly in and out of the continent, but the kind of urban sprawl from which they travel should be discouraged. This potentially provincial view of African development is dangerous to ongoing human life on the continent. For reasons like these, debate on the topic must remain lively.

Moreover, the constraints on economic growth created by climate change arguments limit the reductions of poverty achieved most significantly since 1970, and are a threat to human life across the planet. Poverty is tied to almost all known adverse human outcomes ranging from malaria, malnutrition, and child soldiers. If all people cannot access the least expensive means for providing energy in their daily lives then poverty and living constraints are likely to increase. This point is particularly urgent since the propensity to reduce CO_2 emissions while increasing fossil fuel consumption is directly observable in the past fifteen years of data. The United States that used to lead the world in CO_2 emissions has consistently reduced her CO_2 emissions by switching from coal to natural gas electricity generation. Various efficiencies in technology have compounded this process. These empirical realities point to a path in twenty-first-century argumentation that larger nations like India and China can emulate energy choices bound by a free exchange of ideas that allows new technologies like fracking to transform human access to economic affluence and prosperity. We must keep the ecological debates open and not narrowed by partisan ideological or even Jacobin interests aimed at plainly disproven economic models such as socialism. Such hindrances will hurt poor populations in Asia and Africa the most.

The climate change discussion marginalizes debate by representing science incorrectly as a closed discursive system. This elicits phrases such as "settled science." In reality, science which is not falsifiable, is not science. These rhetorical problems are enhanced by melodramatic characterizations of disagreement as "denial." By creating a false analogy with one of the most important genocides of human history—the Holocaust—a false analogy freights the important debate over climate change with emotional language that trivializes the referent event. This is especially egregious when economic development fueled by fossil fuel development dramatically reduces poverty and broad aspects of human suffering.

RWANDA RISING: RWANDA AS A GLOBAL MODEL FOR SUCCESS

At the heart of this book is the case study of Rwanda. In the opening of the book we examined the horrors of the genocide. It is useful to examine the efforts ascending within the nation in the twenty-fifth year anniversary of the genocide. Jean Michel Habineza in leading the iDebate Rwanda Dreamers Academy program provides thousands of young people in Rwanda and the local regions of Africa with high quality debate instruction along with practical teaching on being public advocates, future college students, and entrepreneurs. Habineza provides this explanation of the unique pedagogy ongoing in Rwanda since 2014:

> It was never about the trophies; it was never about winning arguments. Rather, it was about creating a world where each child's voice could be heard. So, we made the move from a purely debate camp to a Dreamers Academy, where we train leaders in debate so that they can impact their communities. This change in vision of the camp meant that we had to also change the activities that take place during the camp.[7]

This change in vision lead to the creation of the Dreamers Academy, which in 2019 trained more than fifty teachers and more than four hundred students with support from a grant provided by the U.S. State Department. The Rwandan model is the basis for lifting global communities up and away from pessimistic models of propaganda and toward empowering critical thinking found in healthy debate.

Programs like this vastly improve the most valuable component of any national economy—human capital. As noted by economist Julian Simon, we cannot predict the means by which humans will overcome adversity because of the intangible yet real power of human imagination.[8] With hundreds of young people from Rwanda, Uganda, Burundi, and elsewhere, transformed by debate, the prospects for the region are growing. New teachers and coaches of debate are emerging. Young entrepreneurs are developing their first business ideas. Confidence in their individual voices is being discovered. The effective imagination and the ability to work toward solutions on many different fields is dramatically expanded because of debate. Rwanda's life expectancy was twenty-seven in 1994 and today it is sixty-eight.[9] Rwanda's neighbor to the south, Burundi, is nearly identical to the ethnic makeup of Rwanda but follows a less deliberative path of politics. Burundi's life expectancy is eight years shorter than Rwanda's. Rwanda's life expectancy is also about eight years higher than the neighboring nation of Uganda. This expansion of discursive complexity points to an empirical basis for urging the replication of Rwanda's educational successes like the iDebate Rwanda program.

GUATEMALA RISING WITH THE CREATIVE PEACE PROCESS

Latin American nations, in their third wave of democracy, experience similar struggles to reignite and foster civil public discourse after violent state-sponsored killings. Human rights prosecutions and the Christian creative peace process represent two ways in which Latin American nations have approached transitional justice and sought to foster discursive complexity. Guatemala's civil war saw a rise of political eliminationism[10] that led to the killing of thousands. The country's use of deliberative models in pursuit of transitional justice exemplify the importance of argumentation and political discourse to build strong democratic institutions. Trials represent a deliberative function that serve to provide a fair forum for argumentation and truth seeking. Grassroots peace approaches foster communication between former enemies at a community level and demonstrate the key role deliberation plays in rebuilding social trust. Continued study and dialogue about events in Central America like this case study are necessary to a truly global vision where deliberation supplants violence as a dominant form of argument.

CHINA RISING: DEBATE PROGRAMS ACROSS CHINA

The relatively recent and profoundly violent history of Maoist China must remain a practical pedagogical concern. The current Communist leader Xi appears successful in creating a hardline retrenchment of party ideology that jeopardizes the emergence of a discursively complex world. Pretending that this closed nature dictated by the Communist party of China is vital or necessary leads to human disasters like the viral pandemic originating in Wuhan, China. The World Health Organization acknowledged in the summer of 2020 that China never notified the WHO about the spread of the virus within China.[11] The virus and stubbornly inaccurate information about its spread contributed mightily to more than seven hundred thousand people dying from the virus by August of 2020.

The street fights in Hong Kong and even along the border between India and China all point to a need to maintain the pressure against the closed authoritarians within the Communist Party of China and for the benefit of the broader Chinese public. With seventy million Communist Party members, it is important to keep in mind the broader interests of more than one billion human beings in China. Communication openness can bring the best results and a stronger China.

As the most populous nation in the world, China must be an international agenda of primary importance if debate is to make a proper global impact. At the forefront of this important work is an American debate academic Stefan Bauschard. His work creating debate leagues throughout Asia, including China, represents important current knowledge on this effort and a vital model going forward. China need not be a purely closed society, and the twenty-first century contains movements for debate enabling the exchange of ideas and greater openness in China.

DEBATE AS A GLOBAL EMPOWERMENT TOOL FOR ENDING INJUSTICE AND GENOCIDE

This chapter offers many examples of serial idealism. Over decades, students take ideas about the human voice, debate, advocacy, and argument and implement them in unique settings. After graduation, many students apply argumentation study to unique aspects of their jobs and personal interests to yield uniquely better communities they live and work in after college. One of the first major efforts came in the summer of 2006 and enabled more than 250,000 per year to hear live testimony from a Holocaust survivor because the United States Holocaust Memorial Museum increased its roster of survivor speakers by more than a dozen through the efforts of Terri Donofrio. Relentless idealism predicated on valuing the human voice can become a decades long pattern contributing to the end of human injustice. This work can at times be perilous but it remains inspiring and fundamentally hopeful. This and other examples demonstrate that practical efforts to increase discursive complexity through speech and debate instruction can confront the cycle of cynicism that leads to dangerous ideological outcomes of violence.

President Bush continues to emphasize a deliberative model as highlighted by his biography *Decision Points*. The Decision Points Theater at the Bush Library is one of the most popular exhibits among the thousands who visit the library each year. Decision Points Theater highlights the discursively complex notion that deliberation among competing advisors is useful toward making the best decision possible. This notion was amplified in the earliest projects of the Bush institute with special debate programming in 2012 and 2013. Those debates focused on the Dallas Urban Debate Alliance led by Nicole Serrano who is now the head of the National Speech and Debate Association for high school speech and debate competitions. President Bush personally encouraged those high school students to continue with their activities as a basis for improving future leadership.

The Bush Center's focus on Human Freedom allowed public speaking programs to equip dissidents in Asia. One program focused on individuals who have escaped from the dangerous repressive government of North Korea. The program was conducted with a translator and speeches were given by each student. Another program aimed to equip the voices of Burmese dissidents seeking to establish a new democracy in their homeland. In at least one case, dissidents trained in these programs went to jail in Burma during the democratic elections. Efforts like these demonstrate the mutuality of learning. Teachers learn from students important lessons in idealism and practical daily perseverance. Coaches of debate will often discover later in life that the tools of debate provided to the debater brought brave challenges that now inspire the coach anew.

COOLIDGE DEBATE PEDAGOGY: A HISTORIC AND INCLUSIVE MODEL FOR TODAY

We are approaching the one-hundred year anniversary of the Coolidge presidency. Ironically, the number associated with Coolidge is thirty—

because he is America's thirtieth president. Ironically, the number thirty is also often associated with a perfect speaking score in American competitive debate. Understanding President Calvin Coolidge as a rhetorical ideal is reformative to general debate practice today and also useful for inspiring debate as a global pedagogy. Coolidge was himself inspired toward leadership while in college and taking debate classes. He took multiple classes in debate and these studies increased both his proficiency and confidence in speaking. Coolidge famously observed the humble strength that ought to be observed in good arguments:

> While everyone knows that evil exists, there is yet sufficient good in the people to supply material for most of the comment that needs to be made. The only way I know to drive out evil from the country is by the constructive method of filling it with good. The country is better off tranquilly considering its blessing and merits, and earnestly striving to secure more of them, than it would be in nursing hostile bitterness about its deficiencies and faults.[12]

Coolidge is one of the least yet most misunderstood American presidents. With a nickname of "Silent Cal" it is easy to dismiss and even diminish the president. In academic rankings he is typically ranked rather low. His silence is a misunderstanding of his deliberate calculations to be careful with what he said in public. The problem of Coolidge's memory is compounded by the partisan intransigence of academic cultures that take a reactionary view of Republican presidents. While excelling at fiscal responsibility and economic policies that made his decade "roar," Coolidge did more than manage the books of America effectively. He was a profound advocate for equality among Blacks and Whites. Speeches and actions as vice president and president point to an individual deeply convicted on the matter of racial equality. In defiance of his ideological predecessor Woodrow Wilson, Coolidge, and Harding both sought to demolish through argument the false notion of Black inferiority in the United States. In our one-hundred year anniversary of his presidency, we do well to challenge the ideological norms of an intellectual culture that sought to reject Coolidge while reifying the racist policies of Wilson. The words and actions of Coolidge can be a practical argumentation guide for the twenty-first century aimed at an Afro-idealist agenda for improving race relations in the United States.

A far-ranging Coolidge debate curriculum emerged at the historic foundation based at Plymouth Notch, Vermont. Aimed at improving economic literacy through debate, the curriculum reaches thousands of high school students and reached all the way to Rwanda in December of 2019. An array of economic briefs on immigration, trade, economic shutdowns, and collegiate education help students discover the highest degree of discursive complexity on the complicated yet urgent issues of the day. The Coolidge project remains one of the most important efforts toward maintaining and dramatically improving forensics (speech and debate) training in the United States and worldwide. Coolidge debate also emphasizes the notion of citizen judges. Debate formats regularly devolve into specialized practices that a narrower and narrower band of individuals can participate in within educational settings. Whether technical jargon that arises or the rapid rate of delivery associated with time limits, debate styles can become an exclusive club for building up an elite. The citizen judge focus of Coolidge is designed to disrupt this outcome.

PROSPECTUS FOR UTILIZING DEBATE AS A PEDAGOGY FOR ENDING GENOCIDE

The examples provided in this book suggest that debate can serve as a global pedagogy for improving the human condition. The contexts of action from Dallas to Plymouth Notch, Vermont; to Kigali, Rwanda, to Guatemala; and Israel to Beijing all indicate that there is not a particular place where debate cannot operate. The inherent values of education centered upon debate are many: (1) maximizing individual potential by improving the ability to express ideas, (2) improving individual resilience with regard to adverse circumstances, (3) encouraging the emergence of community-based rubrics for discovering the greater good, (4) jeopardizing the chief prerequisite to genocide: propaganda. Each of these values establishes a strong academic basis for debate as global pedagogy toward the end of genocide in the twenty-first century.

As noted in the successful QEP of debate across the curriculum at Wiley College, debate did equip students to be better critical thinkers. Students experienced debate directly in many different educational contexts and this improved individual abilities to express ideas. As noted by economist Julian Simon, human beings embody a unique immeasurable value. Much of that vast value is enmeshed in the ideas contained within each mind. If the dreams, visions, and better ideas are locked away in those minds because of an inability to express ideas, then everyone in the immediate society is adversely affected. The ability to express and argue for better ideas will lift a society more than material abundance and wealth. Intellectual property as it originates in the mind of the individual is the dominant precursor to the material world, and as Jurgen Habermas observed, it may be the truer root of key concerns on inequality. Our aim for justice will be improved when we realize that the silence of individuals is a fundamental catalyst to inequality, injustice, and even the most dramatic instances of human cruelty.

Human resilience is an important outcome of debate. Human suffering ranges from mental illness, malnutrition, disease, family disruption, incarceration, terrorism, isolation, war, and accidents. These are only a few adversities that millions of human beings suffer as a matter of circumstance, which produce inclinations to give up or forfeit the dreams noted earlier. Resilience is the capacity to endure and thrive again after adversity. Debate is an excellent conditioning toward resilience. Debate combines some of the most naturally stressful aspects of being human—public speaking and public conflict—to create a temporary enjoyable intellectual activity. Students who attend a debate tournament acquaint themselves with their own internal mental terrain regarding anxiety. What will my opponent say? How will I respond? What will the judge think of my arguments? All of these natural questions will occasionally be answered in affirming ways and occasionally be answered in adverse ways. This cycle of winning and losing during debates prepares students to endure the stress of a job interview where someone will judge whether their case for being employed is convincing. This is an intimate psychological journey toward resilience which psychological experts increasingly believe is an area of growing need for young people. Debate makes participants consider both sides and more of an argument. This critical thinking makes us ready for understanding and cooperation.

Debate as an educational practice encourages team leaders to develop rubrics for evaluating arguments. What are the elements of a good argument? Stephen Toulmin has a specific answer, what more can we add to this as we teach debate? What are the characteristics of a good debater? These characteristics may vary from one community to another and the process of building these rubrics is helpful in providing a better local means for sharpening the mental axes of young minds. The emergence of debate in various locations around the world will naturally give rise to different approaches. These differences are themselves a manifestation of discursive complexity which is ethically and philosophically desirable. These differences will make some national exchanges more difficult as students and individuals more broadly try to adapt themselves to different formats. All of this can contribute to a local ethic that appreciates what has been created to build up the future of the community whether in Guatemala, Plymouth Notch, Vermont, Burma, Rwanda, North Korea, Sudan, or Europe. In this framework, four key principles are outlined for recognizing the consistent approach of debate: (1) a resolution, (2) two sides, (3) equal time limits for speaking, and (4) a balloted means of adjudication. The local emergence of debate rubrics and practices does not need to be a major obstacle to the pedagogical drive toward discursive complexity.

Finally, and perhaps most importantly, debate jeopardizes the primary prerequisite of genocide: propaganda. Chapter 1 provided this definition of propaganda from *The New Oxford American Dictionary*: "information, especially of a biased or misleading nature, used to promote or publicize a particular political cause or point of view."[13] The struggle to understand what information is biased or misleading is difficult. Often partisan lenses will accuse any point of difference as being mere "propaganda." Therein lies an important paradox about debate. Becoming committed to an internally biased notion of how propaganda is defined and intellectually defining those individuals who dissent with as being outside reasonable debate impairs and deters the ideal debate activity. There is no easy answer to this dilemma but the continuously inclusive and open approach to debate that seeks growing membership is the best means for preventing this problem. Propaganda is the key communication ingredient that establishes the prelude to genocide. The growing efforts of dehumanization become the sharpened rhetorical edges of this propaganda as genocidaires prepare themselves for the most violent expression of propaganda in the form of a genocide.

The stages of genocide are well detailed by Greg Stanton, a professor at Mary Washington University.[14] Ironically, this is the same university James Farmer Jr. was a professor at in his final days. The ten stages of genocide are:

1. Classification
2. Symbolization
3. Discrimination
4. Dehumanization
5. Organization
6. Polarization
7. Preparation
8. Persecution
9. Extermination
10. Denial

Many, if not all of these stages are intimately associated with communication processes. Stage two is the most centrally based upon communication. In stage two, the framework for genocide is established. A pattern of oppositional and potentially demeaning symbols will begin to form. If debate is not established within the society, then a "losing" side of the social conversation will gradually be established as impending victims. This is apparent in stage four where dehumanization begins to happen. Dehumanization relies upon arguments that describe groups of people like the Tutsis as "cockroaches." That word and argumentation frame has travelled significant rhetorical distance from a missing debate in an earlier time that would have recognized the Tutsis as "my esteemed opponent." "Esteemed opponent," is the kind of language educators would expect to hear in a good debate. This would implant the key ideas of respect and understanding necessary to prevent genocide. The absence of the critical pedagogy of debate in stage two dramatically increases the risk that a society will continue along the dangerous ten step path outlined by professor Stanton. By stage six "polarization," individuals in a society are being asked to "choose sides" and essentially forswear debate as a social process. This is how the steep downhill rhetorical regression descends from order, to chaos, and ultimately genocide. A society committed to deliberative processes like debate can thwart the ultimate emergence of genocide.

It is not simply that debate methods thwart genocide, the inherent nonviolence of this means of social and political change makes it profoundly more successful than violent alternatives. A study of major political movements made in the twentieth century demonstrate empirically that methods like these are much more successful in achieving good results for humanity. The study was conducted by a researcher who expected that the study would show violent movements as at least more efficient in bringing about change. Professor Erica Chenoweth and her colleague Maria Stephan painstakingly collected data on 323 violent and nonviolent political campaigns since 1900. To qualify for the analysis, the movement had to be substantial in size, involving at least one thousand people active in the movement. They counted a campaign as successful if the goal had been achieved within one year of the peak of the event (as when Corazon Aquino and the People Power Revolution peacefully ousted dictator Ferdinand Marcos from the Philippines in 1986).[15]

Key findings to this study include:

- Nonviolent campaigns have a 53 percent success rate and only about a 20 percent rate of complete failure.
- Violent campaigns were successful 23 percent of the time, and complete failures about 60 percent of the time.
- Violent campaigns succeeded partially in about 10 percent of cases, again comparing unfavorably to nonviolent campaigns, which resulted in partial successes over 20 percent of the time.[16]

This study and others like it suggest that nonviolent pedagogical precursors that condition its participants to conceptualize political solutions in a nonviolent way are placing the future in the hands of those most likely to succeed in bringing positive future change. It is important for successful societies to be led by processes of argumentation and debate. The habits cultivated in an educational environment founded upon debate will yield a future committed to nonviolent processes of social change. Such change can yield a world without genocide.

As noted in the study above, this is not theoretical. Nonviolent argument strategies are empirically ridding the world of catastrophic violence. Researchers such as Steven Pinker and Hans Rosling demonstrate the profound progress being made. A skeptical review of Pinker's thesis helps clarify how profound the success toward reducing violence has become. Will Koehrsen, a data science communicator at Cortex Intel, concludes that Pinker is correct and global violence is in dramatic decline.[17] He concludes in an examination of the data:

The US and Europe from 1900 through 1960, even with two world wars, saw less than 1 percent of their population perish in armed conflicts. In 2007, just 0.04 percent of deaths in the world were from international violence. If this data is correct, the world in 2007 was at least an order of magnitude safer than most prehistoric societies.[18]

In this statistical data set, deaths from war and genocide in the twentieth century produce a rate of death equal to six deaths per year per one hundred thousand people in that century. By comparison, France in the nineteenth century had a death rate of seventy deaths per year per one hundred thousand people—more than ten times greater than the global era that followed. The Chippewa native population of Minnesota in 1825 to 1832 experienced a death rate of seven hundred fifty per year per one hundred thousand and the numbers escalate in far more dire statistics the further back in history one goes. For 2007, the death rate was thirty-three per year per one hundred thousand worldwide. Comparing this twenty-first century statistic to the composite statistic of the twentieth century suggests that violence has declined in the outset of this century by 90 percent. Pinker's research documents that human violence of a recent nature reached a peak in the World War II era and has been in sharp decline since then.[19] Our World in Data with compiled data from Integrated Network for Societal Conflict Research finds that genocides since 2000 have vacillated between zero and two for at least fifteen years. By comparison, genocides were numbered as high as eleven in the mid twentieth century.[20]

The United Nations provides a definition to classify acts of genocide.[21] Genocide is the most extreme expression of human evil. Debate pedagogy that reaches every human member of a community with an idea of reducing communication capacity disparities will be a powerful insurance that these trends of violence continue to decline in the present century. This provides an empirical basis for expecting that broader and deeper commitments to nonviolent pedagogies like debate can further enshrine this trend and make 2100 dramatically less violent for humanity in the same way that 2000 differed from 1900.

Two years after writing her important work *Hate: Why We Should Resist It with Free Speech, Not Censorship*, Nadine Strossen wrote this new conclusion to the book after travelling extensively to discuss the book's arguments for free speech:

> In the two years since I wrote this book, I have made hundreds of public presentations, discussing its themes with diverse audiences in forms all over the United States, as well as in multiple other countries. Many participants have told me that these vigorous exchanges of ideas and experiences have had the positive impact that I certainly have appreciated from them: enhanced understanding in both key senses of that word—increased knowledge and empathy. Therefore, I am more convinced than ever that open, inclusive channels of communication

constitute an essential engine for resisting hate and promoting "liberty and justice for all."[22]

Those open channels of communication are best insured by building the widest and deepest possible global base for debate. This book delivers empirical models for doing this and an elaboration of the communication theories that undergird the process of genocide abolition in the twenty-first century. The world is robust with difference. Those differences create sensations among individuals that they are doomed to irreconcilable differences. Violent conflict like genocide that can arise from these differences accentuated with propaganda are the most dire indictment of human hope and dreams of tranquility. In the human darkness of genocide, enlightening pedagogical tools like debate remedy and forestall the worst of our human nature. Debate teaches us to listen to one another across those differences that seem too far. In teaching communication through debate, we love one another. Rwanda in the past twenty-five years demonstrates the path to global tranquility in its fledgling debate program.

CONCLUSION

The example of Rwanda overcoming one of the twentieth century's worst genocides can serve as a pedagogical model for all of the world regardless of their unique and current difficulties. The deep empirical trough of suffering indicated by a twenty-six years life expectancy in 1994 rising in 2017 to sixty-eight years points to an incredible recovery. Rwanda is now a shining example of economics, health care, public policy, genocide recovery, and so many other positive indicators. An important recent signal of this larger success is the iDebate Rwanda program led by Jean Michel Habineza. Thousands of students are being taught to debate along with dozens of high school teachers in Rwanda and nearby regions. All of this bolsters the social infrastructure of discursive complexity. These debaters can become better teachers, lawyers, community leaders, entrepreneurs, parents, and leaders of all kinds.

When I was working at the Dreamers Academy debate workshop in Rwanda in December of 2019, I was standing outside and looking toward the horizon after the sun had set. One of the other staff members asked if I was curious about the red and green lights flashing across the evening sky. I told him I was. "Those are part of a regional drone system that distributes blood supplies to area hospitals." He explained that this was a unique technological development in Rwanda that allowed doctors to prevent one of the most common causes of death among mothers who hemorrhage after giving birth. The drones carry blood supplies from a distribution center to the remote hospitals far faster than conventional vehicle delivery can be achieved. The green lights on the drone indicate that it is carrying blood to a hospital and the red light indicates that it has completed its mission and is returning to the base. The World Health Organization provides this description of the blood supply issue in Rwanda:

> Blood transfusion services started in Rwanda in 1975, and since 1985 they have been exclusively from voluntary, unpaid blood donors. The 1994 genocide devastated the health infrastructure and systems, but the government prioritised the rebuilding of blood transfusion services, realizing how pivotal access to blood is in saving lives. Stringent measures were put in place to improve the safety and availability of blood countrywide—this has contributed to the drop in child mortality by two-thirds between 2000 and 2015, and maternal mortality by three-quarters.[23]

Though the blood supply program has been successful, getting blood to rural areas is a special challenge. The drone technology plays an important role in saving lives in those areas:

> One of the country's major challenges in providing blood to those in need, especially in rural and remote areas, is the country's terrain—including impassable mountains—and damaged roads. Rwanda uses a drone technology called "Zipline" which cuts blood delivery times down from four hours to just 15 minutes in some cases. "Every second you gain in saving a life is critical. When we saw that Zipline was a solution, we didn't hesitate," said Dr. Diane Gashumba, Rwandan Minister of Health.[24]

Rwanda was the first nation to implement such a system and now it is being modeled in other nations to save lives.[25] Medical technology like Zipline is an example of discursive complexity at work allowing human societies to overcome the worst aspects of human suffering. Medical robots are improving care in hospitals during the coronavirus epidemic as face to face contact becomes more perilous.[26] Kigali is home to innovative electric car and electric motorcycle technologies that aim to preserve the green environment of the nation.

The nation is buoyed by additional good news. In May of 2020, one of the most important perpetrators of the genocide was captured near Paris.[27] Felicien Kabuga was a key architect of the 1994 genocide against the Tutsis:

> Kabuga is accused of creating two key killing instruments that whipped up the genocide: the Interahamwe militia that carried out a large portion of the massacres, and the Radio-Television *Libre des Mille Collines* that incited people to murder Tutsi "cockroaches."[28]

The persistence of public conscience found him and brought him to justice. Additional good news for Rwanda is that the political rights of women are higher than anywhere else in the world. Female participation in elected political office is the highest in the world. More than 60 percent of legislative seats are held by women—almost 10 percent higher than any other nation in the world.[29] In the 1990s, women made up 19 percent of the parliament.[30] The 2016 NPR article notes the role of debate in Rwanda as empowering women to believe they can serve in politics and the transformative role the activity plays.[31] In the 2019 debates, I was pleasantly surprised to see women interrupting men with "points of information," without lack of confidence or angry reactions from the men. In our final award ceremony, women won both top speaker awards for the debate tournament—something I do not regularly see in the United States.

Rwanda is rising. Though this nation suffered devastating human losses in a genocide now more than twenty-five years ago, her people are rising in a way that serve as a global model. The iDebate Rwanda Dreamers Academy is a powerful illustration of how global humanity can come together in dialogue to improve the human condition and prevent genocide. The method for coming together is to encourage debate and deliberation anywhere and everywhere. Debate created the "Beloved Community" of the American civil rights movement and unleashed a wide array of advocates. Many of these leaders came to Africa to further their own education and a more practical sense of how to pursue human freedom. Case studies of successful debate instruction around the world from China, to India, to Burma, to Korea, and to Rwanda, demonstrate that debate can serve as a catalyst among people for building discursive complexity within societies: the healthy respect for dissent and disagreement that we need to overcome the angry threat of political differences. Ideological and reactionary arguments on the environment and colonialism can skew debate in ways that impair the deliberative path forward. All of these chapters examining specific case studies and arguments point to an academic and pedagogical path for defeating the disturbing human enemy of the twentieth century: propaganda. It was propaganda that took too many Herores[32] and Tutsis to their genocidal ends in the beginning and end of the twentieth century. Debate is the antithesis of propaganda. Debate creates new generations of leaders willing to listen and consider multiple points of view. A discursively complex global environment enriched by debate instruction can bring to an end the propaganda-driven violence of genocide, eliminationism, and democide. Holocaust survivor Elie Wiesel's painful observation that "silence is what hurts the victim most" is a truism that can be inverted to make a world of many voices unwilling to be silent and ready to be upstanders. In the final analysis, debate instruction should continue its global advance so that the rising community of Rwanda can be a metaphor for a world rising as well with the joy of many voices.

In one of the many learning activities in Rwanda during the iDebate Dreamers Academy, instructors were asked to construct and deliver a four-minute elevator speech justifying debate. The conclusion of my speech is appropriate here:

> The true problem in society is not material inequity but communication inequity. Those who have the ability to communicate will succeed in any society. Those who cannot communicate will not succeed. Debate is our best teaching tool for raising the status of any individual from a point of silence to a point of expression.[33]

When the final round of the iDebate Dreamers Academy was over, the two top teams stood as more than ten judges deliberated over who should be crowned "the winner." When the decision was announced, the team that won second, danced and shouted with the same enthusiasm as the team the judges voted for on their ballots. It was as if *they had all won* in debate. It was hard to see who *lost*. Joyful faces dancing and singing in jubilation spread like wildfire among the judges and hundreds of observers—including representatives from the U.S. State Department and the Rwandan Education Ministry. Humanity wins because of debate, and I saw that vividly in the iDebate Rwanda Dreamers Academy. Now, it is time for the world to rise with Rwanda and her beautiful programs of debate. Debate can be a lifeblood for humanity worldwide. We should rise to the challenge of delivering this precious educational commodity.

NOTES

1. Jacques Ellul, *Propaganda: The Formation of Men's Attitudes* (New York: Random House, 1973).
2. Ben Voth, *The Rhetoric of Genocide: Death as a Text* (Lanham, MD: Lexington Books, 2004).
3. Elie Wiesel, foreword, in C. Rittmer and S. Myers (Eds.), *The Courage to Care* (New York: New York University Press, 1986).
4. Evan Andrews, "What Was the Sword of Damocles," History Channel, August 22, 2018, https://www.history.com/news/what-was-the-sword-of-damocles.
5. George Ayittey, *Africa Unchained: The Blueprint for Africa's Future* (New York: Palgrave Macmillan, 2005).
6. Monica Anderson, "Look at Historically Black Colleges and Universities as Howard Turns 150," *Pew Research*, February 17, 2017, retrieved July 8, 2020, https://www.pewresearch.org/fact-tank/2017/02/28/a-look-at-historically-black-colleges-and-universities-as-howard-turns-150/?amp=1.
7. "Dr. Ben Voth Interview with Jean Michel Habineza," unpublished, December 18, 2019.
8. Julian Simon, *The Ultimate Resource 2*, revised ed. (Princeton: Princeton University Press, 1996).
9. Google search for "Rwanda life expectancy," accessed July 8, 2020, https://www.google.com/search?client=safari&sxsrf=ALeKk01gbRa5dKiYMYX68fg070BPbI76oApercent3A1594248948472&source=hp&ei=9E4GX_mIGo22swXBtY3QBQ&q=rwanda+life+expectancy&oq=Rwanda+life+ex&gs_lcp=CgZwc3ktYWIQAxgAMgIIADICCAAyAggAMgIIADIGCAAQFhAeMgYIABAW-EB4yBggAEBYQHjIGCAAQFhAeMgYIABAWEB4yBggAEBYQHjoECCMQJzoFCAAQsQM6CAgAELEDEIMBOgQIABAKULYFWOYSYO4haABwAHgAgAGjA4gBjxcSCAQk3LjQuMi4wLjGYAQCgAQGqAQdnd3Mtd2l6&sclient=psy-ab.

10. Daniel Jonah Goldhagen, *Worse than War: Genocide, Eliminationism, and the Ongoing Assault on Humanity*, 1st ed. (New York: PublicAffairs, 2009).

11. Adam Kredo, "China Never Reported the Existence of the Coronavirus to the World Health Organization," *Washington Free Beacon*, July 2, 2020, retrieved on July 8, 2020, https://freebeacon.com/national-security/china-never-reported-existence-of-coronavirus-to-world-health-organization/.

12. Calvin Coolidge, *Autobiography*, 186.

13. *New American Oxford Dictionary*.

14. Greg Stanton (2013), *The 10 Stages of Genocide*, accessed August 10, 2020, https://genocideeducation.org/wp-content/uploads/2016/03/ten_stages_of_genocide.pdf.

15. Douglas Kendrick, "Violent Versus Nonviolent Revolutions: Which Way Wins? Why Boycotts Outperform Bombs," *Psychology Today* (2014), accessed August 10, 2020, https://www.psychologytoday.com/us/blog/sex-murder-and-the-meaning-life/201404/violent-versus-nonviolent-revolutions-which-way-wins?fbclid=IwAR2lTM0xGOJUEpAt9o4LGgxkmfULKKbAR8sD-70GZ64j-oTPBTff-1GVme8.

16. Kendrick, "Violent Versus Nonviolent Revolutions: Which Way Wins? Why Boycotts Outperform Bombs."

17. Will Koehrsen, "Has Global Violence Declined? A Look at the Data," *Towards Data Science* (2019), accessed August 10, 2020, https://towardsdatascience.com/has-global-violence-declined-a-look-at-the-data-5af708f47fba.

18. Koehrsen, "Has Global Violence Declined? A Look at the Data."

19. Steven Pinker, *The Better Angels of Our Nature: Why Violence Has Declined* (New York: Viking, 2011).

20. Max Roser and Mohamed Nagdy (2013), "Genocides," *OurWorldInData.org*, accessed August 10, 2020, https://ourworldindata.org/genocides [Online Resource].

21. Genocide is defined as: "any of the following acts committed with intent to destroy, in whole or in part, a national, ethnical, racial or religious group, as such: killing members of the group; causing serious bodily or mental harm to members of the group; deliberately inflicting on the group conditions of life calculated to bring about its physical destruction in whole or in part; imposing measures intended to prevent births within the group; [and] forcibly transferring children of the group to another group," United Nations Resolution 96 (I), "The Crime of Genocide," December 11, 1946.

22. Nadine Strossen, *Hate: Why We Should Resist It with Free Speech, Not Censorship* (New York: Oxford University Press, 2019).

23. "Drones Take Rwanda's National Blood Service to New Heights," World Health Organization, June 12, 2019, retrieved July 27, 2020, https://www.who.int/news-room/feature-stories/detail/drones-take-rwandas-national-blood-service-to-new-heights.

24. "Drones Take Rwanda's National Blood Service to New Heights."

25. Aryn Baker, "The American Drones Saving Lives in Rwanda," *Time*, May 31, 2018, retrieved July 27, 2020, https://time.com/rwanda-drones-zipline/.

26. Clement Uwiringiyimana, "Rwandan Medical Workers Deploy Robots to Minimize Coronavirus Risk," *Reuters*, May 30, 2020, retrieved July 27, 2020, https://www.reuters.com/article/us-health-coronavirus-rwanda-robots/rwandan-medical-workers-deploy-robots-to-minimize-coronavirus-risk-idUSKBN2360EW.

27. "Key Rwanda Genocide Suspect, Felicien Kabuga, Arrested Outside Paris," *RFI*, May 16, 2020, accessed August 5, 2020, https://www.rfi.fr/en/africa/20200516-key-rwanda-genocide-suspect-felician-kabuga-arrested-outside-paris?fbclid=IwAR3myu6Xgn1UKbpEdQQQzy-RiDhYMEZxWICbSVfa8yJ513yH65_UoUC6FI8.

28. "Key Rwanda Genocide Suspect, Felicien Kabuga, Arrested Outside Paris."

29. Gregory Warner, "It's the No. 1 Country for Women in Politics—But Not in Daily Life," NPR, July 29, 2016, accessed May 5, 2020, https://www.npr.org/sections/goatsandsoda/2016/07/29/487360094/invisibilia-no-one-thought-this-all-womans-debate-team-could-crush-it.

30. "Revisiting Rwanda Five Years after Record-Breaking Parliamentary Elections," *UN Women*, August 13, 2018, accessed August 5, 2020, https://www.unwomen.org/en/news/stories/2018/8/feature-rwanda-women-in-parliament.

31. Warner, "It's the No. 1 Country for Women in Politics—But Not in Daily Life."

32. "Herero and Nama Genocide," United States Holocaust Memorial Museum, August 18, 2020, https://www.ushmm.org/collections/bibliography/herero-and-nama-genocide.

33. Ben Voth, "Elevator Speech for Debate," December 14, 2019, iDebate Dreamers Academy–Rwanda.

Bibliography

"16 Ways the World Is Getting Remarkably Better: Visuals by Statistician Hans Rosling." *Open Culture.* May 26, 2020. http://www.openculture.com/2020/05/16-ways-the-world-is-getting-remarkably-better.html.

Aegis Trust Genocide Research hub. Accessed July 15, 2020. http://www.genocideresearchhub.org.rw/document/?fwp_search_library=Post%20GEnocide%20Trauma.

"After the Verdict: What Ríos Montt's Conviction Means for Guatemala." *WOLA.* Accessed March 11, 2018. https://www.wola.org/analysis/after-the-verdict-what-rios-Ríos Montts-conviction-means-for-guatemala/.

Ahlburg, D. "Julian Simon and the Population Growth Debate." *Population and Development Review* 24, no. 2 (1998): 317–27. doi:10.2307/2807977.

Alinsky, Saul. *Rules for Radicals: A Practical Primer for Realistic Radicals.* New York: Random House, 1971.

Allers, Rudolf and Sigmund Freud. *The Successful Error; A Critical Study of Freudian Psychoanalysis.* London: Sheed & Ward, 1940.

Altman, Irwin and Dalman Taylor. *Social Penetration: The Development of Interpersonal Relationships.* New York: Holt, Rinehart, and Winston, 1973.

Alvarez, Enrique and Tania Palencia Prado. "Guatemala's Peace Process: Context, Analysis and Evaluation." *Conciliation Resources.* February 7, 2012. http://www.c-r.org/accord/public-participation/guatemala-s-peace-process-context-analysis-and-evaluation.

Applebaum, Anne. *Red Famine: Stalin's War on Ukraine.* First United States edition. New York: Doubleday, 2017.

"Attackers Carve Jewish Star into Back of Iraqi Poet in S. Louis." *Israel Faxx.* Electronic World Communications, Inc., 2011.

Ayittey, George. *Africa Unchained: The Blueprint for Africa's Future.* New York: Palgrave Macmillan, 2005.

Bachmann, Sascha-Dominik Dov and Naa A. Sowatey-Adjei. "The African Union-ICC Controversy before the ICJ: A Way Forward to Strengthen International Criminal Justice?" *Washington International Law Journal* 29, no. 2 (2020): 247+. *Gale Academic OneFile.* Accessed August 10, 2020. https://link.gale.com/apps/doc/A629150909/AONE?u=txshracd2548&sid=AONE&xid=50e95ee2.

Bakewell, Sarah. "Steven Pinker Continues to See the Glass Half Full." *New York Times.* March 2, 2018. Accessed July 10, 2019. https://www.nytimes.com/2018/03/02/books/review/steven-pinker-enlightenment-now.html.

Barnes, Catherine. *Journey from Jim Crow: The Desegregation of Southern Transit.* New York: Columbia University Press, 1983.

Bartanen, Michael and Robert Littlefield. *Forensics in America: A History.* Lanham, MD: Rowman & Littlefield, 2013.

Bates, Karen Grigsby. "Stokely Carmichael. A Philosopher behind the Black Power Movement." NPR. March 10, 2014. Accessed August 1, 2020. https://www.npr.org/sections/codeswitch/2014/03/10/287320160/stokely-carmichael-a-philosopher-behind-the-black-power-movement.

Beecher, Henry Ward. Quoted in *Forty Thousand Quotations: Prose and Poetical.* Comp. by Charles Noel Douglas. New York: Halcyon House, 1917; Bartleby.com, 2012. www.bartleby.com/348.

Belkin, Douglas. "Exclusive Test Data: Many Colleges Fail to Improve Critical-Thinking Skills." *Wall Street Journal*. June 5, 2017. https://www.wsj.com/articles/exclusive-test-data-many-colleges-fail-to-improve-critical-thinking-skills-1496686662.

Benton, Bond. *The Challenge of Working for Americans: Perspectives of an International Workforce*. New York: Palgrave Macmillan, 2014.

Benton, Bond. "Debate, Diversity, and Adult Learners: The Experiences of Foreign Nationals in the U.S. State Department." *Argumentation and Advocacy* 49, no. 2 (2012): 100+. Gale Academic OneFile. Accessed August 12, 2020. https://link.gale.com/apps/doc/A332892396/AONE?u=txshracd2548&sid=AONE&xid=5662644e.

Billings, Andrew. "Increasing Diversity in the 21st Century: Minority Participation in Competitive Individual Events." *Forensic* 85, no. 4 (2000).

Blair, J. "A Time for Parting: The Negro during the Coolidge Years." *Journal of American Studies* 3, no. 2 (1969): 177–99.

Blomfield, Adrian. "Going, Going, Gone: African Dictators Losing Luxury Lifestyle amid Money Laundering Crackdown." *Telegraph*. October 6, 2019. Accessed July 15, 2020. https://www.telegraph.co.uk/news/2019/10/06/going-going-gone-african-dictators-losing-luxury-lifestyle-amid/.

Bloom, Benjamin, Max Englehart, Edward Furst, Walter Hill, and David Krathwohl. *Taxonomy of Educational Objectives, Handbook One*. Nashville, TN: Vanderbilt University, 1956: 201–7. https://cft.vanderbilt.edu/guides-sub-pages/blooms-taxonomy/.

Bothmann, Astrid. *Transitional Justice in Nicaragua 1990–2012: Drawing a Line under the Past*. London: Springer, 2015.

Branham, James. "I Was Gone on Debating: Malcolm X Prison Debates and Public Confrontations." *Argumentation and Advocacy* 31 (1995): 117–37.

Brar, Dhanveer Singh and Ashwani Sharma. "What Is This 'Black' in Black Studies? From Black British Cultural Studies to Black Critical Thought in UK Arts and Higher Education." *New Formations*, no. 99 (2019): 88+. Gale Academic OneFile. Accessed August 10, 2020. https://link.gale.com/apps/doc/A626207381/AONE?u=txshracd2548&sid=AONE&xid=9d678ae9.

Brockriede, Wayne. "Arguers as Lovers." *Philosophy and Rhetoric* 5, no. 1 (Winter 1972): 1–11.

Burke, Kenneth. *A Grammar of Motives*. Berkeley: University of California Press, 1969.

Burke, Kenneth. *The Philosophy of Literary Form: Studies in Symbolic Action*. New York: Vintage, 1941.

Burke, Kenneth. *A Rhetoric of Motives*. 1st ed. New York: Prentice-Hall, 1950.

Bush, G. W. "President Bush Speaks at Goree Island in Senegal." *White House*. July 8, 2003. Accessed July 10, 2020. https://georgewbush-whitehouse.archives.gov/news/releases/2003/07/20030708-1.html.

Buxton, Julia. "Venezuela: Deeper into the Abyss/Venezuela: A las puertas del abismo." *Revista de Ciencia Politica* 38, no. 2 (2018): 409.

Byrd, Jodi. "Weather with You: Settler Colonialism, Antiblackness, and the Grounded Relationalities of Resistance." *Journal of the Critical Ethnic Studies Association* 5, no. 1–2 (2019): 207. Gale Academic OneFile. Accessed July 28, 2020. https://link-gale-com.proxy.libraries.smu.edu/apps/doc/A608784113/AONE?u=txshracd2548&sid=AONE&xid=b677b2e7.

Cabrera, Roberto. "Guatemala—The Brudnick Center on Violence and Conflict." Accessed April 6, 2018. http://www.northeastern.edu/brudnickcenter/past_conferences/third_world_views-2/transcriptions-of-presentations/roberto-cabrera-guatemala/.

Campbell, Karlyn Kohrs and Susan Huxman. *The Rhetorical Act*. 3rd ed. Belmont, CA: Thomson Wadsworth, 2003.

Canby, Peter. "The Maya Genocide Trial." *The New Yorker*. May 3, 2013. https://www.newyorker.com/news/daily-comment/the-maya-genocide-trial.

Caputo, Marc. "'He Is Not Going to Be the Nominee': Dems Slam Sanders over Maduro Stance: The Just-Announced 2020 Contender Declines to Say Whether the Socialist Venezuelan Dictator Should Go." *Politico*. February 21, 2019.

Carmichael, Stokely. "Black Power." *Voices of Democracy*. October 29, 1966. Accessed September 22, 2019. https://voicesofdemocracy.umd.edu/carmichael-black-power-speech-text/.

Carmichael, Stokely. "Pan Africanism: Land and Power." *Black Scholar* 27, no. 3/4 (1969): 36–43.

Carmichael, Stokely and Ekwueme Michael Thelwell. *Ready for Revolution: The Life and Struggles of Stokely Carmichael (Kwame Ture)*. New York: Scribner, 2003.

Carson, Rachel and Evelyn Oppenheimer. *Silent Spring*. Boston: Houghton Mifflin, 1962.

Case, C. "Germans Reconsider Religion: Pope Benedict XVI's Challenge to Secularism Meets with Receptivity during His German Visit." *The Christian Science Monitor*. September 15, 2006. Accessed August 10, 2020. http://www.csmonitor.com/2006/0915/p01s01-woeu.html.

Case, Roland and Ian Wright. "Taking Seriously the Teaching of Critical Thinking." *Critical Discussions*, 1997.

Chakravarty, Anuradha. *Investing in Authoritarian Rule: Punishment and Patronage in Rwanda's Gacaca Courts for Genocide Crimes*. New York: Cambridge University Press, 2016.

Coates, Taneshi. "Bigotry and the English Language." *The Atlantic*. March 12, 2013. Accessed August 10, 2020. https://www.theatlantic.com/national/archive/2013/12/bigotry-and-the-english-language/281935/.

Cobb, Charles. "From Stokely Carmichael to Kwame Ture." *Callaloo* 34, no. 1 (2011): 89–97.

Collison, Michelle N.-K. "Ressurecting the Thurman Legacy for the Next Millennium." *Black Issues in Higher Education* 24 (November 1999). *Gale Academic OneFile*. Accessed August 11, 2020. https://link.gale.com/apps/doc/A58036234/AONE?u=txshracd2548&sid=AONE&xid=2dba1bc3.

Coolidge, Calvin. "At the Dedication of a Government Hospital for Colored Veterans of the World War, Tuskegee, Alabama, Lincoln's Birthday." February 12, 1923. *The Price of Freedom: Speeches and Addresses*. Fredonia Books.

Coolidge, Calvin. *Autobiography of Calvin Coolidge*. 1929.

Coolidge, Calvin. "Black River Academy Commencement." May 1890. Calvin Coolidge Presidential Foundation website. Accessed August 12, 2020. https://www.coolidgefoundation.org/resources/oratory-in-history/.

Coolidge, Calvin. "President Calvin Coolidge, First Annual Message to Congress on the State of the Union." December 6, 1923.

"Coronavirus Disease 2019 (COVID-19) Situation Report–82." *World Health Organization*. August 15, 2020. https://www.who.int/docs/default-source/coronaviruse/situation-reports/20200411-sitrep-82-covid-19.pdf?sfvrsn=74a5d15_2.

"Corte de Constitucionalidad Guatemala." [Guatemalan Constitutional Court] No. 1904–2013. May 20, 2013 at 002067 (Guat.). http://www.right2info.org/resources/publications/votos-razonados-may-21-2013.

Courtois, Stéphane and Mark Kramer. *The Black Book of Communism: Crimes, Terror, Repression*. Translated by Jonathan Murphy and Mark Kramer. Consulting editor Mark Kramer. Cambridge, MA: Harvard University Press, 1999.

Csaky, Zselyke. "Dropping the Democratic Façade." *Freedom House*. 2020. https://freedomhouse.org/report/nations-transit/2020/dropping-democratic-facade.

Dallas Holocaust Museum. https://www.dhhrm.org/about/.

Damascene, Jean Bizimana. "Some Key Activities that Characterized the Preparation of Genocide against Tutsi between Dates of 13–19 January 1991–1994." *KGM*. January 16, 2020. Accessed July 15, 2020. https://www.kgm.rw/some-key-activities-that-characterized-the-preparation-of-genocide-against-tutsi-between-dates-of-13-19-january-1991-1994/.

Darby, J. and Roger Mac Ginty. *Contemporary Peacemaking: Conflict, Peace Processes and Post-War Reconstruction*. London: Palgrave Macmillan Limited, 2008.

Davies, Steven. "The Great Horse Manure Crisis." *FEE*. September 4, 2004. Accessed July 13, 2020.https://fee.org/articles/the-great-horse-manure-crisis-of-1894/.

Dean, John W. *Warren G. Harding: The American Presidents Series: The 29th President, 1921–1923*. New York: Times Books, 2004.

De Heusch, Luc. "Rwanda: Responsibilities for a Genocide." *Anthropology Today* 11, no. 4 (1995): 3–7.

"Dehumanisation—How Tutsis Were Reduced to Cockroaches, Snakes to Be Killed." *Africa News Service*. COMTEX News Network, Inc., March 14, 2014.

Denton, R. and Ben Voth. "The Epistemological Poisoning of America." In *Social Fragmentation and the Decline of American Democracy*, 85–111. Cham, Switzerland: Palgrave, 2017.

Denton, Robert and Ben Voth. *Social Fragmentation and the Decline of American Democracy*. London: Palgrave Macmillan, 2017.

Denton, Robert and Ben Voth. "What Can We Do? An American Renaissance Predicated on Communicative Idealism." In *Social Fragmentation and the Decline of American Democracy*, 161–65. London: Pagrave Macmillan, 2016.

Desilet, Gregory. *Cult of the Kill: Traditional Metaphysics of Rhetoric, Truth, and Violence in a Postmodern World*. New York: Xlibris Corporation, 2002.

Dilanian, Ken, Courtney Kube and Carol Lee. "Did the Coronavirus Really Escape from a Chinese Lab? Here's What We Know." *NBC News*. May 4, 2020. https://www.nbcnews.com/politics/national-security/did-coronavirus-really-escape-chinese-lab-here-s-what-we-n1199531.

Donofrio, Theresa Ann. "Ground Zero and Place-Making Authority: The Conservative Metaphors in 9/11 Families' 'Take Back the Memorial' Rhetoric." *Western Journal of Communication* 74, no. 2, (March 2010): 150–69.

Dovidio, John, Samuel Gaertner, Kerry Kawakami, and Gordon Hodson. "Why Can't We Just Get Along? Interpersonal Biases and Interracial Distrust." *Cultural Diversity and Ethnic Minority Psychology* 8, no. 2 (2002): 88.

Doxtader, Erik W. "The Entwinement of Argument and Rhetoric: A Dialectical Reading of Habermas' Theory of Communicative Action." *Argumentation and Advocacy* 28, no. 2 (1991): 51+. *Gale Academic OneFile*. Accessed August 10, 2020. https://link.gale.com/apps/doc/A12983009/AONE?u=txshracd2548&sid=AONE&xid=9d012d1f.

"Drafting Document Education." UNICEF. Accessed July 1, 2019. https://www.unicef.org/rwanda/education.html.

Driessen, Paul. "Destroying the Environment to Save It." *Townhall*. May 2020. Accessed July 13, 2020. https://townhall.com/columnists/pauldriessen/2020/05/30/destroying-the-environment-to-save-it-n2569710.

Edwards, Lee. "The Legacy of Mao Zedong Is Mass Murder." *Heritage Foundation*. February 2, 2010. https://www.heritage.org/asia/commentary/the-legacy-mao-zedong-mass-murder.

Ehrlich, Paul R. *The Population Bomb*. New York: Ballantine Books, 1968.

"#83 Ellen Johnson Sirleaf." *Forbes*. Accessed July 15, 2020. https://www.forbes.com/profile/ellen-johnson-sirleaf/#6f20c5a044fb.

Eisele, Robert. *The Great Debaters* [screenplay]. Beverly Hills, CA: 2007.

"Electric Cars Pose Environmental Threat." BBC. October 5, 2012. https://www.bbc.com/news/business-19830232.

Ellul, Jacques. *Propaganda: The Formation of Men's Attitudes*. Translated by Konrad Kellen and Jean Lerner. Introduction by Konrad Kellen. New York: Vintage Books, 1974.

Ezekiel 37:1–14. The Bible. *The New Jerusalem Bible*.

Fanon, Frantz. *The Wretched of the Earth*. New York: Grove Press, 1963.

Fanon, Frantz and Constance Farrington. *The Wretched of the Earth*. Translated by Constance Farrington. Preface by Jean-Paul Sartre. New York: Grove Press, 1967.

Farber, Daniel. "Coping with Uncertainty: Cost-Benefit Analysis, the Precautionary Principle, and Climate Change." *Washington Law Review* 90, no. 4 (December 1, 2015): 1659–82.

Farmer, James, Jr. *Lay Bare the Heart*. Fort Worth: TCU Press, 1985.

Farmer, James, Jr. "Lecture." Mary Washington University. Accessed August 11, 2020. https://jamesfarmerlectures.umwblogs.org/lectures-audio/.

Farmer, James, Jr. 1945. "Plan for a Two Month or Three Month Full Time Campaign against Jim Crow." James Leonard, Jr., and Lula Peterson Farmer papers. Dolph Briscoe Center for American History. The University of Texas at Austin. Box 2R566.

Farmer, James, Jr. April 16, 1968, TV Interview. Transcript. James Leonard, Jr., and Lula Peterson Farmer papers. Dolph Briscoe Center for American History. The University of Texas at Austin. Box 2R635.

Farr, Christina and Michelle Gao. "How Taiwan Beat the Coronavirus." *CNBC*. July 15, 2020. https://www.cnbc.com/2020/07/15/how-taiwan-beat-the-coronavirus.html.

Feigenbaum, Evan and Jeremy Smith. "How Taiwan Can Turn Coronavirus Victory into Economic Success." *Foreign Policy*. June 1, 2020.

Felzenberg, A. S. "Calvin Coolidge and Race: His Record in Dealing with the Racial Tensions of the 1920s." Presented at "Calvin Coolidge: Examining the Evidence" conference. Boston, 1998.

Ferry, Victor. "What Is Habermas's 'Better Argument' Good For?" *Argumentation and Advocacy* 49, no. 2 (2012): 144+. *Gale Academic OneFile*. Accessed August 10, 2020. https://link.gale.com/apps/doc/A332892402/AONE?u=txshracd2548&sid=AONE&xid=2ed30c90.

Fisas, Vicençe. *La Paz Es Posible*. Barcelona, Spain: Intermon Oxfam, 2002.

Fisher, Bernice. "Confessions of an Ex-Liberal." James Leonard, Jr., and Lula Peterson Farmer papers. Dolph Briscoe Center for American History. The University of Texas at Austin. Box 2R648.

Fisher, Walter. "Homo Narrans the Narrative Paradigm: In the Beginning." *Journal of Communication* 35, no. 4 (Fall 1985): 74.

Fleser, Arthur. *The Rhetoric of Calvin Coolidge*. Dissertation. Indiana University, 1962.

Ford, James H. *The Peddler's Son*. BLURB incorporated, 2016.

Foucault, Michel. "Politics and Reason." In *Politics, Philosophy, Culture: Interviews and Other Writings: 1977–1984*. New York: Routledge, 1988.

Foucault, Michel and A. M. Sheridan Smith. *The Archaeology of Knowledge*. Translated from the French by A. M. Sheridan Smith [1st American ed.]. New York: Pantheon Books, 1972.

Freeley, Austin J. and David Steinberg. *Argumentation and Debate: Critical Thinking for Reasoned Decision Making*. 12th ed. Boston, MA: Wadsworth Pub. Co., 2008.

Freire, Paulo. *Pedagogy of the Oppressed*. New York: Continuum, 2000.

Gage, Beverly. "Our First Black President?" *New York Times*. April 6, 2008.

Ganesan, N. and Sung Chull Kim. *State Violence in East Asia*. Lexington: University Press of Kentucky, 2013.

"Gasoline and Additives." encyclopedia.com. Accessed July 13, 2020. https://www.encyclopedia.com/environment/encyclopedias-almanacs-transcripts-and-maps/gasoline-and-additives.

George W. Bush Presidential Center. Accessed August 17, 2020. https://www.bushcenter.org/explore-our-work/index.html.

Ghebreyesus, Dr. Tedros Adhanom. "Director-General Dr. Tedros Takes the Helm of WHO: Address to WHO Staff-Director-General of the World Health Organization." World Health Organization. Geneva, Switzerland. July 3, 2017. https://www.who.int/dg/speeches/2017/taking-helm-who/en/.

Giles, Howard. *Communication Accommodation Theory*. Los Angeles: Sage Publications, 2008.

Gilley, Bruce. "The Case for Colonialism." *Academic Questions* 31 (2017): 167–85.

Gilley, Bruce. "The Case for Colonialism." *Third World Quarterly* (2017). DOI: 10.1080/01436597.2017.1369037.

Gilmore, Betty. "Going to Rwanda to Train Security Forces in Dispute Resolution." April 2017. Accessed July 14, 2020. https://www.smu.edu/News/2017/betty-gilmore-18april2017Gk.

Goidel, Kirby, Craig Freeman, and Brian Smentkowski. *Misreading the Bill of Rights Top Ten Myths Concerning Your Rights and Liberties*. Santa Barbra, CA: Praeger, 2015.

Goldhagen, Daniel Jonah. *Worse than War: Genocide, Eliminationism, and the Ongoing Assault on Humanity*. 1st ed. New York: PublicAffairs, 2009.

"Goodbye to All That? Liberia: (Liberia's Despot Resigns)." *The Economist* (US) 368, no. 8337 (August 16, 2003).

Grady, Denise. "Coronavirus Is Spreading, but W.H.O. Says It's Not a Global Emergency." *New York Times*. January 23, 2020. https://www.nytimes.com/2020/01/23/health/china-virus-who-emergency.html.

Granovetter, Mark. "Economic Action and Social Structure: The Problem of Embeddedness." *American Journal of Sociology* 91, no. 3 (1985): 481–510.

Gross, A. G. "The Roles of Rhetoric in the Public Understanding of Science." *Public Understanding of Science* 3, no. 1 (1994): 3–23. https://doi.org/10.1088/0963-6625/3/1/001.

Guest, Iain. "For Rwandan Genocide Survivors, It's Pragmatism vs. Revenge." *The Christian Science Monitor*. August 30, 1996. https://www.csmonitor.com/1996/0830/083096.opin.opin.1.html.

Haberman, Clyde. "Rachel Carson, DDT and the Fight against Malaria." *New York Times*. January 22, 2017. https://www.nytimes.com/2017/01/22/us/rachel-carson-ddt-malaria-retro-report.html.

Habermas, Jurgen. *Communication and the Evolution of Society*. Boston: Beacon Press, 1979.

Habermas, Jurgen. *The Theory of Communicative Action*. Cambridge, UK: Polity Press, 1984.

Habineza, Jean Michel, Dr. John Rief, and Rachel Wilson. "The iDebate Rwanda Tour of the U.S.: Cross-Cultural Perspectives on Debate and Social Justice Memory." National Communication Association Conference. November 7, 2018. Salt Lake City, UT.

Han, Soo-Hye and Colene J. Lind. "Putting Powerfulness in Its Place: A Study on Discursive Style in Public Discussion and Its Impact." *Argumentation and Advocacy* 53, no. 3–4 (2017): 216. *Gale Academic OneFile*. Accessed August 10, 2020. https://link.gale.com/apps/doc/A543611048/AONE?u=txshracd2548&sid=AONE&xid=2af50b41.

Hanscom, Aaron. "Confronting a Worldwide Jew-Hatred." *History News Network*. April 24, 2007.

Hart, Hanna. "How to Say 'I Don't Know' with Grace and Authority: A Leadership Lesson from Ta-Nehisi Coates." *Forbes*. October 31, 2019.

Hart, Julie. "Grassroots Peacebuilding in Post Civil War Guatemala: Three Models of Hope." *Mennonite Life* 60, no. 1 (March 2005). https://ml.bethelks.edu/issue/vol-60-no-1/article/grassroots-peacebuilding-in-post-civil-war-guatema/.

Haynes, Jeffrey. *Handbook of Religion and Politics*. New York: Routledge, 2008.

Heffernan, James. "For JMU Students, Refugee Plight Hits Home." James Madison University News. November 1, 2012. https://www.jmu.edu/news/2012/11/lost-boys-noland.shtml.

Heffron, Florence. *Organization Theory and Public Organizations*. Princeton: Princeton University Press, 1968.

Heinze, Eric. "The Rhetoric of Genocide in U.S. Foreign Policy: Rwanda and Darfur Compared." *Political Science Quarterly* 122, no. 3 (2007): 359–83. www.jstor.org/stable/20202884.

Henderson, David. "1.6%, Not 97%, Agree That Humans Are the Main Cause of Global Warming." *Econ Log*. March 2014. Accessed August 10, 2020. https://www.econlib.org/archives/2014/03/16_not_97_agree.html.

Hentoff, Natatorium. "The World's Oldest Hatred Hasn't Gone Away." *Aspen Daily News*. August 20, 2006.
Hilker, Lyndsay McLean. "The Role of Education in Driving Conflict and Building Peace: The Case of Rwanda." *Prospects* 41, no. 2 (2011): 267–82.
Hisham, Aidi. "Malcolm X and the Sudanese." *Al Jazeera*. March 19, 2020.
Hitler, Adolf. *Mein Kampf*. Translated by Ralph Manheim. Boston: Houghton Mifflin Company, 1943.
Hitler, Adolf. *What about Germany?* New York: Dodd, Mead & Co., 1942.
Hixson, Walter L. *American Settler Colonialism: A History*. 1st ed. New York: Palgrave Macmillan, 2013.
Hobday, Richard A. and John W. Cason. "The Open-Air Treatment of Pandemic Influenza." *American Journal of Public Health* 99, no. S2 (October 1, 2009): S236–S242.
Hoekema, David A. "Risking Peace: How Religious Leaders Helped End Uganda's Civil War." *Commonwealth*. January 25, 2019, 10+. *Gale Academic OneFile*. Accessed August 10, 2020. https://link.gale.com/apps/doc/A573715695/AONE?u=txshracd2548&sid=AONE&xid=333f8703.
"Howard Thurman." National Cathedral Website. Accessed August 11, 2020. https://cathedral.org/what-to-see/interior/howard-thurman/.
"'How Dare You?' Greta Thunberg Asks World Leaders at UN Summit." *International Business Times*-US Ed. Newsweek Media Group. September 23, 2019.
Huang, Chaolin, et al. "Clinical Features of Patients Infected with 2019 Novel Coronavirus in Wuhan, China." *Lancet* 395, no. 10223 (2020): 497–506. https://www.thelancet.com/journals/lancet/article/PIIS0140-6736(20)30183-5/fulltext.
Huff, Ethan. "Harvard Study Finds That Wind Turbines Create MORE Global Warming than the Fossil Fuels They Eliminate—And the Same Is True for Scooters and Electric Cars." *Ecology News*. August 26, 2019. Accessed July 13, 2020. https://www.ecology.news/2019-08-26-wind-turbines-create-more-global-warming.html.
"ICC's Toughest Trial: Africa vs. 'Infamous Caucasian Court.'" *Reuters*. October 28, 2016. https://www.reuters.com/article/us-africa-icc/iccs-toughest-trial-africa-vs-infamous-caucasian-court-idUSKCN12S1U3.
Idso, Craig. "Projecting Impacts Rising CO_2 Future Crop Yields in Germany." *CATO*. 2016. Accessed July 13, 2020. https://www.cato.org/blog/projecting-impacts-rising-co2-future-crop-yields-germany.
Iribagiza, Glory. "102-Year-Old Genocide Survivor Who Lost All Her 17 Children Reminisces about Meeting the King, Old Times." *The New Times*. March 9, 2020.
Isaiah 58:12. The Bible. *New International Version*.
"Italy Launched 'Hug a Chinese' Campaign to Fight Coronavirus Induced Racism." *The Indian Express*. March 30, 2020.
Jacob, Frank. *Genocide and Mass Violence in Asia*. Berlin: DeGruyter, 2019.
Jakubowski, Aleksandra, et al. "The US President's Malaria Initiative and Under-5 Child Mortality in Sub-Saharan Africa: A Difference-in-Differences Analysis." *PLoS Medicine* 14, no. 6 e1002319 (June 13, 2017). doi:10.1371/journal.pmed.1002319.
Jenkins, Colin. "Burning Down the American Plantation: An Interview with the Revolutionary Abolitionist Movement." *Truth Out*. September 16, 2017.
Johnson, C. *Why Coolidge Matters: Leadership Lessons from America's Most Underrated President*. New York: Encounter books, 2013.
Johnson, Ian. "Who Killed More: Hitler, Stalin, or Mao?" *New York Times Book Review*. February 5, 2018. https://www.nybooks.com/daily/2018/02/05/who-killed-more-hitler-stalin-or-mao/.
Johnson, Kevin A. "Speech and Debate as Civic Education." *Argumentation and Advocacy* 55, no. 1–2 (2019): 82. *Gale Academic OneFile*. Accessed August 10, 2020. https://link-gale-com.proxy.libraries.smu.edu/apps/doc/A615915869/AONE?u=txshracd2548&sid=AONE&xid=15fb55e4.
Kashyap, Monika Batra. "Unsettling Immigration Laws: Settler Colonialism and the U.S. Immigration Legal System." *Fordham Urban Law Journal* (June 2019): 548. *Gale Academic OneFile*. Accessed July 28, 2020. https://link-gale-

com.proxy.libraries.smu.edu/apps/doc/A592339979/AONE?u=txshracd2548&sid=AONE&xid=fba3ca73.

Keane, Kiara. "Ted Cruz Says San Antonio's Decision to Label the Term 'Chinese Virus' as Hate Speech Is 'Nuts.'" *Business Insider.* May 9, 2020.

Kelsie, Amber. "Blackened Debate at the End of the World." *Philosophy and Rhetoric* 52, no. 1 (2019): 63–70.

Kendi, Ibram X. "The 11 Most Racist U.S. Presidents." *Huffington Post*, May 28, 2017. Accessed July 10, 2019. https://www.huffpost.com/entry/would-a-president-trump-m_b_10135836.

"Key Rwanda Genocide Suspect, Felicien Kabuga, Arrested outside Paris." *RFI*, May 16, 2020. Accessed August 5, 2020. https://www.rfi.fr/en/africa/20200516-key-rwanda-genocide-suspect-felician-kabuga-arrested-outside-paris?fbclid=IwAR3myu6Xgn1UKbpEdQQQzy-RiDhYMEZxWICbSVfa8yJ513yH65_UoUC6FI8.

Kim, H. J., et al. "Health Development Experience in North and South Korea." *Asia-Pacific Journal of Public Health* 1, no. 3_Supplemental (2001): S51–7.

Kim, Hunjoon and Kathryn Sikkink. "Explaining the Deterrence Effect of Human Rights Prosecutions for Transitional Countries." *International Studies Quarterly* 54, no. 4 (December 1, 2010): 939–63. https://doi.org/10.1111/j.1468-2478.2010.00621.x.

King, Elisabeth. *From Classrooms to Conflict in Rwanda.* Cambridge: Cambridge University Press, 2013.

King, Elisabeth. "The Role of Education in Violent Conflict and Peacebuilding in Rwanda." PhD Dissertation. University of Toronto, 2008.

King, Martin Luther, Jr. "An Address by the Reverend Dr. Martin Luther King Jr." Cornell College, Mount Vernon, Iowa. October 15, 1962. Accessed on August 10, 2020. https://news.cornellcollege.edu/dr-martin-luther-kings-visit-to-cornell-college/.

King, Martin Luther, Jr. "I Have a Dream Speech." March on Washington. August 28, 1963. Accessed August 10, 2020. https://www.americanrhetoric.com/speeches/mlkihaveadream.htm.

Kirkpatrick, David D. "U.S. Criticizes Egypt's Leader for Anti-Semitic Remarks: Foreign Desk." *New York Times.* January 16, 2013.

Krieger, Hilary. "Jewish World Marks Rise in Antisemitism." *Jerusalem Post.* August 1, 2006.

Kristof, Nicholas. "2019 Was the Best Year." *New York Times.* December 28, 2019. https://www.nytimes.com/2019/12/28/opinion/sunday/2019-best-year-poverty.html.

Krushelnycky, Askold. "Stalin's Government Created the Ukrainian Famine-Genocide." *Contemporary Issues Companion: Genocide.* New York: Greenhaven, 2008.

Kuhn, Thomas. *The Structure of Scientific Revolutions.* University of Chicago, London, 1962.

Kurmanaev, Anatoly. "Evo Morales and Bolivia: What We Know about the President's Resignation." *New York Times.* November 12, 2019. https://www.nytimes.com/2019/11/12/world/americas/evo-morales-resignation-bolivia-facts.html.

Kushkush, Isma'il. "Protesters in Sudan and Algeria Have Learned from the Arab Spring." *The Atlantic.* April 13, 2019. Accessed July 10, 2020. https://www.theatlantic.com/international/archive/2019/04/protesters-sudan-and-algeria-have-learned-arab-spring/587113/.

"Kwame Ture 1941–1998." *Race and History.* November 15, 1999. Accessed August 1, 2020. http://www.raceandhistory.com/historicalviews/111599.htm.

Langbert, Mitchell. "Homogenous: The Political Affiliations of Elite Liberal Arts College Faculty." *Academic Questions* 31, no. 2 (Summer 2018).

Lederach, John Paul. *The Moral Imagination: The Art and Soul of Building Peace.* New York: Oxford University Press, 2005.

Levitt, Laura. *American Jewish Loss after the Holocaust.* New York: New York University Press, 2007.

Lewis, C. S. *The Screwtape Letters.* New York: MacMillan Co., 1943.

Li, Chi-Do. *Buy This Land*. 2012.
"Liberia." *World Bank*. Accessed July 21, 2020. https://data.worldbank.org/country/liberia.
"List of Federal and State Recognized Tribes." National Conference of State Legislatures. Accessed July 28, 2020. https://www.ncsl.org/research/state-tribal-institute/list-of-federal-and-state-recognized-tribes.aspx.
Lombrana, Laura Millan. "Saving the Planet with Electric Cars Means Strangling This Desert." *Bloomberg News*. June 11, 2019. Accessed July 13, 2020. https://www.bloomberg.com/news/features/2019-06-11/saving-the-planet-with-electric-cars-means-strangling-this-desert.
Lott, John. "Public Schooling, Indoctrination, and Totalitarianism." *Journal of Political Economy* 107 (1999).
Lovelock, James. *The Vanishing Face of Gaia: A Final Warning*. New York: Basic Books, April 2009.
Lula Peterson's High School Yearbook. James Leonard, Jr., and Lula Peterson Farmer papers. Dolph Briscoe Center for American History. The University of Texas at Austin. Box3U250.
MacDougall, Clair and Helene Cooper. "George Weah Wins Liberia Election." *New York Times*. December 28, 2017. https://www.nytimes.com/2017/12/28/world/africa/george-weah-liberia-election.html.
Mallin, Irwin and Karrin Vasby Anderson. "Inviting Constructive Argument." *Argumentation and Advocacy* 36, no. 3 (2000): 120. *Gale Academic OneFile*. Accessed August 12, 2020. https://link-gale-com.proxy.libraries.smu.edu/apps/doc/A59044832/AONE?u=txshracd2548&sid=AONE&xid=e85d2d6e.
Mare, Admire. "Popular Communication in Africa: An Empirical and Theoretical Exposition." *Annals of the International Communication Association* 44, no. 1, (2020): 81–99.
Matthew 5–7. *New American Standard Bible*. Anaheim, CA: Lockman Foundation, 1997.
Matthew 25: 37–40. *New American Standard Bible*. Anaheim, CA: Lockman Foundation, 1997.
Matthews, Dylan. "Secret Love Child Aside, Warren Harding Was a Solid President." Vox. August 13, 2015.
Max Rettig. "Gacaca: Truth, Justice, and Reconciliation in Postconflict Rwanda?" *African Studies Review*, no. 3 (December 2008): 25–50. Accessed April 1, 2020. www.jstor.org/stable/27667378.
Mbembe, Achille. *On the Postcolony*. Berkeley: University of California Press, 2001.
Mcdoom, Omar Shahabudin. "War and Genocide in Africa's Great Lakes Region since Independence." In *The Oxford Handbook of Genocide Studies*, 1–41. Edited by Donald Bloxham. Oxford: Oxford University Press. *ResearchGate*. January 2012. https://www.researchgate.net/publication/.48911153_War_and_genocide_in_Africa's_Great_Lakes_region_since_independence.
McKean, Erin. *The New Oxford American Dictionary*. 2nd ed. New York: Oxford University Press, 2005.
"Medgar Evers." Mississippi Writers website, University of Mississippi English Department (2015). Accessed August 11, 2020. http://mwp.olemiss.edu//dir/evers_medgar/.
Medina, Christopher, Denise Vaughan, Sean Allen, and Dawn Lowry. "Perceived Racial Discrimination and Its Effects in Collegiate Forensics." Manuscript, 2017.
Mellen, Ruby. "Wildfires in Indonesia Have Ravaged 800,000 Acres. Palm Oil Farmers Are Mostly to Blame." *Washington Post*. September 18, 2019. https://www.washingtonpost.com/world/2019/09/18/wildfires-indonesia-have-ravaged-acres-palm-oil-farmers-are-blame/.
Mendez, Juan E. "Accountability for Past Abuses." *Human Rights Quarterly* 19, no. 2 (1997): 255–82. https://doi.org/10.1353/hrq.1997.0018.
Meredith, James. *Three Years in Mississippi*. Jackson: University of Mississippi Press, 2019.

Meredith, James and William Doyle. *A Mission from God: A Memoir and Challenge for America*. New York: Atria, 2012.

Middle East Media Research Institute. 2020. Memri.org.

Milliken, Frances and Luis Martins. "Searching for Common Threads: Understanding the Multiple Effects of Diversity in Organisational Groups." *Academy of Management Review* 21, no. 2 (1996): 402–33.

Mishler, William and Richard Rose. "What Are the Origins of Political Trust? Testing Institutional and Cultural Theories in Post-Communist Societies." *Comparative Political Studies* 34, no. 1 (February 1, 2001): 30–62. https://doi.org/10.1177/0010414001034001002.

Mitchell, Gordon R. "Pedagogical Possibilities for Argumentative Agency in Academic Debate." *Argumentation and Advocacy* 35, no. 2 (1998): 41. *Gale Academic OneFile*. Accessed August 10, 2020. https://link.gale.com/apps/doc/A53650192/AONE?u=txshracd2548&sid=AONE&xid=34d0a1a7.

Mitter, Rana. "The World's Wartime Debt to China." *New York Times*. October 17, 2013. https://www.nytimes.com/2013/10/18/opinion/the-worlds-wartime-debt-to-china.html.

Moore, Peter. "One Third of Millenials View Socialism Favorably." *Yougov poll*. 2019. Accessed August 10, 2020. https://today.yougov.com/topics/politics/articles-reports/2015/05/11/one-third-millennials-like-socialism.

Moore, Stephen. "How Fracking Has Reduced Greenhouse Gases." *Real Clear Politics*. April 16, 2016. Accessed June 1, 2020. https://www.realclearpolitics.com/articles/2016/04/16/how_fracking_has_reduced_greenhouse_gases_130303.html.

Naimark, Norman M. *Stalin's Genocides*. Princeton: Princeton University Press, 2010.

Ndahiro, Kennedy. "In Rwanda, We Know All about Dehumanizing Language: Years of Cultivated Hatred Led to Death on a Horrifying Scale." *The Atlantic*. April 13, 2019. https://www.theatlantic.com/ideas/archive/2019/04/rwanda-shows-how-hateful-speech-leads-violence/587041/.

Neubeck, Kyle. "DeSean Jackson Shares Anti-Semitic Quotes Attributed to Hitler on Instagram." *Philly Voice*. July 7, 2020. https://www.phillyvoice.com/eagles-desean-jackson-anti-semitic-instagram-farrakhan-hitler-quotes/.

Nigam, Sonya. "The Internet Campaign Urging Capture of Ugandan Rebel Leader Joseph Kony Is a Good Thing." *Internet Activism*. January 1, 2013.

Olaka, Musa Wakhungu. *Collaborating to Preserve and Disseminate Testimonies of Child Survivors of the 1994 Genocide in Rwanda*. Paper Presented at the IFLA/WLIC Conference in Capetown, South Africa in 2015.

Oltmann, Shannon M. "Intellectual Freedom and Freedom of Speech: Three Theoretical Perspectives." *The Library Quarterly* 86, no. 2 (April 2016): 153–71.

"Omar Al-Bashir Steps Down, Transitional Government Announced: Al-Arabiya TV." TCA Regional News. Chicago: Tribune Content Agency LLC, April 11, 2019.

Orbe, Mark and Tina M. Harris. *Interracial Communication: Theory into Practice*. Los Angeles: Sage Publications, 2013.

"Otto Warmbier, American Recently Released by North Korea, Dies at 22." Morning Edition. National Public Radio, Inc. (NPR), 2017.

Özdemir, Cem. "Controversy over Turkish Movie: Beyond the Valley of the Wolves." *Speigel Online*. February 22, 2006. Accessed August 1, 2007. http://www.spiegel.de/international/0,1518,401565,00.html.

Page, Clarence. "Learning from Andrew Young's Blunder." *Chicago Tribune*. August 21, 2006.

Paliewicz, Nicholas S. and George F. (Guy) McHendry, Jr. "When Good Arguments Do Not Work: Post-Dialectics, Argument Assemblages, and the Networks of Climate Skepticism." *Argumentation and Advocacy* 53, no. 3–4 (2017): 287. *Gale Academic OneFile*. Accessed August 10, 2020. https://link.gale.com/apps/doc/A543611053/AONE?u=txshracd2548&sid=AONE&xid=27fb938a.

Parry, Sam. "US Imperialism in Venezuela, and the Legacy of Colonialism." *Undod*. January 29, 2019. Accessed August 1, 2020. https://undod.cymru/en/2019/01/29/venezuela/.

Pearl, Robert. "American Healthcare 2040." *Fortune*. October 1, 2019. https://www.forbes.com/sites/robertpearl/2019/10/01/american-healthcare-2040/#25ae29ff71b0

Perelman, C. and L. Olbrechts-Tyteca. *The New Rhetoric: A Treatise on Argumentation*. Notre Dame, IN: University of Notre Dame Press, 1969.

"Peru's Fujimori Gets 25 Years Prison for Massacres." *Reuters*. April 7, 2009, https://www.reuters.com/article/us-peru-fujimori/perus-fujimori-convicted-of-human-rights-crimes-idUSTRE5363RH20090407.

Pietrusza, David. "Calvin Coolidge and Civil Rights—The Rest of the Story." *The Coolidge Quarterly* 1, no. 3 (November 2016): 10.

Pinghui, Zhuang. "Chinese Laboratory That First Shared Coronavirus Genome with World Ordered to Close for 'Rectification', Hindering Its Covid-19 Research." *South China Morning Post*. February 28, 2020. https://www.scmp.com/news/china/society/article/3052966/chinese-laboratory-first-shared-coronavirus-genome-world-ordered.

Pinker, Steven. "Why Violence Is Vanishing." *Wall Street Journal*. Accessed on September 24, 2011. http://www.wsj.com/articles/SB10001424053111904106704576583203589408180.

Platt, Carrie Anne and Zoltan P. Majdik. "The Place of Religion in Habermas's Transformed Public Sphere." *Argumentation and Advocacy* 49, no. 2 (2012): 138. Gale Academic OneFile. Accessed August 10, 2020. https://link.gale.com/apps/doc/A332892400/AONE?u=txshracd2548&sid=AONE&xid=29f70fdb.

"Plunge in Carbon Emissions from Lockdowns Will Not Slow Climate Change." *National Geographic*. May 2020. https://www.nationalgeographic.com/science/2020/05/plunge-in-carbon-emissions-lockdowns-will-not-slow-climate-change/.

Power, Samantha. *Problem from Hell: America in the Age of Genocide*. New York: Harper Collins, 2002.

Priyadarsini, Lakshmi S. and M. Suresh. "Factors Influencing the Epidemiological Characteristics of Pandemic COVID-19: A TISM Approach." *International Journal of Healthcare Management* 13, no. 2 (April 2, 2020): 89–98.

"Professor Fired after 9-11, Nazi Comparison." *NBC News*. July 24, 2007. Accessed August 10, 2020. http://www.nbcnews.com/id/19940243/ns/us_news-education/t/professor-fired-after-nazi-comparison/#.UkJL8RY9roM.2013.

Proverbs 29:18. *New American Standard Bible*. Anaheim, CA: Lockman Foundation, 1997.

Radu, Sintia. "Countries with the Highest Incarceration Rates." *U.S. News and World Report*. May 13, 2019.

"Ranking America's Worst Presidents." *U.S. News and World Report*. November 6, 2019. Accessed August 10, 2020. https://www.usnews.com/news/special-reports/the-worst-presidents/articles/ranking-americas-worst-presidents.

"Revisiting Rwanda Five Years after Record-Breaking Parliamentary Elections." *UN Women*. August 13, 2018. Accessed August 5, 2020. https://www.unwomen.org/en/news/stories/2018/8/feature-rwanda-women-in-parliament.

Rice, Condoleeza. *Stories from the Long Road to Freedom*. New York: Twelve, 2017.

Richter, Elihu and Alex Barnea. "Tehran's Genocidal Incitement against Israel." *Middle East Quarterly* 16, no. 3 (June 22, 2009).

Rieke, Richard D. and Malcolm O. Sillars. *Argumentation and Critical Decision Making*. New York: Pearson, 1997.

Rogin, Josh. "State Department Cables Warned of Safety Issues at Wuhan Lab Studying Bat Coronaviruses." *Washington Post*. April 14, 2020. https://www.washingtonpost.com/opinions/2020/04/14/state-department-cables-warned-safety-issues-wuhan-lab-studying-bat-coronaviruses/.

Roser, Max and Esteban Ortiz-Ospina. "Global Extreme Poverty." *Our World in Data.* 2019. Accessed July 13, 2020. https://ourworldindata.org/extreme-poverty.
Rosling, Hans. "200 Countries in 200 Years." BBC/YouTube. https://www.youtube.com/watch?v=jbkSRLYSojo.
Rosling, Hans. *Factfulness: Ten Reasons We're Wrong about the World—And Why Things Are Better than You Think.* New York: Flatiron Books, 2018.
Ruiz, María Teresa. *Los Cristianos Y Los Derechos Humanos En Guatemala.* Colección Análisis. San José, Costa Rica: DEI, 1994.
Rummel, Rudolph. *Death by Government.* London: Transaction Publishers, 2004.
Rummel, Rudolph J. "Democracy, Power, Genocide, and Mass Murder." *The Journal of Conflict Resolution* 39, no. 1 (1995): 5.
Rummel, Rudolph J. *Power Kills: Democracy as a Method of Nonviolence.* New Brunswick, NJ: Transaction Publishers, 1997.
"Rwanda Genocide: 100 Days of Slaughter." BBC. April 4, 2019. https://www.bbc.com/news/world-africa-26875506.
"Rwanda: In Brief." *Congressional Research Service.* Updated May 14, 2019. https://fas.org/sgp/crs/row/R44402.pdf.
Saad, Lydia. "Americans' Take on the U.S. Is Improved, but Still Mixed." *Gallup.* January 27, 2020. Accessed August 10, 2020. https://news.gallup.com/poll/284033/americans-improved-mixed.aspx.
Sargent, Albert. Boston Traveler, Scrapbook. Forbes Library. August 16, 1923.
Sayapin, Sergey. "Raphael Lemkin: A Tribute." *European Journal of International Law* 20, no. 4 (November 2009): 1157–62.
Schorr, Daniel. "Iran's Holocaust-Denial Conference: A Community of Hate; The Iranian Effort to Mount a Holocaust Denial Campaign Is Linked with the Israeli-Palestinian Crisis: ALL Edition." *The Christian Science Monitor.* Boston: The Christian Science Publishing Society, 1983.
Schuessler, J. "Woodrow Wilson's Legacy Gets Complicated." *New York Times.* November 29, 2015. https://www.nytimes.com/2015/11/30/arts/woodrow-wilsons-legacy-gets-complicated.html.
Schwartz, Howard and Stanley Davis. "Matching Corporate Culture and Business Strategy." *Organizational Dynamics* 10, no. 2 (1981).
Seay, Laura. "Rwanda's Gacaca Courts Are Hailed as a Post-Genocide Success. The Reality Is More Complicated." *Washington Post.* June 2, 2017.
Seelye, Katharine. "Thomas Freeman Debate Coach with Broad Influence Dies at 100." *New York Times.* June 16, 2020. https://www.nytimes.com/2020/06/16/us/thomas-freeman-debate-coach-with-broad-influence-dies-at-100.html.
Sharon, Jeremy. "Farrakhan Compares Jews to Termites, Says They Are 'Stupid.'" *The Jerusalem Post.* Jerusalem: The Jerusalem Post Ltd, October 18, 2018.
Shellenberger, Michael. *Apocalypse Never: Why Environmental Alarmism Hurts Us All.* New York: Harper Collins, 2020.
Shellenberger, Michael. "If Solar Panels Are So Clean Why Do They Produce So Much Toxic Waste?" *Forbes.* August 28, 2018. https://www.forbes.com/sites/michaelshellenberger/2018/05/23/if-solar-panels-are-so-clean-why-do-they-produce-so-much-toxic-waste/#54d0e713121c.
Shiffrin, Steven. "Dissent, Democratic Participation, and First Amendment Methodology." *Virginia Law Review* 97, no. 3 (2011): 559–65. www.jstor.org/stable/41261522.
Shlaes, Amity. *Coolidge.* 1st ed. New York: Harper, 2013.
Sikkink, Kathryn. *The Justice Cascade: How Human Rights Prosecutions Are Changing World Politics.* 1st ed. New York: W. W. Norton & Co, 2011.
Sikkink, Kathryn and Carrie Booth Walling. "The Impact of Human Rights Trials in Latin America." *Journal of Peace Research* 44, no. 4 (2007): 427–45.
Simon, Julian L. *The Economic Consequences of Immigration.* Oxford: Basil Blackwell, 1990.
Simon, Julian L. *The Economics of Population Growth.* Princeton: Princeton University Press, 1979.

Simon, Julian L. *Population Matters: People, Resources, Environment, Immigration*. New Brunswick, NJ: Transaction Publishers, 1981.
Simon, Julian L. *Theory of Population and Economic Growth*. Oxford and New York: Basil Blackwell, 1989.
Simon, Julian L. *The Ultimate Resource*. Princeton: Princeton University Press, 1986.
Simon, Julian L. *The Ultimate Resource 2*. Princeton: Princeton University Press, 1996.
Smith, Thomas E. *Emancipation without Equality: Pan-African Activism and the Global Color Line*. Amherst: University of Massachusetts Press, 2018.
Song, X., M. C. Hansen, S. V. Stehman, et al. "Global Land Change from 1982 to 2016." *Nature* 560 (2018): 639–43. https://doi.org/10.1038/s41586-018-0411-9.
Song, Xiongwei. "Why Do Change Management Strategies Fail? Illustrations with Examples." *Journal of Cambridge Studies* 4, no. 1 (2009): 6–15.
Specia, Megan. "How a Nation Reconciles after Genocide Killed Nearly a Million People." *New York Times*. April 25, 2017.
Staub, Ervin. "Basic Human Needs and Their Role in Altruism and Aggression." In *The Psychology of Good and Evil*, 52–68. Cambridge University Press, 2003.
Staub, Ervin. *The Roots of Evil: The Origins of Genocide and Other Group Violence*. Cambridge: Cambridge University Press, 1989.
Stevenson, Angus and Christine A. Lindberg. "Propaganda." In *The New American Oxford Dictionary*. New York: Oxford University Press, 2018.
"Sudan Repeals Omar Al-Bashir-Era Law Regulating Women's Behaviour and Dissolves Former Ruling Party." *The Telegraph Online*. November 29, 2019.
"Sudan's Bashir Accuses ICC of Facilitating Colonisation in Africa." *Middle East Monitor*. April 3, 2017. Accessed July 10, 2020. https://www.middleeastmonitor.com/20170403-sudans-bashir-accuses-icc-of-facilitating-colonisation-in-africa/.
"Survivors of the 1994 Genocide in Rwanda." Cape Town IFLA WLIC. June 2015: 1–12. http://library.ifla.org/1161/7/206-olaka-en.pdf.
"Taiwan Beat the Virus with Efficient Government and Advanced Technology—The Same Ingredients That Power the Economy." *Foreign Policy*. June 1, 2020. https://foreignpolicy.com/author/evan-a-feigenbaum/.
Talbott, Strobe. "Unilateralism: Anatomy of a Foreign Policy Disaster." *Brookings Institute*. 2007. https://www.brookings.edu/opinions/unilateralism-anatomy-of-a-foreign-policy-disaster/.
"The 10 African Strongmen Who Left Power since 2011." *Agency France Press*. April 25, 2019. https://www.france24.com/en/20190423-timeline-10-african-strongmen-deposed-gaddafi-bashir-mugabe-bouteflika.
"The Beloved Community." *The King Center*. Accessed March 1, 2016. http://www.thekingcenter.org/king-philosophy#sub4.
"The Law of Return 5710 (1950)." Article 1. July 5, 1950. https://knesset.gov.il/laws/special/eng/return.htm.
"The Legal Case against Gonzalo Sánchez de Lozada Moves into High Gear." *The Democracy Center*. Accessed January 15, 2018. https://democracyctr.org/the-legal-case-against-gonzalo-sanchez-de-lozada-moves-into-high-gear/.
"The Open Mind: Race Relations in Crisis." PBS. June 1963 and 1993. [Video]. https://www.pbs.org/video/the-open-mind-race-relations-in-crisis/.
"The Stunning Statistical Fraud behind the Global Warming Scare." *Investor Business Daily* Editorial. March 29, 2018. Accessed July 13, 2020. https://www.investors.com/politics/editorials/the-stunning-statistical-fraud-behind-the-global-warming-scare/.
Tisdall, Simon. "Sudan Fears US Military Action over Darfur Clinton Warns of 'Need to Sound Alarm' over Crisis: Obama Urged to Keep Pledge to End Genocide." *Guardian*. January 16, 2009.
"Top Ten Myths Concerning Your Rights and Liberties." Oxford: Praeger, 2015.
Toulmin, Stephen. *Uses of Argument*. London: Cambridge University Press, 1958.
"Truth Commission: Guatemala." *United States Institute of Peace*. Accessed March 27, 2018. https://www.usip.org/publications/1997/02/truth-commission-guatemala.

Ture, Kwame. "We Are All Africans: A Speech by Stokely Carmichael to Malcolm X Liberation University." *Black Scholar* 1, no. 7 (1970).
"Ukrainians Honour Victims of Stalin-Era Famine." BBC monitoring former Soviet Union. November 24, 2018.
"United Nations, Activists Urge Guatemala to Continue Trial of Deceased Dictator Efraín Ríos Montt." *Telesur*. April 6, 2018. https://videoenglish.telesurtv.net/video/665736/the-1954-us-coup-in-guatemala/.
"Venezuela 2017 Annual Inflation at 2,616 Percent: Opposition Lawmakers." *Reuters*. January 8, 2018. Accessed on 10 February 2018. https://www.reuters.com/article/us-venezuela-economy-inflation/venezuela-2017-annual-inflation-at-2616-per-cent-opposition-lawmakers-idUSKBN1EX23B.
Volf, Miroslav. *The End of Memory: Remembering Rightly in a Violent World*. Grand Rapids, MI: William B. Eerdmans Publishing Company, 2006.
Voth, Ben. "Academia and Republican Presidents." *American Thinker*. August 21, 2019. https://www.americanthinker.com/articles/2019/08/academia_and_republican_presidents.html.
Voth, Ben. *James Farmer Jr.: The Great Debater*. Lanham, MD: Lexingon, 2017.
Voth, Ben. "President Bush's Rhetoric and Policy against Genocide." In *The George W. Bush Presidency, Volume III: Foreign Policy*. Edited by Meena Bose and Paul Fritz. New York: Nova Publishers, 2016.
Voth, Ben. *The Rhetoric of Genocide: Death as a Text*. Lanham, MD: Lexington Books, 2014.
Voth, Ben and Aaron Noland. "Argumentation and the International Problem of Genocide." *Contemporary Argumentation and Debate* 28 (September 2007): 38–46. http://search.ebscohost.com.proxy.libraries.smu.edu/login.aspx?direct=true&db=cms&AN=40305088&site=ehost-live&scope=site.
"Voth Helps Holocaust Survivors Tell Their Stories." *Miami Report*. July 13, 2006. https://miamioh.edu/news/article/view/9919.
Wander, Philip C. "The Rhetoric of Science." *Western Speech Communication* 40, no. 4 (1976): 226–35. DOI: 10.1080/10570317609373907.
Wang, William. "Meet Yang Jisheng: China's Chronicler of Past Horrors." *The Atlantic*. September 20, 2013. https://www.theatlantic.com/china/archive/2013/09/meet-yang-jisheng-chinas-chronicler-of-past-horrors/279858/.
Warner, Gregor. "It's the No. 1 Country for Women in Politics—But Not in Daily Life." NPR. July 29, 2016. Accessed May 5, 2020. https://www.npr.org/sections/goatsandsoda/2016/07/29/487360094/invisibilia-no-one-thought-this-all-womans-debate-team-could-crush-it.
"Watch President Clinton Speak at the Dedication of the George W. Bush Presidential Library." PBS/YouTube. April 25, 2013. Accessed August 10, 2020. https://www.youtube.com/watch?v=F8zS23nAy5k.
Weinstein, Adam. "Blood for Oil Is Official US Policy Now." *The New Republic*. October 28, 2019. Accessed July 15, 2020. https://newrepublic.com/article/155507/blood-oil-official-us-policy-now.
"What's So Sinister about Jews' Buying Land from Arabs?" *Washington Post*. January 23, 1988.
Wheelis, Alien. Cited in B. Brummett. "Some Implications of Process or Intersubjectivity: Postmodern Rhetoric." *Philosophy and Rhetoric* 9 (1976): 39–40.
"Why Taiwan Has become a Problem for WHO." BBC. March 20, 2020. https://www.bbc.com/news/world-asia-52088167.
Wike, Richard and Shannon Schumacher. "Democratic Rights Popular Globally but Commitment to Them Not Always Strong." *Pew Research*. February 27, 2020. Accessed August 11, 2020. https://www.pewresearch.org/global/2020/02/27/democratic-rights-popular-globally-but-commitment-to-them-not-always-strong/.
Wiesel, Elie. Foreword. In *The Courage to Care*. Edited by C. Rittmer and S. Myers. New York: New York University Press, 1986.

Wilderson, Frank. *Red, White and Black: Cinema and the Structure of U.S. Antagonisms*. Durham, NC: Duke University Press, 2010.

"Wiley College's Quality Enhancement Plan." 2012. Unpublished manuscript, Wiley College, Marshall.

Williams, Abigail and Dan De Luce. "DHS Report: China Hid Coronavirus' Severity in Order to Hoard Medical Supplies." *NBC News*. May 4, 2020. https://www.nbcnews.com/politics/national-security/dhs-report-china-hid-coronavirus-severity-order-hoard-medical-supplies-n1199221.

Wilson, Edward. *The Social Conquest of Earth*. 1st ed. New York: Liveright Pub. Corp., 2012.

World Health Organization. Twitter. January 14, 2020. https://twitter.com/who/status/1217043229427761152?lang=en.

X, Malcolm and Alex Haley. *The Autobiography of Malcolm X*. New York: Grove Press, 1965.

Yanagizawa-Drott, David. "Propaganda vs. Education; A Case Study of Hate Radio in Rwanda." *Oxford Handbook of Propaganda Studies*. Oxford: Oxford University Press, 2013.

Young, Vershawn Ashanti and Aja Martinez. "Code-Meshing as World English." *Pedagogy, Policy, Performance*. Chicago: National Council of Teachers of English, 2011.

Ziegelmueller, George W. and Jack Kay. *Argumentation: Inquiry and Advocacy*. Boston: Allyn & Bacon, 1997.

Index

Africa, vii, x, xi–xiii, 6, 8, 12, 26, 27, 29, 34, 35, 38, 48, 57, 58, 60, 61, 62–63, 64, 65–68, 71, 100, 109, 117, 135, 181, 213, 214, 227
Afro-idealism, 28
Afro-pessimism, 28–29, 30
Ahmadinejad, Mahmoud, 175
AK-47, xii, 21
ALARM, 47, 52
Alinsky, Saul, 29, 48, 173–174
Altman, Taylor, 81, 82
American Forensics Association (AFA), 24–25
Amin, Idi, 212
Aniston, Alabama, 31
Annan, Kofi, xii
anti-colonialism, 57, 63, 64, 67, 212, 214
anti-imperialism, 57, 207, 212
Arab Spring, 66
argumentation, ix, xiii, xiv, xvi, xvii, 16, 25, 33, 49, 87, 89, 174, 178, 185, 211
Armenians, xv, 1, 169, 209
Arusha Accords, 5, 8
Ayittey, George, 61, 62, 212
Aylward, Bruce, 158, 159, 160

Baron, Chris, vii, xiii, 119, 125, 126
Bartannen, Michael, 75
Bashir, Omar, xviii, 27, 57, 60, 64, 66, 71, 181, 186, 210, 212–213
Bauschard, Stefan, xx, 161–162, 163
Beecher, Henry Ward, 160
Belgium, 58
Beloved Community, xvii, 28–38
Benton, Bond, 52
Bin Laden, Osama, 8
Birmingham Jail, xi
The Birth of a Nation, 193
Black power, 29, 35, 64
blood libel, 178, 179

Boko Haram, 66
Bolivia, xviii, 57, 68, 69, 135
Boston University, 33
Brockriede, Wayne, 49
Burke, Kenneth, 26, 178
Burundi, xiv, xix, 5–6, 11, 46, 216
Bush Presidential Center, ix, xi
Bush, George W., xi, xii, 180–181
bystander effect, ix, 5, 6, 7, 19, 181, 210

Cambodia, xv, 1, 27, 153, 169, 209
capitalism, 60, 201
Carmichael, Stokely, 29, 35, 58, 65, 93. *See also* Ture, Kwame
Carson, Rachel, 99, 214
Catholic Church's Trauma Healing Project, 144
Chakravaty, Anuradha, 46, 48
Chavez, Hugo, xviii, 57, 68
Chenoweth, Erica, 223
Chicago, 31, 35–36
China, xx, 151–165, 217
Chomsky, Noam, 68
Christianity, x, xiii, 24, 30, 44, 51, 132, 136, 147, 153, 169, 182, 193, 213, 216
Churchill, Ward, 70
CIA, 64
Cicero, 210
civil rights movement, xv, xvii, 28–38, 48, 64, 66–67, 182, 211, 227
climate change, xviii, 97–109, 214–215
climate denial, xviii, 97, 100, 215
Clinton, William Jefferson, 7, 8
CO_2 emissions, 97, 100, 102, 103–104, 107, 214–215
Coates, Taneshi, 29, 30
"cockroaches," 4, 10, 209, 222, 226
code-meshing, 82–83, 85
code-switching, 82–85

College Learning Assessment (CLA), 91
colonialism, xviii, 35, 57–71, 182, 207, 212–213, 214, 227
Committee for Historical Clarification, 146, 147
Communication Accommodation Theory (CAT), 81
communism, xv, 151, 155, 171, 173
Community and the Evolution of Society, 23
conflict resolution, xvii, xix, 43, 47–50, 207, 211
Congo, 6, 46
Congress of Racial Equality (CORE), 28, 30–32, 35–38; thirteen rules, 36
Coolidge, Calvin, 189–198; "Silent Cal," 196, 219
CORE. *See* Congress of Racial Equality
Cornell University, 33
coronavirus, 158, 159, 160, 226
creative peace process, 131–141, 147, 216

Dallaire, Romeo, 2, 7, 8
Damocles's sword, 210
Darby, John, 136
DDT, 99–100
debate, xiii–xiv, xvi, 24–25, 32–33, 75–76, 78, 86–87, 118–125, 161–165, 189–190, 198–203; Debate across the Curriculum, xviii, 78, 85–94, 214
Decision Points Theater, 180, 218
decoloniality, 63
dehumanization, ix, 6, 9, 10, 12, 137, 221
democide, xix, 5, 21, 97, 151–152, 154, 227
Denton, Robert, 172
dialectic materialism, 23
Dipont Education Management, 161, 163
discursive complexity, ix, xii, xiii, xvi, xvii, xxi, 3, 6, 16, 19–38, 45, 58, 64, 100, 107, 151, 157, 171, 209–211
Donofrio, Terri, vii, ix, 53, 175, 217
Dreamers Academy, xiv, xix, 119–125, 201, 215–216, 225, 227, 228
Du Bois, W. E. B., 192

Ebola, 68, 157
eliminationism, xix, 5, 21, 151–152, 154, 169, 209, 216, 227
Ellul, Jacques, 4, 115, 151, 209
Evers, Medgar, 30, 33, 38, 78, 123, 211

Farmer, James, Jr., xvii, 28, 33, 35, 47–49, 50, 64, 78, 94, 119, 182, 190, 222
Farmer, Lula, 30, 31, 38, 78, 123, 211
Farrakan, Louis, 178
FDR, 193
First Amendment, xvii, 19, 21, 172
Fisher, Bernice, 30, 35
Fleser, Arthur, 190
Floyd, George, 54, 192, 212
fossil fuels, 97, 100, 103–104, 105, 214
4% Growth Unit, 180
fracking, 103, 215
France, 2, 6–8, 58, 194, 224
Francophone, 6
Frankfurt School, 23
Frantz, Fannon, 29, 58–60
Freedom Rides, 31
Freeley, Austin, 25, 33
Freeman, Dr. Thomas, 33, 34, 38, 211, 213
Freire, Paulo, 116, 121, 174
Freud, Sigmund, 60
Freudian critiques, 60
Fujimori, Alberto, 133

Gandhi, Mohatmas, 35, 182
Garman, Charles Edward, 190
Garvey, Marcus, 192
Gaza Strip, 19, 170
genocidaire, x, xi, xiii, 4, 12, 13, 14, 15, 25–27, 181, 210, 212, 221
genocide, ix, xi, xiii–xiv, xvi, 1–15, 16, 21, 26–28, 97, 98, 113, 142, 151, 169; definition, 151, 224
Ghebreyesus, Tedros Adhanom, 159
Gilmore, Betty, vii, 44, 47
Gitera, Joseph Habyarimana, 6
Global Academic Commons, 163
Goldhagen, Daniel, xix, 97, 152, 154
Goree Island, xi
Gramsci, Anthony, 24
Great Debaters, vii, 34, 78, 118, 119, 123

Guatemala, vii, xix, 131–148, 216
Guatemalan Civil War, 141, 144, 145
Guatemalan Constitutional Court, 142
Guinea, 64, 67

Habermas, Jurgen, 23, 24, 27, 38, 220
Habyarimana, Juvenal, 2, 5, 6, 8
Harding, Warren, 189, 190, 191–192, 195, 219
Harvard, xi, 33, 68, 75, 105, 123, 156, 160; Debate Summer Workshop, 161
HBCUs, xvi, xviii, 33, 75–94
Hereroes, 169
Hindu, 35, 51, 182
Hitler, Adolf, 4, 133, 178, 210
Holmodor, 152, 209
Holocaust, vii, ix, xv, xix, 4, 5, 9, 174–178, 210; denial, xviii, 97
Hong Kong, xviii, 19, 57, 156, 217
Hoover, Herbert, 180, 198
"Hotel Rwanda," 54
Howard University, 29, 30, 123, 195, 196, 211
human rights, xi, xviii, 24, 57, 58, 64, 67, 131, 132, 133–136, 137–141, 143–148, 181, 185, 194, 216
Humphrey, Hubert, xiv
Hurricane Katrina, 192
Hussein, Saddam, xi, 181
Hutu, 2, 4–6, 7–9, 10–11, 12–13, 14, 46, 113, 115, 116, 117

ICC International Criminal Court, 64, 66, 135, 151
iDebate Rwanda, xiii, xix, 52, 114, 117, 121, 125, 201, 216, 225, 227, 228
IDF, 183
imperialism, xviii, 57, 67, 153, 155, 185, 207
International Criminal Court (ICC), 64, 66, 135, 151
Iraq, xi, 22, 27, 67, 179, 181
ISIS, 22, 66
Ivory Coast, xi

Jackson, DeSean, 178
Jackson State University, 32
Jack Spratt, 35
Jacobin, xxi, 29, 93, 207, 215

Jews, xv, 1, 109, 169, 178–179, 183
Jordan, Barbara, 33, 38, 123
Judaism, 24

Kabuga, Felicien, 226
Kagame, Paul, 13, 53
Kai-sheck, Chiang, 155
Kay, Jack, 25
Kelsie, Amber, 30
Kennedy, John F., 31
Kennedy, Robert, 172
Khartoum, Sudan, 66
Kigali, xvii, 7, 13, 43, 53, 54, 55, 57, 124, 220, 226
King, Martin Luther, Jr., xi, xvii, 30, 33–35, 48, 50–51, 66, 123, 172, 211
Kinyarwanda, 47
KKK, 193
Koehrsen, Will, 223
Kony, Joseph, 27
Kosovo, 27
Kyi, Aun Sung, 180

Lacanian critiques, 60
Latin America, 132, 143, 148, 207, 216
Lederach, Paul, 136–137, 138–140
Lemkin, Raphael, 151
Lemon, Don, 192
Lewis, C. S., 15, 16
Lewis, John, 28
Liberia, x, xi, xii, 64, 66, 67–68, 181
Lincoln, Abraham, 192, 193, 194
Lord's Army, 27
Louden, Al, 75
Lovelock, James, 98
Luddy, Bob, 202

MacGinty, Roger, 136
malaria, xix, 68, 97, 99–100, 160, 214
Malthus, Thomas, 98, 99, 108, 109
Mandela, Nelson, xi
March on Washington, 34
Marx, Karl, 60, 156, 210
Marxism, 156
Mary Washington University, 222
Matthew 25, 51, 182
Mbembe, Achille, 29, 60, 62
mediation, 136, 138, 143, 146, 178
Mein Kampf, 4

Meredith, James, 28, 29, 32, 34, 38, 71, 78, 93, 123, 211
Methodist Social Gospel, 51, 182
Middle East Media Research Institute, 179
A Mission from God, 34
MIT, 33
Mitchell, Gordon, 24
Mogadishu, Somalia, 8
Monrovia, xi
Montgomery Bus Boycott, 36
Morales, Evo, xviii, 68, 69
Moscow, 19
Moton, Dr. Robert, 192, 194
Mugabe, Robert, xviii, 10, 57, 60, 66
Muslim/Bosnia, 8, 169
muted group theory, 79

NAACP, 33, 38
National Cathedral, 31
Nazi fascism, 46, 171, 177, 179, 183, 210, 216
NGOs, 21
Nigeria, xi, xii, 14, 67
Nkrumah, Kwame, 64
Noland, Aaron, vii, 26, 118, 178
nonviolence, 16
North Korea, xx, 21, 27, 180, 218, 221
NPR, 64, 226
Ntaryamira, Cyprien, 5
Nyamata, 44, 53

OAS, 145–146
Obasanjo, xii
Orbe, Mark, 79
otherization, 115

pedagogy, xii, xiii, xvii, xviii, xix, xx, xxi, 14, 21, 24, 30, 38, 54, 93, 94, 125, 203
PEPFAR, 100
Peru, 133
Pinker, Steven, xx, 16, 104, 169, 170
Plato's *Republic*, 24
Plymouth Notch, Vermont, 189
pogrom, 6
Poland, 133
postmodernism, 172
Powell, Colin, 26

Power, Samantha, xi, 5, 7
praxis, ix, xiv, xviii, 25, 30, 35, 37, 57, 121, 174, 211
propaganda, ix, xiii, 3–6, 15, 16, 21–22, 27, 66, 115, 163, 164, 209, 211, 222, 227
The Protocols of the Elders of Zion, 179
Pyun, Jieun, vii, 180

Quality Enhancement Plan (QEP), 85, 220

Reconciliation Commissions, 45
reconciliation courts, Gacaca, 14, 45, 46, 48, 148
renewable energy, 97, 104, 105
Rhetoric of Genocide, ix, xii, xiv, 151
Rice, Condoleeza, xii, 164
Rios Montt, Efrain, 135, 141, 143
Robben Island, xi
Rosling, Hans, xx, 108, 170, 171, 223
Rummel, R. J., ix, 97, 152, 154, 155
Russia, xv, 21, 179
Rwandan genocide, xiv, 1–6, 8, 9–13, 14, 26, 66, 67, 209
Rwandan Patriotic Front (RPF), 5, 13

SAC-SCOC, 85
Salinas, Roberto, 201
Sanches, Jose Mauricio Rodriguez, 142
SCLC, 32
Screwtape Letters, 15
Seidel, Maggie, 201
Senegal, x, xi
settler colonialism, 70–71
Shaw, Lori, vii, 47
Shi Shi Qiu Shi, 156, 161
Shintoism, 153, 155
Shinto supremacism, 163, 171
Shlaes, Amity, vii, 196, 199
Sikkink, Kathryn, 133, 134
Silent Spring, 99–100, 214
Simon, Julian, 104, 108, 216, 220
Sirleaf, Ellen Johnson, xi, xii, 68
Skinner, Beth, xiii
SMU Conflict Resolution Program, xvii, 44, 47
SNCC, 32
Snyder, Chris, 47

social penetration theory, 81
Somalia, xi, 7–8, 26, 64, 67
Southern Methodist University, vii, xvii, 43, 44, 47, 90
South Korea, 21, 161, 180
Soviet Union, 152, 165
Spanish Flu, 106
Stanton, Greg, 222
Staub, Ervin, 114, 118
Strossen, Nadine, 224
Sudan, xviii, 26–27, 57, 64, 65, 66, 125, 135, 178, 181, 186, 210, 212, 213, 221

Taiwan, 155, 158, 159–161, 163
Taylor, Charles, x, xi, xii, 67
Tel Aviv, 19
Thunberg, Greta, 100
Thurman, Howard, 30–31, 211
Tolson, Melvin, 30, 34, 38, 75, 78, 119, 123, 190, 211, 213
Tombstone, 156
Towson University, xiii, 186
Trapp, Robert, 163
Tse Tung, Mao, xx, 155, 158
Ture, Kwame, 64–65. *See also* Carmichael, Stokely
Turkey, 1, 27
Tuskegee, 192, 194, 196

Uganda, xiv, xix, 122, 125, 212, 216
Ukrainians, xv, 152
United Nations, 2, 7, 143, 144, 155, 224
United States Holocaust Memorial Museum, vii, ix, xv, 9, 53, 151, 174–178, 217
University of Mississippi, 32
U.S. Constitution, 19

U.S. State Department, vii, ix, xiv, 8, 14, 158, 216

Venezuelan Supreme Court, 134
Voices from a Post-Genocide Generation, 123

Walker, Wyatt, 33
War on Terror, 67
War without Violence, 35, 48
Washington, Denzel, 34, 75, 78, 123, 213
West, Kanye, 192
WHO, 158–161, 217, 225
Wiesel, Elie, ix, 5, 6, 13, 24, 181, 210
Wilderson, Frank, 29
Wiley College, xviii, 75–76, 78, 83, 84, 85–94, 210, 214, 220
Wilson, E. O., xv, 14, 70
Wilson, Woodrow, 192–193, 196
World School Debate Championship, 119
Wuhan, 151, 157–161, 217

X, Malcolm, 28, 30, 33, 34, 38, 64, 65–66, 78, 93, 123, 211

Yad Vashem, 5
Yale, 33
Yang, Jisheng, 156
Young, Andrew, 179
Yugoslavia, 209

Zane, Billy, 178, 179
Ziegelmueller, George, 25
Zimbabwe, xviii, 10, 27, 57, 62, 68
Zipline, 226

About the Author

Ben Voth is associate professor of rhetoric and director of speech at Southern Methodist University. Voth's teaching and research mission is to equip individuals to have their voice. With more than thirty years of teaching and directing competitive forensics, he coached numerous state, national, and world champions of speech and debate. He is a leading international scholar on debate and argumentation and has worked in consulting roles with major institutions including: the United States Holocaust Memorial Museum, the Calvin Coolidge Presidential Foundation, and the Human Freedom Initiative of the George W. Bush Institute. An award-winning author, Voth's books include *The Rhetoric of Genocide: Death as a Text* (2014); *James Farmer Jr.: The Great Debater* (2017); *and Social Fragmentation and the Decline of American Democracy* (2016) with political communication scholar Robert Denton. His analysis of debate appears in outlets such as the *Washington Post, Dallas Morning News, Fortune Magazine, American Thinker, Washington Examiner,* and *KERA* Dallas.

www.ingramcontent.com/pod-product-compliance
Lightning Source LLC
Chambersburg PA
CBHW072110010526
44111CB00038B/2480